I0125979

WHEN
REBELS
WIN

WHEN REBELS WIN

Ideology, Statebuilding, and Power After Civil Wars

Kai M. Thaler

CORNELL UNIVERSITY PRESS   **ITHACA AND LONDON**

Copyright © 2025 by Kai M. Thaler

All rights reserved. Except for brief quotations in a review, this book, or parts thereof, must not be reproduced in any form without permission in writing from the publisher. For information, address Cornell University Press, Sage House, 512 East State Street, Ithaca, New York 14850. Visit our website at cornellpress.cornell.edu.

First published 2025 by Cornell University Press

Librarians: A CIP catalog record for this book is available from the Library of Congress.

ISBN 9781501784194 (hardcover)
ISBN 9781501784934 (paperback)
ISBN 9781501784217 (epub)
ISBN 9781501784200 (pdf)

*To those Liberians, Nicaraguans, and Ugandans
continuing to struggle for more peaceful, just, and responsive states.*

Contents

Acknowledgments

Rebel victory is the end of a winding path of individual and collective decisions and interventions, and this book is similar: it is the product of well over a decade of learning, thinking, and discussions about ideology, rebel victory, statebuilding, politics, and life thanks to many mentors, colleagues, interviewees, and friends.

My largest debt of gratitude is to those who made possible the primary research underlying this book. In Nicaragua, Liberia, and Uganda, many people took time to talk about their experiences and ideas with me. Edmundo Jarquín was extraordinarily generous in connecting me with key individuals I hoped to interview in Nicaragua, even lending me an office for meetings. Murphy Bella and Alex Kendima helped me find interviewees in Liberia and navigate Monrovia and beyond, while Nat Daygbor introduced me to several interviewees and the ways of Liberia's capitol building. In Uganda, interviews were difficult when I was there, but Paul Kabango helped set several up. Archivists and librarians at the Instituto de Historia de Nicaragua y Centroamérica at Managua's Universidad Centroamerica (now seized by the government, but may it be resurrected soon!); the Hoover Institution at Stanford University; and the Makerere Institute for Social Research, Makerere University Library, Centre for Basic Research, and Parliamentary Library in Uganda also helped me access critical local primary sources.

The seeds of this book and much of my research were planted at Yale University learning from Jasmina Besirevic-Regan, Stathis Kalyvas, Ben Kiernan, Matthew Adam Kocher, Mike McGovern, Thomas Jeffrey Miley, and Elisabeth Jean Wood. Stathis supported my random desire to conduct research on identity in Ceuta, Melilla, and their Moroccan surroundings, and then suggested I start attending Program on Order, Conflict, and Violence (OCV) seminars. The question of how victorious rebels behave in power grabbed my attention in a course with Libby Wood and has held it since, and Libby has been a golden example of a rigorous and caring scholar and has continued supporting me. OCV also introduced me to many then-PhD students and fellows who welcomed me, with thanks to Ana Arjona, Laia Balcells, Christine Cheng, Luis de la Calle, Corinna Jentzsch, Paul Kenny, Matthew Longo, Joshua Simon, Abbey Steele, Dawn Teele, and others.

I let the rebel victory idea rest for a few years before returning to it while I was part of a great intellectual community at Harvard University. Steve Levitsky was a fantastic mentor and offered a model for how to be not only a successful scholar but also an excellent teacher, leader, and community member. His stamp on this book is evident: my initial focus on victorious rebels having to wage counterinsurgency turned to one with much more emphasis on institutions. My other mentors—Robert Bates, Melani Cammett, and Fotini Christia—similarly provided both advice on my work and important lessons about how to think, research, and figure out academia and life beyond it. I also benefited from scholarship and advice from Dara Kay Cohen, Jeffry Frieden, Peter Hall, Alastair Iain Johnston, Joshua Kertzer, Gwyneth McClendon, and Roger Petersen.

My peers played a huge part in my time at Harvard. Jonathan Weigel and I became not only friends but eventually roommates. Janet Lewis, James Loxton, Jason Warner, and Yuri Zhukov all particularly helped me feel included in a department that was not always the most natural fit for my eclectic research interests. Tyler Jost suffered through reading my writing and has remained a great friend. I also benefited from comments and friendship from many other colleagues, including Sean Paul Ashley, Peter Bucchianeri, Chase Foster, Mai Hassan, Jingkai He, Dana Higgins, Connor Huff, Sam Imlay, Mayya Komisarchik, Dominika Kruszewska, Shelley Liu, Christopher Lucas, John Marshall, Daniel Moskowitz, Noah Nathan, Andrew Ong, Stephen Pettigrew, Jonathan Phillips, Arjun Ramamurti, Melissa Sands, Jason Sclar, Anton Strezhnev, Lydia Walker, and Julie Weaver.

I had the great fortune that one of my best friends from home, Nicholas Miller, started at the Massachusetts Institute of Technology (MIT) a couple years before me, and he is still an excellent friend and sounding board. I met many MIT students who became friends and helped shape my work then and now, with special mention to Noel Anderson, Lena Andrews, Mark Bell, Christopher Clary, Daniel de Kadt, Marika Landau-Wells, Philip Martin, Cullen Nutt, Reid Pauly, and Alec Worsnop. From the Tufts University Fletcher School, I was also lucky to meet Meg Guliford, Benjamin Naimark-Rowse, Benjamin Spatz (whose knowledge of Liberia far outstrips my own), and Rebecca Tapscott.

My research on Nicaragua was supported by the Weatherhead Center for International Affairs and the David Rockefeller Center for Latin American Studies at Harvard University, and by the Tobin Project. A Harvard Frederick Sheldon Traveling Fellowship funded research in Liberia and Uganda. Fellowships from the Harvard Kennedy School's Ash Center for Democratic Governance and Innovation, the Harvard Government Department, and the Harry Frank Guggenheim Foundation provided crucial writing support.

At the University of Denver Korbel School, I was especially welcomed then and still by Marie Berry, Cullen Hendrix, and Oliver Kaplan, and I got feedback, fun, and tips on good hiking and skiing trails from them and Deborah Avant, Rebecca Galemba, Jill Hereau, Julia MacDonald, Kelsey Norman, Tricia Olsen, and others. I also reconnected with Singumbe Muyeba and Abigail Kabandula many years after meeting in Cape Town. Sinduja Raja and Will Calhoun provided excellent research assistance.

At the University of California, Santa Barbara (UCSB), the Department of Global Studies has provided a home for me to work on difficult questions, regardless of the methods used. Colleagues in Global Studies, Latin American and Iberian Studies, Political Science, and elsewhere across the university have supported me, and I must give special shoutouts to Javiera Barandiarán, Alison Brysk, Jia-Ching Chen, Charmaine Chua, Nadège Clitandre, Bridget Coggins, Aashish Mehta, Kevin Whitehead, and Hannah Wohl. UCSB's Academic Senate and the Hellman Fellows program have each funded work on this book and related projects, and UCSB funds helped subsidize this book's production costs.

Other academic colleagues and friends have influenced me and my research over the years. Don Leonard has gone from academic friend to another brother. Mateo Jarquín and Eric Mosinger have been excellent compañeros over many years of work on Nicaragua. I also want to thank Naazneen Barma, Dara Kay Cohen, Sarah Zukerman Daly, Christopher Day, Danielle Gilbert, Jarrod Hayes, Marina Henke, Reyko Huang, Morgan Kaplan, Nelson Kasfir, Peter Krause, Adam Lichtenheld, Meredith Loken, Terrence Lyons, Romain Malejacq, Zachariah Mampilly, Zoe Marks, Jonathan Leader Maynard, Dipali Mukhopadhyay, Sarah Parkinson, Evan Perkoski, Sam Plapinger, Blair Read, William Reno, Rachel Schwartz, Kunaal Sharma, Anastasia Shesterinina, Niloufer Siddiqui, Dan Slater, Paul Staniland, Megan Stewart, Michael Weintraub, Michael Woldemariam, Catherine Worsnop, Sherry Zaks, and many more who I apologize for not naming! Dozens of nonacademic friends around the world helped to keep me mostly sane and happy while working on often depressing topics. I cannot list them all here, but they have my eternal gratitude.

As the book came together, Mateo Jarquín, Peter Krause, Romain Malejacq, Rebecca Tapscott, and Gregory Thaler provided comments to improve it, and two excellent anonymous reviewers pushed me to sharpen the book and its contributions. Jackie Teoh at Cornell University Press has been encouraging, and offered great suggestions throughout the publishing process.

My family instilled in me a curiosity about other histories and cultures and a sense of the importance of politics. I owe many thanks to my grandparents, Manley and Dodie Thaler and the late Charles and Jean Massey, for encouraging me to read, travel, and enjoy life. My parents, Karen Massey and Jeff Thaler, have supported my pursuits, academic and otherwise, and shared my enthusiasm for exploring new places, even if they might have sometimes preferred that I was not living so far away. My brother, Gregory Thaler, has been an amazing friend and provider of new friends, a supportive (and critical when needed) reader and adviser, and a traveling companion across the Ecuadorian Amazon, the caves of Capadoccia, and many other places.

The last stages of this book's long process came in Santa Barbara where I would not have been able to finish it without the love and support of my partner Jennifer, who also cleaned up the figures. Our dog Ada provided companionship and important reminders to get up from the computer and go outside. Our son Mica arrived in the middle of revisions, offering perspective on what is important in life and strong incentives to get the book finished. May he grow up in a more just and peaceful world where there are fewer good reasons for rebels to take up arms.

Portions of the introduction and chapters 1–4 were previously published in 2025 as "From Insurgent to Incumbent: Ideology, Rebel Governance, and Statebuilding After Rebel Victory in Civil Wars" in *Comparative Politics*, and are adapted and reprinted with permission from *Comparative Politics*.

Abbreviations

ADF	Allied Democratic Forces
AFL	Armed Forces of Liberia
AFDL	Alliance des Forces Démocratiques pour la Libération du Congo
ATU	Anti-Terrorist Unit
CBR	Centre for Basic Research
CCP	Chinese Communist Party
CDS	Comité de Defensa Sandinista
CIA	Central Intelligence Agency
CIJ	Coalition for International Justice
CIPRES	Centro para la Investigación, la Promoción y el Desarrollo Rural y Social
CNA	Cruzada Nacional de Alfabetización
CPN-M	Communist Party of Nepal-Maoist
DGSE	Dirección General de Seguridad del Estado
DN	Dirección Nacional
DP	Democratic Party
DRC	Democratic Republic of the Congo
ECOMOG	ECOWAS Monitoring Group
ECOWAS	Economic Community of West African States
ENI	Ente nazionale idrocarburi
EPRDF	Ethiopian People's Revolutionary Democratic Front
EPS	Ejército Popular Sandinista
FAO	Frente Amplio Opositor
FLEC	Frente para a Libertação do Enclave de Cabinda
FLN	Front de Libération Nationale
FNLA	Frente Nacional de Libertação de Angola
Frelimo	Frente de Libertação de Moçambique
Fretilin	Frente Revolucionária de Timor-Leste Independente
FRONASA	Front for National Salvation
FSLN	Frente Sandinista de Liberación Nacional
GN	Guardia Nacional
GPP	Guerra Popular Prolongada
GRAE	Governo Revolucionârio de Angola no Exilio
HTS	Hayat Tahrir al-Sham

IDP	internally displaced person
IFIs	international financial institutions
IGNU	Interim Government of National Unity
IHNCA	Instituto de Historia de Nicaragua y Centroamérica
IMF	International Monetary Fund
INEC	Instituto Nacional de Estadísticas y Censos
INPFL	Independent National Patriotic Front of Liberia
IS-K	Islamic State-Khorasan Province
JGRN	Junta de Gobierno de Reconstrucción Nacional
LDU	Local Defence Unit
LPC	Liberia Peace Council
LURD	Liberians United for Reconciliation and Democracy
M-26-J	Movimiento 26 de Julio
MIDINRA	Ministerio de Desarrollo Agropecuario y Reforma Agraria
MINED	Ministerio de Educación
MINSA	Ministerio de Salud
MINT	Ministerio del Interior
MOJA	Movement for Justice in Africa
MPEA	Ministry of Planning and Economic Affairs
MPLA	Movimento Popular de Libertação de Angola
NGO	nongovernmental organization
NHP	National Health Plan
NPFL	National Patriotic Front of Liberia
NPP	National Patriotic Party
NPRAG	National Patriotic Reconstruction Assembly Government
NRA	National Resistance Army
NRC	National Resistance Council
NRM	National Resistance Movement
OAU	Organization for African Unity
PAIGC	Partido Africano para a Independência da Guiné e Cabo Verde
PAL	Progressive Alliance of Liberia
PDPA	People's Democratic Party of Afghanistan
PRA	People's Resistance Army
RC	Resistance Council
Renamo	Resistência Nacional Moçambicana
RPF	Rwandan Patriotic Front
RUF	Revolutionary United Front
SCSL	Special Court for Sierra Leone
SMP	Servicio Militar Patriótico
SNUS	Sistema Nacional Único de Salud

SOD	Special Operations Division
SSU	Special Security Unit
TPLF	Tigray People's Liberation Front
TPU	Tropas Especiales Pablo Úbeda
TRC	Truth and Reconciliation Commission
UFF	Uganda Freedom Fighters
ULIMO	United Liberation Movement of Liberia
UN	United Nations
UNAMA	United Nations Assistance Mission in Afghanistan
UNDP	United Nations Development Programme
UNEPI	Ugandan National Programme on Immunisation
UNESCO	United Nations Educational, Scientific, and Cultural Organization
UNICEF	United Nations Children's Fund
UNITA	União Nacional para a Independência Total de Angola
UPA	União das Populações de Angola
UPC	Ugandan People's Congress
UPM	Uganda Patriotic Movement
WHO	World Health Organization
ZANU	Zimbabwe African National Union

Part I

THEORIZING REBEL VICTORY AND ITS CONSEQUENCES

INTRODUCTION
From Fighting the State to Controlling It

When the Frente Sandinista de Liberación Nacional (FSLN) took power in Nicaragua in 1979 after over a decade of guerrilla struggle, the group's leaders felt they were stepping into a void because the prior dictatorial regime had done little to serve most Nicaraguans. As FSLN guerrilla and postvictory government minister Lea Guido told me in an interview, "This was truly a revolution: the annihilation of the armed forces, the disintegration of national institutions, the transformation of institutions, changes in the leadership of the government, of ministers, of everything. The disappearance of parliament. The state was gone, there were only buildings. But the institutions needed to be reestablished, reformed, and given content to work with." The FSLN set about building a new state: developing new ministries, mass organizations, and security forces; expanding provision of public services; and trying to extend the state's reach to previously neglected regions.

When the National Patriotic Front of Liberia (NPFL) and its leader, Charles Taylor, gained control of the country in 1997 after fighting since late 1989, there were hopes amid state collapse that the group would fulfill its promises to bring Liberians democracy, provide economic opportunities, and end longstanding patterns of violence and ethnic favoritism. An early NPFL officer I interviewed told me, "We were expecting that to happen, to build roads and schools and things, but it didn't happen that way. Charles Taylor only focused on war . . . his only plan was to rule the country as president." The NPFL made little effort to rebuild the state or provide services to the population, with Taylor and associates instead focusing on their own security in power and using ministries to fill their own bank accounts.

Rebels emerge victorious in civil wars around one-fourth of the time (Fearon and Laitin 2003; Pettersson and Wallensteen 2015; Toft 2009). But as the FSLN and NPFL cases suggest, when rebels do win, their governing behavior varies dramatically. Some victorious rebel organizations may reshape political, economic, and social systems. When Taliban rebels took over Afghanistan's capital of Kabul in 1996, for instance, they set about transforming the state based on an Islamist ideology. The Taliban created new ministries and institutions and used state resources to enforce religious laws. They worked with and through local leaders and clerics to implement their political program throughout Afghanistan's territory and society until they were toppled in 2001 (Gopal and van Linschoten 2017; Maley 2009; Rashid 2001).

Other rebel leaders and the organizations they build may be more interested in the personal benefits state power can yield (Reno 1998). Before he led a victorious rebellion and gained power in Liberia, Charles Taylor reportedly dismissed other young opposition leaders who called for remaking Liberian state-society relations, saying, "I'm not interested in ideology. I just want money and I want to be on top" (Schuster 1994, 52). In the Republic of Congo, former dictator Denis Sassou-Nguesso and his Cobra rebel forces, who fought their way to power in 1997, halted the country's nascent democratization process and diverted oil revenues and other state resources toward their own benefit. Sassou-Nguesso failed to develop or maintain state institutions beyond security forces and agencies for extracting the country's resource wealth, working only to benefit a limited loyalist constituency and ruling through repression up until the present (Clark 2008; Shaw and Carter 2021).

What determines how a rebel group will govern once in power? Does it retain characteristics from the civil war period once it moves from opposing the state to controlling it? Drawing on data from Nicaragua, Liberia, Uganda, and other cases, this book offers an original theory of rebel victory and its impacts. I show that the ideologies motivating and developed by rebel leaders shape rebel organizations' internal institutions and rebels' interactions with civilians. Rebels' ideologies vary in the degree of societal transformation they seek and the constituencies they aim to serve, pushing groups toward different types of governance in the rebellion period.

Controlling territory as rebels and governing an internationally recognized state are clearly different enterprises, and one might expect victorious rebels to change their aims and policies drastically when faced with demands from new sectors of the population they must govern, as well as the opportunities and constraints presented by international actors and laws. As rebels, organizations must primarily manage the expectations and demands of those in areas under their influence—though they may seek to make broader appeals—and civilians may be more understanding if they are unable to put plans into action while still fighting against the state. Rebels also have more limited opportunities for support through official international channels like UN agencies and international development banks. Once in power, however, victorious rebels face the demands of the entire country's citizens and civil society organizations, though they will have the state's institutions to try to address them politically—or suppress citizens coercively. Victorious rebels also gain greater opportunities to leverage their legitimacy in the international state system to secure support for their initiatives or blunt some international pressure, although they also face a higher burden of compliance with international laws and regulations. Despite these contextual differences, this book shows that previctory ideology continues guiding statebuilding plans and efforts for public good and service provision—or the lack thereof—through at least the first postvictory decade.

Rebel Ideologies, Policies, and Practices

Civil wars have replaced interstate wars as the most prevalent form of large-scale armed conflict since World War II (Gleditsch et al. 2002; Themnér and Wallensteen 2012), and rebels continue to threaten state power—and sometimes seize it. For instance, in April 2021, Chad's long-standing dictator Idriss Déby was killed while at the front lines of his government's fight against the Front pour l'Alternance et la Concorde au Tchad, prompting political uncertainty and then a military takeover. Later that year, the United States withdrew its remaining military forces from Afghanistan, leading to the collapse of the Afghan National Army and the Taliban's recapture of power after two decades of struggle. Syrian rebels in December 2024 launched a rapid offensive that broke a long stalemate and unexpectedly toppled the Assad family regime. Unlike victories by incumbent regimes, which generally exhibit strong continuity between pre- and postconflict politics, rebel victories result in the creation of new regimes with the potential to build a new state and transform a country's political, social, and economic institutions and practices. Negotiated settlements may also create space for reforms, but victory gives a rebel organization the most latitude to pursue its goals and ideal vision of the postwar state and society.

Comparative knowledge about how victorious rebel groups govern remains sparse. Most analyses focus on rebel governance while opposing the state rather than once controlling it (e.g., Arjona, Kasfir, and Mampilly 2015; Mampilly 2011; Stewart 2021). Victorious rebel organizations must build a new state apparatus or decide what institutions of the old state to inhabit, abandon, or rebuild. I focus on the development of rebel organizations and then follow their trajectory through victory, demonstrating how rebel ideology carries over from groups' time fighting against the state to then shape their postvictory state-building and service provision efforts. Looking within rebel organizations is crucial because it is organizations that engage in conflict, strategic interaction, and policy formulation and implementation (Parkinson and Zaks 2018; Sinno 2008). Following victory, rebel organizations have unique power among actors to put their ideals and plans into practice, having displaced rivals and possessing a predominance—if not a monopoly—in the use of force.

This book demonstrates that the ideological principles and aims that motivate rebel organizations shape the structure of the state and the patterns of governance they adopt once in power. I define "ideologies" as relatively clear, coherent sets of beliefs or ideas that delimit a constituency and what sociopolitical goals and actions should be pursued in that constituency's interests, at times with prescriptions for the strategies best suited for achieving these goals (Gutiérrez Sanín and Wood 2014; Thaler 2012). Rebel leaders orient organizations toward certain visions of what postwar society should look like based on a given ideology. Ideologies are translated into action through the institutions and practices developed within organizations and in relations with civilians during the civil war period, which then carry over into government after rebel victory.

I distinguish between ideological "types" of rebel organizations on two dimensions: (1) the degree to which they aim to transform society, and (2) the breadth of the population they wish to benefit. I distinguish organizations' desired degree of social transformation on a spectrum from *programmatic* to *opportunistic*, and their degree of popular incorporation and benefits on a spectrum from *inclusive* to *exclusive*, with groups falling somewhere between the end points on each dimension (see figure 1.2 in chapter 1).

More programmatic organizations attempt to achieve long-term goals involving transforming or reforming existing socioeconomic and political relations and are more likely to be inclusive: trying to incorporate more of the population into the political sphere under their influence and seeking to deliver public goods and services in alignment with ideological goals. Rebellions often erupt in highly unequal societies—whether economically, politically, or ethnically (e.g., Cederman, Gleditsch, and Buhaug 2012; Gurr 1970), so inclusive organizations likely must programmatically transform existing structures and systems to achieve their aims of serving a broader population. More opportunistic organizations are less interested in changing social relations than in exploiting a political opening to change who controls the state and its resources. Leaders and members in more opportunistic organizations are more likely to be motivated primarily by individual interests and short-term economic benefits or using power for private gain, usually seeking exclusive benefits for a select, limited group, versus working for public interests. Opportunistic-inclusive and programmatic-exclusive organizations are rarer types among rebel victors (see chapter 1).

These ideal types describe distinct organizational logics and imply distinct sets of relations between organizational leadership and followers and between a rebel group and the civilian population. Organizational type then shapes the state structure and governing practices that a victorious rebel group adopts once it takes power. I focus on two types of state power that victorious rebels may try to develop: coercive and infrastructural. Coercive power is the ability to use state security forces and institutions to establish a hold over society and an ability to control it by force if necessary (Mann 1988; Weber 1946). Infrastructural power entails state elites' ability to penetrate society and use societal structures to coordinate the population toward elites' desired ends (Mann 1988). States can increase their infrastructural power and influence over and through society with activities such as promoting literacy, improving physical infrastructure and communications, carrying out censuses (Lee and Zhang 2016; Soifer 2012), or increasing administrative presence throughout the territory to make the population more "legible" by increasing the state's information about it (Scott 1998). Infrastructural power aids state control, but if the government so chooses, it also permits provision of goods and services beyond order (Soifer 2015; Soifer and vom Hau 2008). While both programmatic and opportunistic organizations seek to gain coercive power to secure their hold on the state, programmatic organizations also focus on developing infrastructural power, extending the state's reach and actions across territory and throughout the population. The ability to generate revenues through taxation, another key facet of state capacity (Hanson and Sigman 2021), tends to be low across post–civil war states, which often depend heavily on foreign aid and natural resource extraction (Besley and Persson 2008). Throughout the book, I use the term "statebuilding" to refer specifically to building infrastructural power (see also Saylor 2014; Soifer 2015).

More opportunistic groups will use or develop state institutions only if they can provide security and exclusive benefits for the organization's leaders, members, and select constituencies. More programmatic groups, in contrast, will seek to expand the state's reach to implement their transformative political program, and especially if they are inclusive, they may invest in state provision of vital services like health care and education to the population. We can measure coercive power and statebuilding efforts by looking at how organizations structure, fund, and use security forces and government agencies, and by examining their ability to project power across the national territory and throughout society and their attempts to expand infrastructure and programs that enable the state to reach more of the population and territory (Mann 1988; Scott 1998), as outlined in table 1.1.

For example, the more programmatic-inclusive Frente de Libertação de Moçambique (Frelimo), which developed a Marxist-Leninist nationalist ideology in its fight against the Portuguese colonial regime in Mozambique, worked after independence to reorganize society. Frelimo adopted a state-directed economic model, challenged traditional authorities, and shifted rural populations into collective villages (Dinerman 2006; Marcum 2018), a transformation that required developing and expanding the state apparatus. Frelimo leader and inaugural Mozambican president Samora Machel envisioned state authority manifested in every corner of the country's territory, despite Mozambique's low population density and "difficult political geography" (Herbst 2000, 150). Without building new institutions, Machel argued, Frelimo's victory would be hollow, leaving it sitting in the capital of Maputo, "isolated like limbs without a trunk" (Munslow 1985, 25), unable to reach people it wished to include politically and benefit with education, health care, and infrastructure.

Unlike Frelimo, the leaders of the more opportunistic-exclusive Alliance des Forces Démocratiques pour la Libération du Congo (AFDL) were motivated by gaining personalized wealth and power rather than pursuing societal transformation in the former Zaire. In 1965, Cuban Revolution leader Ernesto "Che" Guevara arrived in eastern Congo to assist future AFDL leader Laurent-Désiré Kabila's rebel forces. He lamented, however, that Kabila "lets the days pass without concerning himself with anything other than political squabbles, and all the signs are that he is too addicted to drink and women" (Guevara 2001, 69). At the end of the failed campaign in 1966, Guevara reflected that "a man with leadership skills does not become, ipso facto, a revolutionary leader. One has to be serious, and possess an ideology and a spirit of sacrifice. Until now, Kabila has not shown any of these traits" (Guevara 2001, 244).

Guevara's doubts proved correct decades later. In 1996, with backing from Rwanda and Uganda, Kabila cobbled together a coalition of diverse opposition groups in the AFDL, a front united only in name and militarily effective only thanks to its foreign allies' direct intervention (Reyntjens 2009, 102–8; Schatzberg 1997, 80–81). The AFDL swept to power in Kinshasa in 1997, but leaders had little idea what to do afterward—beyond filling their own bank accounts. The rest of the population was an afterthought. Kabila centralized and personalized power within the ADFL and constructed a weak state that he could control through patronage networks (de Villers and Tshonda 2002; Reyntjens 2009). His rhetoric and practices rarely matched; "many of Kabila's initiatives [were] purely rhetorical and never realized" (Dunn 2002, 66).

The lack of a longer-term vision for statebuilding or benefiting the public led to weak state authority even in core, heavily populated areas because Kabila's government failed to develop state capabilities beyond coercion and economic extraction.

The ideologies motivating rebel leaders clearly matter, but their importance in shaping groups' behavior remains an underexplored, although growing area in the study of civil war (Gutiérrez Sanín and Wood 2014; Maynard 2019) and statebuilding. My focus on rebel group ideologies—on their ideas and envisioned political futures—helps untangle otherwise unexplained variation in wartime and postwar outcomes, improving our understanding of how and why rebel organizations develop institutions and governing strategies, as well as showing how patterns and preferences established during rebellion carry over after victory.

Answering Unanswered Questions About Civil War and Statebuilding

This book integrates and expands upon three literatures: scholarship on civil wars and rebel governance, theories of statebuilding, and studies of post–civil war governance. This synthesis provides a more comprehensive theorization of victorious rebels' paths and how their ideologies manifest in policies and practices before and after taking power.

The civil wars literature has largely focused on war onset, wartime dynamics, and war resolution or recurrence (see Blattman and Miguel 2010; Cederman and Vogt 2017; Kalyvas 2009; Walter 2017b). Scholars have more rarely considered civil wars as a process in which factors at war onset or rebel group formation may carry through the conflict and continue afterward to affect postwar governance or society (Shesterinina 2022; Wood 2015). Works on how civil wars endure and end focus on how violence evolves and how wars are resolved (Balcells and Kalyvas 2014; Staniland 2014; Toft 2009; Walter 2004). The civil war literature at times engages with work on social revolutions, which can remake societies, although comparative scholars of revolutions have tended to focus more on the causes of revolution (Foran 2005; Goodwin 2001; Skocpol 1979) than their domestic political consequences (Lawson 2019, ch. 6; Selbin 1999). I offer a more unified picture of the course of rebellion from organizational inception through fighting against the state to controlling the state and governing. This permits analysis of what remains the same and what changes as rebel organizations develop and their political status shifts. Studying rebel victory more generally rather than only successful "revolutions" lets us understand not only rebel movements seeking to change social or political structures but also those seeking power alone.

Classic studies of statebuilding have focused on the role of interstate war in stimulating the construction of strong states and projection of state power throughout a national territory. War is seen as creating a new relationship between the rulers and the ruled (Olson 1993; Tilly 1990) and expanding state extractive capacity (Bates 2010; Rasler and Thompson 1989), with wartime institutions and increased state power persisting after hostilities end (Mann 1986). There is conflicting evidence, however, about whether this theory applies outside Western Europe (e.g., Centeno 2002; Herbst 2000), nor does this "bellicist" perspective examine the role of internal conflict in statebuilding. Whether and how civil wars lead to statebuilding remains debated: several studies suggest that civil wars may lead to sociopolitical transformation and state strengthening (Porter 1994; Slater 2010; Vu 2010), but others find that civil wars have weakened states (Thies 2005, 2006; Wimmer 2012). Looking at the particular outcome of rebel victory, I show how civil wars *can* lead to statebuilding, but it depends on the ideology of the winning organization.

Uniting the civil war and statebuilding literatures, the rebel governance research agenda examines the institutions and patterns of interactions arising between a rebel organization, civilians, and outside actors when the group undertakes functions normally associated with states (Arjona, Kasfir, and Mampilly 2015; Loyle et al. 2023; Mampilly and Stewart 2021). Rebel governance research builds on the guerrilla warfare theory of Mao Tse-Tung (1962) and Che Guevara (1961) and classic works on rebel-civilian relations (Johnson 1962; Popkin 1979; Wickham-Crowley 1987) to understand when and how rebel groups develop a social contract with communities and begin collecting taxes, providing public goods and services, creating participatory institutions, and developing and enforcing laws and regulations. This literature, however, has largely concentrated on governance during civil wars, not what rebel groups do with the state when they win. Existing studies of rebel victory and its impacts have generally been restricted to single cases or regions (Dorman 2006; Fisher 2020; Lewis 2020; Liu 2022, 2024; Martin 2021; McDonough 2008; Podder 2014; Young and Florea 2025). There remains a need for further comparative work on how processes of social transformation and wartime institutions created by rebels during civil wars may persist into the postwar period (Arjona 2014; Huang 2016b; Shesterinina 2022; Wood 2008), beyond rebel transformations into political parties and their electoral performance (Daly 2022; Ishiyama 2016; Manning, Smith, and Tuncel 2024; Zaks 2024). By examining how rebels across regions and time have turned from rebel governance to managing the state, this book shows how rebellion-era institutions and practices carry over into power, and what new opportunities victorious rebels have to enact their ideological visions.

Much scholarship has likewise recognized that rebel victory potentially leads to especially durable authoritarian regimes (Lachapelle et al. 2020; Levitsky and Way 2022; Lyons 2016a, 2016b), but sometimes it leads to regime collapse (Ashley 2023; Day and Woldemariam 2024; Lachapelle et al. 2020, 561). Yet *what form the state takes after civil wars and why*, especially after rebel victory, has not been fully explored. As Slater (2010, 5) points out, much work on internal conflicts treats them "as an outcome to be explained—as a product instead of a producer of political institutions." Toft (2009, 2010) has suggested rebel victories may lead to more durable peace (see also Licklider 1995; Luttwak 1999) and may also lead to some improvements in economic outcomes and more democratic politics (see also Huang 2016b), at least compared to the pre-war regime. These outcomes depend significantly on how victorious rebels decide to govern.

Not all rebel groups are the same, and the peace that prevails under some rebel victors, like in Taliban-ruled Afghanistan, may not align with global ideals of equality, democracy, and human rights. This point follows Galtung's (1969) distinction between negative peace (absence of war) and positive peace (improving human security and development). I argue that the states built by victorious rebels also diverge in their structures and policy priorities based on the organizational type of the group that comes to power. Only by looking inside the organizations that seize power can we understand the variation in statebuilding efforts pursued and the outcomes achieved by victorious rebel governments in some of the world's territorially largest and most populous countries (Angola, Bangladesh, China, Democratic Republic of the Congo) and some of the smallest (Nepal, Nicaragua, Rwanda).

Alternative Explanations

I test my argument against alternative explanations for rebel group political orientation and behavior and for government statebuilding and service provision efforts. On rebel organizational type, Weinstein (2007) argues that rebel leaders' decisions about recruitment and how to engage with the population are structurally determined depending on the availability of natural resources or foreign funding when groups are founded. In resource-rich environments or with foreign funding, an organization will be able to grow quickest by attracting recruits seeking short-term material awards versus recruits interested in longer-term prospects of political change. For Weinstein, ideologically motivated rebel groups tend to take root only in the absence of material resource endowments, whereas more opportunistic organizations develop where such endowments are present. Reliance in early recruitment on material resources rather than grievances or ideological commitments leads to a path-dependent situation in which opportunistic recruits join an organization and prey on civilians, crowding out ideologues even if some leaders initially had longer-term political goals. If Weinstein is correct, we should see rebel leaders and fighters making recruitment, socialization, and governance decisions based on organizations' access to economic resources or lack thereof, with structural conditions—rather than leaders' agency and ability to influence recruits' and followers' preferences (see e.g., Kalyvas 2006)—shaping how a rebel organization develops.

The quality of particular leaders could also affect organizational type and the potential for an organization to mobilize the population for rebellion or statebuilding. Building on Weber's (1968) idea of charisma enabling some rulers to generate loyalty and compliance from subjects, Gerdes (2013) suggests charisma rather than material resources can enable a rebel leader to outcompete rivals and mobilize support for their faction or organization without developing institutions. This could extend to statebuilding as well, with charismatic leaders able to mobilize the population and maintain their desired order without engaging in statebuilding. The effects of charisma or "visionary leadership" may ultimately depend, however, on the ends toward which a leader uses it (Aminzade, Goldstone, and Perry 2001) because both opportunistic-exclusive leaders like Charles Taylor and programmatic-inclusive leaders like Fidel Castro can be charismatic.

Reno (2011) posits that rebel organizational type may be determined by the political opportunities available in the domestic and international sociopolitical environment to gain support and power. If Reno is correct, then we should see rebel leaders adopt political programs for reasons of political expediency rather than sincere commitments or grievances, at least in some cases.

Another set of arguments focuses on the particular social networks and socioterritorial constituencies that rebel groups develop and rely on while opposing the state, which could then shape rebels' governance once in power. As Staniland (2014) and Parkinson (2023) show, the social networks rebel organizations are built on or tap into affect their ability to survive, the relationships they have with particular populations, and thus their patterns of coercion or governance among different communities. Liu (2022, 2024) sees rebels' wartime territorial control and social constituencies as key to subnational variation in the types of governance they enact after taking power (see also Sharif and Joshi 2023). Liu argues that where rebels develop ties to civilian populations they enjoy control after victory and can mobilize the population to implement policies and plans; in areas that were rivals' strongholds, they deploy coercion; and in areas where neither the rebel victors nor rivals had much influence, they build the bureaucracy and use funding to try to coopt citizens. If these theories hold, we should expect to see rebel organizations' aims and behavior shaped by their civilian constituencies, with their postvictory governance in different areas depending on rebellion-era networks and territorial influence.

Regarding statebuilding patterns and the ends governments seek in power, related to the above points about social constituencies, the ethnic structure of a rebel organization could determine the social networks it has developed and then shape statebuilding and governance decisions once the rebels are in power in order to benefit favored ethnic groups (e.g., Horowitz 1985; Lijphart 1977; Posner 2005). If ethnicity outweighs other factors, we should expect to see organizations as rebels and then as rulers making decisions primarily based on ethnic cleavages, leveraging them to maximize benefits for leaders and their preferred ethnic constituencies.

The prewar state structure could also determine the structure of the postwar state, as Herbst (2000) suggests. If this is the case, we should see continuity in state structures and activities between the old and new regime following rebel victory, with little change or expansion of the state's institutions and what the state does among the population and across the territory.

Security threats could also stimulate statebuilding (Slater 2010; Lachapelle et al. 2020; Levitsky and Way 2022). Almost all rebel groups that seize power face serious domestic and/or international threats (e.g., Walt 1996). Severe threats require greater societal mobilization—absent significant allied foreign intervention—so if threats determine organizations' cohesion and ability to retain power (Levitsky and Way 2022), groups should become more likely to try to build infrastructural power—ensuring regime durability—the more severe the threats they face.

Both when rebels are fighting the state and when they control it, foreign aid and the international environment may shape organizational goals and policies. For example, Cold War–era funds and weaponry from superpowers enabled certain organizations to wage more robust rebellions than others (Kalyvas and Balcells 2010), while rebel organizations' survival and success may depend on the ties they develop to foreign states or activist networks (Bob 2005; Coggins 2015; Huang 2016a). Once victorious rebels are in power, international actors may mandate certain types of state institutions and governance activities as part of peacekeeping operations or conditions of loans or aid (Barma 2017; Berg 2022; Lee 2022; Paris 2004). International incentives and obligations may constrain organizations' behavior once they are in power

TABLE 0.1.   Alternative explanations

VARIABLE	IMPLICATIONS
Resource availability	Rebel group political orientation and decisions about recruitment and civilian relations determined by resource availability.
Charismatic leadership	Organizations with charismatic leaders may be less likely to pursue institutionalized rebel governance and postvictory statebuilding.
Political opportunities	Rebel organizations' decisions based on potential political opportunities to gain domestic and international support.
Territory and constituencies	Rebel aims and behavior shaped by territory and social base while opposing the state.
	Postvictory coercion and statebuilding efforts vary based on social networks and territorial control.
	Ethnic composition and constituencies may have especially strong effects on groups' decisions and resource distribution as rebels and as rulers in power.
Prior state	Statebuilding patterns determined by structures of preexisting state.
Threat severity	More severe threats should increase statebuilding efforts.
International influence	International pressure and incentives should shape policies and practices as rebels and as rulers in power.

and may lead to certain institutional design features. International actors have varied interests so in adjudicating the role of international pressures or incentives in shaping rebel organizations' policies and practices while they are rebelling and once they are in power, we must look at which international actors attempted to exert influence over rebel organizations and the countries they governed and how these efforts interacted with organizations' ideals and goals.

Table 0.1 summarizes these alternative explanations. Throughout the rest of the book, I examine the applicability of these alternative explanations to rebel organizations' ideologies and behavior while fighting against the state and the statebuilding and service provision policies they pursued once they were in power. This illustrates how groups' ideological orientation interacted with these other variables to evaluate when rebel ideology and its organizational effects held independent sway, were moderated by other variables, or were overpowered.

Methods and Case Selection

This study is restricted to the period after World War II ended in 1945, during which civil war has outstripped interstate war as the most common form of large-scale violent conflict. This is also a period for which significant qualitative and quantitative data are available at both the case and cross-national levels to enable internally valid case studies and cross-case comparisons. To analyze the processes through which rebel groups forge plans to implement upon victory and what they actually pursue once in power, I conduct a controlled comparison of three cases located between programmatic-inclusive and opportunistic-exclusive, the most common types for rebel victors: the FSLN in Nicaragua (more programmatic-inclusive), the National Resistance Movement (NRM) in Uganda (middle-ground), and the NPFL in Liberia (more opportunistic-exclusive). The NRM as rebels were called the National Resistance Army (NRA), with the NRM the political wing; the NRM is Uganda's ruling party to this day, so this book refers to both the rebel group and political party as NRM for simplicity.

Comparative case studies are ideal when the total number of potential cases is limited (Skocpol and Somers 1980; Slater and Ziblatt 2013) and the processes to be examined are complex and contingent such that causal inference using statistical analysis is not feasible. Given the limited number of cases of rebel victory after 1945 and the difficulties of gathering nuanced data on ideology and postvictory intentions, close examination of fewer cases is preferable to more general cross-national statistical or qualitative comparative analysis methods. In each case, using evidence from in-depth interviews and archival research, I draw on principles of process tracing (Bennett and Checkel 2015; George and Bennett 2005) and trace the development of organizational type, the role of organizational type throughout the statebuilding process, what other variables intervened at different points, and how the hypothesized causal variable of ideology interacted with the different contextual settings (see Falleti and Lynch 2009). Process tracing offers an "invaluable tool" in understanding "why (and how) outcomes are produced in civil war settings" (Lyall 2015, 186), especially given my focus on ideology and its effects on organizational development and behavior over time (Jacobs 2015).

If civil wars are critical junctures during which the nature of the state and state-society relations are potentially transformed (Thaler 2024a), then it is necessary to examine not only behavior and events during the war but also those that may have precipitated the war in the first place or that shaped the type of group that formed to oppose the state. Controlling for these "critical antecedents" (Slater and Simmons 2010) permits a clearer, more nuanced specification of the workings of causal processes within each case. I break down the historical process into the prewar period, the civil war when organizations were fighting as rebels, and the period after coming to power, and I pay explicit attention to rebel organizations' origins and evolution and to alternative explanatory variables. This allows me to analyze how divergences in organizational goals and ideologies during wartime and the transition to power affected postvictory institutions and practices.

I selected the three cases of the FSLN, NPFL, and NRM for close examination based on variation in organizational type established *during the period of fighting as rebels*, avoiding selecting on the dependent variable (Geddes 1990). I also assessed and selected cases for research feasibility on three criteria: (1) availability of information from primary documents and potential interviewees; (2) my language skills—namely, in French, Portuguese, and Spanish—to conduct interviews and evaluate sources independently; and (3) ability to conduct research without danger to myself or to my informants and without significant government interference.

When assessing statebuilding after rebel victory, I focus on organizations' first decade in power. In this immediate post–civil war period, structural constraints remain relaxed, organizations may enjoy significant popularity for toppling the prior government, and there is thus wide scope to implement transformative programs if desired. The NPFL and its leader, Charles Taylor, were forced from power after only six years, but the NPFL controlled significant territory for most of its time fighting as rebels, giving greater confidence about its governance trajectory. Given that victorious rebel organizations are likely to endure in power, potentially for decades (Lachapelle et al. 2020; Levitsky and Way 2022; Lyons 2016b), the initial period after victory is when organizational type and the experience of rebellion hold the most influence over policy and behavior because the ideology and aims of the organization and leaders may change over time. Some opportunistic organizations may begin with programmatic pretensions (Mampilly 2011; Weinstein 2007, 303–5), while many programmatic groups' ideological adherence diminishes over increasing time in power (Lowenthal 1970; Thaler 2012). Leaders' priorities also often change the longer they stay in power (Bunce 1981; Chiozza and Choi 2003) so this initial postvictory decade is when we should be most able to see the effects of decisions made during the rebel period and to separate them from shifts in goals endogenous to ruling.

My case selection controls for possible alternative explanations by maintaining similarity in the characteristics of the countries where the three victorious rebel organizations formed and fought and the regimes they toppled. The FSLN, NPFL, and NRM as rebels all represented vanguard movements, with relatively strong horizontal ties within the organizations but more limited vertical ties to the population, which can reduce social pressure to engage in governance benefiting civilians (Staniland 2014). The movements also all arose in countries ruled by clientelistic authoritarian regimes with poor statebuilding and poor records in service provision, although in each case there was precedent for prior regimes seeking to build greater state influence throughout the territory and society. While secessionist groups face pressures to engage in state-like rebel governance (Mampilly 2011; Stewart 2018), all three movements sought to gain control of the central state; thus, rebellion-era divergences in governance are not explained. All three rebel organizations experienced tensions in terms of factionalization and attempts at unification among antigovernment armed opposition during their civil wars. The organizations all enjoyed some foreign support and training, but they were unambiguously controlled by domestic national leaders versus serving as proxies for foreign powers. All three movements came to power in contexts of political, economic, and infrastructural collapse, inheriting enormous reconstruction tasks. All three also had to wage new civil wars, this time as the incumbent, soon after taking power, and yet they all governed very differently.

There are some key distinctions across the cases. Most notably, the NPFL came to power through a political victory rather than outright military victory like the FSLN and NRM. NPFL leader Charles Taylor and the NPFL's National Patriotic Party (NPP) won internationally organized elections in 1997 after a peace accord. Yet this electoral victory came in a context where the NPFL remained Liberia's most powerful military actor, having outcompeted all rivals and withstood a non-neutral international intervention. Taylor threatened to return to war if the NPFL did not win electorally, NPFL fighters intimidated opposition candidates and supporters, and many Liberians therefore voted for the NPFL to avert a return to war (Harris 1999; Lyons 1998b). The NPFL and NPP also did not represent a preexisting party or social movement so their legitimacy was based entirely in their military rebellion. The NPFL may not have seized power militarily, but it was the organization's coercive capabilities that won it control of the state.

The three organizations also all fought in different regions and time periods. While Central America, West Africa, and East Africa are quite different, within their regions Nicaragua, Liberia, and Uganda were among the poorest, most underdeveloped, and most mismanaged countries. The countries all had histories of strong foreign influence in their politics, with both Nicaragua and Liberia under US influence for most of the twentieth century, while Uganda emerged from British colonialism and later experienced a Tanzanian military intervention.

The FSLN fought and came to power at the height of the Cold War in the 1970s and 1980s. NRM leaders had been involved in rebel movements throughout the 1970s but gained power only in the mid-1980s, as the Cold War was waning. The NPFL emerged from opposition movements active in the 1970s, and its initial core military forces had attempted a failed coup in 1985, but the organization did not begin rebelling until late 1989, as the Cold War was ending, and began governing in the mid-1990s. The world historical context, while a powerful explanation in many cases for the funding sources available to rebels and governments and prospects for foreign intervention in their politics, does not necessarily explain differences in the ideals and aims pursued by rebel leaders and whether they were oriented toward inclusive or exclusive interests. More programmatic rebels came to power in Ethiopia, Eritrea, and Rwanda around the same time that the NPFL was fighting in Liberia (Fisher 2020), for instance, and the end of the Cold War also did not mean the end of new programmatic-inclusive leftist rebellions: Nepal's Maoists fought a successful civil war from 1996 to 2006.

Comparing these three cases illuminates the pathways from group formation and goal setting to victory and to policy formulation and implementation in power, while examining sources of variation to test my organizational theory. In the conclusion of the book, I also consider how organizational type may evolve and ideological commitments change or wane over the course of time in power. Many programmatic organizations become more opportunistic and leaders more personalistic, for instance among the liberation movements of Southern Africa (Melber 2002; Southall 2013) and in the extended authoritarian presidencies of Yoweri Museveni in Uganda and Daniel Ortega in Nicaragua.

It is possible that the national and world-historical contexts in which the FSLN, NPFL, and NRM emerged overdetermined their organizational type, with circumstances favoring leaders and ideals at particular points on the programmatic-opportunistic and inclusive-exclusive axes. To address this, in chapter 5, I compare the three independent rebel organizations that developed during the Angolan war of independence against Portugal. The Movimento Popular de Libertação de Angola (MPLA), Frente Nacional de Libertação de Angola (FNLA), and União Nacional para a Independência Total de Angola (UNITA) all took up arms around the same time in the 1960s, facing a common enemy within the same territory. Yet other than ending colonial rule, their ideals and goals diverged, which continued shaping their behavior after independence when the MPLA controlled the state and UNITA kept fighting as rebels. In chapter 6, I examine three cases of victory by Islamist groups, assessing my theory's applicability to rebel victors with the most common ideological basis today across Africa and Asia (e.g., Walter 2017b).

Data and Sources

Data on the FSLN, NRM, and NPFL draw on a mix of interviews and archival sources from sixteen months of research in Nicaragua, Liberia, Uganda, and the United States conducted over five years, along with information from documentary and secondary sources. A list of archival sources and interviewees are located, respectively, in the references and in appendix B. Research plans were approved by Harvard University's Committee on the Use of Human Subjects. While I tried to focus interviews on events in the past and individuals' contemporaneous perceptions, there is inevitably some retrospective bias or potential for more recent political events to have shaped what interviewees told me (see Thaler 2021). Where possible, I provide qualitative and quantitative evidence from the time of the groups' rebellions and periods in government to complement interview evidence.

Interviews gathered factual and perceptual information about organizational history, ideology, policies, and practices from military and political members of the organizations, nonmembers who became government officials, civil society members, and some opponents. Interviews are cited in text and listed in appendix B with codes beginning with N for Nicaragua, L for Liberia, U for Uganda, and an interview number (for instance, N-5 or L-17). In archives, I examined internal and public documents from the rebel organizations before and after victory, domestic and international periodicals, and documents from foreign governments and nongovernmental or intergovernmental organizations. Documents intended for private communication within organizations are especially valuable, helping me establish the nature and effects of groups' ideologies (Jacobs 2015, 48–56). I supported and checked my primary research with the existing secondary literature on each case. Together, these data allow for detailed analyses of decision making, policy formulation, and implementation for the victorious rebel organizations, and how people affected by policies and outside analysts perceived organizations' ideals and actions.

I conducted archival research on the FSLN case in Nicaragua over several trips between 2013 and 2017, and in the United States in 2014. The US-based archives help combat potential selection biases in the documents available in the Nicaraguan archives. Nicaragua's military archives have unfortunately been closed to outside researchers since the return of the FSLN and Daniel Ortega to power in 2007, and in August 2023, Ortega's government seized the Universidad Centroamericana and the Instituto de Historia de Nicaragua y Centroamérica, where I conducted much of my research, leaving access and materials' availability uncertain.

I conducted nineteen interviews with eighteen participants in Nicaragua in 2015 and two further interviews in 2017, speaking with former FSLN political leaders, government ministers, and military officers and with members of opposition groups and civil society organizations. I selected interviewees for the roles they had played in the FSLN and government or for their sectoral expertise.

Interviewees were generally part of Nicaragua's political and socioeconomic elite, so I did not offer compensation and no one asked about payment. I offered the option of anonymity, and while one interviewee requested that their comments not be directly quoted or cited, no one asked for their identity to be withheld. However, political conditions in Nicaragua have changed following mass protests in 2018 and a subsequent wave of fierce repression (Mosinger et al. 2022; Thaler and Mosinger 2022), continuing through the time of writing in early 2025. Out of an abundance of caution, I withhold names for quoted or cited living interviewees who are not prominent public figures today.

In Liberia, I interviewed 102 participants in fifty-four sessions over three months in late 2015, talking to former NPFL military officers and political officials; former officers in the government Armed Forces of Liberia (AFL); some NPFL opponents; and scholars, journalists, and civil society actors. Interviewees were selected through purposive sampling followed by limited snowball sampling, where interviewees suggested additional contacts, a common practice in conflict-affected contexts (Malejacq and Mukhopadhyay 2016). Two local research assistants and a local journalist helped me arrange interviews. Enmities among former combatants have largely subsided, and there was little foreseeable risk to my research assistants.

Interviews were conducted in and around Monrovia, Liberia's capital and economic core and home to one-fourth of the national population in 2015. Former fighters and civilians from throughout Liberia migrated to Monrovia, reducing the risk of interview data being unrepresentative of national experiences and views. I concentrated initially on interviewing military figures to understand the NPFL's development because its members prioritized military over political activities when they were rebels. As I reached saturation of information from interviewees, and after a few particularly challenging experiences interviewing individuals who had committed human rights abuses but were seeking to present themselves in a different light (see Thaler 2021, 26–27), I switched to primarily nonmilitary interviewees.

Military interviewees often preferred group interviews, but I conducted these only when interviewees suggested and mutually agreed to them. I told interviewees they did not need to relate any personal experiences of violence, and I asked no questions about these issues to try to avoid retraumatization. Almost all interviews were recorded; however, on two occasions, interviewees requested no recording, and I took handwritten notes. I asked military interviewees not to state their names while the recorder was on (and did not write them down). Omitting ex-combatants' names aligns with other interview-based works on Liberia's civil wars (Gerdes 2013; Lidow 2016), and safeguards against potential future legal risks (Reno 2013).

I told interviewees that while I had limited funds, I recognized that they were sharing their time and experiences, and so I offered compensation of around US$3 cash and a soft drink or US$4 cash, a not insignificant amount but not high enough to be a pressuring incentive for participation. Nonmilitary interviewees were generally national-level public figures in Liberia in government or civil society and were not compensated. While I offered anonymity, almost all elite interviewees declined it. In my judgment, there is minimal risk of negative future consequences (Knott 2019) for named interviewees based on their statements.

Liberia's documentary record was largely destroyed during the civil wars and the NPFL's time in power. I rely mainly on documents from NPFL leader and former Liberian president Charles Taylor's war crimes trial before the Special Court for Sierra Leone, declassified US government documents, media reports, and secondary sources. Through interviewees and other contacts, I was also able to examine some rare publications from the 1990s, including a book of Taylor's speeches during his presidency (Taylor n.d.).

For the NRM case, I conducted research in Uganda from January to June 2016, but political tensions around the 2016 national elections meant only five people were willing to grant interviews during my time there, despite contacting dozens of current and former NRM military and political officials, civil society figures, opposition figures, and journalists. Evidence from the five interviews is used for brief quotations and examples to support archival or secondary source data, which span books, NRM documents and speeches, reports, working papers, and newspaper articles located in various archives and libraries in Uganda.

To analyze the three Angolan rebel organizations and three Islamist cases, I rely primarily on secondary sources. Where possible, I also use primary documents from rebel organizations, governments, and international organizations available online, along with media reports.

Outline of the Book

This book is divided into three parts. Part I, which includes this introduction and chapter 1, establishes the book's theoretical framework and definitions. In chapter 1, I develop my theory in depth, explaining the programmatic and opportunistic and inclusive and exclusive dimensions of rebel organizations and their effects, and providing precise specifications of key concepts and measurement strategies to analyze them. I argue that where a rebel organization falls on the programmatic-opportunistic and inclusive-exclusive axes affects the extent and type of statebuilding and service provision it attempts once installed as the national government. I discuss ideology's importance in setting organizations' trajectories and then develop hypotheses about what we should expect more programmatic or opportunistic and more inclusive or exclusive groups to do with their power once controlling the state.

Part II comprises chapters 2, 3, and 4, which present the case studies of the FSLN, NPFL, and NRM, respectively. I trace each organization's emergence, leadership consolidation, and the development of the ideals and goals around which the group was organized and which it used to recruit and socialize fighters and followers and practice rebel governance. I then turn to analyzing their statebuilding and service provision policies and efforts once in power.

Part III, which includes chapters 5 and 6 and the conclusion, extends the analysis and theory testing beyond the three main cases and discusses the book's broader lessons for research and policy. To demonstrate that rebel organizational type is not necessarily contingent on the country in which rebels are fighting, the regime they are opposing, or when they fight, chapter 5 compares three Angolan rebel groups that formed in the 1960s and fought to topple the Portuguese colonial regime and rule an independent Angolan state but developed distinct ideologies and goals. To probe my arguments' potential applicability to Islamist rebel organizations across time and in diverse contexts, in chapter 6 I analyze the Front de Libération Nationale (FLN) in Algeria, Iran's Islamist revolutionaries, and the Taliban in Afghanistan. In the conclusion, I summarize my findings and discuss how analyzing ideology and variation across rebel groups and their postvictory behavior contributes to the study of civil wars, statebuilding, postconflict politics, and other areas of inquiry. I also discuss the book's implications for policymakers and practitioners. I highlight the need to analyze each organization on its own terms versus assuming organizations with the same general ideological leaning (e.g., leftist or Islamist) will behave the same. Whatever their aims, ideology remains key to engaging with rebel groups before and after victory and understanding what incentives or pressures might be effective and which are likely to be rejected.

STATEBUILDING AFTER REBEL VICTORY

Ideological Orientation and Governing Behavior

How do we explain the way a rebel group is organized and how it interacts with civilians? And how might these rebellion-era factors carry over into power if rebels emerge victorious? I argue that once a rebel organization's leadership is consolidated, the ideology that leaders develop affects how an organization appeals to and recruits members and what institutions it develops internally and in relation with civilians. Civil wars are critical junctures in states' evolution and social relations (Thaler 2024a), times in which structural constraints are relaxed and "there is a substantially heightened probability that agents' choices will affect the outcome of interest" (Capoccia and Kelemen 2007, 348). Rebel leaders' efforts to institutionalize ideological principles can create a self-reinforcing political trajectory throughout the process of rebelling and governing, with path-dependent effects on both wartime behavior and patterns of statebuilding and service provision after taking power, independent of other processes endogenous to the war (see Shesterinina 2022).

Leadership and Ideology

I argue that a rebel organization's ideological type solidifies when leadership has been consolidated so that the organization's goal orientation and agenda are established. The civil wars literature has largely overlooked leaders' agency until recently (Acosta, Huang, and Silverman 2022; Doctor 2021; Prorok 2016), despite leaders like Che Guevara, Mao Tse-Tung, and Võ Nguyên Giáp shaping modern theories of irregular warfare. The weight of structural factors in conflict situations depends on how they are "used, adapted, or manipulated" by leaders (McGovern 2010, xxiii), so leaders' ideas and goals logically will shape rebel organizational development and subsequent policies.

A foundational work in leadership studies is James Downton's (1973) book on rebel and revolutionary leadership, in which he developed a typology of transactional versus transformational leadership. Transactional leadership is based on exchange relationships, with leaders rewarding followers for compliance and for fulfilling specific required tasks. Transformational leaders create a new "shared vision for the future" (Hater and Bass 1988, 695) to tackle more ambitious goals. Transformational leadership motivates followers by raising consciousness of the value and means of achieving certain outcomes, pushing followers to "transcend" self-interest in favor of collective benefits and altering or expanding followers' conception of their needs and wants (Bass 1985, 20). Rebel leaders' aims and how they are enacted are thus key to determining what organizations attempt to achieve while fighting for state power and while exercising it.

In most rebel organizations, multiple potential leaders or leadership groups exist with competing visions for how they believe the organization should behave and what it should pursue (e.g., Bakke, Cunningham, and Seymour 2012; Mampilly 2011). This competition may be resolved through compromise between leaders, elimination of competition through purges or the resignation or sidelining of less powerful contenders, or through fragmentation into multiple competing organizations. In El Salvador, five different armed organizations and additional popular groups peacefully united into the Frente Farabundo Martí para la Liberación Nacional, developing shared leadership around a common vision of political and social transformation (McClintock 1998; Montgomery 1982). The Frente de Libertação de Moçambqiue (Frelimo) in Mozambique, in contrast, consolidated its leadership through purging; the Marxist-Leninist wing violently purged leaders like Lázaro Nkavandame, Uria Simango, and Mateus Gwenjere who sought to promote different ethnic, racial, or economic visions for the organization (Marcum 2018; Pearce 2020).

The leader or group of leaders who win in these struggles can orient the rebel organization toward their preferred ideology and goals. These goals will be endogenous to the sociopolitical dynamics in which the organization arises. But while resource availability (Weinstein 2007), preexisting institutions (Mampilly 2011), and international actors may have some effects on the governance goals and policies adopted by organizations, they do not necessarily outweigh leaders' agency in pursuing their preferences while rebelling or when governing (e.g., Clapham 1998; Selbin 1997; Vu 2010, 240). Once a particular set of leaders consolidates control, the ideology they adopt and develop orients the

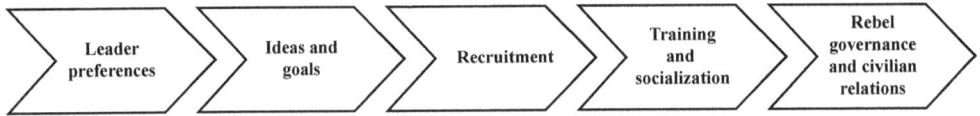

FIGURE 1.1. Process of rebel ideological institutionalization

organization in a path-dependent manner, shaping recruitment practices, internal institutions for training and socializing members, and rebel governance of civilians (see also Gutiérrez Sanín and Wood 2014; Maynard 2019), as depicted in figure 1.1.

Ideological Variation and Organizational Type

When an ideology has clear organizational and political strategies built into it, as in Marxism-Leninism, Maoism, or jihadist Islamism, there may be a road map for leaders to follow in pursuing their goals. Transnational ideologies must always be adapted to domestic political contexts, however, creating different local versions that frequently clash and making it impossible to predict how leaders will apply a transnational ideology. In Colombia, for example, several Marxist-Leninist guerrilla groups emerged with competing aims and strategies (see Arjona 2016, 88–99).

Leaders do not necessarily construct or draw on a well-articulated ideology, however, and may seek instead to mobilize followers based on short-term interests versus the long-term benefits promised by a proposed political future (Hanson 2010). In developing their plans for the rebellion and potential future governance once in power, however, rebel leaders must still have a vision for whom they wish to benefit and what actions might achieve that, forming at least a "thin ideology" addressing limited aspects of politics and society (Freeden 2003, 97–100). Whether the ideology is thick or thin and goals and strategy are clearly or nebulously specified, "all armed groups engaged in *political* violence . . . do so on the basis of an ideology, that is a set of ideas that include preferences (possibly including means toward realizing those preferences) and beliefs" (Gutiérrez Sanín and Wood 2014, 214, emphasis in original).

Rebel leaders must be able to control their followers' violent and nonviolent actions, which they do through rewards and coercive punishments and/or institution building and socialization mechanisms, with variation from group to group (Gutiérrez Sanín and Wood 2014; Hoover Green 2016;

Worsnop 2017). Fighters and cadres have a variety of motivations for joining organizations, many of which may be unrelated and at times opposed to the ideologies leaders espouse. Socialization then channels individual efforts toward collective goals and can potentially change individuals' expectations from seeking personal benefits to thinking about how a broader public may collectively benefit.

Convincing followers of a broader common purpose is only necessary if leaders have a transformative ideological program they wish to enact. Opportunistic leaders can offer fighters a pathway to pursue more personalized aims (as long as they do not challenge leaders' personal interests) because they have little desire for change beyond seizing power and resources, and in exclusive groups no sense of obligation to a broader public. For more programmatic leaders, however, training and socialization are critical because political education can lead followers to internalize an ideology's messages or can reinforce sympathizers' beliefs, enabling the pursuit of more ambitious, transformative goals. If an organization is inclusive, socialization can instill in followers a desire to benefit the population at large. The sense of a long-term, collective purpose produced by ideological development and political education can potentially constrain leaders and induce lower-level members—even those with less sincere ideological adherence—to accept short-term personal costs in exchange for possible future benefits and advancement within the organization (Cremer 1986; Rauch 2001; Soskice, Bates, and Epstein 1992).

In building and testing this theory, I distinguish between rebel groups on two axes based on the ideologically motivated goals they pursue and the policies they enact while fighting as rebels: first, on an axis from *programmatic* to *opportunistic* based on the degree of societal transformation sought (see also Stewart 2021, 49), and second, on an axis from *inclusive* to *exclusive* based on the proportion of the population they seek to benefit. These ideological variations shape how exactly rebel leaders and organizations pursue their goals, what downstream outcomes they desire, and who in society may benefit or lose.

Programmatic Organizations

Programmatic organizations attempt to achieve long-term goals that extend beyond taking power to transforming or significantly reforming socioeconomic and political relations. Ideological principles promoted by leaders guide the groups' formation and structure, as well as their conduct of war and relations with civilians. These principles are institutionally transmitted to cadres and civilian constituents through political education and socialization processes in rebel camps or territory where rebels have control or influence, with the aim to develop compliance with leaders' goals and to shift sociopolitical consciousness

(Hoover Green 2016; Oppenheim and Weintraub 2017; Wood 2003). In territory under their control, programmatic organizations may begin implementing programs and exercising political and economic functions through rebel governance before capturing the central state (e.g., Arjona, Kasfir, and Mampilly 2015; Mampilly 2011; Stewart 2021). Wartime dynamics may make it difficult to consolidate territory and implement such plans until the existing regime is defeated, although an inability to control territory does not necessarily keep rebels from attempting to carry out governance activities (Chakrabarti 2021; Waterman 2023). Limited experience implementing rebel governance also does not preclude pursuing extensive statebuilding after rebel victory, as the Frente Sandinista de Liberación Nacional (FSLN) did in Nicaragua.

More programmatic organizations can vary widely in their ideological content and civilian relations—the Taliban, Khmer Rouge, or Islamic State differ greatly from Frelimo or Cuba's Movimiento 26 de Julio (M-26-J) in these areas. Groups with differing ideologies may adopt similar strategies, with many twentieth-century rebels taking up the Chinese Communist Party's (CCP) model of people's war and building rebel governance institutions (Stewart 2021)—although nonprogrammatic organizations also used the CCP's military strategy toward different political goals—and programmatic organizations may seek to change similar aspects of society, such as the education system or the state's economic role. The types of states that programmatic organizations seek to build will have similar goals of effecting broad impacts on social, political, and economic life and extending state influence throughout the national territory and society, even if the population may disagree with an organization's conception of what is in the public interest (Scott 1979). More programmatic organizations are also more likely to extend the scope of the state's activities, such as seeking central control or influence over social services. Programmatic groups may differ, however, in how inclusive or exclusive they want the postvictory state to be and how they think institutions should be rebuilt, regardless of whether they follow the same strategic model or share a similar transnational ideology that is then adapted to their own circumstances and aims.

Opportunistic Organizations

More opportunistic organizations are motivated primarily by expectations of personalized economic and status benefits or by the use of power for private gain (Collier and Hoeffler 2004; Reno 1998; Weinstein 2007). These groups try to take advantage of opportunities for rebellion to carve out power and profits for themselves. Opportunistic organizations do not seek transformation beyond a change of who is in charge, viewing the state as a prize to win to then "stay in office and collect the fruits of monopolizing political power" (Wintrobe 1990, 849).

Opportunistic organizations display more limited articulation of ideological principles or political and socioeconomic plans, with socialization of members and followers directed mainly at ensuring compliance with leaders' orders, not politicization. Opportunistic leaders may profess wide-ranging and publicly-oriented goals when addressing outside audiences, but these pronouncements tend to be insincere (Collier 2007, 17–32; Thaler 2022), presenting a "pseudoideology, easily shed when convenient" (Markoff and Baretta 1985, 184). Even if opportunistic groups have collective sets of attitudes and goals organizing and motivating their members, they will not have a more comprehensive "thick" ideology (see Linz 1975, 266–69) that offers "an explicit and desirable picture of the political future" (Hanson 2010, xiv), operating instead on a thinner ideology of self-interest and self-aggrandizement.

Opportunistic organizations can still forge sufficient unity and military power to capture the state through a number of means (Stewart 2021, 67–68). They may gain popular support simply by opposing hated and repressive governments or by insincerely exploiting popular grievances (Thaler 2022). Even without popular support, an opportunistic organization may emerge victorious if it benefits from significant natural resources, external intervention or foreign fighters, or international efforts to weaken the incumbent government (Maynard and Thaler 2018; Weinstein 2007). The collapse of government forces can also enable an opportunistic organization to gain control of the state, although it might still have to outcompete other contenders for power.

State weakness and unpopular regimes have helped several opportunistic African rebel organizations take power, including the Alliance des Forces Démocratiques pour la Libération du Congo (AFDL) in the Democratic Republic of the Congo (DRC) and the Mouvement Patriotique du Salut in Chad. Some Kosovo Liberation Army leaders were allegedly profit seeking and tied to organized crime, harnessing popular grievances and using ethnonationalism as a vehicle for private ambitions in an independent Kosovo (Pugh 2004; Judah 2000). Some Southeast Asian rebel groups have also been more interested in riches than in developing robust governance structures and practices, with the remnants of the Khmer Rouge, for instance, becoming opportunistic in the 1990s (Berdal and Keen 1997). Different fronts within the Fuerzas Armadas Revolucionarias de Colombia in Colombia and Sendero Luminoso in Peru also, over time, turned from a more programmatic-inclusive focus on sociopolitical transformation to prioritizing private profits (Weinstein 2007). If they seize power, opportunistic organizations pursue much narrower aims than programmatic groups and have a more limited impact on society beyond coercion, seeking to use the state for economic extraction and perpetuation in power while largely ignoring the broader population's interests.

Inclusive versus Exclusive Benefits

Beyond the degree of societal transformation they are seeking, rebel ideologies can be distinguished by the extent of the population an organization aims to benefit in the country they seek to control, varying along a spectrum from inclusive to exclusive. All organizations may be inclusive in some ways or areas and exclusive in others, so I focus on their predominant orientation (Mudde and Rovira Kaltwasser 2013, 167).

Inclusive organizations aim to provide public goods including and beyond order to the majority of the population without significant favoritism or discrimination (Stewart 2018, 2021; Wickham-Crowley 1987), thereby bringing more of the population under the state's political influence when in power. While rebelling, they are thus more likely to devote resources not just to war but also to providing services to most people under their control, versus providing goods and services only to committed supporters or members of their own ethnic group. In rebel governance and in power, any type of organization may provide goods and services to seek popular support (Bell 2011; Mampilly 2011; Stewart 2018, 210), but more programmatic-inclusive organizations, who feel ideologically compelled to provide goods and services, will do so even among groups who do not want their interventions (Hale 1994; Scott 1998; Stewart 2021, 11).

Exclusive organizations aim primarily to secure private welfare for leaders and group members and direct goods and services to limited constituencies or client groups (Azam 2006; Stewart 2018; Weinstein 2007). Exclusive groups may provide order in areas under their control while rebelling, but it is either an extractive order, with little benefit for civilians beyond violence being more predictable (Reno 2015), or an order with benefits for a selected constituency, "exclud[ing other] people from services by simply barring access to goods, by expelling them from a territorial space, or by killing them" (Stewart 2018, 208). This exclusivity may sometimes escalate into mass violence against populations outside an organization's conception of its ideal public or nation (Straus 2015).

Groups fall somewhere in the four quadrants of programmatic-inclusive, programmatic-exclusive, opportunistic-inclusive, and opportunistic-exclusive, with most victorious rebel organizations located somewhere on the diagonal between programmatic-inclusive and opportunistic-exclusive, as illustrated in figure 1.2.

I classify as *middle-ground* those organizations falling closer to the center, where the axes meet. One example is the Zimbabwe African National Union (ZANU), which fought to end the white minority's discriminatory rule in then-Rhodesia. ZANU leaders were not simply seeking enrichment, yet beyond overturning the racial hierarchy they were not seeking more extensive socioeconomic transformation or public goods and services provision for most

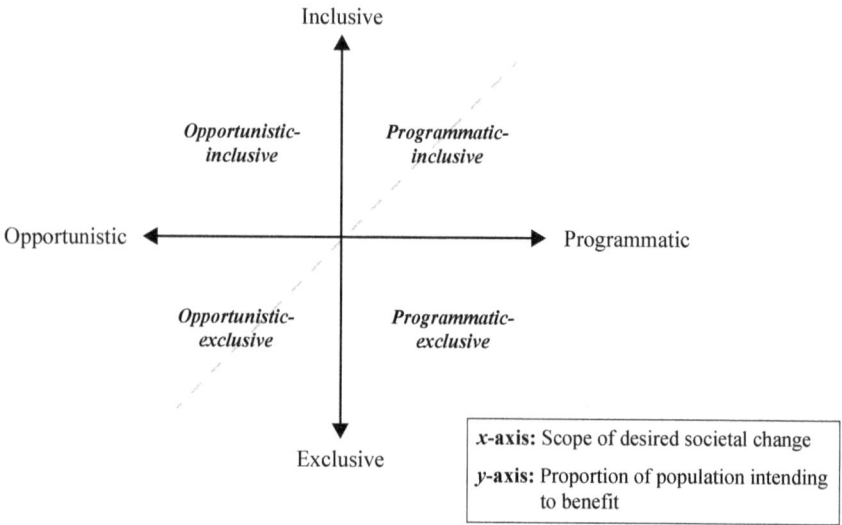

FIGURE 1.2.   Rebel organizational type

Zimbabweans (Alexander 1994; Brett 2005; Moore 1991; Phimister 1987), which would have required greater infrastructural power once ZANU controlled the state. In power, ZANU undertook some meaningful reform efforts, creating workers' committees and a new national trade union (Yates 1980, 76) and taking some steps to address inequities in health and education (Barry et al. 1990; Brett 2005; Kanyongo 2005, 66–67). ZANU disappointed many Zimbabweans, however, who had hoped for a transformative social revolution and a stronger, more inclusive state (Alexander 1994; Brett 2005).

Ideology is complex and contested, and case experts may disagree with one another (and with me), so I classify rebel organizations and their ideologies qualitatively rather than creating quantitative scores. When it comes to the nuances of ideology, this is a case where "the task of producing quantifiable measures of the relevant variables" for cross-case comparison "requires such oversimplification that the resulting proxies distort reality beyond reasonable limits" (Hall 2006, 26), offering only an illusion of precision.

Rhetoric and Reality

Ideological discourse may shape goals and is a component of a rebel organization's political identity (Gutiérrez Sanín and Wood 2014; Kalyvas 2015b), and it does sometimes sincerely reveal intentions (Stewart 2021, 17–18). A group's true intent and nature may be revealed, however, through practice more than doctrine

(Kasfir 2015, 40). To conceptualize and measure rebel organizational type, we must consider not only what organizations and their leaders claim to believe and seek but also what they *do*, whether they achieve their aims or not. Organizations may have incentives to write policy proposals and stage demonstrations for domestic and international audiences to present themselves as concerned with public interests and human rights (Jo 2015; Stanton 2016) while, if they are opportunistic and exclusive, still directing their energies toward accumulating private power and material wealth or marginalizing significant populations.

I therefore focus on both the *expressed preferences* rebel leaders articulate through their discourse and documents or media and their *revealed preferences* demonstrated through organizational behavior and how attempts are made (or not) to put pronouncements into action. This helps distinguish ideological "cheap talk" (Collier 2007, 17–20; Walter 2017a) from more sincere intentions and the costly signal of moving from expression to action. Examining both discourse and practice, I coded the FSLN in Nicaragua as more programmatic-inclusive; the National Patriotic Front of Liberia (NPFL) as more opportunistic-exclusive; and the National Resistance Movement (NRM) in Uganda as a middle-ground case slightly more toward the programmatic and inclusive ends of those spectrums, seeking to transform politics but with less interest in rebuilding Uganda's economy and social structures. Figure 1.3 depicts these three groups on the organizational type axes.

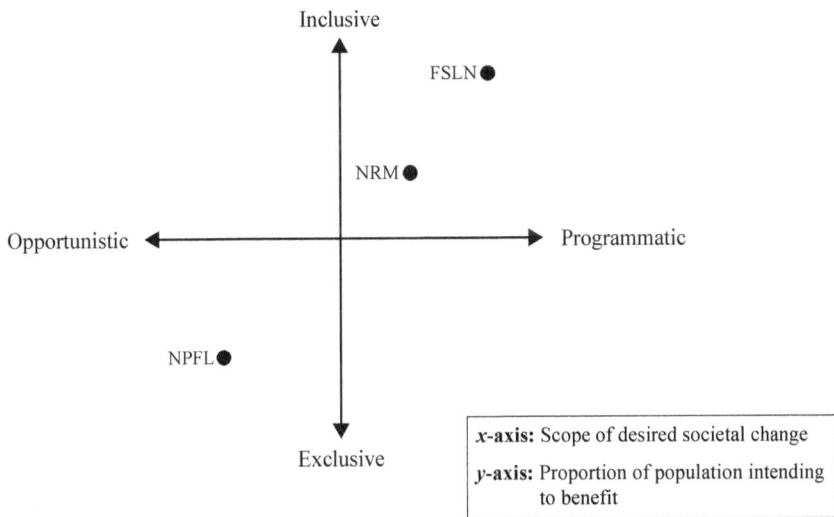

FIGURE 1.3. Organizational types of the Frente Sandinista de Liberación Nacional (FSLN), National Patriotic Front of Liberia (NPFL), and National Resistance Movement (NRM)

From Rebellion to Statebuilding

After victory, rebel leaders and the organizations they have built face both opportunities and constraints as they transition from fighting against the state to controlling it. Victorious rebels must decide, for instance, which of their practices and institutions to maintain or if they wish to rely on the previous state's structures. Either way, "they have become different kinds of governments with different pressures and resources, particularly if they receive international recognition" (Kasfir 2015, 25).

The international system and remaining state institutions present both possibilities and potential barriers for achieving organizational goals. International actors can provide or withhold aid or advice, and postconflict international assistance may come with conditions or be given freely depending on the provider (Barma 2017; Coggins 2016; Lake 2016). Aid can be useful in building state capacity, but leaders can also use aid to substitute for state action or privately appropriate aid instead of directing it toward the population. Membership in the international system could constrain victorious rebels by making them subject to more international laws and norms, yet it also offers access to new resources, influence in international organizations, and the protections of sovereignty.

The extent to which preexisting state institutions persist or have been destroyed similarly provides opportunities or constraints, with at least some institutions or personnel remaining after most revolutions or rebel victories (Skocpol 1979). An existing bureaucracy may provide a basis for statebuilding projects, or it could serve to redirect or block victorious rebels' goals. Maintaining old state institutions and structures may be the path of least resistance but could lead victorious rebels to emulate the pathologies of the government they just defeated, or existing structures might be used only as a foundation, avoiding the costs of statebuilding from scratch but aiming for reform and transformation.

Domestic interest groups will seek to make claims on the new government and international actors will pressure it, whatever its organizational type. Such outside influences may make it difficult for victorious rebels to carry out their intended plans but will not necessarily force an ideological shift or foreclose the possibility of attempting policy implementation. Outside demands can be defied, and external pressures ultimately place potential limits on victorious rebels *achieving* their desired outcomes but not what they attempt.

How organizations interact with and respond to these opportunity structures varies depending on how they developed ideologically and organizationally during the rebellion period, with regimes' founding ideologies powerfully affecting their behavior (Straus 2015). It is certainly possible that a programmatic-inclusive organization's leaders *could*, upon taking over the state, decide pursuing private wealth is more important than enacting the vision they professed and sought to implement as rebels. An opportunistic-exclusive organization's leaders *could* feel a new responsibility to govern in the interests of a broader public and forgo extracting private wealth from the state. In the near term, however, these possibilities are highly unlikely. The political visions and institutions of recruitment, socialization, and rebel governance that organizations developed have carried them to victory so there is little incentive to change tack.

Changing political circumstances while rebelling or once in power may lead organizations to adapt the *means* by which they are attempting to implement their goals (see Tapscott and Urwin 2024) but should not change the ultimate *ends* toward which they are working. External constraints and pressures may provoke a shift in goal orientation over time and move the victorious rebel organization along the spectrums toward programmatic or opportunistic and inclusive or exclusive. The path dependencies produced by decisions made as rebels when constructing the organization are likely to endure at least through the first decade in power, however, highlighting the importance of looking at not only rebel governance but also its legacies (e.g., Ibáñez et al. 2023; Kubota 2017; Martin, Piccolino, and Speight 2022).

Predicted Governing Behavior

What types of statebuilding decisions will victorious rebels make? Will they focus mainly on coercive power and some degree of resource extraction, or will they also seek to build infrastructural power? All governments pursue coercive power and some revenue sources, but not all pursue extensive statebuilding projects (Herbst 2000; Slater 2010; Soifer 2015; Vu 2010). This will be the key difference between opportunistic and programmatic groups, with only programmatic groups seeking to build infrastructural power.

Coercive power is fundamental to the nature of the state (Weber 1946), and the capacity to mobilize violence to pursue their goals is also inherent to rebel organizations. Power is always contested to varying extents between state and society (Mann 1993; Migdal 1988, 2001; Scott 1998), but coercive power enables the state to try to impose its will on society rather than compromising or investing in other means of influencing the population. All rebel groups and governments also seek to generate revenues, which are necessary for organizing a coercive apparatus and for other activities, like providing goods and services (Bates 2010; Levi 1988; Tilly 1990). Tax collection capacity has frequently been employed as a measure of state strength (see Lieberman 2002), but post–civil war governments (and lower-income states more generally) are likely to be highly dependent on foreign aid or easily collected trade taxes requiring limited bureaucratic capacity (Besley and Persson 2008, 2014). Sources of revenues therefore may not be as important as the ends to which funds are directed.

What remains more contested is why state leaders invest in developing infrastructural power by extending noncoercive state influence through society and throughout the territory (Herbst 2000; Slater 2010; Soifer 2015; Waldner 1999), especially when, in many lower-income states, "government sovereignty often does not extend far beyond capital cities" (Vu 2010, 9). The ability to project force and coercive dominance is a natural goal for victorious rebels, who have gained power through insurrection and worry about befalling a similar fate against domestic enemies while also often facing threats from foreign rivals (Clarke 2023; Lachapelle et al. 2020; Levitsky and Way 2022; Walt 1996). This desire for security does not necessitate developing infrastructural power, however; some leaders may feel they can take advantage of the post-1945 international system's sovereignty protections to avoid the imperative to develop territorial control felt by rulers in earlier eras (Herbst 2000; Jackson and Rosberg 1982). More programmatic organizations' goals of transforming political, economic, and social institutions, however, demand attempts to build infrastructural power and expand the state's reach beyond the capital or a small elite stratum.

Victorious rebel organizations may confront unfavorable conditions for successful statebuilding given the constraints they may face and the difficulties of learning to govern a sovereign state, but this does not prevent them from attempting statebuilding if they so desire. Some rebel groups already seek to engage in more programmatic governance even when they have limited resources and lack territorial control (Chakrabarti 2021; Waterman 2023), and victorious rebels usually have to outcompete other opposition groups and state forces (Krause 2017), thereby demonstrating capacity to pursue and potentially implement desired policies. As Soifer (2015) points out, there is a crucial distinction between statebuilding *efforts* and statebuilding *success* when pursuing infrastructural power, and the factors behind each may be different, so I therefore focus on statebuilding attempts and not only outcomes.

Prior theories of statebuilding efforts have emphasized leaders' calculation of the costs and benefits of building infrastructural power (Herbst 2000; Soifer 2015; Waldner 1999), but programmatic organizations have an ideological imperative to engage in statebuilding efforts. These groups have engaged in armed struggle for transformative goals and have indoctrinated followers, built institutions, and developed and promoted policies toward these ends. Programmatic-inclusive organizations may also feel obliged to honor a "social contract" created with civilians during the civil war through rebel governance (Wickham-Crowley 1987) and believe the state under their control should be used to change the broader public's circumstances, in line with group leaders' conception of what would be good for them. We should expect programmatic groups' leaders to maintain their goals even after taking power, for "principled ideologues do not immediately turn into stereotypical Machiavellians the moment they gain control of the state" (Hanson 2010, xvi). Programmatic organizations are thus pushed to develop infrastructural power, whether they succeed or not, while opportunistic organizations are more likely to remain content with building coercive power and securing access to material resources.

Opportunistic organizations are also more likely to choose to deliver exclusive benefits to a narrower population. For more programmatic organizations, expanding infrastructural power and more direct, noncoercive state involvement "in the routinized practices of quotidian politics" (Waldner 1999, 3) often requires increased state provision of goods and services to a wider, more inclusive constituency. This is especially the case if the organization wants to level societal hierarchies. Inclusive benefits also help incorporate people into the state's sphere of influence while sidelining alternative local or regional power holders by developing citizens' loyalty to or dependence on the state (Waldner 1999). Engaging with society through civic organizations and controlling services like education and health care are goals that programmatic organizations aim to achieve and offer means to promote their ideological vision. For programmatic-inclusive groups, this involves expanding access to services, but programmatic-exclusive organizations might seek control over services to privatize them or restrict accessibility.

Hypothesized Behavior in Government: Programmatic-Inclusive Organizations

Programmatic-inclusive organizations were among the most common victors during the Cold War. Inspiration, strategies, and material support from the Soviet Union, China, and Cuba especially helped leftist organizations wage "robust insurgencies" (Kalyvas and Balcells 2010), and they often emerged as winners. Programmatic-inclusive rebels in Asia took power in anticolonial rebellions in countries like North Korea, Vietnam, and Laos. After the end of European and Japanese colonization, there have also been two successful independence movements in Bangladesh (Baxter 1998) and Timor-Leste (Strating 2016; Kammen 2019), both aided by eventual foreign intervention. Most recently, the Communist Party of Nepal-Maoist (CPN-M) fought a civil war from 1996 to 2006 that ended monarchical rule; its members accepted a democratic political system, winning the first elections (Adikhari 2014; Lawoti and Pahari 2010). Around Africa, programmatic-inclusive, Marxist-Leninist rebels won power in anticolonial uprisings, like Frelimo in Mozambique in 1975 (Marcum 2018) and the Eritrean People's Liberation Front in 1991 (Pool 2001), though other late Cold War rebel victors like the NRM and ZANU had less transformative ideologies (Fisher 2020). In Latin America, Cuba's M-26-J rebel victors directly inspired and aided the FSLN, along with many other movements who could not achieve the same success (Kruijt 2017; Wickham-Crowley 1992).

Changing sociopolitical and economic systems and relations and inclusively delivering services requires the ability to access and monitor regions and populations. To pursue their transformative goals, programmatic-inclusive organizations must work to establish state influence throughout society, building mechanisms for political education to incorporate more citizens into their project, and building institutions to extend state influence and activities geographically.

State absence in the periphery has been the norm in lower and middle-income countries. Herbst (2000, 19) describes rural areas in Africa as lacking "even the most basic agents of the state—agricultural extension workers, tax collectors, census takers." O'Donnell (1993) characterized Latin American peripheries as zones of state absence. Large swathes of Southeast Asia remained "zones of weak or no sovereignty" for central states until the late twentieth century (Scott 2009, xii). A more programmatic organization must be able to reach into these areas and social spheres to effect or even attempt changes. We should therefore see programmatic-inclusive victors increasing state personnel's territorial coverage and attempting to deliver public goods where they were previously lacking, extending infrastructural power and not only coercive capacity.

Alongside institutions, expanding physical infrastructure and communications links can help integrate peripheral areas with the national core (Herbst 2000; Soifer 2015). Extending roads or railroads and building ports or airports enables faster movement of security forces to areas, increasing coercive power. Extending physical infrastructure, however, also enables greater exchange of people, goods, and ideas between regions, and ensures the state's ability to deliver the supplies and personnel necessary for inclusive organizations to expand public service provision in health, education, sanitation, or other sectors (Müller-Crepon, Hunziker, and Cederman 2021). Developing administrative capacity to track demography, geography, and socioeconomic status also facilitates further statebuilding and service provision efforts (Lee and Zhang 2016; Soifer 2012). Censuses, surveys, and national identity registration can help target and deliver social or economic programs, and aid in formal military conscription. Cadastral surveys and mapping help target physical infrastructure projects and are necessary for land reform and redistribution programs. Telecommunications capacity enables state monitoring of territory and the population, and offers opportunities to transmit political education material to draw citizens to an ideological program (e.g., Warren 2014). Satellites, drones, and internet data can help map and monitor territory and people more easily than in the past, but governments must still decide to invest in this capacity, and many administrative activities like census taking and vaccination still require state agents physically reaching people and places to ensure coverage and reliability.

Beyond extending physical infrastructure and administrative capacity, programmatic-inclusive organizations may seek to increase the scope of activities the state undertakes (Fukuyama 2004), creating or reforming institutions to shape or carry out a wider array of political, social, and economic activities. They may also seek influence over and through civil society through means such as popular mobilizations or building government-affiliated corporatist organizations. This mobilizing capacity and delivering a range of public services allows organizations to reach more of the populations they wish to benefit and to involve them in pursuing political goals, as well as ensuring that delivery of goods and services aligns with ideological preferences. The mobilization and service provision that programmatic-inclusive groups pursue also offer means to shape citizens' normative commitments and perceptions of the state's potential role in their lives, ideational influence that facilitates further statebuilding efforts (see e.g., Thornton 2007). Expanded state education provision, for example, lets victorious rebels influence educational content, shaping the national mentality and building popular allegiance. Public health-care provision can be part of reducing societal inequalities, but state control also offers opportunities to determine which services are delivered; groups might, for ideological reasons, decide to provide or deny reproductive health or addiction treatment services, for example.

We should observe programmatic-inclusive organizations channeling resources toward expanding state influence, implementing new programs, and delivering public goods and services. We should not see leaders or members accruing significant personal wealth based on their positions in the first decade after victory because diverting resources to private coffers would diminish organizations' ability to noncoercively effect change.

Hypothesized Behavior in Government: Opportunistic-Exclusive Organizations

Opportunistic-exclusive rebellions have remained common globally, especially since the end of the Cold War (Reno 2011; Kaldor 2013; Stearns 2022), and several have seized power. Chad has been taken over by opportunistic-exclusive rebels three times since the 1970s: the Forces Armées Populaires/Gouvernement d'Union Nationale de Transition in 1979, the Forces Armées Nationales in 1982, and the Mouvement Patrotique du Salut in 1990 (Nolutshungu 1996; Azevedo 1998). In 1997, the same year the AFDL took power in the DRC, corrupt former Republic of Congo president Denis Sassou-Nguesso and his Cobra militia gained control across the Congo River in Brazzaville (Clark 2008).

More opportunistic groups engage in minimal statebuilding once in power, largely maintaining or ignoring preexisting state structures. Building state institutions and expanding state influence are difficult tasks that require significant investments of resources, effort, and time (Rueschemeyer and Evans 1985). Opportunistic-exclusive organizations are driven more by short-term, personalistic concerns of quick returns for their efforts and thus limit such costly investments, even if they have long-term goals of continued extraction for private gain. Opportunistic-exclusive organizations therefore turn existing institutions and the country's resources toward securing their own interests and exclusive benefits for narrow constituencies rather than governing for a broader public.

Opportunistic-exclusive organizations should devote resources primarily to two sectors: security and the economy. They have less interest in a fully functioning state that can serve public interests, but they are quite content to develop a "shadow state," with state institutions providing a façade for private relationships and parallel structures channeling resources toward leaders' and their allies' own benefit (Reno 1995a, 1998). Because their priority is private (i.e., personalized) security, not protecting the population at large, opportunistic victors have less incentive to extend state influence and even security forces' reach into peripheral areas. Their focus geographically is primarily on core areas where the organization and its leaders have political and economic interests. Opportunistic-exclusive organizations may create order, but it will likely be a coercive, predatory governance instead of the development of a social contract (Reno 2015), mirroring Tilly's (1985) vision of war making and state making as a criminal protection racket.

In the economic sector, opportunistic-exclusive organizations may build or maintain ministries to manage production and extraction of natural and agricultural resources, or parallel structures may be created to funnel wealth to group leaders. We should thus see most state bureaucratic resources devoted to extraction and security, with investments in physical infrastructure primarily around resource-rich areas, military installations, and leaders' or selected constituencies' home areas. Increasing state reach through society is unlikely to be a priority beyond coercive power and intelligence collection, and neither is delivering inclusive benefits to improve social and economic outcomes for the masses, so we should see limited or very targeted investment in state provision of goods and services. Administrative structures that opportunistic-exclusive organizations develop are likely to be hollow and used for patronage for members or supporters rather than public goods provision.

Because opportunistic-exclusive organizations do not have the goal of ideologically converting or indoctrinating the population, they may be more willing to let nongovernmental or religious organizations pick up the slack in social service provision (Mampilly 2011) as long as these nonstate actors do not try to undermine the organization's political authority or interfere with resource extraction. Nongovernmental organizations' resources and foreign development aid may also be seen as sources of rents to divert from public projects toward government officials' own accounts—sometimes with donors' acquiescence (Brautigam 2000; Easterly 2006).

Programmatic-Exclusive Rebel Victors: Reactionary or Ethnic Paths

While little represented among victorious rebel organizations and not examined in depth in this book, there may sometimes be programmatic-exclusive organizations that pursue societal transformation to benefit a narrower slice of the population, like elites, members of their own ethnic group, or cosectarians. In some cases, programmatic-exclusive rebels might be more conservative actors seeking to undo transformations undertaken by prior regimes in order to return to idealized past values and systems. Nationalist forces under Francisco Franco fought in the Spanish Civil War to transform society by uprooting social changes enacted by the prior Republican regime and reestablishing a hierarchical political and social order benefitting socioeconomic and religious elites (Balcells 2017; Graham 2005; Preston 2006). The Nationalists aimed to create an elitist "dictatorship of the bourgeoisie" (Esteban 1976, 82–83) and, once in power from 1939 to 1975, they collaborated with the Catholic Church to exclude the Republicans' leftist and working-class supporters from state services and benefits (Mangen 2001, chap. 2).

Since 1945, however, political actors seeking to preserve the status quo or return to the past have taken power more often through coups than rebellions. In Chile, for example, right-wing politicians and economic elites grew unhappy with the more inclusive socialist policies adopted under President Salvador Allende's government from 1970 to 1973. Rather than start a rebellion, however, right-wing paramilitaries assassinated some government and left-wing figures but worked primarily to foment a military coup; military leaders behind General Augusto Pinochet seized power in 1973 and built a more exclusionary regime inspired by Francoist Spain while rapidly liberalizing Chile's economy

(Ortiz de Zárate 2003; Weld 2018). Right-wing rebels during the Cold War, such as the contras in Nicaragua and Resistência Nacional Moçambicana (Renamo) in Mozambique (Thaler 2022), often had more opportunistic aims and focused on destabilization more than governance and controlling the state—and they rarely emerged victorious.

A more likely source of programmatic-exclusive rebel victors is ethnic minority rebel organizations, who can take advantage of state collapse or strong military capabilities to seize control of the central state (versus seceding) and may aim to build a new state, but one disproportionately benefiting in-group members. This was arguably the case in Rwanda. The Rwandan Patriotic Front (RPF) had significant military experience from fighting alongside the NRM in Uganda and was dominated by members of the Tutsi ethnic minority. The RPF had clear programmatic goals of transforming Rwanda into a modernized and "de-ethnicized" society (Buckley-Zistel 2006; McDoom 2022; Purdeková 2008) in response to instability, discrimination, and violence by governments controlled by the Hutu ethnic majority, which culminated in the 1994 Rwandan genocide. The RPF stopped the genocide and swept to power in 1994, although its forces committed atrocities of their own against Hutus during the campaign (Reyntjens 1996; Straus 2019; Verwimp 2003). The RPF sometimes proclaimed a goal of broadening its base across ethnicities (Reed 1996, 479) and while in power it has sought to suppress ethnicity as a societal cleavage in favor of "consensus" and "unity" (McDoom 2022). The infrastructural improvements, economic development, and poverty reduction the RPF oversaw in power have benefited all Rwandans—but they are not intended to do so toward equal ends. The RPF and its leader, Paul Kagame, believed building up public infrastructure and improving service delivery were key to keeping the Hutu majority quiescent and preserving security; while many Hutus appreciate improvements in public services, they remain politically excluded (Ingelaere, Ndayiragije, and Verpoorten 2022; Mann and Berry 2016). The RPF ultimately geared infrastructural power and economic growth toward ensuring Tutsis remain secure and prosperous in Rwanda, directing greater benefits toward Tutsis and RPF elites and centralizing power in an increasingly authoritarian manner (Desrosiers and Thomson 2011; Reyntjens 2006; Straus and Waldorf 2011; Weerdesteijn 2019). The RPF was thus not as exclusive as a group that actively denies goods and services to members of other ethnic groups, but in practice it has not actually been inclusive in terms of who it intends state power to benefit. There remains little prospect of this changing as long as Kagame remains in power, and Rwanda's electoral authority declared him the winner of the unfair 2019 and 2024 elections with 99 percent of the vote, while constitutional reforms allow him potentially to serve until at least 2034 (Reyntjens 2024; Ssuuna 2024).

When an ethnic minority takes power as part of a rebel coalition, more exclusive aims might need to be subordinated to consolidate power, but they could then emerge over time. For example, the NRM's base was among leader Yoweri Museveni's western Banyankole ethnic group and the Baganda with whom they allied. The group was initially somewhat inclusive (but excluded northerners), yet after the NRM's first decade in power, control and state benefits became even more concentrated with Museveni's western Ugandan constituency (Lindemann 2011).

Many ethnic minority rebel organizations, however, start by seeking secession or autonomy and only later shift to national-level aims, like the Frente Nacional de Libertação de Angola (FNLA) did in Angola, incentivizing them to try to build pan-ethnic coalitions. One such coalition, the Ethiopian People's Revolutionary Democratic Front (EPRDF), collapsed into conflict in 2020, three decades after taking power. The EPRDF was led by the Tigray People's Liberation Front (TPLF), a nationalist rebel group formed in the 1970s to seek independence for the Tigrayan ethnic minority. The TPLF's planning and rebel governance concentrated on serving Tigrayans (Matfess 2022; Vaughan 2011), but as war continued into the 1980s, the TPLF forged ties with other ethnic groups and formed new allied movements among the more populous Amhara and Oromo peoples (Vaughan 2003; Lyons 2019; Young 1997; Berhe 2009). After taking power in 1991, the relatively programmatic EPRDF undertook a "radical restructuring of the Ethiopian polity [including] the introduction of formal multi-party politics, recognizing ethnicity as the political idiom of public life, holding elections, redrawing administrative boundaries, decentralizing bureaucracy, and liberalizing different sectors of the economy" (Hagmann and Abbink 2011, 582). The EPRDF initially promoted an inclusive vision of an Ethiopian state that would provide autonomy, economic development, and benefits to all the country's ethnic groups. Yet the TPLF continued dominating the EPRDF, and frustrations grew about ethnic favoritism, cronyism, and failures to distribute resources and power equitably beyond TPLF elites and their allies (Abbink 2009; Vaughan and Gebremichael 2011; Gebregziabher and Hout 2018).

TPLF dominance finally ended in 2018, when the Oromo Democratic Party's leader, Abiy Ahmed, took over as EPRDF chair and Ethiopia's prime minister. Abiy challenged the TPLF and Tigrayan elites' control, sparking conflicts over elections and the resources Tigray received, and the TPLF refused to join the Prosperity Party that Abiy created to succeed the EPRDF (Lyons 2021). This escalated to war in late 2020. TPLF officials and Tigrayan forces said that they were seeking to preserve ethnoregional autonomy in the face of central government overreach and Abiy's personalization of power, while Abiy suggested Tigrayans were trying to secede or reclaim control and that they needed to be crushed. The conflict spiraled as the government mobilized militias and received support from Eritrean troops; Tigrayan forces allied with the Oromo Liberation Army and called for overthrowing Abiy; and all parties committed (and denied) atrocities (Matfess and Lyons 2023; Plaut and Vaughan 2023; Verhoeven and Woldemariam 2022; Woldemariam and Woldgabreal 2023). Setting aside questions of blame, TPLF unwillingness to accept changes in the internal EPRDF balance of power suggests they were ultimately concerned more with Tigrayan welfare than an inclusive Ethiopian nation, an exclusivity the TPLF had initially cloaked behind the EPRDF's coalitional nature.

Victories by programmatic-exclusive rebels are clearly possible, but future research can specify the conditions under which they occur. Ethnic fractionalization may play a role in what type of rebel organization minorities seek to form. Rwanda has two major ethnic groups, so the Tutsis who led the RPF may have been more likely to go it alone, while Ethiopia and Uganda's kaleidoscope of ethnic groups could have created incentives for early TPLF and NRM leaders to seek coalition partners. Specifying how civil-military relations affect sociopolitical or ethnic minority actors' decisions about whether to rebel or launch a coup (see, e.g., Roessler 2016) can also improve our understanding about the prospects for both civil war onset and rebel victory. Finally, investigating the development of minority rebel organizations' ideologies can shed light on when they adopt programmatic aims (e.g., Stewart 2023), and when they pursue inclusivity or form a broader coalition at least initially versus seeking exclusive benefits.

The Elusive Opportunistic-Inclusive Rebel Victor

Rebels interested in using state power to benefit the broader public tend to want to transform the status quo beyond only who is governing because they are generally fighting in highly unequal societies (e.g., Cederman, Gleditsch, and Buhaug 2012). This means opportunistic-inclusive groups, the fourth rebel organizational type, are unlikely to take control of a state. We can think of opportunistic-inclusive types as Robin Hood–style social bandits (Hobsbawm 1959): aiming to redistribute resources to the popular majority but otherwise wanting to preserve their own well-being and not seeking to systematically overturn sociopolitical systems. Organizations concerned with regionally specific distribution of resources and revenues, who might fall into Reno's (2011) category of "parochial rebels," need not control the state to pursue inclusive aims. Even under repressive central governments, they can use their coercive power to carve out space to deliver services and can seek autonomy rather than independence.

When a more exclusive regime collapses, those actors trying to shift the state toward inclusivity tend also to want programmatic changes. In Libya, early leaders of rebel forces opposing the Gaddafi regime declared intentions to carry out a relatively programmatic and inclusive rebuilding of the state and society (Interim National Council 2011). More opportunistic and exclusive members of the rebel coalition seized the initiative during the transition, however, sparking a new civil war and fragmenting authority to their own benefit (Lacher 2020). One could imagine a social democratic rebel organization in a democracy fighting not for major societal transformation but still seeking wider, more inclusive resource distribution and service provision. Yet when leftist rebel groups have taken up arms against democratic governments, they tend to want to pursue more radical, extensive statebuilding and inclusion if they gain power (Staniland 2021).

An opportunistic-inclusive rebel organization might conceivably take state power if a split within an already inclusive government escalated to a civil war and the resulting rebel victors maintained or expanded inclusive public policies but had little interest in further statebuilding beyond ensuring their own political standing and security. While not a civil war, we can see these dynamics in the 1980 coup within the Partido Africano para a Independência da Guiné e Cabo Verde (PAIGC), the victorious rebel organization that freed then-united Guinea-Bissau and Cape Verde from Portuguese rule in 1975. PAIGC had programmatic-inclusive aims, but its postindependence statebuilding efforts were slow, and many people in Guinea-Bissau (where the bulk of the fighting had taken place) felt the distribution of power and resources unevenly favored Cape Verdeans and urbanites. Ethnic, rural-urban, and interpersonal conflicts escalated in the late 1970s between President Luis Cabral, a Cape Verdean, and prime minister and army commander João Bernardo Vieira, who was from Guinea-Bissau and was supported by the military, peasants, and Guinea-Bissau's major ethnic groups. Vieira seized power in a 1980 coup, and while he did not seek to build state infrastructural power, he initially tried to make the government and its resource distribution more inclusive within Guinea-Bissau, home to most of the population (Forrest 1987; Levitsky and Way 2022, 308–14). Having been pushed out by Vieira, Cape Verdeans in PAIGC quickly split off to establish their own party and country, and Vieira's own governance gradually grew more exclusive. Former allies in coups or rebellions often wind up in conflict with each other (Ashley 2024; Roessler 2016), and while this particular conflict resulted in a coup in Guinea-Bissau, elsewhere it could theoretically lead to an opportunistic-inclusive rebellion.

Defining and Measuring Key Variables

I define *victorious rebel groups* as those who engage in a sustained civil war against the government lasting at least six months and then gain total or majority control over the central state or seceded country for at least one year after the capture of the capital city or cessation of hostilities, becoming broadly internationally accepted as governing a state. The six-month war duration threshold only excludes the case of the more programmatic-inclusive Ejército de Liberación Nacional in Costa Rica, which won a forty-four-day war in 1948 (see Bell 1971), while capturing the capital is critical for any group's sovereignty claims being recognized (Landau-Wells 2018). This definition is thus based on political victory, which may or may not coincide with a complete military victory (Toft 2009) but includes rebel groups who successfully forced new elections that they then won, like Nepal's CPN-M (Huang 2016b, chap. 6). This specification of rebel victory avoids including coups where acting government officials and/or security forces depose the executive leadership. It also excludes groups that only temporarily capture the capital and thus lack time to control and alter state institutions, like Séléka rebels who briefly controlled the Central African Republic in 2013 and early 2014 (Vlavonou 2014). Hayat Tahrir al-Sham (HTS) in Syria seized power in December 2024 after forming in 2017 (with roots in Jabhat al-Nusra, which formed in 2011), but has not yet been in power for a year as the book is going to press—though it seems likely to hold on to power long enough to meet my definition. Only groups controlling internationally recognized states may, among other things, ratify or be subject to international treaties; hold full membership in international organizations; be responsible for state debt; and, most important, claim the protections and privileges of sovereignty under international law. Separatist and irredentist groups sometimes control territory and set up de facto states (Florea 2014), but without broad international recognition, they do not face the same opportunities and constraints as governments integrated into the international system. There may also be cases, like the Taliban in Afghanistan, where victorious rebels are not officially internationally recognized as the new government but are de facto widely accepted as such, which I take as an indicator of rebel victory. Appendix A lists victorious rebel groups since 1945 (with HTS perhaps soon to join their ranks).

For *rebel organizational type* to provide useful inferences about how it affects outcomes once groups come to power, it must be measured during the period when groups are fighting as rebels. Measurement is tricky when leadership competition is ongoing and policy stances may be shifting, but we can trace the threads of organizational type throughout the rebel period to uncover its development and consolidation. Within a case, I thus examine (1) contenders for leadership within an organization and in broader antigovernment movements (see Krause 2017); (2) who gained hegemony over organizational agenda setting; (3) discourse used by leaders, organizational documents, and fighters in developing and presenting an ideology; and (4) how stated ideological principles and goals were or were not borne out in practice in institutions and civilian relations and in the use and distribution of power and resources.

It can be difficult to know what exactly happens in rebel-held or contested territory during a civil war, yet by using a variety of primary and secondary evidence, we can reconstruct wartime dynamics among leaders, how organizations behaved, and what institutions they developed. This lets us evaluate a rebel organization's placement on the programmatic-opportunistic and inclusive-exclusive axes. For each case, I analyze the content and depth of political education. For what and whom were recruits told they were fighting? What efforts were made to educate civilians about the organization's ideals and goals? The degree of political, economic, or social reorganization and inclusion attempted by a group in areas it controls also reveals preferences, potentially offering a costly signal of a group's ideological sincerity if they proclaim programmatic or inclusive goals. In terms of rebel governance, I examine how organizations administered territory and if they incorporated local populations into decision making, imposed their will through force, or left preexisting power structures in place. I also analyze whether organizations attempted to provide social services like health care and education, which can reveal concerns with broader public interests and whether an organization is aiming to inclusively benefit the majority of people under their control or only an exclusive constituency (Huang 2016b; Stewart 2018).

How do we measure the dependent variables, *statebuilding* and *service provision*? I separate state capacity into the elements of coercive and infrastructural power, using statebuilding to refer to the development of infrastructural power. Coercive power is based on force and state elites' ability to impose their will unilaterally on the population. Infrastructural power, in contrast, is "the capacity of the state actually to penetrate civil society, and to implement logistically political decisions throughout the realm" (Mann 1988, 113), working through the population to achieve state aims.

Even without infrastructural power, coercive power may be used to create order because both rebels (Arjona 2016) and state elites (Huntington 1968; Mann 1988; Olson 1993) prefer order to disorder (order enables more efficient resource extraction and control over territory and people). To measure victorious rebels' coercive power, I examine how they developed and deployed their security apparatuses along four dimensions. *Structure* is the organization of different forces across the security apparatus. *Strength* is not only security forces' size and equipment but also their technical capabilities (whether strength is used effectively is another matter). *Territorial coverage* is security forces' geographic presence and the state's ability to project coercive power across space. *Use* is the ends toward which security forces are employed.

Infrastructural power captures the state's ability to affect citizens and enact leaders' aims without relying on coercion or threats. Physical infrastructure enables travel and communication across space and populations, so I examine efforts to extend transportation and communications infrastructure and how these were distributed within the national territory. There is also "human infrastructure": How were administrative officers distributed throughout the territory and how did the state incorporate the population, or not, in the process of governing and administration? State agents' presence in an area does "not automatically translate into the state's ability to implement policy" (Soifer and vom Hau 2008, 226), so a state seeking to build infrastructural power must also organize the population to make it legible to the state (Scott 1998). We can measure this social component of infrastructural power in part by looking at efforts to increase state administrative capacity through census administration (Lee and Zhang 2016; Soifer 2012), cadastral surveys, and statistical capacity (Hanson and Sigman 2021), plus efforts to build mass institutions like government-affiliated labor unions or women's and youth organizations (Kasza 1995).

State capabilities to reach across territory are not always translated into action, however, so I seek to analyze the "weight" of the state (see Soifer 2008) and the ends toward which it is deployed to affect citizens and other sociopolitical actors. What are the types, quantity, and quality of public goods and services the state aims to provide and ultimately delivers, and is the government directing benefits inclusively or exclusively? I concentrate my analyses on two of the most essential services states can deliver: health care and education. Health care and education constitute social welfare goods (Cammett and MacLean 2014) recognized by the United Nations as human rights, and that, as they entail "substantial externalities . . . lie within the state's comparative advantage" (Lake and Baum 2001, 599). Civil wars frequently destroy health-care and education systems, making their reconstruction one of the most vital tasks a new government can undertake, especially with outcomes in both sectors usually intertwined (Ghobarah, Huth, and Russett 2004; Iqbal 2010; Lai and Thyne 2007).

I look at state efforts to improve health-care access by increasing the number and location of health-care facilities and personnel, other health-sector investments, vaccination campaigns, and trends in these efforts. Vaccination campaigns are particularly good examples of a state's ability to reach populations throughout its territory and can be accomplished either through direct implementation using state employees or through mass mobilization, making them a useful measure of administrative or mobilizational capacity and service provision (Soifer 2012).

TABLE 1.1.   Categories and indicators of statebuilding and service provision

Security forces and coercive power	Structure Strength Territorial coverage Use
Physical infrastructure	Transportation Communications
Administrative power	State agents' territorial coverage Census and survey administration Statistical capacity
Public goods and service provision	Health care Education

In analyzing education, I focus on state efforts to expand public access to schooling, improve literacy, and expand and invest in the teaching corps. Education builds knowledge and skills that are goods in and of themselves and can bolster economic development, but education can also be used to try to shape a national narrative and identity (Abbott, Soifer, and vom Hau 2017; Darden and Grzymala-Busse 2006) and to facilitate citizens' mobilization and political engagement through ideological indoctrination (see Paglayan 2022).

The scope of public goods and services that are delivered depends in part on states' capacity to do so, but many powerful states like the United States limit the scope of their activities and interventions in society (Fortin 2009; Fukuyama 2004), and a range of states fail to act on their rhetorical promises (e.g., Manion et al. 2017). Efforts to provide public goods and services therefore measure outputs of state intents and actions (Fukuyama 2013). Corruption, a frequently used indicator of "bad governance," is highly difficult to measure, but I also discuss in each case the extent to which state revenues were used inclusively for public-facing projects versus for the more exclusive interests of those in government and their cronies. Table 1.1 summarizes the indicators of statebuilding and service provision used in this book.

From Theory Building to Testing

This chapter presented a theoretical argument about how ideology shapes rebel leaders' goals and is used to motivate organizations, in turn affecting organizations' institution building and behavior while fighting as rebels and subsequent statebuilding and service provision efforts once they control the state. Distinguishing between the dimensions of programmatic and opportunistic organizations and organizations seeking to deliver inclusive or exclusive benefits, I outlined the motives and hypothesized behavior we should see following victory by each type of group. While all groups seek to develop coercive power, only more programmatic organizations devote effort and resources to building infrastructural power. Organizations' relationships with the civilian population and whether they are devoting resources to the masses or to narrow constituencies depend on whether the group intends to deliver inclusive or exclusive benefits. The next three chapters test this theory in the cases of the more programmatic-inclusive FSLN, the more opportunistic-exclusive NPFL, and the middle-ground NRM.

Part II

COMPARATIVE EVIDENCE FROM NICARAGUA, LIBERIA, AND UGANDA

FROM IDEALISM TO ACTION

The Frente Sandinista de Liberación Nacional in Nicaragua

After years of clandestine guerrilla struggle, Nicaragua's Frente Sandinista de Liberación Nacional (FSLN) took power in 1979 at the vanguard of a broad popular uprising in Nicaragua. The FSLN developed a programmatic and inclusive ideology and worked to build cooperative relationships with civilians in its limited areas of influence while fighting as rebels. Once in power, the organization sought to expand state influence territorially and throughout society, and aimed to foster more inclusiveness in politics and provision of social and economic benefits—although many Nicaraguans disagreed with their efforts. Civil war and economic struggles led to pragmatic shifts, at times, with the FSLN scaling back some transformative ambitions (Gilbert 1988; Ramírez 2012), but the ideology and organizational ethic forged by FSLN leaders as rebels was institutionalized, guiding both FSLN rebel governance and then behavior in power through a decade of rule. This was the case until, in an exception among victorious rebels, the FSLN ceded control in 1990 after losing democratic elections.

The Nicaraguan Political Context

Central America's largest country territorially, Nicaragua was long at the whims of great powers. The United States regularly intervened economically and militarily in Nicaragua throughout the nineteenth century, and Britain maintained influence on Nicaragua's "Atlantic Coast," more accurately called

51

the Caribbean Coast today (Gobat 2005; Meringer 2019; Walker and Wade 2011). State strength remained ephemeral after Nicaragua's independence from Spain, with various oligarchical families holding control amid disputes between the rival Conservative and Liberal parties. Three decades of Conservative rule beginning in the 1860s brought relative stability before, after an 1890–1893 war, Liberal leader José Santos Zelaya sought to centralize power and build the state's capacity and reach (Cruz 2002; Holden 2004, 80–88). Zelaya's government worked to extend state influence across the national territory to the Atlantic Coast, built new transit and communications links, and aimed to develop public education and other services to pursue Zelaya's vision of a unified, modernized Nicaragua from the Pacific to the Atlantic. Zelaya's state-building desires clashed with US commercial and strategic interests, however. US Marines intervened in 1909 on the Atlantic Coast and supported Zelaya's opponents, who toppled him in a rebellion later that year.

US Marines returned for good in 1912, backing Conservative governments that "depended almost completely on the United States for their continued hold on power" (Holden 2004, 87–89). Following a 1926 coup by a hardline Conservative general, Liberals launched a rebellion with support from Mexico's revolutionary government. After US Marine reinforcements arrived in 1927, most Liberal forces accepted a peace agreement in 1928. Liberal general Augusto César Sandino refused to surrender his arms, however, and began a nationalist rebellion, while the Marines organized and trained a new Nicaraguan military, the Guardia Nacional (GN, or National Guard). Sandino's forces evaded capture and harassed the Marine occupiers until they withdrew in 1933 (Millett 1977; Schroeder 1993; Walter 1993). The occupation's legacy lived on, however: Guardia commander Anastasio Somoza García assassinated Sandino in 1934 during negotiations, and Somoza then seized power in 1936. This began forty-three years of Somoza family rule. Elder son Luis Somoza Debayle governed after his father's 1956 assassination, and younger son Anastasio Somoza Debayle took over after Luis died in 1967, ruling until the FSLN overthrew him in 1979.

FSLN Origins and Organizational Development

The FSLN formed in 1961 following several years of student organizing and protest by its early leaders, taking up arms to topple the Somoza family's repressive, corrupt, US-supported dictatorship. The Somozas provided limited social services in Managua (the capital) and other urban areas but ruled mostly coercively elsewhere and largely ignored the Atlantic Coast region (Millett 1977; Walker and Wade 2011; Booth 1982).

The 1956 assassination of Somoza García invigorated a new generation of dissidents. Among them were Carlos Fonseca and Tomás Borge, students who helped found the Frente de Liberación Nacional (FLN). Fonseca became the chief ideologue, and Borge was the only founder who survived to see victory in 1979. In 1963, at Fonseca's insistence, the group latched onto Sandino's image as a nationalist liberator who had fought for exploited Nicaraguans against dictatorship and imperialism, adding "Sandinista" to the FLN's name and becoming the FSLN (e.g., Zimmermann 2001). That year also saw the group's first guerrilla attacks, which ended in failure.

Early FSLN communiqués focused primarily on the armed struggle itself, but the group began forming and expressing its ideology over the course of the 1960s. A 1960 statement by one of the FSLN's predecessor student organizations discussed the need for both armed struggle and developing popular support while also rejecting terrorism and violence against civilians or prisoners (FSLN 1960). Early "Marxist-Leninist and anti-clerical" leader Leonel Rugama reportedly taught fellow student dissidents about both Sandino's anti-imperialist, nationalist struggle and Ernesto "Che" Guevara's political and military ideas (Cabezas 1985, 12). While imprisoned, Fonseca (1964) described an ideology drawing on Marxist identification with the impoverished and repressed masses, liberalism's emphasis on individual rights, and social Christianity's popular appeal and calls for social change. This fusion became *sandinismo*, the FSLN's ideology throughout its rebellion and once in power (Gilbert 1988; Nolan 1984; Reed 2002; Wright 1995), creating a "revolutionary ethic" driving FSLN members to work for the benefit of the masses and largely to avoid corruption and human rights abuses (N-1, Dora María Téllez; N-4, Joaquín Cuadra; N-6 and N-10, Hugo Torres; N-13, Luis Carrión).

Political education socialized FSLN members into a culture of self-sacrifice and a focus on long-term goals. Commander Javier Pichardo said, "We had the idea that we would die along the way . . . we knew the people would triumph, but that we would not see it" (Baltodano 1999). FSLN guerrilla Omar Cabezas (1985, 121–22) reflected that political education instilled in fighters that "we had to die for an ideal. We had to put aside our dreams, hopes, and ambitions . . . and break through."

Early FSLN political development culminated in the 1969 release of the Historical Program, which was developed through a process of dialogue and consensus among the organization's several dozen core members at the time (N-18, Oscar René Vargas). The Historical Program maintained the FSLN's focus on militarily defeating the Somoza dictatorship but also began laying out a broader plan "for the establishment of a social system that liquidates the exploitation and misery that our people have historically suffered" (FSLN 1969). The program emphasized individual rights and popular participation in politics and outlined specific policy ideas including improving access to education and a campaign to eliminate illiteracy; reducing unemployment; free public medical care, building hospitals and clinics nationwide, and campaigns to eliminate endemic diseases and prevent epidemics; ending corruption; integrating the Atlantic Coast with the rest of Nicaragua; and creating a new, more disciplined military with stronger relations with civilians (FSLN 1969). FSLN guerrilla commander and later general Hugo Torres told me that "this was not an armed group fighting only to take power, but to advance the interests of the people and the working class in general" (N-6). These themes and policy ideas were largely maintained and instilled in members as the FSLN began to grow and push toward victory in the 1970s, and they were then carried over into power.

In the mid-1970s, the FSLN began having more military success and developed closer ties to communities, especially after a devastating 1972 earthquake destroyed Managua and Anastasio Somoza Debayle and his cronies embezzled reconstruction funds. The FSLN developed urban guerrilla cells and support networks, but most forces in the early 1970s were located in rural areas, where the FSLN began successfully recruiting peasants from 1970 on, having gradually built up trust (Booth 1982, 140–41).

The group also engaged in a high-profile hostage taking in 1974 at a party thrown by Somoza acolytes. The FSLN treated hostages well, and their demands included not only money and releasing prisoners but also improved conditions and wages for workers. After taking National Assembly members hostage in 1978, FSLN commandos' demands included government concessions to protesting health-care workers, demonstrating solidarity and attempts to ally with the working class (FSLN 1978b; Torres 2005, 116, 417; also mentioned in N-4, J. Cuadra; N-6, Torres). These two prominent operations increased the FSLN's visibility and public support.

Throughout the 1970s, FSLN leaders were careful in recruitment to maintain secrecy and discipline, waiting for a person to earn recruiters' trust. Recruits then had to swear an oath "to defend the nation's dignity with arms in hand, and to fight for the redemption of the oppressed and exploited of Nicaragua and the world" (Kinzer 2007, 62–63). Socialization then included both political education and military training. In Nicaragua, fifty-nine FSLN schools reportedly trained around 1,200 cadres from 1973 to 1976, and nineteen camps in Costa Rica trained around 1,500 people from 1976 to 1979 (Hernández 1982, 72). Recruits there were taught military strategy and tactics and given weapons training while also being indoctrinated with the FSLN's ideology and analysis of Nicaraguan history (Herrera 2013, 190).

By the mid-1970s, however, disagreements emerged within the FSLN over the best tactics and strategy to defeat the regime. As a former FSLN guerrilla and later military staff officer saw it, "We could not keep going in the mountains. If you kill 100 guardias in the mountains, no one knows about it. If you kill one guardia in Managua or León, everyone finds out" (N-11). Leaders' strategic disagreements split the FSLN into three factions, known in Nicaragua as "tendencies," around 1975 and 1976. The Guerra Popular Prolongada (GPP) tendency of Tomás Borge and Henry Ruiz sought to maintain the FSLN's original rural guerrilla warfare strategy. The Proletarian tendency led by Jaime Wheelock, Luis Carrión, and Roberto Huembes emphasized mobilizing wage laborers and uniting the urban and rural fronts in the fight, and strongly endorsed a socialist economic system. The Insurrectional or Tercerista tendency, led by Eduardo Contreras and brothers Daniel and Humberto Ortega, focused on escalating military operations around the country and was politically pragmatic; the Terceristas sought to develop civil society alliances to support a broad popular insurrection and advocated for a mixed economic system to attract international support. The split was primarily about strategic differences: Dora María Téllez (N-1) said that the three tendencies had disagreements in how they "conceptualized the situation of Somocismo—if it was strong, if it was weak, if it was in crisis, or if it was consolidating itself." Ideological and interpersonal disputes also played a role, however, especially after the death of leading ideologue Carlos Fonseca in 1976 (Booth 1982; Mosinger 2019; Nolan 1984).

There was still significant coordination among the tendencies, however, and lower and mid-level cadres retained cross-tendency ties (N-6, Torres). These differences were smoothed over in early 1979 when Fidel Castro, who had been primarily supporting the GPP, began trusting the Terceristas and pushed the tendencies to unify in order to topple Anastasio Somoza Debayle. The Terceristas took the lead strategically, but power remained distributed across the tendencies. The regime had been weakened by the insurrectional strategy's growing success in urban areas, falling public support after the 1978 assassination of journalist Pedro Joaquín Chamorro, and declining US backing. Castro and many FSLN leaders also saw unification and a quick push to victory as necessary to avoid any US efforts to intervene unilaterally or through the Organization of American States, which might install a new government that would perpetuate "somocismo without Somoza" (FSLN 1979).

The FSLN's ideology and goals had not changed significantly since the 1969 Historical Program, which continued throughout the 1970s to be presented to followers as the organization's guiding principles (N-7, Lea Guido; N-13, Luis Carrión). The war's all-consuming nature in the face of a brutal counterinsurgency campaign (see Fragoso and Artucio 1980; Inter-American Commission on Human Rights 1978) meant it was difficult for the FSLN to consolidate liberated areas in which to implement ideas and experiment with governance or for the organization to forge more concrete plans for the postvictory state (N-1, Téllez; N-13, Carrión; N-15, Jaime Wheelock; N-16, Víctor Hugo Tinoco). FSLN student leaders, especially in León, organized residents of marginalized neighborhoods to advocate for improved health services and public water and electricity, while in Managua and other cities, the FSLN organized the population into neighborhood committees to support the rebellion (N-6, Hugo Torres). These relatively limited experiences were the closest the FSLN came to implementing its social and administrative vision prior to the final stages of the rebellion. As the war progressed between 1977 and 1979, the Proletarios' and Terceristas' insurrectional strategy paid dividends. The ranks of FSLN fighters and collaborators rapidly expanded, and broad sectors of civil society aligned themselves with the FSLN against the Somoza regime in a "multiclass coalition" (Everingham 1996). The Terceristas also forged links with the Panamanian, Venezuelan, and Costa Rican governments to gain material and diplomatic support (Jarquín 2024).

Tercerista efforts to broaden the FSLN base most concretely affected policy formulation through the Grupo de los Doce (Group of Twelve). This informal committee of prominent Nicaraguans, some of whom were secretly FSLN members, joined together at the Terceristas' behest in 1977 to issue a proclamation supporting the FSLN and worked to organize middle- and upper-class opposition to the regime. These efforts led to the formation in 1978 of the Frente Amplio Opositor (FAO, or Broad Opposition Front). The FAO issued a program of government calling for the end of the dictatorship, political reforms, and protection of civil liberties but also for undertaking agrarian reform, tackling illiteracy, and "urgent action to solve the problems of health and welfare in the cities and countryside, in all aspects related to social security, medical and hospital care, and maternal and child health" (Envío Team 1984). This mirrored many of the concerns in the FSLN's Historical Program, although without the Historical Program's call for military conscription and popular militias. The Terceristas' own policy discourse retained Historical Program principles, with communiqués in 1978 describing some of the motivations for the FSLN's struggle: forming a more democratic government and nonrepressive security forces; providing health care, education, water, and electricity for all Nicaraguans; and integrating and developing the Atlantic Coast (FSLN 1978a; 1978c; 1978d).

In 1979, the FSLN began advancing militarily throughout Nicaragua, yet political planning remained secondary to fighting until June and July 1979, when the Somoza regime's defeat began to appear not only possible but imminent. Working with the Grupo de los Doce, the FSLN in June 1979 organized in Costa Rica the Junta of the Government of National Reconstruction (JGRN), a five-person transitional government composed of FSLN Dirección Nacional (DN, or National Directorate) member Daniel Ortega; leftist activists Sergio Ramírez, from the Grupo de los Doce, and Moises Hassan (both secretly FSLN members); and conservative opposition leaders Violeta Chamorro and Alfonso Robelo. The JGRN began developing plans for a transition to a post-Somoza state, releasing a program of government on July 9 outlining future executive, legislative, and judicial institutions (Junta de Gobierno de Reconstrucción Nacional 1979).

In July 1979, FSLN forces captured several cities, but administrative plans remained relatively limited. Efforts focused on establishing order, ensuring the availability of food and water, starting to restore public services, and organizing local governments, usually through committees of trusted collaborators, so FSLN forces could continue onward toward Managua and the final defeat of the Somoza regime (N-1, Téllez; N-13, Carrión; N-16, Tinoco). In León, Dora María Téllez (N-1) and her forces, "first organized civil defense committees. Then the [JGRN] named Juntas Municipales that functioned like mayors," with commanders and the committees working with communities on food and childcare, and then seeking to restore electricity and water service. The Somoza regime's rapid collapse and the disintegration of the GN in mid-July, however, caught everyone by surprise (e.g., Kinzer 2007, 72–73). On July 19, the JGRN and DN were thrust into government to organize and administer a state and society ruined by years of dictatorship and war.

The FSLN in Power, 1979–1990

The new government's immediate task was establishing order. Cities were in ruins and filled with thousands of armed men and women, many of whom had only joined the insurrection in its last few weeks and thus were not trained or under FSLN commanders' control (N-1, Téllez; N-16, Tinoco; Borge 1980, 86; Kruijt 2008). FSLN leaders therefore reinforced the importance of political education for all new recruits when forming official militias and once fighters were organized into the new military (N-10, Torres; *Barricada* 1979o; Chamorro 1979; Dirección Política E.P.S. 1984; Gorman and Walker 1985). Training emphasized "the legitimacy of the FSLN's role as vanguard of the revolutionary process, the need to defend the well-being of the poor masses and the nation, as well as the responsibility of soldiers to set a moral example for the population" (Horton 1998, 121). Once order had been imposed and the FSLN either disarmed or incorporated the armed masses into new security forces, the broader tasks of governing began in earnest.

The FSLN had the benefit of building on its Historical Program and the group's "relative ideological coherence" (N-21, Alejandro Bendaña). Public hopes were high, and transformation and rebuilding were foregrounded in FSLN's public pronouncements and planning. The new FSLN newspaper, *Barricada*, crowed, "This military and political victory of the FSLN has brought our people a true revolution that must transform—gradually but surely—the social, political, and economic structures of our country" (*Barricada* 1979h), changes "for the benefit of the people" (*Barricada* 1979a). After the hardships of the war and with FSLN promises of inclusion, "the general expectation was the rapid resolution of the problems of the poor" (N-1, Téllez). Initial support was broad and genuine because "a revolution that, in its discourse, offered the opportunity to construct a utopia obviously made people very happy and very willing to participate" (N-3, Elvira Cuadra).

The members of the DN and JGRN spent several days together deciding who would be named to head new and preexisting government institutions. The JGRN was involved in most decision making, but the FSLN kept control over decisions about ministries that it deemed critically important, such as Defense, the Interior Ministry (MINT), and the Ministry of Agricultural Development and Agrarian Reform (MIDINRA), as well as keeping significant influence over the Ministry of External Cooperation (N-5, Edmundo Jarquín; N-13, Carrión; N-15, Wheelock).

Government institutions were largely created and rebuilt from the ground up, and within FSLN-controlled institutions, posts were distributed to create parity among the tendencies and ensure each had influence over areas in which it had more experience and skills. The Terceristas had hegemony in defense, the GPP in the MINT, and the Proletarios in MIDINRA. Dividing posts based on competencies and parity helped reduce intertendency tensions, with Alejandro Bendaña describing the process as characterized by "coherence and collectivism" (N-21). Cuban advisers helped organize the security forces but had less influence in other areas and "respected Nicaraguan autonomy" (N-21, Bendaña), despite US beliefs that the FSLN would be a Cuban puppet.

Most FSLN leaders and members were young, in their twenties and thirties, and cadres did not necessarily have technical training for their new roles in government ministries, but they improvised and learned on the job. Víctor Hugo Tinoco had no background in diplomacy or foreign affairs yet was named ambassador to the United Nations (N-16). Lea Guido (N-7) was informed on July 17, when entering Managua, that she would be named minister of social welfare and had to ask, "But what is social welfare?" Posts in the Ministry of Health (MINSA), Ministry of Education (MINED), and Ministry of Social Welfare were initially assigned based on technical competence (if anyone had it) and the idea of continuing to ensure national unity (N-15, Wheelock; N-16, Tinoco). Many lower and mid-level functionaries who had served in these social ministries and other "non-strategic" institutions under the Somoza regime returned to work, which produced culture clashes at times (N-11, former guerrilla and Ejército Popular Sandinista [EPS] staff officer; N-13, Carrión), but the FSLN planned to replace holdovers once a new generation of trained bureaucrats and professionals emerged from the reformed and now more accessible university system (Cabezas 1980, 9–10).

The JGRN and DN moved quickly to put their broad preexisting plans into action in key areas of security, statebuilding, and service delivery: reorganizing the security forces; seizing lands belonging to the Somoza family and associates and redistributing them; and launching major education and health campaigns. The DN also made clear its serious plans to integrate the Atlantic Coast with the rest of the country politically, economically, and militarily; Carlos Núñez promised that the FSLN would not visit and value *costeños* (Atlantic Coast residents) only to demand their votes, as occurred under the Somozas (*Barricada* 1979q). The new government had a clear, inclusive, public-minded orientation, with even conservative JGRN member Alfonso Robelo stating that there was a need for changes in the orientation of private and public spending from "cold utility" to social benefit and a "communitarian spirit" (*Barricada* 1979e).

The revolution's political pluralism began eroding, however. Chamorro and Robelo resigned from the JGRN in 1980, decrying excessive DN control over policy and arguing that the FSLN was pushing the new government in a more leftist, centralized direction than they and others in the anti-Somoza civic opposition had initially envisioned (Booth 1982; Weaver and Barnes 1991). These resignations corresponded with the rise of initial peasant resistance to FSLN policies, especially the agrarian reform program (Horton 1998; Brown 2001; Bendaña 1991; CIPRES 1991; MIDINRA 1984); conflicts with Indigenous leaders on the Atlantic Coast (Dennis 1993; Hale 1994); and efforts by US and Argentine intelligence to organize former GN members into an armed opposition force, which became the military organizational base of the contras (see, e.g., Kornbluh 1988, 1991). "Contras" was the broad name for the emerging set of armed opposition groups—the Fuerza Democrática Nicaragüense, Miskitu, Sumo, Rama, Sandinista All Together (MISURASATA), and Alianza Revolucionaria Democrática—ultimately comprised of former guardias, peasants, civic opponents of the Sandinistas, Indigenous peoples, and disaffected former Sand-inistas. As the 1980s wore on, the civil war intensified, and an economic crisis born of the war, a US economic blockade, and falling commodity prices took its toll. Military needs took precedence, but the FSLN persisted with statebuilding and service provision efforts, especially trying to reach populations underserved by the Somoza regime (Arnove 1986; Booth 1982; Donahue 1986; Garfield and Williams 1992; N-1, Téllez; N-7, Guido; N-19 Fernando Cardenal).

Developing Coercive Power

The FSLN's first task in expanding state influence territorially was organiz-ing security forces to establish control and defend their new power. With Cuban aid, the FSLN transformed its guerrilla columns into a more regular army, the EPS, and Panamanian and Cuban advisers helped the MINT build its intelligence and police forces. The EPS began developing specialized units like other regular militaries and created seven military regions correspond-ing to the country's sixteen departments to organize the military throughout Nicaragua, while also continuing popular involvement through the creation of militias in both urban and rural areas nationwide (Barbosa Miranda 2009, chap. 7; Gorman and Walker 1985; Walker 1991). The EPS had less strength in remote frontier regions, the central mountains, and the Atlantic Coast, which were where contra resistance developed, leaving the rebels initially opposed only by poorly trained and armed border guards, militias, and reserves (Close 1990).

The war grew in 1982 and 1983 because of continued popular grievances in rural areas, failures to confront the insurgency with sufficient forces, and increased US funding for the contras. The FSLN began to recognize these prob-lems, however, and the EPS's territorial and societal influence soon expanded (Horton 1998, 199; Kruijt 2008; Walker 1991, 89; N-4, J. Cuadra; N-6 and N-10, Torres; N-11, former guerrilla and EPS staff officer; N-13, Carrión). The FSLN, now fully in charge of the government, implemented nationwide military con-scription for young men, dubbed Servicio Militar Patriótico (SMP), in 1983. This allowed the creation of specialized counterinsurgency units, including units designed to keep soldiers in territory with which they were familiar, cre-ating more permanent military presence in many of the areas where the EPS previously held only tenuous control (Portocarrero 1986; *Revista Segovia* 1986; N-4, J. Cuadra; N-6 and N-10, Torres; N-11, former guerrilla and EPS staff offi-cer; N-13, Carrión). Conscription saw 149,950 young men mobilized between 1983 and 1989, and in 1985, mandatory reserve service was created for men aged twenty-five to forty, mobilizing a total of 175,695 men between 1985 and 1989 (Barbosa Miranda 2009, 369) in a country of 3 to 3.5 million people. This massive percentage of citizens passing through military training and service does not include militias (which included women), or the internal security, intelligence, and police forces.

Between regular forces and reserves, the EPS had about 20,000 personnel in 1983 before conscription began; by 1986, including militia forces, there were 134,000 troops under arms, and in 1990, at the end of the war, the EPS had 87,000 troops. In contrast, the Somozas' Guardia Nacional, which fulfilled both military and police functions, generally had fewer than 10,000 personnel before peaking late in the 1970s at about 20,000 to 25,000 (Barbosa Miranda 2009; Cajina 1996; Millett 1977). General Joaquín Cuadra, EPS chief of staff during the 1980s, summed up the EPS's territorial and societal strength as "forged during the 1980s when there was war on all sides. With the military service, you needed to know where young people were [to enlist them], since it was obligatory. . . . It's one thing to have conscription in peacetime, another in war. It's a whole different ballgame" (N-4). Conscription was unpopular among many Nicaraguans, but the EPS and the government developed means to enforce it (N-4, J. Cuadra; Cajina 1996, 110), further demonstrating the new regime's coercive power and its reach through society.

The FSLN government also relied on the MINT's forces: the police, Directorate-General of State Security (DGSE), the Tropas Pablo Úbeda (TPU) paramilitary unit, and other intelligence units. The DGSE and its agents were in charge of ensuring contra activity could not develop in major cities or in the Pacific Coast region, as well as sending moles to infiltrate the contra leadership and field units (N-4, J. Cuadra; Cardenal 2003, 572–73; Kinzer 2007, 179). The DGSE was also blamed, however, for the majority of government human rights abuses committed in contested regions (Americas Watch 1985a, 1985b; Amnesty International 1989; N-14, nongovernmental organization [NGO] worker). The TPU was used for occasional joint operations with the military. The police were the most visible (and popular) segment of the MINT's forces and were spread throughout urban and rural areas. The police developed strong community ties (Kruijt 2008, 109–10), and their discipline and close relations with the population, in contrast to the much-despised GN, contributed to falling reported crime rates in the first few years under the FSLN (Ministerio del Interior 1989). Close police-community relations were seen as assets for both crime prevention and defense: "There was the creation of an idea of . . . community policing, of the police being embedded at street levels in communities. This was a necessity for defense to impede the war from entering the cities, and the Contra from establishing any territorial control" (N-5, Jarquín).

From the beginning of the FSLN's time in power, the government emphasized citizens' role in securing their communities and the entire revolutionary project, with Borge saying in July 1979 that "the best method for the defense of the revolution is the two million eyes of the Sandinista people" (*Barricada* 1979j). The FSLN itself, as a party, developed strong ground-level territorial and societal reach through the Comités de Defensa Sandinista (CDSs), neighborhood-level committees formed shortly after victory. CDSs worked on issues like health and sanitation campaigns and neighborhood improvement but also functioned as neighborhood watch organizations to report suspicious activity and coordinate crime prevention with the police, furthering the reach of the developing party-state (*Barricada* 1979d; Booth 1982, 193; N-8, security analyst; N-9, journalist). CDSs' extent and influence declined over time, but they remained highly influential in urban areas, where FSLN support was stronger (Booth 1982, 193).

After implementing conscription and strategic adjustments, the EPS waged a highly successful counterinsurgency campaign, preventing contra forces from consolidating stable territorial control within Nicaragua, and forcing frequent retreats to rear bases in Honduras in the north and Costa Rica in the south. The MINT also successfully prevented any attacks in Managua or other major cities (N-4, J. Cuadra; N-10, Torres; N-13, Carrión). Even late in the war, EPS officers and professional publications continued emphasizing the importance of political education (e.g., Aráuz Ruiz 1989). The increasing number of conscripts and growing frustrations as the conflict continued undermined discipline in combat areas, however, leading to more violence against civilians in the late 1980s (Americas Watch 1989; Horton 1998; Thaler 2024b).

While the FSLN was forced into negotiations by US pressure and the population's war fatigue, the contras had been strategically defeated and would have collapsed without continued US support, with state control consolidated in most of the country (Cajina 1996; Close 1990). State influence on the Atlantic Coast remained more limited, but the FSLN had negotiated with leaders there to increase local involvement in government, undercutting popular support for Indigenous Miskitu rebels and eventually agreeing to a form of autonomy for the regions of the Atlantic Coast (N-9, journalist; N-13, Carrión; N-15, Wheelock). The project of integrating the Atlantic Coast remained unfulfilled or unfinished, but the FSLN had imposed more state authority than ever before in the region, even after drawing back and agreeing to autonomy (Sollis 1989; Vilas 1988; Hale 1994). This extension of state influence was not only because of the FSLN's coercive forces but also because of its more enduring efforts to build infrastructural power and inclusively provide goods and services.

Expanding Infrastructural Power

Security was the FSLN's top priority after victory, but efforts very quickly turned to establishing infrastructural power. Despite the FSLN's limited territorial base as rebels, once in power they quickly undertook efforts to develop nationwide influence and to intervene in Nicaraguans' political, social, and economic lives through new mass organizations (Cochran and Scott 1992; Luciak 1990; Serra 1985), state enterprises (Colburn 1990), and communications and infrastructure links. The FSLN created the Commission for the Organization of the Masses that in August 1979 began holding workshops in each department to try to understand local problems and develop social organizations and workers' and peasants' unions (*Barricada* 1979l). FSLN organization and oversight of labor unions helped channel dissent and implement top-down directives from the government (Cochran and Scott 1992; Connell 2002; Serra 1985). The FSLN also centralized previously dispersed student organizations (*Barricada* 1979g) into the Juventud Sandinista 19 de Julio (Sandinista Youth), which became a key resource for civic mobilization.

The FSLN organized municipal elections in key cities (e.g., *Barricada* 1979m), but neighborhood-level committees provided a further means to organize the population, transmit political directives, and implement the FSLN program through mobilization in education, health, and sanitation campaigns. These initiatives were driven by the FSLN's ideological commitments and by leaders' experiences living and fighting in underserved areas. For guerrilla commanders like Joaquín Cuadra, developing territorial influence was in "the Sandinista DNA, the mode of thinking, the modus operandi" (N-4). As a journalist found in the mountain regions where FSLN guerrillas had been active, "There wasn't much healthcare, there were no schools. Once you got out past a certain point, there was no state. . . . So the idea of bringing healthcare and schools and elevating people was a necessary part of what they wanted to do that Somoza wasn't doing" (N-9). Guerrilla commander Francisco Rivera recalled how, in rural areas, the FSLN would encounter "illiterate people without schools, where teachers had never appeared. They did not have electricity or medicine" (Rivera Quintero and Ramírez 1989, 87–88). These enormous socioeconomic and geographic inequalities were what the FSLN set out to remedy, and among some communities they succeeded in leading *campesinos* (rural peasants) to "develop a new way of looking at life," with a greater sense of social and national belonging (N-11, former guerrilla and EPS staff officer).

Beyond the security forces, the government institution most clearly manifesting the new state's territorial reach was MIDINRA, the agriculture and rural development agency. Within a week of victory, MIDINRA worked to expand state influence, creating a vice ministry for the development of the Atlantic Coast and making initial land distributions to over one thousand families around León (*Barricada* 1979b, 1979k). As the main institution acting on land and agriculture issues in an agrarian country, and holding the power to seize and redistribute land, MIDINRA had a great influence both politically and geographically (see, e.g., Enriquez 1991). According to Jaime Wheelock, the DN member who led MIDINRA, the ministry "had a deployment in all of the departments, in all municipalities. It was probably the ministry most spread throughout the national territory and with resources—with trucks, with personnel, with enterprises" (N-15). MIDINRA expropriated and redistributed hundreds of thousands of acres of agricultural land belonging to the Somoza family and alleged associates or collaborators, as well as giving official land titles to many small farmers and Indigenous groups for the first time—although local FSLN administrators also seized land from less wealthy individuals in many areas (Torres 2010). From 1978 to 1988, over 48 percent of Nicaragua's agricultural land (over 2.7 million hectares) passed into or through MIDINRA's hands and was "reformed" into state enterprises, peasant collectives, or newly titled smallholder farms and delineated Indigenous territories (Wheelock Román 1990, 84). The land reform strategy later shifted from collectivization toward titling smallholder plots to undercut peasant grievances that fed support for the contras, but changing rural economic relations remained the underlying goal (Schwartz 2023a, 2023b).

Like the rest of the FSLN state, MIDINRA had difficulties achieving its goals on the Atlantic Coast among its large Indigenous and Afro-descendant communities, failing to understand the cultural context. Yet MIDINRA undertook significant projects in the region around forestry, cattle ranching, and other agricultural activities, expanding the state's role in a regional economy previously dominated by foreign corporations (Bourgois and Grünberg 1980; Hale 1994; MIDINRA 1984; Sollis 1989; Vilas 1988; N-15, Wheelock).

A major component of the efforts to integrate the Atlantic Coast and other peripheral areas was developing new roads and other transport and communications links. Inaugurating a highway project in November 1979, Víctor Hugo Tinoco proclaimed, "Even if the Atlantic Coast did not exist, we would still need to resolve problems of communication, but because [the Atlantic Coast] is ours and because we have a Revolution in progress, we can consider this route an economic, political, and social reference point for our connection with the Caribbean" (*Barricada* 1979c). Vilas (1988, 124) describes how the FSLN sought to bring the state to the Atlantic Coast infrastructurally in the 1980s:

> The construction of the Río Blanco-Siuna-Puerto Cabezas highway, and the extension of the telephone network to the mining region and Puerto Cabezas, contributed to physically integrating the national

territory. Various *costeña* communities were electrified and potable water and sewer systems improved. Public health and education services improved and expanded.

Even as contra activity escalated, the FSLN sought to ensure that nonmilitary state institutions, infrastructure, and service provision expanded into the periphery. A 1984 document touting the FSLN's achievements claimed, "Brigades of workers have brought roads, water, electricity, telegraph and telephone communications to the most remote areas of Nicaragua. . . . Television and radio have been brought to the north of the country and the Atlantic Coast. . . . We will continue bringing electricity, drinking water, and communications to the whole country, especially peasant communities and rural centers" (FSLN 1984, 11). The war, economic difficulties, and road maintenance problems in rainy seasons kept the FSLN from achieving all its desired infrastructure expansion outcomes, but government ministries continued working to bring the state to the people, whether they wanted it or not.

Given agrarian reform's centrality to the FSLN's program, MIDINRA still played a large role inside war zones and in resettling displaced rural populations. MIDINRA developed close ties to the military to redistribute land within war zones and arm peasant cooperatives, while also arming ministry workers in the face of frequent contra attacks (N-4, J. Cuadra; N-11, former guerrilla and EPS staff officer; N-14, NGO worker; N-15, Wheelock). In conflict-affected areas, the goal was "not to regress, and to rebuild that which was destroyed" (N-15, Wheelock). Other state institutions also tried to keep operating in war zones, demonstrating a commitment to continue delivering services to the whole population, for instance, sending in mobile teams for vaccinations and medical checkups (Donahue 1986; Garfield and Williams 1992; N-1, Téllez). The FSLN's determination to serve the whole country inclusively, and especially those who had been left behind by the capitalist economy (Ryan 1994), was most visibly manifested in health-care and education programs.

The Transformation of Health Care

Health care under the Somoza regime was largely private, and public health-care provision was limited to the Managua area. The state social welfare system covered only 8.4 percent of the population in an impoverished country (Donahue 1986, 9–13; MINSA 1981, 11–13). Health care was fragmented among different state institutions with limited coordination, giving the Somozas opportunities to manipulate health-care provision and engage in favoritism, using the health system for their own exclusive political ends (Donahue 1986, 17). Fighting destroyed much of Nicaragua's health-care infrastructure, so reconstruction was the FSLN's immediate health-sector priority following victory, with additional plans to start vaccination campaigns quickly (*Barricada* 1979n).

As part of their vision of creating a more equal society in which "health is a right of every individual" (MINSA 1981), the FSLN and JGRN planned not only to make health care free for all Nicaraguans, but also to expand health-care access greatly by developing human resources and infrastructural capacity in the most underserved places first: rural areas outside the Pacific region (N-1, Téllez). The new government's first health minister, César Amador Khüll, described MINSA's mission as "bringing health to all corners of Nicaragua" (*Barricada* 1979i). A decree in August 1979 created a national unified health system, Sistema Nacional Único de Salud (SNUS), aligning with the primary healthcare model suggested by the World Health Organization (WHO). The SNUS was seen as the vehicle to "substantially elevate the level of health and well-being of the Nicaraguan people" after the Somoza regime's harm and neglect (MINSA 1989a, 1–2).

The FSLN's effort succeeded in many ways. Lea Guido, Minister of Health from 1980 to 1985, argues, "There was a great expansion in access to health—economic access because people did not pay; geographic access because wherever people were, they had access; cultural access because people learned to work in Miskito or English" (N-7). Beyond expanding coverage territorially and demographically, the FSLN's commitment to popular mobilization led to greater citizen involvement in preventive efforts and health-care provision through special campaigns and everyday service delivery in poor neighborhoods and rural areas. FSLN popularization of health care sometimes provoked clashes with the professional medical establishment, which emphasized treatment in established hospitals and clinics, although this did not prevent great qualitative and quantitative improvements in outcomes (Donahue 1986; Garfield and Williams 1992; Ortega Saavedra 1985; N-1, Téllez; N-7, Guido). The infant mortality rate under Anastasio Somoza Debayle had hovered around 120 per 1,000 births and was estimated at over 200 in rural areas from a lack of services, compared to rates of 43.7 in Venezuela, 30.3 in Panama, and 19.4 in Cuba (MINSA 1980, 23). Under the FSLN, infant mortality fell to 80.2 by 1982 and then to 61.7 in 1988, while overall mortality and life expectancy also improved (Donahue 1986; Garfield and Williams 1992; MINSA 1989b).

Vaccination was another key emphasis. MINSA worked with Sandinista mass organizations and local communities to educate the population about the importance of vaccinations and then organized what they called Popular Health Days to carry out vaccination and sanitation campaigns throughout the country. This led to massively improved vaccination coverage. The measles immunization rate for infants rose from 15 percent in 1980 to 43 percent in 1981, while the polio vaccination rate jumped in this one-year period from 20 percent to 51 percent, and reached 82 percent in 1982 (MINSA 1989b). Polio was effectively eradicated in Nicaragua by 1982, accomplishing what the US-aided Somoza regime never did (Donahue 1986; Garfield and Williams 1992; MINSA 1989b).

Popular health campaigns were accompanied by expansion of the numbers of medical personnel and by improvement in infrastructure. There were efforts to construct new hospitals in chronically underserved areas, but the greatest infrastructural expansion was through smaller health centers and health posts. MINSA laid out plans for health areas, each consisting of approximately twenty thousand to thirty thousand people, "with specific geographic limits and served by the basic unit of the Health Center," and then divided the areas into sectors of three thousand people, with each sector served by a smaller health post or mobile units with nurses or *brigadistas*, trained local popular health workers (MINSA 1980, 12–13). This shift to a regional system and hundreds of new health centers and posts was key in expanding health-care access and uptake because people could now receive more immediate attention close to home and then be referred for more advanced care if necessary (MINSA 1980, 15–19, 1989b; N-1, Dora María Téllez; N-7, Lea Guido).

To staff the expanded health system, the government invested in and improved training for doctors, nurses, technicians, and auxiliaries. The number of people per doctor, for instance, fell from 16,700 in 1977 to 15,400 in 1981 and down to a low of 11,100 in 1986, despite population growth over this period (MINSA 1989b). The process was initially uneven, however. Dora María Téllez (N-1), minister of health from 1985 to 1990, recalled that "the government had trained doctors at a much higher rate than nurses or auxiliary nurses, so there was a moment when the quantity of doctors produced was enormous, and the system had to absorb all of these doctors" before the government gradually increased support personnel.

Health-care provision predictably worsened over the course of the 1980s amid the war and economic difficulties. Resource distribution—for instance, concentrating on rural areas to the neglect of improving urban health care—and health worker attrition both became ever-larger problems. The FSLN's project succeeded, however, in health care becoming viewed as a right, and one the state had a duty to protect and serve. Access to health care and medical education vastly expanded, public health was established as an academic and policy field in Nicaragua, and infant and maternal mortality and infectious disease rates were significantly reduced (Donahue 1986; Garfield and Williams 1992; N-1, Téllez; N-7, Guido). Qualitative and quantitative improvements in health-care access and outcomes were matched in the education sector.

Educational Expansion and Popular Incorporation

As with health care, education access had been very low for most of the population under the Somoza regime, with very limited state provision or support of education. Inclusive education had long been on the FSLN agenda, with the Historical Program including provisions for "a massive campaign to eliminate illiteracy," making education free at all levels (and obligatory at the primary level), and making universities open to all Nicaraguans (FSLN 1969). These earlier prescriptions were adopted and further formalized once the FSLN was in power (Junta de Gobierno de Reconstrucción Nacional 1979). The FSLN's major initiatives throughout the 1980s sought to treat education as a right, aiming to make education accessible "even in the most isolated place in Nicaragua" (*Barricada* 1979p) and developing a new educational model adapted to Nicaragua's characteristics and needs.

One of the FSLN government's first major initiatives was the 1980 national literacy crusade, the Cruzada Nacional de Alfabetización (CNA). Eradicating illiteracy in Nicaragua was seen as a core mission of sandinismo, drawing on the example of Sandino teaching his troops and campesinos to read and write, and Carlos Fonseca legendarily exhorting FSLN guerrillas not just to give campesinos weapons training but "also teach them to read" (e.g., MINED 1980a, viii). Combating illiteracy was considered necessary not only for development and reconstruction but also as "a just task, a moral commitment of our Revolution to our people" (Arríen and Matus Lazo 1989, 94). The minister of education, Carlos Tünnerman, began planning the CNA within two weeks of the July 1979 revolutionary victory (N-20, Carlos Tünnerman; *Barricada* 1979f).

Limited data existed about educational provision or attainment after the Somoza regime eliminated regional statistics offices in 1974 (Ocón 1981). Thus, in preparation for the CNA, the new national statistics and census institute, the Instituto Nacional de Estadísticas y Censos (INEC), and MINED were tasked with organizing a literacy census of Nicaraguans over age ten, which was Nicaragua's first nationwide census since 1971. United Nations Educational, Scientific, and Cultural Organization (UNESCO) advisers were convinced that such a census would take two years to organize and complete and cost millions of dollars. Yet MINED recruited Sandinista Youth members to serve as enumerators and completed a relatively comprehensive census (although missing some remote areas) in October and November 1979, for a cost of approximately US$10,000 and with a "minimal" margin of error per UNESCO (Cardenal 2003, 390; Cardenal 2008, 20). The census also provided an opportunity to gather data on populations in rural areas where the Somoza regime had not maintained informational capacity, which proved useful for planning other government initiatives. The census revealed that over 50 percent of Nicaraguans over age ten were illiterate, with the problem especially acute in rural areas and among those aged ten to fourteen; almost 80 percent of ten- to fourteen-year-olds were illiterate in some rural areas (MINED 1980a; Arnove 1986).

Now knowing the size of the task, the JGRN declared 1980 the Year of Literacy and government institutions coordinated with MINED to organize the literacy crusade, launching the five-month campaign that March. Most literacy teaching was done by about fifty thousand brigadistas, mainly high school students, who went into rural areas to live with local families and teach them to read and write, while tens of thousands of other volunteers carried out the literacy campaign in urban areas (e.g., Arnove 1986; Cardenal and Miller 1981). The CNA was a huge success in education, with illiteracy reduced from 50.3 percent to about 23 percent nationally (INEC 1990, 54), although MINED claimed a reduction to 12.9 percent after excluding people deemed "unteachable or learning impaired" (Arnove 1986, 27). By late August 1980, the initial literacy campaign had helped over 400,000 people achieve basic literacy, while a later campaign on the Atlantic Coast taught an additional 12,664 people to read and write (MINED 1982, 19). MINED also launched widespread adult education and popular education programs in rural areas to sustain and build on the CNA's educational gains, with a 1985 survey finding that illiteracy in rural areas had fallen from 75.4 percent before the campaign to 40.0 percent (INEC 1990, 54).

Alongside improving literacy and educational opportunities, the CNA also worked as a form of statebuilding and nation building, indoctrinating and incorporating the population into the Sandinista vision for a new Nicaragua. Brigadistas were told that one of their tasks was to "contribute to national unity, integrating the countryside with the city, the worker with the student, the Atlantic with the rest of the country" (MINED 1980b, 3). The CNA also represented the first time many urban students had been to rural areas of their own country and the first time many campesinos had interacted with urban Nicaraguans (Arnove 1986; Cardenal and Miller 1981; N-2, education researcher; N-3, E. Cuadra; N-19, Cardenal; N-20, Carlos Tünnerman). Brigadistas also undertook other activities advancing state priorities and knowledge, including health promotion and distributing medicines; surveying rural workers; collecting information about local plants, animals, and traditions; and improving rural infrastructure. According to MINED, brigadistas built "2,862 latrines, 75 wells, 96 schools, 34 roads, 50 bridges, 37 health centers" (Arnove 1986, 42n26). For the special literacy campaign in late 1980 on the Atlantic Coast, materials were prepared in Miskito, Mayangna, and English, bringing state-sponsored educational activity and health services to a region and Indigenous and Afro-descendant communities previously served almost exclusively by the Moravian Church (e.g., Arnove 1986, 36–37; Vilas 1988, 130). As Arnove (1986, 25) argues, these state-building and nation-building elements were possibly the CNA's most important effects, demonstrating "the concern of the new political regime for the most neglected areas and populations of the country" with "the extension of national authority and services into previously unreached corners of the society."

Beyond the CNA, state support for education greatly increased compared to the Somoza era, and access to education expanded across Nicaragua to incorporate underserved regions and populations. The FSLN emphasized new primary schools in rural areas and new secondary schools in small cities that could draw students from surrounding rural communities (Arnove 1986, 74). Educational access was considered a matter of justice but also a way to instill the FSLN's ideas and national vision in new generations. State education spending as a percentage of gross domestic product increased significantly from the Somoza years, rising from 2.6 percent in 1978 to 3.7 percent in 1980, and it reached a peak of 6.2 percent in 1986 (Arríen and Matus Lazo 1989, 517–20). The number of primary schools jumped drastically, with the most growth in rural areas. Nicaragua shifted from having 2,402 primary schools in 1978, 69 percent of which were in rural areas, to having 4,061 primary schools in 1983, with 85 percent in rural areas (Arríen and Matus Lazo 1989, 496). Educational enrollment increased dramatically at all levels, with primary school matriculation jumping from 369,640 students in 1978 to over 500,000 by 1982 and continuing to rise throughout the 1980s (Arríen and Matus Lazo 1989, 428). To serve these students, the number of primary and secondary school teachers nearly doubled over the course of the 1980s, while preschool teachers' ranks were nine times larger in 1987 than in 1978 (Arríen and Matus Lazo 1989, 385).

As in the health system, this massive expansion was not without problems. There were constant concerns about the quality of education, teacher training, and student retention (Arnove 1986; Arríen and Matus Lazo 1989). According to former DN member and vice minister of the interior Luis Carrión, the revolution achieved "expansion of access, at times at the cost of quality. Under Somoza, the quality of education was a little better, but its access was very restricted, the system was very small" (N-13). Educational opportunities in war zones were also curtailed because contra forces destroyed schools and targeted teachers for assassination (Arnove 1986; N-14, NGO worker; N-19, Cardenal). Despite these issues, the expansion of education brought a new level of state services to the population and spread state influence throughout Nicaragua. It helped enshrine education as a right rather than a privilege, fulfilling the FSLN's long-standing promises and goals.

Considering Alternative Explanations

How does this book's ideology-focused theory compare to alternative explanations of rebel organization and statebuilding in explaining FSLN plans and behavior? The FSLN did not enjoy significant natural resource wealth or foreign funding as rebels, but they also did not explicitly develop their ideology in order to appeal to recruits (Weinstein 2007) or to potential international funders and allies. Many principles and the Historical Program were established before the FSLN had consolidated significant territorial presence or managed to engage in much outreach, and when recruitment did begin to pick up, only certain ideological elements drew broad popular engagement—most members' understanding of Marxism-Leninism, for instance, remained limited (Kruijt 2008; Torres 2005; Rivera Quintero and Ramírez 1989). The FSLN also did not modify its ideals and plans based on geopolitical opportunities, instead focusing on what they perceived as domestic needs and their preferred means of addressing them.

The FSLN's most charismatic leader, Carlos Fonseca, did not view personal popularity as a substitute for developing policies that would serve Nicaragua's people, especially those who had been excluded and ignored by the Somoza regime, for instance following Sandino in prioritizing literacy education for rural peasants. Even before Fonseca's death in 1976, the FSLN had a collective leadership structure that was not dominated by any one figure, and when the group divided into the three tendencies, each continued developing plans for programmatic-inclusive transformation. Collective leadership continued after victory. The most charismatic figure in the final years of the FSLN's struggle, Edén Pastora, was excluded from the top-level DN leadership body and split off from the FSLN in disappointment. Meanwhile, the decidedly uncharismatic Daniel Ortega received top posts and even managed to gain greater power than the more charismatic and ideologically committed Tomás Borge, the lone surviving FSLN founder (e.g., Kinzer 2007; Ramírez 2012). Although the FSLN struggled for material resources as rebels and once in power, they relied on ideological appeals and socialization rather than personalities to mobilize the population and pursue the group's goals.

Rebel territorial control affords opportunities for governance, but as the FSLN case reveals, it does not necessarily predict effective statebuilding or administration after capturing the central state. Rather, the quality and intent of rebel governance, guided by an organization's ideology, provides a better indicator of what postvictory governance will look like—although experiences in liberated territory can still shape downstream governance. Compared to the National Patriotic Front of Liberia (NPFL) and National Resistance Movement

(NRM), the FSLN had the least territorial control as rebels but still engaged in popular outreach, trying to provide education in rural areas and working to help urban communities get better services. The FSLN gained sustained control of significant populated territories only in the final months of the conflict against the Somoza dictatorship, lacking a chance to build new administrative structures. Once in power, however, they still pursued extensive infrastructural power building and inclusive service delivery throughout Nicaragua, regardless of rebellion-era presence and constituencies. While Liu's (2022, 2024) theory would suggest that statebuilding efforts outside the FSLN's areas of rebellion-era influence were seeking to co-opt residents' support in exchange for goods and services, the FSLN's statebuilding and service provision were instead undertaken to enact ideological principles and aims of the state working for the benefit of all Nicaraguans and connecting the Atlantic Coast more with the rest of the country. The FSLN's base in terms of recruits and followers was in urban areas, but they still sought to engage in statebuilding and govern noncoercively across rural areas and on the Atlantic Coast, even as contra rebel forces began gaining ground in these regions.

Ethnicity could have played a bigger role in shaping FSLN policies and practices in the Atlantic Coast region. Nicaragua is relatively ethnically homogeneous, with a clear mestizo majority living mainly in the Pacific Coast and central regions, while the smaller Indigenous and Afro-descendant populations are concentrated on the Atlantic Coast and in the sparsely populated northeast and southeast. Nicaragua's ethnic and geographic divides would have made it easy for the FSLN to maintain the Nicaraguan state's historic neglect of the Atlantic Coast by ethnically differentiating public goods provision. Because of their ideological commitment to transform society and to inclusively serve all Nicaraguans, however, the FSLN sought to extend state authority to the Atlantic Coast and serve its residents, redistributing resources from Nicaragua's core to the periphery. FSLN engagement on the Atlantic Coast was often blunt, betraying the group's lack of roots in the region and the paucity of costeño leaders (e.g., Hale 1994; Vilas 1988). Luis Carrión (N-13), who headed a commission working on Atlantic Coast issues, reflected, "We had a minimal understanding of the reality [on the coast]. Of the desires and culture of groups, especially Indigenous groups. . . . We tried to transport institutions and structures of the state and municipalities from the Pacific to the coast, but they were not coming from the people, like they had in much of the rest of the country, where it was more natural." The FSLN eventually recognized some of its mistakes in attempting to transplant the state to the Atlantic Coast without sufficient local buy-in. Beginning in 1984, Carrión and other FSLN leaders began working to design autonomy statutes, and more local leaders were involved in decision making (N-9, journalist; N-13, Carrión). This push toward greater political autonomy did not end efforts to build state presence on the Atlantic Coast but rather increased the extent to which they were pursued cooperatively with local leaders and communities.

Prior state institutions did not significantly shape FSLN statebuilding intentions or efforts. Under the Somozas, state authority had been consolidated, but it was relatively hollow and was absent from much of the country, with the dictators maintaining power through clientelism, cooptation, and coercion (Millett 1977; Everingham 1996; Walter 1993). The Somoza regime and its institutions then largely disintegrated in 1979 (e.g., Booth 1982). Bureaucratic structures remained in some of the government ministries, and many Somoza-era civil servants were willing to return to work, but it was precisely in those surviving institutions that the FSLN sought to enact some of the most dramatic changes. As Luis Carrión (N-13) said, "When Carlos Tunnermann took over the Ministry of Education, there was already a structure, there was already organization, an institution," yet this institution was then remade in the service of the FSLN's ideologically driven goals of mass literacy, universal education, and reshaping Nicaraguans' consciousness and values. Surviving institutions may have aided in implementing programs, but they were not preconditions for statebuilding or service provision efforts. MIDINRA was a completely new institution and undertook land reform, one of the FSLN government's most difficult tasks. The construction of mass organizations did not depend on pre-existing state structures. The FSLN was also willing to pursue statebuilding and service provision even in the face of serious resource constraints, using popular mobilization to compensate for a lack of funding and resources, for example in the literacy census and campaign (Cardenal 2003, 390; Cardenal 2008, 20) and vaccination campaigns.

International and domestic threats were constant factors for the FSLN when they were fighting as rebels and then in power (e.g., Ortega Saavedra 2004, 342), but while FSLN leaders anticipated and sought to counter the threat of a US intervention, their policies and behavior remained guided by their rebellion-era ideology. The Atlantic Coast was considered a "weak flank" where US intervention might concentrate and where the FSLN's ideological program was unlikely to receive buy-in because of the region's historical exclusion and orientation toward foreign powers (N-9, journalist), and so this is where external threats should have been most salient in stimulating statebuilding. The FSLN reacted accordingly in terms of coercive power, increasing troop presence and ensuring that the Atlantic Coast was "full of radar stations" (N-8, security analyst). Noncoercive statebuilding on the Atlantic Coast, however, had been the FSLN's stated intention since the Historical Program. Efforts to build infrastructural power and provide social services on the Atlantic Coast and in other peripheral areas were responses not to threats alone but were ideological imperatives, upholding FSLN commitments to serve previously neglected Nicaraguans. Mass organizations, while they provided mobilization and information resources in combating contra forces, were not originally intended to respond to threats but rather to incorporate people into the FSLN project (Cochran and Scott 1992; Luciak 1990; Serra 1985). In many ways, FSLN statebuilding efforts were a cause rather than effect of the contra threat. FSLN projects challenged the "traditions and culture of the peasantry" and Indigenous communities (N-15, Wheelock), offering fuel for contra mobilization (see also Bendaña 1991; CIPRES 1991; Horton 1998, 2004).

Threats did stimulate infrastructural power building, however, in the development of the CDSs. The CDS model was originally put in place to act as grassroots police and help secure the revolution against subversion, although its policing functions were reduced by mid-1980 (Booth 1982, 193), and the CDSs shifted toward concentrating on service delivery and resolving local issues (Cardenal 2003, 344–45; Zwerling and Martin 1985, 80). This was a war setting, however, and the FSLN security services used the CDSs to establish networks of informants, "part of a conception of what each person had to do to contribute in a time of war" (N-3, E. Cuadra), and to be "organized for defense in event of invasion if need be" (Zwerling and Martin 1985, 80).

In terms of international influences more broadly, the FSLN was inspired by the experiences of revolutionary Cuba, and Chile under Salvador Allende, and foreign advisers helped the FSLN organize and, in some cases, staff new institutions (Jarquín 2024). Yet the impetus for programs and ultimate decision making always lay with FSLN leaders (N-15, Wheelock; N-16, Tinoco; N-21, Bendaña). External aid enabled some statebuilding and service provision efforts, but the FSLN continued trying to maintain social services in remote areas, for instance, even amid resource shortages because of the civil war and a US economic blockade (LeoGrande 1996; Pastor 2002). It was sandinismo, the group's ideology, that ultimately led the FSLN to take a programmatic-inclusive approach as rebels and engage in efforts for statebuilding and inclusive service provision once its members were in power.

FSLN Rebel Victory and Its Legacies

The FSLN's programmatic-inclusive policies and behavior reflected leaders' commitments to building a state that would serve Nicaragua's historically neglected majority, increasing the state's territorial and societal influence.

These ideological commitments were instilled in group members and civilians through political education and popular involvement because the FSLN believed changing people's ideas was crucial to success: "The effects of the revolution are in the software, not the hardware" (N-11, former guerrilla and EPS staff officer). This internalization of ideals was critical because the FSLN did not control stable territories as rebels; thus, they had limited opportunities to engage in rebel governance and experiment with policy implementation before controlling the central state.

The FSLN developed as an organization with a vision for transforming Nicaraguan politics and society, committing to expanding state influence territorially and throughout society. In power, the FSLN actively sought to build state institutions and make them serve the majority of the population, not just FSLN members and supporters, and aimed to transform the preexisting market economy. Statebuilding efforts were not always successful, especially as contra attacks and US efforts to damage Nicaragua's economy intensified. And FSLN programs often faced resistance, both from expected sources, like economic elites, and from groups like rural peasants and Atlantic Coast residents who the FSLN sought to benefit. Despite these headwinds, the FSLN continued devoting resources and effort to expanding state influence and public benefits.

Rebel victory created "the opportunity to construct a diversity and quantity of social organizations greater than the country had ever had" (N-3, E. Cuadra), and the FSLN was able to involve vast segments of the population in this new, corporatized civil society. It sought to make the people and territory it governed more "legible" (Scott 1998) by increasing the state's territorial reach and the number of state functionaries and party and mass organization members it could mobilize, implementing and enforcing military conscription and engaging tens of thousands of citizens in educational, health, agricultural harvesting, and defense efforts. The FSLN also rebuilt the state's statistical capacity, beginning to carry out censuses and national surveys (INEC 1990; Ocón 1981; Ministerio del Desarollo Agropecuario 1980).

Efforts to maintain political pluralism were foreclosed in the early 1980s, with the FSLN imposing restrictions on press freedom and freedom of assembly as the contras strengthened. The FSLN were more democratic than the Somoza regime, however, in incorporating the majority of the population in the political sphere and through civil society organizations (Cochran and Scott 1992; Luciak 1990; Serra 1985; Williams 1994). The FSLN held national elections in 1984 in which the opposition largely did not participate and "power was not in play" because the FSLN had no intention of leaving the government if they lost (Cruz 2021; see also Ramírez 2012, 39, 74), but that vote laid the groundwork for more political pluralism later in the 1980s.

State authority was not always evenly spread throughout the territory, and there were significant areas of limited state control in the mountains and on the Atlantic Coast (which closely mirrored the war zones). These areas were smaller than under the Somoza regime, however, and the FSLN-controlled state began establishing state presence and providing services there, despite local unrest. In contrast to the Somoza regime, the FSLN also succeeded in not allowing a rebel group to develop lasting territorial bases within Nicaragua or topple it, despite facing an enemy aided by the United States, a superpower.

The FSLN was not plagued by corruption or widespread personal enrichment by leaders, either. There were isolated incidents of corruption, but they were usually punished heavily when discovered (N-1, Téllez; N-4, J. Cuadra; N-7, Guido; N-12, Antonio Lacayo; N-19, Cardenal). The revolutionary ethic of pursuing the good of the many over the few was maintained throughout the 1980s, and it was not until the FSLN lost the 1990 elections and faced the prospect of losing power that some FSLN leaders began seeking personal benefits from state resources (Close 1999, 2016; Pérez 1992; N-13, Carrión; N-15, Wheelock; N-16, Tinoco; N-18, Vargas).

Whereas health care and education provision were largely left outside the scope of the state under the Somoza regime, they joined land reforms as the FSLN's primary foci for benefiting Nicaraguans. The populations and territory served by the state health-care and education systems expanded exponentially. Vaccination campaigns reflected both the mobilizing and administrative capacity the new state developed, as well as the FSLN's commitment to distributing resources and benefits inclusively. Increased state service delivery, "such as the literacy campaign, the expansion of health services, policies of subsidies and provision of basic food needs . . . changed people's perspectives" (N-5, Jarquín), delivering concrete improvements but also shifting social consciousness about what the Nicaraguan state could and should do for the people.

The FSLN committed errors, and statebuilding and service provision efforts faced often-justified resistance from groups they aimed to benefit. And it is difficult to assess how FSLN governance might have evolved had the contra war not been extended by US backing, or how the organization might have governed if it remained in power beyond 1990. The extent of the organization's statebuilding and service provision efforts and its inclusion of previously marginalized or ignored populations and regions, however, represented sharp breaks from prior political patterns in Nicaragua, and the FSLN left lasting legacies, especially reformed security forces (Cajina 1996) and institutionalization of democratic elections. The FSLN was also relatively unique among revolutionary regimes in peacefully ceding power after electoral defeat and transitioning to an opposition party, a democratic legacy that many FSLN leaders saw as their greatest achievement (Ramírez 2012; Cardenal 2003; Jarquín 2024).

The democratically elected governments that succeeded the FSLN in the 1990s and early 2000s sought to roll back the FSLN's statebuilding efforts systematically by implementing a neoliberal vision of a limited state and capitalist development (see, e.g., Close 1999, 2016). The FSLN, meanwhile, lost its programmatic-inclusive nature. Where the FSLN once had collective leadership, over the course of the 1990s and early 2000s, it was transformed into a clientelist, personalistic machine controlled by Daniel Ortega and his family (Close 2016; Jarquín 2016; Martí i Puig 2010). As historical FSLN leaders left the party or were forced out, Ortega built alliances with the FSLN's past rivals, courting business elites and the conservative Catholic Church hierarchy and cutting deals with the corrupt right-wing president, Arnoldo Alemán (Thaler 2017).

Ortega took advantage of these new allies and popular discontent with post-1990 corruption and cutbacks to public services to win the presidency in 2006, leading a new version of the FSLN. He remains in power today in 2025. Ortega used the FSLN's party apparatus and revolutionary legitimacy to build a repressive authoritarian regime, using revolutionary rhetoric as a cover for neoliberal economic policies; clientelism and crony capitalism; and the entrenchment in power of Ortega, his wife Rosario Murrillo, and their family (Close 2016; Jarquín 2016; Martí i Puig and Serra 2020; Thaler 2017). Ortega and his allies gradually eroded and then destroyed the democratic legacies and public trust in security forces that the revolution had achieved, turning elections into fraudulent, noncompetitive nonevents and making state employment and benefits for citizens contingent on supporting the FSLN (Thaler and Mosinger 2022; López Baltodano 2020; Cuadra Lira 2020; Jarquín 2020).

When mass prodemocracy protests erupted in 2018 in response to proposed social security cutbacks, Ortega sent police and progovernment paramilitaries to crush the uprising lethally, recalling Somoza-era repression (Mosinger et al. 2022; Cabrales Domínguez 2020). Since then, Ortega has further consolidated power around himself and his family, maintaining an ever-tightening totalitarian grip on Nicaragua and attacking any historical FSLN comrades who criticize his abandonment of revolutionary ideals (Thaler and Mosinger 2022; Rocha 2021). Ortega has become a violent dictator like the Somozas, undoing what good the FSLN had achieved as rebel victors before.

How did the programmatic-inclusive FSLN of the 1960s to 1980s turn into today's *orteguista* organization that governs far more like an opportunistic-exclusive group? The FSLN, like most victorious rebel organizations (Lachapelle et al. 2020; Lyons 2016a, 2016b), formed an authoritarian government, even if it was democratizing compared to the Somoza regime in its greater inclusion of Nicaragua's population. The orientation, however, was clearly toward building a state that would inclusively serve Nicaraguans. During the 1980s, the FSLN maintained its collective leadership structures, and while Ortega was installed in the most prominent leadership positions, if he already had personalist ambitions, they were constrained by this collective structure, an issue I explore further in the conclusion to this book.

After the shock of losing the 1990 elections, Ortega was single-minded in his desire to return the FSLN and himself to power, regardless of what alliances or policy positions it required. This path was not predetermined by the post–Cold War global dominance of liberal capitalism, however, because several other former leftist militants in Latin America, like Uruguay's José Mujica, Brazil's Dilma Rousseff, and Colombia's Gustavo Petro, maintained more programmatic and inclusive policy orientations and preserved democratic rule after winning post-2000 elections. When Ortega succeeded in regaining control of the state, he was more concerned with benefiting his family and associates along with dedicated supporters exclusively than with advancing a new political program to rebuild the infrastructural power his predecessors had dismantled (Jarquín 2016; Martí i Puig and Serra 2020; Thaler and Mosinger 2022). Ortega instead took advantage of economic growth to enrich his family and relied on coercion alone when serious challenges emerged, a strategy the NPFL's Charles Taylor embraced from his earliest days as a rebel.

PREDATION AND POWER GRABBING
The National Patriotic Front of Liberia

The National Patriotic Front of Liberia (NPFL) emerged in the mid-1980s around a failed coup attempt and then fought its way to power, winning elections in 1997. Rebels quickly threatened the NPFL's new government starting in 1999, while NPFL leader Charles Taylor also stoked insurgencies elsewhere in West Africa, until his and the NPFL's downfall in 2003. This tumultuous political trajectory was guided by Taylor and the NPFL's opportunistic-exclusive ideology, which shaped the organization and its practices as the NPFL exercised limited, coercive rebel governance and then failed to engage in state-building or service provision once in power.

Liberia's Ethnopolitical History

The Republic of Liberia was founded in 1847 after settlement by formerly enslaved people from the United States. The settlers, known as Americo-Liberians, created a colonial society along the coast, gradually expanding their power and subjugating local populations (Liebenow 1969; Sawyer 1992; Levitt 2005; Lowenkopf 1976). Americo-Liberian rule continued through most of the twentieth century. Outside the capital, Monrovia, most Indigenous Liberians' only experience with the state was coercion, forced labor, and extractive taxation (Munive 2011).

The administrations of William Tubman (1944–1971) and William Tolbert (1971–1980) began governing in a more developmentalist manner, seeking to build state infrastructural power. They enacted policies that slowly but mean-ingfully expanded opportunities and access to services for Liberia's Indigenous majority, although without conceding single-party and America-Liberian political primacy (Liebenow 1987; Sawyer 1992, 2005; Lowenkopf 1995). Tubman and Tolbert also expanded physical infrastructure, giving Liberia the largest increase in road network density of any African country between 1963 and 1997 (Herbst 2000, 163). Services previously concentrated only "in places where the power elite have lived" began to see "some attempt at trickling down services to smaller cities" and towns, expanding state reach (L-51, Byron Tarr). Rural religious schools and clinics began to be supplemented by government facilities from the 1960s through the 1970s (David 1993, 61; Liebenow 1987), although much of the periphery remained beyond state influence and interest. Indigenous Liberians continued lacking influence at the center of power, how-ever, until a 1980 coup led by Master Sergeant Samuel Doe finally ended America-Liberian hegemony.

Despite initial hopes that the coup would usher in political openness and benefits for Liberia's poor majority, Doe's rule quickly devolved into a personal-ized dictatorship, with patronage and power dispensed based on ethnic affinity with Doe. From among Liberia's sixteen Indigenous groups (referred to locally as tribes), Doe's rule chiefly benefited members of his own Krahn tribe and the Mandingo. Doe's regime gradually lost US support as corruption and human rights violations increased, alienating Liberia's most important ally (Dunn 2009), and resentment and disillusionment grew domestically and among Liberians abroad, sowing seeds for new conflicts.

The Origins and Leadership of the NPFL

One of Doe's fellow coup makers was Thomas Quiwonkpa, who became com-mander of the military, the Armed Forces of Liberia (AFL). As Doe consoli-dated power around himself and other Krahn officers and officials, he grew uneasy with the popularity of Quiwonkpa, a Gio, and so tried to demote him in 1983, which Quiwonkpa rejected. Doe then accused Quiwonkpa of plotting a coup alongside Samuel Dokie, a Mano also from the eastern Nimba county, leading Quiwonkpa to flee the country (Huband 1998, 19–20; Ellis 2007; Gerdes 2013, 31). In 1985, shortly after Doe won sham elections to continue his rule, Quiwonkpa attempted a coup with support from exiles and Mano and Gio Nimbaians angry at Doe's treatment of them, dubbing these small "patriotic forces" (James 1986) the National Patriotic Front of Liberia.

The coup failed, Quiwonkpa was killed, and Doe sought violent vengeance on the Mano and Gio in Nimba County, Monrovia, and in the military. A few coup participants survived, and they continued searching for ways to topple Doe, although it took time for a new military organization to coalesce among angry Nimbaians and diverse exile groups (Huband 1998; Lidow 2016, 115–16). Multiple potential opposition leaders emerged, but one ultimately became the new rebel movement's figurehead and commander: Charles Taylor.

The son of an Americo-Liberian father and Gola mother, Taylor grew up mainly among the Americo-Liberian community. He attended university in the United States, where he became involved in exile politics during the Tolbert government. Peers remembered Taylor as highly politically ambitious even as a student activist (Schuster 1994). Tolbert invited Taylor and other young exile leaders to visit Liberia in early 1980, so Taylor was in the country when Doe's coup occurred. Because of his education and marriage to Quiwonkpa's niece, Taylor became head of the General Services Agency, in charge of state procurement and distribution. Taylor swiftly developed a reputation for criticizing government policies and opposing Doe's and other officials' improper use of government property. Doe demoted Taylor in November 1983 and then accused him of embezzling funds himself (Huband 1998, 15–20), leading Taylor to flee the country. In January 1984, Taylor wrote a secret letter to Doe, discussing his ambitions to climb higher in the government and suggesting he wanted to challenge Doe in the 1985 presidential elections (Huband 1998, 23–24). Taylor was arrested in the United States in May 1984, but he escaped jail in September 1985 during extradition proceedings, eventually landing in Ghana and Côte d'Ivoire.

Several factions existed among Liberian exiles organizing around West Africa, the United States, and Europe (L-40, Emmanuel Bowier; L-53, Conmany Wesseh). Taylor took up the NPFL mantle from Quiwonkpa and began collecting his own supporters, both Liberians and other West African dissidents. In 1987, now based in Burkina Faso, Taylor began traveling to Libya to seek Muammar Gaddafi's support, competing with other nascent Liberian armed movements (L-47, Tarr; L-53, C. Wesseh). Taylor sought support from more established Liberian dissident leaders, but they frequently rejected him. There were concerns over Taylor's plans for a sustained armed rebellion rather than a coup, and his demands that "military [force] would determine who would dictate everything . . . [and] that he would be the head of everything and that everybody could tag along" (L-53, C. Wesseh). When groups led by dissident activists Joe Wiley and Boima Fahnbulleh tried to join the NPFL in Libya for training, Taylor treated them as threats. He wanted to be the undisputed leader of the challenge to Doe and was determined to become president in a postvictory administration (Huband 1998, 53–57; Ellis 2007, 72). Tonia King, who was affiliated with the NPFL in 1989, said it became clear Taylor was uninterested in cooperation: he "didn't want a democratic organisation, and in fact just wanted something for himself" (Huband 1998, 58).

During this late 1980s period, Taylor focused on leveraging West African political rivalries to support military mobilization rather than undertaking planning for a future Liberian state, as the left-leaning Movement for Justice in Africa (MOJA) and the Progressive Alliance of Liberia (PAL) did after being disappointed by the lack of transformation Doe's coup had brought (see, e.g., Dunn 1999; Kieh 2024). An early Taylor associate said that political planning in Libya mainly focused on undermining West African governments that Taylor and Gaddafi disliked, while "MOJA militants and the leaderships of all the Liberian political parties would be eliminated" (Huband 1998, xxiii). As invasion plans accelerated in December 1989, Taylor made NPFL fighters pledge loyalty to him personally (Huband 1998, 59). He also opened the NPFL to opposition fighters from around West Africa and Burkinabé soldiers, who understood that Taylor would support their own attempts to seize power if they helped him take over Liberia (Duyvesteyn 2004, 55; Alao 1998, 34; Adebajo 2002b).

When the invasion came on December 24, 1989, the main NPFL force under Prince Johnson crossed into Nimba County from Côte d'Ivoire. Two other prongs of the invasion collapsed, however, and Taylor fled to Burkina Faso, the NPFL's staunchest regional supporter, whose leader, Blaise Compaoré, allegedly relied on assistance from Johnson and early NPFL members in the 1987 assassination of Thomas Sankara that brought Compaoré to power (L-28, NPFL general and later Special Security Unit [SSU] commander; RFI 2008). Once in Liberia, Johnson, a Gio and ex-soldier, gathered strong support among Nimbaians angered by Doe's repression, and his forces became the nucleus for the NPFL and its operations in Liberia. The NPFL later developed ties to foreign companies to exploit natural resources, but at this initial stage, most recruits were motivated by antigovernment grievances.

Ideology, Aims, and Rebel Governance

Prince Johnson established a base in Gborplay near the Ivoirien border and gathered and trained Mano and Gio recruits. Taylor, along with Libyan weapons, arrived in March 1990. As NPFL forces grew, they advanced through eastern Liberia, capturing large swathes of territory and eventually establishing a new base at Gbarnga in Bong County, a mining area. The NPFL's goals were presented to recruits and outsiders as battling to "liberate Liberians who were supposed to be in bondage" (Aning 1998, 17) and create "a new Liberia" through a "revolution," while offering few specifics (Huband 1998, 77).

Former NPFL officers said the organization's aims were defeating Doe and ending tribalism and nepotism, which were largely understood as Doe's policies favoring the Krahn and Mandingo and his anti-Mano and Gio repression. Mano and Gio fighters saw deposing Doe as a form of liberation, telling civilians from their ethnic groups that "we came to free you people from suppression. . . . You need to be with us to go and move this government from power, because they kill our people" (L-3, NPFL intelligence officer). Prince Johnson recruited fighters by saying that removing Doe would "give the country to the sovereign people" (L-2, NPFL commander); most early recruits understood this, however, as meaning Nimbaians would now be in power, maintaining tribalism but with new exclusive beneficiaries. One NPFL commander (L-4) said that the organization was fighting to "bring democratic change" but also that the fight was "to change the government and put a rightful government there. And we were the rightful government," rather than holding elections. The strong popular desire in Nimba to fight back against Doe and his allies helped the NPFL grow to an estimated ten thousand members by late 1990 (Bøås 2001, 709).

Taylor later claimed that time in Libya infused him and his forces with a "revolutionary and liberating ideology" (*Prosecutor v. Charles Ghankay Taylor* 2012, SCSL-03-01-T-0784, 25258). Yet Taylor and other NPFL leaders "did not promulgate a political ideology as much as a political theology, an all-encompassing" reverence for power and desire to hold it (Reno 1998, 93), with only 10 percent of NPFL fighters in an ex-combatant survey reporting joining because of the organization's political goals (Pugel 2007). The NPFL motto of "Liberty, Justice, Discipline, Work," was, according to Reno (1993, 183), "not to be confused with any developmentalist urge" but instead focused on "domination of society, accumulation and power." The NPFL became "a vehicle" (Adebajo 2002b, 58) for Taylor's opportunistic-exclusive project. One of Taylor's allies, former NPFL official John Richardson (L-52), said that Taylor "had a vision, but he didn't have the foggiest idea of how to implement [it]," although they also discussed "running Liberia as a corporate entity, rather than a government bureaucracy."

Leadership Consolidation

The issue of who would be in charge was contentious among NPFL leaders, too. Taylor sought to ensure loyalty to himself rather than to a higher cause, and left leadership hierarchies below him poorly defined. With disaffected Nimbaians quickly outnumbering early Libyan-trained recruits, Taylor felt increasingly threatened. In early June 1990, NPFL commander and former US marine Elmer Johnson was killed behind NPFL lines, allegedly because Taylor felt threatened by his combat skills (Huband 1998, 111–13). NPFL secretary general Moses Duopu told outsiders that the NPFL was run by an executive council that would vote to decide the president in case of victory and stated that he intended to run for president, challenging Taylor's supremacy—then Duopu was killed, too (Ellis 2007, 84, L-2, NPFL commander).

Prince Johnson's military prestige and his ethnic affinity with recruits also worried Taylor, who viewed Johnson as "frisky" (L-2, NPFL officer) and potentially interested in controlling the NPFL. Johnson was less interested in taking power for himself, however, than he was focused on toppling Doe and instituting democracy. Johnson felt Taylor was "overambitious for power" and "wanted to seize and hold power" for himself as president (L-44, Prince Johnson). By May 1990, Johnson and forces he commanded had effectively separated from Taylor-led NPFL forces (Ellis 2007, 81–82). The NPFL had been successfully advancing toward Monrovia and controlled most of Liberia's territory, but these leadership disputes undermined the group.

Prince Johnson decided in July 1990 to split officially from the NPFL and Taylor rather than risk being killed by his ostensible comrades (L-44, Johnson) and formed the Independent National Patriotic Front of Liberia (INPFL). Johnson has consistently stated that he split not because of bad blood on his part but because of Taylor's dictatorial tendencies, even writing a book advocating for democratic government and executive accountability called *The Gun That Liberates Should Not Rule* (Johnson 1991). Other interviewees concurred that the issue of democracy was the reason for Johnson's and Taylor's disagreements and the INPFL's separation (L-1, NPFL general; L-21, United Liberation Movement of Liberia [ULIMO] officer).

Worried about NPFL advances, Ghana and Nigeria pushed the Economic Community of West African States (ECOWAS) to create the ECOWAS Monitoring Group (ECOMOG) peacekeeping force. Taylor and the NPFL attacked ECOMOG forces as they arrived in August 1990, while President Doe and Prince Johnson welcomed the multinational force. ECOMOG then oscillated over the course of the conflict between neutral peacekeeping, actively opposing the NPFL, and tacitly cooperating with the group (Adebajo 2002b; Alao 1998; Howe 1996).

After the NPFL's fragmentation and ECOMOG's arrival, popular Nimbaian politician Jackson Doe, who had joined the NPFL side in early July 1990, disappeared. Taylor allegedly ordered his death, fearing he would win any open national presidential election (Ellis 2007, 83–85). Over three months in mid-1990, other military and political leaders on the NPFL side were killed, allegedly to stamp out alternative visions for the NPFL and possible challenges to Taylor's control, a "purge [that] removed all of Taylor's most dangerous rivals" (Ellis 2007, 85; see also Alao 1998, 34–35; Kieh 1992). This centralized and personalized leadership to the point that one former NPFL officer (L-3) said, "There is no NPFL but Charles Taylor." Even after purging leading competitors, Taylor "systematically neutralized potential 'number 2s'" (Weissman 1996, n18), and retained control over military and financial resources to ensure that he remained alone atop the NPFL.

NPFL Rebel Governance

Through late 1990, Taylor presided from his base at Gbarnga over NPFL commanders around Liberia. While Taylor denied responsibility for commanders who committed atrocities, he maintained strong communications and intelligence networks and so was well aware of events throughout the country (Innes 2005a; Lidow 2016; Weissman 1996), with Taylor's presidential ambitions driving overall war dynamics (Duyvesteyn 2004, 35; Gershoni 1997, 228). After Prince Johnson and INPFL forces captured and killed President Samuel Doe in September 1990, Taylor became Liberia's de facto most powerful person. NPFL forces continued pressing toward Monrovia whenever possible, at times fighting ECOMOG. Taylor also began forming an administrative apparatus in Gbarnga and started attracting more educated Liberians to work with him (L-39, George Mulbah). In early 1991, the NPFL created the National Patriotic Reconstruction Assembly Government (NPRAG) to rule over the territory they called Greater Liberia, colloquially known as Taylorland. In 1990 and 1991, the NPFL controlled an estimated 80 to 90 percent of Liberia's territory (Harris 2012, 130–31; Lidow 2016, 100), with the group's control then fluctuating between half and three-quarters of the national territory from 1993 to 1995 (Adebajo 2002b, 127; Lowenkopf 1995, 93).

The NPRAG mimicked the Liberian state's structures, with government ministries, a legislative body of selected representatives of Liberia's counties, and centrally supervised regional and local administrators (Gerdes 2013, 64–65). These structures were largely hollow, however, existing to make Taylor and the NPFL appear equal to or more legitimate than the internationally supported Interim Government of National Unity (IGNU) that formed in October 1990. To an extent, the NPRAG governed Liberia's interior, with IGNU having little territorial or material influence; IGNU was comprised mostly of elites who had fled the country (Gerdes 2013; Huband 1998; Reno 1995b).

NPRAG institutions "were little more than a thin façade. What Taylor really had was personal control over commodity-rich territory" (Steinberg 2011,

95–96), ruling through "intensely personalized, almost completely de-institutionalized political networks" (Reno 1993, 181). Close to Gbarnga and the core of NPFL territory, there was "rudimentary state infrastructure, featuring schools, medical clinics, currency, transportation, and a system of public communications" (Innes 2005a, 294). Civilians there could generally continue farming or worked in resource extraction to benefit Taylor and other NPFL commanders—as long as they paid taxes and provided young men as fighters (Ellis 1995, 186; Reno 2015). Elsewhere, however, relations with civilians were almost entirely and brutally coercive (Ellis 2007; Innes 2005a, 294; Lidow 2016; Reno 1995b), except for the few areas the NPFL was uninterested in controlling (see, e.g., Defense Intelligence Agency 1990). NPFL commanders would place a military officer in charge of a captured town or district and then name a local deputy to help administer the area, but control and discretion remained firmly with NPFL officers (Liberty 1998, 163; L-5, NPFL general). Especially further from Gbarnga, organizational cohesion and direction diminished: "Things went wrong because there were no trust, no confidence. . . . Because everybody works not together. . . . It's everybody doing their own thing" (L-11, NPFL colonel; see also Johnston 2008; Lidow 2016).

This neglect of governance or civilian welfare was reflected in the NPFL's treatment of civilians as a resource for labor, supplies, and information without emphasizing conversion to a political program. Interviewees agreed that NPFL fighters were ordered to avoid looting, rape, and murder, on possible penalty of death. NPFL officers instructed their troops that, on capturing a town, "you first rescue civilians, because civilians are the ones that will give you information, if you have any enemies in the area. So you cannot kill any civilians, because if you kill them, who will work for you? Who will cook for you?" (L-1, NPFL general). Another officer concurred that the NPFL needed to protect civilians "because they will talk for you [provide information] tomorrow" (L-17, NPFL officer and later Executive Mansion official). It was only in mid-1990, however, that the NPFL began developing informal efforts to provide food for civilians, and not only fighters, after persistent civilian complaints about abuse and food being stolen (L-52, Richardson). This very limited service provision was exclusive, however; it did not extend to Krahn and Mandingo civilians, who were often rounded up and killed despite the NPFL's supposed goal of ending tribalism (Defense Intelligence Agency 1990; Innes 2005a; Waugh 2011; L-28, NPFL general and later SSU commander). NPFL leadership sometimes sought to curb such ethnic violence (Lidow 2016, 127), but Taylor also may have "encourage[d] massacres in some cases for political reasons" (Ellis 1995, 182).

NPFL fighters overall committed very high levels of violence against civilians (e.g., Republic of Liberia 1993; Truth and Reconciliation Commission of Liberia 2008); in a study of Liberia's full 1989–2003 conflict period, the NPFL was found responsible for 40 percent of catalogued human rights violations (Truth and Reconciliation Commission of Liberia 2008, 215–19). Taylor adviser John Richardson (L-52) said that discipline was difficult because fighters were materially motivated: "when rebels are fighting, they move toward capital goals. Rebels will capture a city because it's got televisions, generators, and things. To keep them still, is a problem, because they want to go capture more value." This problem was compounded by leaders' inconsistent disciplinary enforcement and the lack of institutions or efforts to develop fighters' commitment to any cause beyond themselves and Taylor. Fighters were sometimes executed for harming civilians, but enforcement varied widely, and Taylor and other leaders often protected favored officers and fighters. For instance, in Gbarnga during the NPRAG period, "some guys they would go and in broad day commit these atrocities. And sometimes they want to prosecute them, but Taylor know that this guy . . . really fought for me [and intervened]. . . . So people began to realize that there were some people that were untouchable" (L-9, NPFL commander and later AFL officer). Taylor also sometimes used punishments for alleged abuses as excuses to eliminate potential rivals (Reno 2015, 272–73).

NPFL leaders' central motivations were (1) personalized accumulation of wealth, and (2) advances on the battlefield and in negotiations to move closer to taking control of the central government, where they would have access to even greater power and resources, while ignoring political transformation and civilian-focused administration. Taylor developed extensive international commercial ties to sell natural resources from NPFL-occupied territory, exploiting Liberia's timber, diamonds, iron ore, and rubber (Gerdes 2013; Johnston 2004; Reno 1993, 1998, 2015). The NPFL prioritized securing lucrative resource-producing areas and seaports to export raw materials, which also helped the organization import weapons and other supplies. Lower-level fighters were often promised material wealth during recruitment and sought to accumulate private wealth through looting (e.g., Aning 1998, 17; Ellis 2007). Valuable looted resources tended to be funneled upward and appropriated by commanders, however, while Taylor rewarded loyal commanders with cash (Ellis 2007; Gerdes 2013; Lidow 2016). Estimates of NPFL funds vary widely. The most recent detailed estimates from Gerdes (2013), while conservative, still suggest millions of dollars in profits per year—from resource extraction, looting and extortion, and appropriated development aid—flowed into NPFL coffers during the rebellion (see table 3.1).

Some funds were used for military purposes, but an unknown amount went into Taylor's and other NPFL leaders' pockets. The NPFL sometimes repaired roads and posted forces to remote areas, but these actions aimed to facilitate and protect resource extraction and supply imports (Gerdes 2013, 253; Lidow 2016, 125) rather than programmatically expanding NPRAG influence or public goods provision.

TABLE 3.1. NPFL profits, 1990–1997

Year	1990	1991	1992	1993	1994	1995	1996	1997
Profits (US$, in millions)	17.3	9.3	16.3	8.8	5.8	13.3	22.1	18.3

Source: Gerdes (2013, 103).

If economic gain was Taylor's and the NPFL's only aim, they could have contented themselves with their significant territory and resource gains because they controlled 80 to 95 percent of Liberia's territory in 1990 and 1991 (Harris 2012, 130–31; Lidow 2016, 100). Yet the NPFL continued pushing to capture Monrovia and install themselves as Liberia's internationally recognized government and Taylor as president. As Harris (2012, 141, 143) writes, Taylor's "ambition to be the real president in the Executive Mansion in Monrovia was never in doubt," although "there were some economic advantages for remaining in a state of perpetual conflict . . . Taylor's personal ambitions overrode this temptation." Even when facing increased competition from the newly emerged United Liberation Movement of Liberia (ULIMO) rebels, other smaller rebel forces, and sometimes ECOMOG, the NPFL devoted forces to capturing Monrovia and the Executive Mansion. Following the NPFL's failed 1992 Operation Octopus attack on Monrovia, ECOMOG commander Ishaya Bakut said, "It is quite clear that Taylor is not sincere about disarmament nor is he willing to let anything stand between him and the Executive Mansion" (Howe 1996, 158).

The NPFL was consistently intransigent in peace negotiations from 1990 onward, either refusing to participate, making bad-faith demands, or undermining ceasefires to which it initially agreed (Adebajo 2002b, 108; Alao 1998, 80–82). In 1993 and 1994, Taylor refused to let NPFL representatives join ongoing peace talks, worried it would undermine his claims to be the only legitimate presidential contender; this led several NPFL officials to split away in March 1994 and join the first Liberian National Transitional Government (Duyvesteyn 2004; Gerdes 2013, 44–45; Lidow 2016, 123–24). Internal NPFL rivals continued preoccupying Taylor even when opposing forces gathered strength and threatened his headquarters at Gbarnga (Defense Intelligence Agency 1994).

Peace Negotiations and the Transition to Power

Taylor only reluctantly entered negotiations in 1994. This came after ULIMO forces seized Gbarnga; another anti-NPFL rebel group, the Liberia Peace Council (LPC), emerged; NPFL fighters began deserting; and Taylor realized he could not fight against ECOMOG and still take power. Having once controlled almost 90 percent of Liberia, the NPFL's domain shrunk to about half the country by 1993 (Adebajo 2002b, 127; *Africa Confidential* 1993). As Conmany Wesseh (L-53), a negotiator for IGNU, saw it, "Every peace conference [Taylor] went to, it was when he perceived a power shift and needed a quick break. Then he would agree and go to the thing. During that period, he used this to mobilize more resources," getting arms through Burkina Faso and consistently refusing to disarm NPFL forces (Adebajo 2002b; Alao 1998).

Despite weakening, the NPFL "remained the largest, most powerful, and best equipped of Liberia's warring groups," boasting about 35,000 members to 10,500 ULIMO fighters and 8,037 remaining AFL members (Innes 2005a, 293). Even in negotiations, Taylor concentrated on ensuring he could retain political primacy and power over rivals. During talks to create the second transitional government in early 1996, "Taylor focused on ministries important for the exercise of political power, rather than the extraction of revenues, which he was well prepared to effectively control without official responsibility," pressing for control over the ministries of foreign affairs, information, internal affairs, and justice (Gerdes 2013, 52–53). Taylor also began campaigning in NPFL-controlled areas in anticipation of eventual elections (L-52, Richardson), using alliances and manipulation to sideline other factions' leaders and push himself closer to sole control (Gershoni 1997).

After elections were scheduled for July 1997, Taylor continued maneuvering to ensure victory for himself and the NPFL, using NPFL resources and control of strategic transitional government ministries to solidify his political supremacy. One community leader (L-12) in Monrovia said, "When Charles Taylor came, he decided to steal the show, saying I got the money, I got the gold, diamonds, I got the logs . . . the iron ore, everything . . . everybody got to talk to me before they talk to you. I want this seat, I want the defense ministry, I want this, and you got to give it because I got a bigger faction than everybody." Taylor's domineering nature led to pushback from Roosevelt Johnson, leader of a Krahn-dominated faction of ULIMO; in April 1996, Taylor tried to arrest Johnson, sparking a bloody battle in central Monrovia and leading to a later assassination attempt on Taylor in October (L-1, NPFL general; L-12, community leader; Alao 1998, 32; Ellis 2007, 106).

With elections approaching, Taylor "dominated the political environment" (Harris 2012, 153), and electoral conditions benefited him. There was little time between negotiations and elections; the NPFL and its newly established National Patriotic Party (NPP) were the largest and best organized groups in the country; and the NPFL still controlled many areas militarily, restricting other parties' access (Harris 2012, 153–54; Tanner 1998). Taylor also manipulated appointments to the electoral commission and then pushed for voting to start as soon as possible, "threatening violence" if there were delays (Innes 2005a, 301; see also Tanner 1998). The NPP did develop a campaign plan (L-50, Reginald Goodridge), and Taylor enjoyed sources of legitimacy beyond coercive power: charisma, financial clout, and some Nimbaians' loyalty to him and the NPFL. The NPFL also controlled Liberia's only nationally available radio station, the primary news medium, and attacked independent media outlets, while a helicopter and local party activists increased the NPP's territorial reach, which was unmatched by any opponents (Innes 2005a, 2005b; Lyons 1998a, 188–90; Tanner 1998).

Taylor and the NPP ultimately owed their election win to the NPFL's coercive power and the pervasive belief that Taylor would plunge Liberia back into war if he lost the vote (Harris 1999, 2012; Lyons 1998b; Seyon 1998; Tanner 1998). Taylor "made it clear that he believes he has a divine mandate to rule Liberia. It was clear to most that he would not take defeat graciously, and that he had the means to go back to war" (Tanner 1998, 138). Taylor won 75 percent of the vote, and the NPP won legislative supermajorities of twenty-one of twenty-six Senate seats and forty-nine of sixty-four House seats. Thus, while the NPFL took control of the state through a political victory, their coercive power and perceived willingness to continue fighting were decisive.

The NPFL and Taylor in Power

During his postelection victory speech, Taylor struck a conciliatory tone, stating, "The good People of Liberia have finally won. You have won. The opposition has won. The International Community has won" (Taylor n.d., 22). In his inaugural address, Taylor (n.d., 28, 31) described the NPFL as committed "to the task of restoring constitutional government to the Republic of Liberia, we marched to ensure that the Rule of Law would guarantee the pursuit of individual liberties, restructure a collective industry, and accelerate the pace of democratization of the Free Market System," and he pledged to govern for all Liberians. Initial cabinet appointments and rhetoric suggested a willingness to work with former enemies and protect civil liberties like freedom of the press, but policy decisions and actions quickly belied this.

Taylor's statements were seen as aiming only "to impress foreigners. The extent of commitment that will drive implementation [was] not there" (L-47, Tarr). Taylor marginalized former rivals as soon as they questioned him or were perceived as threats again (Gerdes 2013, 254). Critical journalists and human rights activists were persecuted and even tortured (Harris 2012, 137;

L-41 Hassan Bility). Taylor filled key positions by moving loyal NPFL and NPRAG leaders into the central state and parastatals, like Benoni Urey at the Bureau of Maritime Affairs (controlling Liberia's lucrative international shipping registry); Roland Massaquoi as minister of agriculture; and Roland Duo at the Oriental Timber Corporation, a company half-owned by Taylor that held 70 percent of Liberia's forestry concessions (Gerdes 2013, 134, 145; Lidow 2016, 121; Munive 2011, 369–70). Taylor and the NPFL had accomplished their goal of controlling the state, beginning a rule "marked by [Taylor's] centrality in terms of both personal control of relations of political domination and appropriation of national economy profits" (Gerdes 2013, 150).

Developing Coercive Power

Instead of trying to expand the Liberian state's infrastructural power and service delivery, Taylor concentrated on coercive power. An official statement in January 1998 announced "that 82% of the new state budget would be devoted to national security," a number then walked back amid public outcry (Tanner 1998, 143). As he did during the rebellion, Taylor established personalized control over security forces to protect his own power and economic interests and to build influence throughout West Africa. Jefferson Kanmoh (L-43) suggested that Taylor was elected with the expectation he would "use that power to justify the numerous sacrifices that were made through the destruction of property, destruction of life, to reconcile our people and put in programs to rehabilitate those areas and facilities and lives that were destroyed. Open up the country to new opportunities for our people. But instead, he was still entrenched and inspired in what we call military expansionism and building a political empire within this sub-region."

Taylor isolated security policy from other aspects of government. Even as he supported rebel movements throughout West Africa and sent former NPFL fighters to support Revolutionary United Front (RUF) rebels in Sierra Leone, he sidelined the Ministry of Foreign Affairs. Former foreign minister Monie Captan (L-48) stated, "Taylor didn't like to discuss those issues with the cabinet. He had a second tier of people that he dealt with on those things. . . . There were times we would ask to bring this to the cabinet and discuss it and he said no. He thought it was a security issue that didn't concern us." Former press secretary and information minister Reginald Goodridge (L-50) described Taylor as having different "layers" of cabinet members and advisers: "You have the boardroom cabinet members, you have the kitchen cabinet members, you have the restroom cabinet people, and then you have the bedroom cabinet people."

Former minister of state for presidential affairs Jonathan Taylor (L-49), Charles Taylor's cousin, agreed that "a lot of stuff [Charles Taylor] managed himself with his Minister of Defense and chief of staff."

Interventions abroad damaged Liberia's and Taylor's international reputation, however, and led to sanctions and aid restrictions. Support for the RUF in Sierra Leone drove a wedge between Liberia and the United States, which had initially been open to working with Taylor (e.g., Adebajo 2002b, 93) but was "skeptical because of the past history with [the NPFL]" (L-50, Goodridge). Undersecretary of State Thomas Pickering on a June 1998 visit threatened "severe consequences" if involvement in Sierra Leone continued (Dunn 2012, 24). Taylor had come to power "thinking of making himself a czar or something of West Africa" (L-41, Bility), however, and he ignored international demands to curb regional interventions.

During the rebellion, Taylor had engaged in efforts to coup-proof his forces through personal loyalty and creation of multiple parallel units (e.g., Ellis 2007; Gerdes 2013, 77), and he replicated this as president. During peace talks, it was agreed that the rebuilt AFL would incorporate members from all the warring factions, including Taylor's former enemies. This made the loyalty of the new AFL suspect, and so Taylor worked to block any ECOMOG-administered AFL restructuring (Adebajo 2002b, 235); entrusted key security positions to loyal NPFL commanders; and created new, personalized units. Taylor "never had explicit confidence in anybody. If Charles Taylor established a group today, he would establish another group to serve as watchdog for that group" (L-18, NPFL officer and later Special Operations Division [SOD] commander).

Shortly after becoming president, Taylor created the Executive Mansion Special Security Unit (SSU), also known as the Special Security Service, as his presidential guard. The SSU later became the Anti-Terrorist Unit (ATU) under the command of Taylor's son Chucky, who became known for his brutality and unpredictability (see Dwyer 2015). Elite NPFL units became paramilitaries devoted to protecting extractive operations and economically important infrastructure, such as logging operations and ports (Gerdes 2013, 139–40). The NPFL-controlled security forces "behaved not the exact way they behaved during the war, but very close to that. They grabbed people, they would beat up people, they would shoot people in the street" (L-41, Bility). As special units were built up, Taylor purged over two thousand AFL members in 1998 to consolidate his and former NPFL officers' control (Adebajo 2002a, 70; Gerdes 2013, 140; L-34, former AFL colonel). Even NPFL fighters who were folded into the AFL received worse equipment and pay than peers in other units (L-26, NPFL colonel later in AFL). The AFL's marginalization and continuing human rights abuses by security forces helped spur new rebellions, which emerged in 1999 with Liberians United for Reconciliation and Democracy (LURD).

The ATU grew to about five thousand members and became an all-purpose special forces unit for suppressing dissent around Monrovia as well as combating rebels once the second civil war began (e.g., Dwyer 2015). As LURD expanded, Taylor relied more heavily on ATU forces, who he trusted because they "were private soldiers, who were taking $150 in salary every month and one bag of rice" (L-29, NPFL general and later ATU commander), even as other government employees were paid infrequently. The ATU also policed other security forces, interrogating and sometimes executing those suspected of disloyalty or crimes (L-27, NPFL general and later ATU officer). Alongside the ATU, the NPFL's intelligence wing became a personalized intelligence and protection service for key regime figures and business partners (Gerdes 2013, 140). In the Liberian National Police, Taylor established the Special Operations Division (SOD), also known as Sons of the Devil, a unit of NPFL veterans "purposely established so as to secure his interests" (L-18, NPFL officer and later SOD commander). SOD was used to persecute "whosoever that opposes Charles Taylor at the time," and SOD officers were placed in the police command structure throughout the country to ensure Taylor's control and access to information (L-18, NPFL officer and later SOD commander).

As the second civil war expanded, Taylor's government also created militias to fight in outlying counties. The militias were largely composed of former NPFL fighters but gradually included new recruits, especially in 2001 and 2002 (Lidow 2016, 109). These forces had limited formal training (Pugel 2007, 42), but they served Taylor directly and so were used instead of the AFL (L-32, NPFL captain and later militia commander). The militias' lack of training and limited pay, however, led many members to desert or defect (L-18, militia officer and later LURD officer; L-29, NPFL general and later ATU commander).

The personalism and parochialism that fragmented the security forces proved to be the undoing of Taylor and the NPFL regime. Taylor's lust for power and economic control led to interventions in neighboring countries, sparking international backlash and leading to increased foreign support for rebels in Liberia. The NPFL's lack of an ethos beyond personal enrichment and loyalty to Taylor became clearer as more forces deserted and the number of rebel groups grew in the early 2000s. This culminated in a 2003 siege of Monrovia and Taylor's decision, under intense international pressure, to resign and enter exile in Nigeria. Amid this violent environment from 1997 to 2003, Taylor's administration largely ignored noncoercive statebuilding and service provision.

Statebuilding and Development: Rhetoric Without Action

Taylor's domestic policy was supposed to be built around "five pillars of Reconstruction and Development (National Security, Strong Economy, Agriculture, Education and Health)" (Taylor n.d., 37). At his trial at the Special Court for Sierra Leone (SCSL), Taylor's defense team argued that he "was the head of a government that was fully functional and engaged in functions domestic and diplomatic, economic and social, all for the betterment of the Liberian people," claiming the budget priorities "under Taylor were development, property renovation, and education; defence was sixth in order of priorities" (*Prosecutor v. Charles Ghankay Taylor* 2012, SCSL-03-01-T-1248, 37047–37048). In July 1998, the new government held the Vision 2024 conference to set planning priorities for the next twenty-five years, and Taylor blamed a lack of progress since the elections on international donors (Taylor n.d., 256–57). Political historian Joseph Saye Guannu (L-35) argued, however, that the conference had no policy follow-through, only signaling Taylor's intention to "still be in power in 2024." The conference was seen as devoid of substance and the postconference plan as "just pieces of paper" (L-47, Nakomo Duche). The one component of infrastructural power that the NPFL prioritized was communications, seeking to monopolize radio and newspapers to control the flow of information (Innes 2005a). They used these tools to promote Taylor and the NPFL and NPP, however, rather than emulating previous governments' use of radio networks for nation building through promoting unity across regions and ethnicities (Innes 2005b).

Taylor's supporters claimed that he had major plans for economic and infrastructural development and improving education but that the LURD rebellion beginning in April 1999 derailed them. According to one NPFL general (L-4), Taylor "tried to control Liberia so that people could benefit. He started road building, but no one let him finish." Another said, "What development can you carry on when you have to worry about the safety of the people?" (L-4, NPFL general later in SSU). Taylor's defenders argued that war "is very expensive, so [Taylor] will not be catering to the citizens . . . [in order] to buy ammunition to protect the people" (L-13, NPFL deputy commander).

Another common refrain was that international aid was insufficient and aid pledges went unfulfilled (Captan 2000; Taylor n.d., 256–57). Much of the over US$200 million pledged at the first donor conference of Taylor's presidency, in 1998, was never delivered, but this was because of the government's failure to meet established conditions for consolidating order and protecting human rights (Gerdes 2013, 151). Relations with donors further deteriorated after

TABLE 3.2. Official development assistance to Liberia, 1997–2002

YEAR	DEVELOPMENT ASSISTANCE (US$, IN MILLIONS)
1997	76.20
1998	71.98
1999	93.95
2000	67.42
2001	38.48
2002	53.51

Source: Organization for Economic Cooperation and Development, in Gerdes (2013, 236).

Taylor's involvement in the Sierra Leone civil war became clear (L-49, J. Taylor). Taylor supporters in turn blamed international assistance shortfalls for the government's lack of concrete development policies or implementation of them: "The international community was restricting. There were great changes going to come in" (L-35, NPFL captain and later militia commander).

Taylor's government *did receive* substantial international assistance (for the size of the national budget), however, getting tens of millions of dollars in development aid each year (see table 3.2), plus billions of dollars in debt relief. There were generally good initial relations with the development funding agencies of the United States, the European Union, and Taiwan and with nongovernmental organizations (NGOs), despite Taylor being "obstinate" about improving relations with the international community (L-36, Nathaniel Barnes). Libya and Taiwan provided significant cash support, but "when that cash came in, it didn't make its way through the formalized budget . . . a lot of it was personalized. It was leader to leader . . . so it wasn't those institutional type of arrangements where you can . . . know where it's going to go" (L-48, Captan).

Anemic statebuilding and service provision efforts ultimately stemmed from Taylor and other NPFL leaders' opportunistic and exclusive priorities. The vast presidential powers granted by the 1986 constitution gave Taylor "personal discretion over a large slice of the national budget and hand[ed] him the power to appoint even minor-level officials" (Tanner 1998, 146). The NPP-majority legislature even passed some bills to improve service provision and accessibility, but Taylor's administration had no political will to implement them, including never rebuilding the government informational capacity that would have been needed for further statebuilding or service provision efforts (MPEA and UNDP Liberia 2006, 36–37).

Public Goods and Services

There is little evidence of any sincere NPFL attempt to enact social policies or provide public goods, even before the eruption of the new civil war. The preexisting state had collapsed so there was wide scope to pursue infrastructural and social services development. Taylor's government, together with international actors, prepared a postwar national reconstruction plan for a donor conference in April 1998, which noted that "social services available to the population in the areas of health and education are virtually decimated. Whatever remains is considerably compromised in quality and accessibility" (Taylor n.d., 47). The majority of Liberians, especially in rural areas, lacked reliable access to health care, sanitation, and safe water (UNICEF 1996).

Yet Taylor's government did not seek to fill the service and infrastructure void, especially disappointing Mano and Gio NPFL supporters who hoped their early support for the NPFL would at least be rewarded by channeling resources to them and favoring Nimba County with development initiatives (L-41, Johnson; L-47, Duche). The Ministry of Information sought to highlight development projects undertaken during Taylor's first year in office, but this was largely limited to restoring or renovating certain government buildings, roads, and hospitals around Monrovia ("Developments in Liberia" 1999). This lack of investment in service provision occurred amid lavish personal spending by top NPFL and government officials, exemplified by Taylor's acquisition of "a £5 [million] presidential jet . . . that failed on its maiden journey" (Tanner 1998, 143). In speeches, Taylor (n.d.) continued discussing the need to repair and expand the health care and education systems, but efforts in these sectors came primarily from international actors, not the government.

Health Care

The somewhat expanded health system built up under presidents Tubman and Tolbert had declined under Samuel Doe's regime as government funding diminished (L-46, Peter Coleman). Then, during the first civil war, approximately "80 percent of the health infrastructure of the country" was destroyed, and in 1998 there were "less than 60 health facilities functional," only around Monrovia, so an enormous reconstruction and rehabilitation program was required (L-46, Coleman). Especially in rural areas, many Liberians were left relying on traditional medicine or occasional visits from "black baggers," roving doctors with questionable qualifications (David 1993).

Former health minister Peter Coleman (L-46) told me that ministry staff wanted to rebuild the health-care system after Taylor took office but lacked funding: "I had to fight with my Minister of Finance for money, even for immu-nization. There were things I couldn't do; my hands were tied." This led to heavy reliance on international organizations and NGOs. Throughout Taylor's time in power, international organizations, NGOs, and religious groups provided the vast majority of health services and implemented vaccination campaigns (Derderian, Lorinquer, and Goetghebuer 2007; Tangermann et al. 2000; Taylor n.d., 274–75). One policy change Taylor's government did pursue was the 2001 introduction of user fees. In an impoverished, war-torn country, fees pushed health care further out of reach for most Liberians, with "disastrous effects"; when fees were suspended in 2003, consultations and people seeking vaccina-tions rapidly increased (Derderian, Lorinquer, and Goetghebuer 2007, 19).

Government disinterest combined with conflict to stall or reverse progress. The mortality rate for children under age five, for instance, dipped to 217 per 1,000 in 1994, but by UNICEF's (1996, 1999, 2005) best estimates, it climbed back to 235 deaths per 1,000 in 1997 and remained at that level through Taylor's time in office. Life expectancy slid from 55 years in 1985 to 47.7 years in 2000 (Kieh 2007, 86), before averaging 42.5 years over the 2000–2005 period (MPEA and UNDP Liberia 2006, 67; UNDP 2006, 287). Health declines are not exclu-sively Taylor and the NPFL's responsibility, but they did little to arrest Liberia's negative health trends and much to precipitate them.

Statistical increases in health-care access during the 1990s and early 2000s were "due to the 'NGO effect,' not state policy" (Kieh 2007, 85) because the gov-ernment let other actors fill provision gaps. Government disinterest particu-larly harmed rural areas, where long distances to reach a health facility deterred many residents from seeking care (Tsimpo and Wodon 2012b, 65–67, 72). No effort was put toward public water and electricity provision to repair war dam-age and ensure public access, which exacerbated public health risks. Even around Monrovia, Liberia's wealthiest area, there was no public electricity, piped water provision, or sanitation from when Taylor came into office until 2006 (Kun 2008; Republic of Liberia 2008; Tanner 1998), increasing the risks of road accidents, house fires, and waterborne illnesses.

Government disinterest in medical education exacerbated personnel short-ages caused by wartime emigration, and health-care facilities were not rebuilt (Challoner and Forget 2011). The NPFL left Liberia with a severe and lasting deficit of medical personnel, with only "4,000 health workers, as compared to 13,000 recommended by the World Health Organization" in 2007 (Tsimpo and Wodon 2012b, 60). A 2006 study found that "only 10% of communities reported having a health facility," leaving half the population without an easily accessible health facility (Republic of Liberia 2008, 30). The Taylor government's failure to expand health-care infrastructure meant that, even after extensive postwar rehabilitation and construction, there were still only 354 "functional" health facilities in 2008 (Republic of Liberia 2008, 110). Improvements in health-care indicators after Taylor resigned in 2003 were due not only to peace but also to "the restoration of basic services in some areas and increased immunization" (Republic of Liberia 2008, 30), issues the NPFL government had ignored.

Education

The NPFL similarly neglected education after gaining power. The Tolbert government had expanded education access between 1970 and 1985, increasing the number of schools and students, even if facilities and personnel failed to keep up with demand and instruction quality was highly uneven (Azango 1997; Liebenow 1987, 162, 243; Nagel and Snyder 1989, 4–6). Before the civil war started in 1989, Liberia had about 2,400 schools with 12,000 teachers on the government payroll; by 2003, over 80 percent of schools were no longer functioning, teacher training institutes were destroyed, and thousands of teachers had left the profession or the country (Dukuly 2004). George Mulbah (L-39), who worked with Taylor in the NPRAG and remained an NPP member, reported that schooling improvements at the beginning of Taylor's presidency were the result of significant international assistance, with education provision left to religious groups and NGOs.

Without a desire to transform Liberian society, the NPFL government had little incentive to use education's potential to shape the national consciousness. The national curriculum was revised in 1996, before Taylor took office, but then remained unchanged during his time in power (Dukuly 2004). The legislature passed a 2001 bill to make primary education free and compulsory, but Taylor's administration did not pursue this (Tsimpo and Wodon 2012a, 37), while a 2002 bill to put 25 percent of the government budget toward education likewise was never implemented. A teacher in Monrovia lamented, "Pronouncements are made on the matter of education, but are never implemented" (Dukuly 2004). NGOs, religious organizations, and communities picked up the slack, but many young Liberians, especially in poorer and rural areas, still lacked access to schooling because of their reliance on government services (Tsimpo and Wodon 2012a). Taylor also actively forbade schools in internally displaced persons camps, "on the grounds that he did not want to encourage dependency," meaning that Liberian refugees who fled to camps abroad had better access to education than people who remained in the country (Heninger et al. 2006, 8).

Education data quality is poor (see Tsimpo and Wodon 2012a), but international organizations' reports offer some insights. From 1986 to 1993, the gross primary school enrollment ratio (total number of children enrolled at an educational level regardless of age, divided by the total age-appropriate population for that level) was 51 percent for boys and 28 percent for girls, a rate that was unchanged from 1990 to 1996, while secondary school enrollment was lower for both boys and girls across both periods (UNICEF 1996, 1999). From 1998 to 2001, "there was an expansive increase in enrollment (289,883 to 794,337), schools (1,507 to 3,135) and primary teachers (9,659 to 17,210)," but this educational recovery was the result of child soldiers and displaced persons returning and of efforts by "communities and development workers," not thanks to government actions (Heninger et al. 2006, 6; see also UNICEF 2005). Students who could attend school received low-quality education: in 2001, "only 42 percent attained the minimal levels of learning achievement" (Heninger et al. 2006, 6). Under the NPFL government's watch, there was "virtually no state-sponsored teacher training in Liberia" because public teacher's colleges were not rebuilt or given resources (Heninger et al. 2006, 13), while higher education was starved of resources and deteriorated (Barclay 2002).

Literacy rates remained low, and they stagnated during the NPFL's time in power. Liberia had a reported 38 percent adult literacy rate in 1995, but the government in 2004 put the country's literacy rate at 28 percent (Dukuly 2004; UNICEF 1999). Conflict and lack of educational investment throughout the 1990s and early 2000s made Liberia "one of very few countries with a high percentage of people under 20 years old in which more adults than children [were] literate" (Heninger et al. 2006, 8, 10), despite the preconflict education system's flaws.

The NPFL government's failure to rebuild or maintain the education system combined with war to restrict educational access. A 2005 study found that over "30 percent of public and 24 percent of community schools were totally destroyed, and a further 16 percent of public and community schools experienced major damage," while about 35 percent of the population had never attended any school (Republic of Liberia 2008, 111). Taylor's government also did not try to address cost or geographic barriers, with the distance from schools keeping many Liberian families from sending their children (Tsimpo and Wodon 2012a, 40). Among households who had never sent children to primary school in 2007, 75.5 percent of urban residents and 55.6 percent of rural residents cited cost as the primary reason (Tsimpo and Wodon 2012a, 40).

When President Ellen Johnson Sirleaf's government took power in 2006, it quickly moved to make primary schooling free and compulsory and reduced secondary school fees, policies Taylor's government never pursued (UNICEF 2011). These changes sent primary school enrollment rates skyrocketing by

82 percent and sparked a 16 percent increase in secondary school enrollment from 2005 to 2008 (Republic of Liberia 2008, 111–12), highlighting Taylor and the NPFL's failures to prioritize and inclusively meet public needs.

Use of Government Resources

Winning an election and becoming legally responsible for serving the Liberian people's interests did not lead Taylor and the NPFL to a change of heart or practices. Instead, "it merely gave [Taylor] political, legal, and military cover to pursue looting by other means" (Adebajo 2002b, 231). The NPFL addressed welfare exclusively through patronage employment for select people—often with heavily delayed or deferred pay (e.g., L-1, two NPFL generals; L-52, Richardson)—and by subsidizing or sporadically giving away necessities, especially around Monrovia, where my interviewees concurred that cheap food and fuel helped Taylor gain popularity. As Hassan Bility (L-41) related, "there was not much social policy. . . . Everything was about security . . . about securing [Taylor's] personal economic interests and those of his cronies" and protecting the regime's control. Jonathan Taylor (L-49) said, "Nothing really much was happening in terms of development, because the priority for [Charles Taylor] was nationally security. . . . Everything was secondary. If teachers were not being paid, whatever."

Looking at the big picture of finances, a Coalition for International Justice (2005, 16) analysis found that, "although the official national budget of Liberia fluctuated between $80 million and $87 million a year from 1997 to 2003, the public budget figures were essentially meaningless. They reflected neither real government revenues nor real expenditures. Most years, virtually none of the money budgeted for infrastructure, health, education or rebuilding was spent on the designated activities." Charles Taylor maintained personal control over state revenues and expenditures, creating parallel structures and companies run by cronies (Coalition for International Justice 2005; Gerdes 2013; Lidow 2016). He pressured the National Assembly to give him "sole power to conclude commercial contracts for exploiting strategic commodities, the clearest sign of his determination to use the trappings of sovereignty to plunder resources" (Adebajo 2002b, 236–37). Tax collection remained informal and limited. To pay for immediate needs, the government sought advances from timber and mining companies that might have concession payments due later in the year, saying, "we know you have $50,000 or $100,000 coming in two months, but we have this emergency, so look, we want you to go ahead and advance this money" (L-49, J. Taylor). Nathaniel Barnes (L-36), the minister of finance under Taylor from 1999 to 2001, said that he had to lie to Taylor to prevent him from diverting public resources for private use:

> I used my naïveté as a public servant to get away with some things. He would say to me, "I need half a million dollars immediately." And I would say, "Oh, Mr. President, I wish you had called fifteen minutes earlier, but I just took that amount and bought Liberian dollars to pay salaries." And then I put the phone down and run and do it.

The proliferation of parallel financial institutions and parastatal companies makes it difficult to pinpoint the financial resources NPFL leaders privatized from 1997 to 2003, but Taylor is estimated to have personally controlled between US$25 million and US$105 million per year during his presidency (Coalition for International Justice 2005; Gerdes 2013), with large amounts presumed to have been sent abroad. Prosecutors discovered documents linking Taylor to a personal bank account used for diverting what should have been state revenues; the account contained millions of dollars of unexplained deposits (*Prosecutor v. Charles Ghankay Taylor* 2012, SCSL-03-01-T-0911-1, 27444– 27451). Journalist Philip Wesseh argued that Taylor ultimately retained popularity by providing his followers with necessities while suppressing free speech to hide corruption and the lack of development efforts: "He had monopoly, he had certain control over the economy. But you could not talk anything, so people didn't know that there were problems there . . . he couldn't deliver. Let people see something being done, there was nothing he can show" (L-38).

Considering Alternative Explanations

This chapter has argued that the NPFL's opportunistic-exclusive ideology best explains its failure to invest in infrastructural power or social service delivery. One contention of my theory is that rebel ideological type does not depend on resource availability at the onset of rebellion. Weinstein (2007) argues rebel organizations with early access to material resources can offer economic inducements to recruit followers quickly and crowd out competing organizations and leaders but at the cost of more predatory behavior toward civilians that is sustained throughout the conflict. The NPFL case, however, complicates this picture. The group's early core of fighters was actually more "activist" in Weinstein's (2007) terms, aiming (somewhat credibly) to replace the Doe regime with a more democratic government. Charles Taylor sidelined these actors in part by using his access to external resources to maintain followers but, more importantly, by ruthlessly killing off more programmatically minded rivals.

Politically motivated Mano and Gio fighters, seeking revenge for past repression by the Doe regime, were also the ones responsible for a great deal of violence against civilians during the first years of the rebellion, even as the more opportunistic, economically motivated Taylor sometimes took action to curtail unsanctioned violence. It was thus not initial access to resources that shaped the NPFL's goals and ideals but the commitments of Taylor and those leaders he cultivated around him.

One possible argument is that Taylor and the NPFL did not engage in more extensive statebuilding efforts because they had very short time horizons and simply wanted to accumulate as much wealth as possible. Yet while Taylor took a different tack from long-run statebuilders like the Frente Sandinista de Liberación Nacional (FSLN), he was not planning just a short-term money grab. Despite controlling most of Liberia's lucrative natural resources in the early 1990s, NPFL forces continued to push to Monrovia at great cost, seeking national and international recognition rather than accepting a stalemate and quasi-independence for their territory. While aiming to be president for life (L-35, Guannu), Taylor also had long-term goals of creating a cross-border "Greater Liberia," capturing territory, resources, and influence throughout West Africa (Sawyer 2004; Silberfein and Conteh 2006; Tanner 1998) for the benefit of himself and NPFL elites rather than for a transformative project.

Prior state structures played little role in determining the NPFL's statebuilding and development trajectory once the organization was in power. The Liberian state decayed under Doe's rule and completely collapsed during the first civil war in the early 1990s so there was little bureaucratic inertia to hold back a programmatic project. The extremely low baseline of state capacity and resources would certainly have made statebuilding success difficult, but it did not preclude statebuilding *efforts*. NPFL leaders' disinterest in programmatic goals was made clear by the NPFL's limited, "predatory" rebel governance (Reno 2015), despite enjoying significant financial and personnel resources, territorial control, and educated supporters who wanted to work with the organization (L-39, Mulbah; L-52, Richardson). In the early 1990s, the NPFL also boasted "some of Liberia's most experienced politicians" (Adebajo 2002b, 58)—who then either left, were forced out, or were murdered as Taylor worked to maintain personalized power. The NPFL's material and human resources could have enabled the pursuit of a more robust governance apparatus or public goods provision if desired. The limited rebel governance they ultimately pursued, however, suggests that political will, rather than resources or capabilities, explains the NPFL's lack of statebuilding and service provision efforts once in power.

Did Liberia's ethnic heterogeneity keep the NPFL from pursuing statebuild-ing and service provision? While the majority of the NPFL's early fighters were Mano and Gio, Taylor and NPFL leadership decried tribalism, punished some of those responsible for ethnic violence, and also relied on foreign fighters with less stake in Liberian interethnic relations; they cultivated a multiethnic organi-zation without a clear ethnic mission (Alao 1998, 34). One early NPFL general (L-28) described how "Taylor executed a lot of these Gio tribe for [killing Krahn]," and "invested in those of us from different tribes to monitor their operations." The purge of Nimbaian officers and politicians in the early 1990s and the INPFL's split further ensured the NPFL did not become a Mano and Gio ethnic project. Taylor and other top NPFL leaders were loyal primarily to them-selves, not their ethnic groups, and this carried over after victory. The NPFL's postvictory government, for instance, did not even seek to benefit the Mano and Gio peoples who had propelled them to victory to maintain their loyalty.

Territorial control also shaped what rebel governance the NPFL *could have* pursued (Liu 2024), but it did not necessarily lead them to build substantial and functional institutions or engage in significant service provision. The NPFL enjoyed the greatest territorial control of any group in Liberia while fighting as rebels—and much more than the FSLN ever had as rebels in Nicaragua or the National Resistance Movement (NRM) had in Uganda—yet it built only a skel-etal administrative apparatus; its provisional government in Gbarnga was more for external appearances than for governance and maintained a largely coercive and extractive order heavily dependent on commanders' whims (Reno 2015). Controlling significant territory therefore did not prepare the NPFL to manage the postvictory state effectively so much as it reinforced the group leaders' and members' convictions that they could personally gain from war and acquiring greater power, leading to little statebuilding or service provision after victory. Nor did the NPFL, while in power, extend the bureaucracy and seek to use development programs to co-opt civilian support beyond rebellion-era strong-holds, only relying on subsidized goods in Monrovia to try to forestall issues in the capital. While this could have been the result of security threats emerging soon after the NPFL took power, as Liu (2024) and some of my former NPFL interviewees suggest, I would argue that there was never any evidence that Tay-lor and his closest associates had sincere plans for statebuilding or more inclu-sive development in the first place, regardless of location or constituency.

Extensive internal and external threats could have provided an impetus for cohesion and statebuilding (Lachapelle et al. 2020; Thies 2006), but they were instead used as excuses for a lack of rebel governance, statebuilding efforts, or development under the NPFL and Taylor. ECOMOG's intervention and the

INPFL's split did not change the NPFL's goal orientation and the plans it would pursue once in power. Taylor and the commanders closest to him were committed to an opportunistic path from the beginning of the conflict. The NPFL did not engage in serious rebel governance efforts when they controlled the majority of Liberia, and they remained Liberia's most powerful armed faction throughout that conflict and during negotiations and elections in 1996 and 1997.

On taking power, the NPFL had to contend with military competitors, but so did the FSLN in Nicaragua and the NRM in Uganda. During the initial, relatively peaceful years of Taylor's administration, from 1997 to 1999, there was little public investment beyond the security forces. This did not change when the second civil war escalated. Taylor also generated serious external threats through his interventionism, especially in Sierra Leone and Guinea (Sawyer 2004). The FSLN's support for Salvadoran rebels and the NRM's sponsorship of Southern Sudanese rebels and intervention in the Democratic Republic of the Congo did not prevent either group, however, from pursuing more robust statebuilding programs than the NPFL did. Overall, the degree of internal or external threat did little to sway Taylor and other NPFL leaders from their preferred path of building their wealth rather than the state.

Did outside pressures or incentives shape NPFL ideology and policies? The NPFL formed around the end of the Cold War, when ideology was no longer a factor in superpower support; this might have made the NPFL unlikely to adopt a more programmatic line and made opportunism bound to win out (Collier 1999; Kaldor 1999; Mueller 2004). Samuel Doe was initially a Cold War ally of the United States, but he lost US support (Dunn 2009), and even if US officials initially disliked Taylor, they "privately admitted that they could have learned to live with him" and the NPFL (Adebajo 2002b, 93). Thus, there was no geopolitical pressure keeping the NPFL from adopting a more publicly oriented program or even embracing socialism had leaders wanted to. The Soviet Union's decline reduced incentives to adopt Marxism-Leninism explicitly, yet other African rebel organizations in the late 1980s and early 1990s still adopted more publicly oriented programs and engaged in more extensive statebuilding once in power (Lyons 2016a, 2016b; Fisher 2020) and the Communist Party of Nepal-Maoist's 2006 victory suggests leftist and programmatic-inclusive organizations can still win twenty-first century civil wars. Liberia had a history of left-wing political activism, with groups like MOJA and PAL active when the NPFL was forming and through the civil war, and some of their leaders were open to armed approaches to challenging the Doe regime (Dunn 1999; Huband 1998; Kieh 2024). Taylor rejected their policy ideas, however, and was worried about such leaders and groups challenging his supremacy while rebelling and after victory.

Meanwhile, Libya, which offered training and arms to the NPFL during the 1980s and throughout the conflict, had minimal ideological influence. NPFL interviewees never mentioned Muammar Gaddafi's *Green Book* playing any role in the organization's training or thinking. Gaddafi's government also engaged in extensive institution building to organize the Libyan population politically (Ibrahim 2009), in contrast to the NPFL.

While rebelling, the NPFL consistently rejected international pressures, including from allies, to negotiate or disarm. The failure of Ivorian pressure to bring concessions from Taylor and the NPFL in 1992 peace negotiations in Switzerland "was the final proof—if any was needed—that the NPFL puppeteer's residence was in Gbarnga and not Abidjan, Yamoussoukro, or Geneva" (Adebajo 2002b, 103). Once in power, Taylor ignored incentives to avoid repression and govern in a less blatantly opportunistic manner, which would have helped secure more international aid. ECOMOG's intervention had forestalled NPFL victory in the early 1990s, international actors organized peace negotiations and Liberia's elections, and international organizations and donors held the purse strings to support reconstruction and development projects: if ever international political and economic incentives *should* have led a new government to change its policies and practices, it should have been in Liberia. Taylor and his government had no ideological opposition to Western donors' and international financial institutions' liberal economic agenda, and Taylor had cultivated international media attention and public opinion while the NPFL were rebels (Ellis 2007; Innes 2005a). Once in office, however, Taylor preferred to continue seeking resources from the same illicit channels that had already enriched him and other NPFL leaders (Global Witness 2001; Johnston 2004; Reno 1998), avoiding demands for good governance or other political reforms. Taylor also actively disregarded donor pressure to curtail interference around West Africa, leading to aid cutoffs and support for NPFL rivals. In contrast, when Ellen Johnson Sirleaf came into office in 2006, she embraced international donors and received significant resources to pursue statebuilding efforts (Gerdes 2013, 256).

NPFL Rebel Victory and Its Legacies

Once a loose organization of dissidents aiming to overthrow a dictator, the NPFL became an opportunistic-exclusive project for personalism and resource extraction, with Charles Taylor at the top. Taylor's "preoccupation with establishing unhindered personal control" (Reno 1995b, 113) was constant across the NPFL's periods as rebels and in government, and Taylor "dominated" the

NPFL "to the extent that it could be considered his personal endeavor" (Gerdes 2013, 60). Yet it did not have to be this way. Taylor was initially unpopular (Gershoni 1997, 199), and his primacy in the NPFL was not preordained because there were several potential leaders who could have emerged at the head of the organization and shaped its trajectory. Whether one views leadership consolidation as occurring through "a series of coincidences," as early NPFL leader Tom Woewiyu later claimed (Ellis 2007, 74), or through purges and splits caused by Taylor's quest for personal control, the end result was Taylor's supremacy. A group whose initial grievance-motivated recruits had joined an organization with limited material resources was reshaped by Taylor around his kleptocratic vision.

When the NPFL took power, Charles Taylor proved impervious to domestic or international pressures to restrain his or other NPFL leaders' warlord tendencies of repressing dissent, looting natural resources and the national treasury, and stoking conflicts abroad (Waugh 2011; Dwyer 2015). Within Liberia, the Tubman and Tolbert regimes offered earlier examples of efforts to implement reforms and build state infrastructural power. The NPFL had the opportunity to pursue similar policies as rebels and while in government, yet they did not offer a new political and economic vision of society, instead fighting "over whose hands the economic power would rest in" (Duyvesteyn 2004, 85). Taylor's government carried on the Doe regime's authoritarianism and dysfunction, a case of "same taxi, different driver" (Lowenkopf 1995, 100).

Personalism and intransigence ultimately proved to be "the undoings of the Taylor administration" (L-50, Goodridge). Taylor rejected international demands to cease military interventions around West Africa, and his government's patterns of corruption, exclusion, and militarization sparked the rebellions that eventually forced them from power in 2003, leaving Liberia in shambles. Taylor's NPP party has a limited electoral constituency today, and many former NPFL commanders have cultivated their own political-economic networks based on personal ties rather than a shared NPFL identity (Lidow 2016; Themnér 2015; Cheng 2018).

After two years under a highly corrupt transitional government, Liberians in 2005 elected Ellen Johnson Sirleaf, Africa's first woman president. Sirleaf's government consolidated state authority and reconstructed or built new institutions. With significant help from international peacekeepers, the new democratic regime maintained security and stability. International actors and NGOs were heavily involved in statebuilding and service provision, but, overall, Sirleaf's government devoted far more effort in these areas than its predecessors (Gerdes 2013). Liberia's state remains relatively weak, and corruption persists, but in January 2018, Sirleaf oversaw the first peaceful, democratic transfer of power in Liberia's history (Spatz and Thaler 2018), and Sirleaf's successor, George Weah, accepted electoral defeat and left office in 2024.

Taylor's rhetorical promises of democracy and development proved hollow and his rule short-lived, but Liberians continued suffering the consequences of his destructive reign. The NPFL's time in power left legacies of state weakness, corruption, and violence (e.g., Blair and Morse 2021; Cheng 2018; Spatz and Thaler 2018). Recent peaceful and democratic turnovers of power, however, offer hope that Liberia can finally leave the NPFL and other actors' opportunistic-exclusive politics behind.

4

FOR PARTY OR PEOPLE?

The National Resistance Movement in Uganda

The National Resistance Movement (NRM) in Uganda represents a middle-ground case: less programmatic and inclusive than the Frente Sandinista de Liberación Nacional (FSLN) in Nicaragua but far from the National Patriotic Front of Liberia's (NPFL) opportunistic and exclusive nature in Liberia. While several NRM leaders had backgrounds in leftist circles, the NRM developed a more moderate program, centered around what it called "Movement ideology." As NRM leader Yoweri Museveni (1992, 18–19) said of the organization's ideological development and policy plans, "We take from every system what is best for us and we reject what is bad for us." The NRM sought to change political structures and representation, challenging prior parties' and ethnic groups' political power to empower itself instead. While rebelling from 1981 to 1986, the NRM developed "resistance committees," governance structures that transformed local-level political participation and representation and provided material goods to communities—although the NRM generally sought to limit its own responsibility for local governance and for services like education and health care. NRM leaders conceived of national interests as including a broader public, and they generally sought political power more than private wealth, but their inclusiveness had limits, with northern Ugandans especially marginalized.

Once in power, the NRM retained this vision of a mixed role for the state, leaving some regions with little noncoercive state presence and not developing mass organizations, but building coercive power through a robust security apparatus and using the renamed resistance councils (RCs) to reach down to the local level when desired (Tapscott 2021, 53–54). The NRM did not bolster RCs with the presence of state bureaucrats in much of the country, however, or employ RCs to pursue transformative social or economic policies. This focus primarily on political change meant that, in many regions, the state had little "weight" (see Soifer 2008) beyond its capacity for violence. While the inclusive transformation and state service provision many Ugandans hoped for did not materialize, the NRM secured its power, retaining control of Uganda for four decades as this book goes to press.

Uganda's History

Different kingdoms ruled and fought over present-day Uganda before the British claimed it as a protectorate in 1897, most prominently the northern Bunyoro and southern-central Buganda kingdoms. After World War II, British administrators gradually gave Ugandans more political power and greater educational and economic opportunities. Different factions began clamoring for more influence or for independence, although there was neither a large-scale rebellion nor heavy repression before negotiations led to independence in 1962 (Byrnes 1992; Reid 2017).

Uganda at independence was one of East Africa's more economically developed countries, but political divisions destabilized it. Buganda was granted limited autonomy within independent Uganda, and two of the country's most prominent early political parties were primarily Baganda (the Bugandan ethnic group): the more moderate Democratic Party (DP) and the more conservative, monarchist Kabaka Yekka party. However, Uganda's first elected prime minister was Milton Obote from the northern Langi ethnic group and the Uganda People's Congress (UPC) party. Obote initially agreed to govern in coalition with Kabaka Yekka but then ended Uganda's brief democratic experiment in 1966. He suspended the constitution, arrested cabinet ministers, dissolved kingdoms' autonomy rights, and sent troops to arrest the king of Buganda (unsuccessfully). Obote increasingly relied on the military for control, until Army Commander Idi Amin deposed him in a coup in 1971 (Kasfir 1976; Kasozi 1994; Mamdani 1976; Mittelman 1975).

Amin ruled through impulse and violent repression, including expelling Uganda's commercially vital South Asian community, which precipitated economic collapse and the decay of national infrastructure and services. Amin overstepped in external relations by invading Tanzania in 1978 to seize part of the Kagera region. The Tanzanian military and Ugandan dissident groups swept into Uganda in January 1979, capturing the capital, Kampala, by April and forcing Amin into exile (Karugire 1996; Kasozi 1994). This led to the 1980 elections that sparked the NRM's formation.

NRM Origins

NRM founder Yoweri Museveni was a student activist and member of Obote's UPC party in the 1960s. Museveni then turned left while studying at the University of Dar es Salaam in Tanzania and visiting areas of Mozambique held by Frente de Libertação de Moçambique (Frelimo) rebels in the late 1960s (Museveni 1971, 1997). After Amin's 1971 coup, Museveni organized the small Front for National Salvation (FRONASA) rebel force alongside friends from Ankole, his home region in western Uganda. FRONASA attempted to infiltrate Uganda from Tanzania during the 1970s but failed to gain traction (Kasfir 2000, 63; Museveni 1997, 54–71). Alongside Museveni's Banyankole ethnic group, FRONASA incorporated many Banyarwanda—Rwandan Tutsi refugees who had been living in western Uganda for years—including future Rwandan rebel leader and president Paul Kagame.

Museveni revived FRONASA to participate in the 1979 invasion that toppled Amin, but his leftist leanings had mostly faded. According to former FRONASA and NRM officer Pecos Kutesa (2006, 53), FRONASA members were motivated less by grand ideals than by personal security and ending Amin's repression. FRONASA joined the Obote-led Kikosi Maalum and two smaller groups to form the Uganda National Liberation Front, which then fragmented after Amin fell.

Uganda had a series of weak interim presidents until national elections in December 1980 (see Gertzel 1980). The elections were contested by two pre-Amin political parties (the DP and Obote's UPC), the Conservative Party (a reboot of the Baganda nationalist Kabaka Yekka), and Museveni's small Uganda Patriotic Movement (UPM). The UPC and Obote had major advantages in funding, name recognition, and support networks, and then gained military support, too; Museveni was convinced, however, that he and the UPM could win—despite being unknown in much of the country (Kasfir 2000, 63; Willis, Lynch, and Cheeseman 2017, 222). Obote and the UPC won in a vote certified as "valid" by foreign observers despite evidence of electoral manipulation and intimidation of DP supporters (Willis, Lynch, and Cheeseman 2017). The UPM won only one parliamentary seat. Museveni rejected the results as fraudulent, but the UPM was highly unlikely to have performed better in a fair election, and Museveni, who was in the transitional government, was informed about the election preparations and administration (Omara-Otunnu 1987, 155).

The DP grudgingly accepted the results, but Museveni decided to return to the battlefield. He gathered FRONASA comrades to form the People's Resistance Army (PRA), while UPM members and followers became the group's early civilian support network (Simwogerere 1996). With twenty-seven initial members, the PRA attacked the Kabamba military academy in February 1981 to seize weapons, then retreated into the heart of Buganda to recruit more forces (Weinstein 2007, 69).

Leadership Consolidation

Initially, "everybody looked to [Museveni] for advice and direction at critical moments" (Ondoga Ori Amaza 1998, 39). In FRONASA, Museveni had been frustrated by the slowness of collective planning efforts (Museveni 1997, 80), but he and other early PRA leaders developed more formalized, distributed leadership structures. Consultations in 1981, reportedly initiated by Museveni (Ngoga 1998, 101), "established the . . . indispensability of collective leadership and . . . the necessity for the movement to develop its collective leadership capacity," instituting regular, nonhierarchical strategy meetings among all members (Ondoga Ori Amaza 1998, 39–40). These discussions led to the creation of the group's commanding body, the National Resistance Council (NRC).

Between February and June 1981, the PRA remained small, working with civilian contacts to create committees to supply food, information, and potential recruits in Buganda's Luwero Triangle region, its base (Kasfir 2005, 281; Weinstein 2007, 69). Then, in mid-1981, the PRA merged with former president Yusuf Lule's Uganda Freedom Fighters (UFF). The primarily Baganda UFF gave the resulting National Resistance Army (NRA) and its political wing, the National Resistance Movement (together the NRM), greater ties to Buganda's population, helping attract support and recruits (Kasfir 2000, 63; Meert 2020, 400–401). Lule became the NRM's political head and Museveni the military commander, but the fifty-two-member NRC remained the "supreme political organ," with subcommittees for finance and supplies, politics and diplomacy, publicity and propaganda, and external operations (NRM 1990, 18–19). The early NRC's collective structure and inclusion of diverse interests helped shape the NRM's ideology and rebel governance.

Ideology and Aims

Obote's return to power suggested to early NRM members that preexisting inequalities would persist. They were convinced "there remained no other method of transforming the country's socio-economic basis apart from armed struggle" (Ondoga Ori Amaza 1998, 21). Early NRM officer Fred Mwesigye (U-2) said, "We didn't go to the bush because of rigged elections. It was a trigger due to historical problems: an undisciplined army, political problems and corruption; the economy was destroyed."

The first edition of the NRM's newsletter, in August 1981, argued that they were invoking the "right of rebellion against tyranny" (NRM 1990, 2). Already at this time the group laid out a program for post-Obote politics, calling for (1) restoring democratic government, including "re-establishment of an effective administration both at the central and local government levels"; (2) disciplined security forces; (3) revitalizing the economy; and (4) writing a new constitution "based on the popular will" of an elected constituent assembly (NRM 1990, 20–21). The aim was not a transformative social revolution but the creation of "accountable structures" and the elimination of "oppression, predation, and irresponsibility" (Brett 1993, 36) because the NRM believed that Uganda's problems were the result of the interests of those in power, not the country's socioeconomic structures.

During the rebellion, the NRM organized its goals into a Ten-Point Programme (Museveni 1986, 44–75; NRM 1986):

1. Democracy
2. Security
3. Consolidation of National security and elimination of all forms of sectarianism
4. Defending and consolidating National Independence
5. Building an independent, integrated and self-sustaining national economy
6. Restoration and improvement of social services and the rehabilitation of the war-ravaged areas
7. Elimination of corruption and misuse of power
8. Redressing errors that have resulted in the dislocation of sections of the population and improvement of others
9. Co-operation with other African countries in defending human and democratic rights of our brothers in other parts of Africa
10. Following an economic strategy of mixed economy

This program of political and economic stabilization and reform contrasted with the more socioeconomically transformative ideology and policies of Frelimo in Mozambique that originally inspired Museveni (Museveni 1971). Museveni—whether for personal or pragmatic reasons—became "*deradicalised* by armed struggle . . . less and less of a socialist" (Mazrui 2000, 128, emphasis in the original), retreating to an ideology of liberal nationalism (Rubongoya 2007, 66, 102). The NRM's initial leftist core, which had "spoken the language of anti-imperialism and socialism" (Brett 1993, 1), began to moderate, or else risk marginalization. Asked in late 1981 what the group's ideology was, the NRM's secretary of political and diplomatic affairs responded, "Democracy is our ideology. We want to establish Democracy first. Since we want to unite with . . . all groups, fighting against Obote, we cannot incline on a particular ideology" (NRM 1990, 64).

The late Cold War global political environment might have closed off some opportunities for forging a more socialist path, but Museveni had shifted independently toward centrist, pragmatic liberalism. In the Cold War context, according to Mwesigye (U-2), "We don't want anyone to dictate who is our friend and who is our enemy," so the NRM was willing to engage with "anyone who can be useful." In 1984, Museveni signaled a willingness to work with the World Bank, the International Monetary Fund (IMF), and foreign capitalist investors while discussing a "mixed economy" (*New Vision* 1990), and, shortly after victory in 1986, Minister of State for Defence Ronald Batta stated that "it is not our idea to define our policy between capitalism and socialism" (Larkin 1987, 163). In 1990, Museveni criticized other African political organizations for presenting themselves as left-wing or right-wing to attract support, saying that the NRM "refused to join these opportunists. We refused even to recognize the so called leftist-rightist categorization" (Museveni 1992, 187).

One of the NRM's main diagnoses of Ugandan politics was that ethnic and partisan polarization prevented national unity and development. NRM leader Eriya Kategaya said that the NRM "is of the strong view that religious and tribal or ethnic differences are not the enemies of the people of Uganda; these differences are not obstacles to unity of the people of Uganda . . . the obstacle to the unity of Uganda is the lazy-minded politicians and opportunists who exploit these differences for their selfish ends" (NRM 1990, 123–24). In this view, there was no need to undermine or transform existing social structures as long as they were kept out of politics. This ideal of unity appealed to Ugandans tired of political dysfunction, while NRM leaders' "commitment to egalitarian, non-sectarian, non-coercive popular support" (Kasfir 2005, 291) shaped the institutions they built as rebels and then when they were in power.

Recruitment, Socialization, and Rebel Governance

The NRM first reached out to communities in the Luwero Triangle through trusted older men known to be anti-Obote, who in turn recruited younger men to act as couriers or spies and began building support for the organization (Tidemand 1994). As they developed more trust, the NRM and local contacts organized resistance committees to procure steadier supplies of food, intelligence, and vetted recruits. The military's indiscriminate counter-insurgency helped the NRM gain more support and influence, with the NRM offering Luwero residents the best hope for survival and change (Meert 2020). By late 1981, a senior officer reported that there were thirty-five committees made up of "hard core supporters" (NRM 1990, 64), although these support-ers were not necessarily motivated by the NRM's policy proposals. An early NRM member wrote that "Museveni and a handful of those with whom he conceived the idea of a protracted people's war may have been motivated by idealism, but for the majority of us it was the demands of physical sur-vival. . . . We fought to win material benefits, to live better and in peace, to see our lives go forward and guard the future of our children!" (Ondoga Ori Amaza 1998, xiv).

Developing resistance committees through the NRM's existing contacts created vulnerabilities. Kategaya recalled that "if you picked upon a wrong man in the village that would be the image of the Movement. . . . That is when we decided that the leadership in these villages should be elected" (Tidemand 1994, 82). Both the NRM and communities in Luwero quickly embraced this unplanned democratic experiment (Museveni 1997, 134), with the NRM offer-ing communities "self-government" and leaving them with the responsibili-ties of administration (Tapscott and Urwin 2024). The resistance committees, later renamed resistance councils (RCs), also helped displace the power of government-affiliated chiefs in many rural areas and offered increased politi-cal opportunities for women (Burkey 1991; Ddungu 1993; Kasfir 2005; Tide-mand 1994).

The NRM did not offer material benefits to recruits; instead, it tried to use political education to build adherence to the organization's program, seeking to instill both discipline and belief in a broader political mission of nonsectarian-ism and economic development (Kabwegyere 2000; Museveni 1997; Weinstein 2007). Mwesigye (U-2) recalled, "Political education [came] first. Convince the people to support you and teach them about the country's problems." Museveni and other NRM leaders initially presided over political education (Weinstein 2007, 141), but they then created a political commissariat and developed a clear code of conduct for members to govern their behavior and their interactions with civilians, whom the NRM was supposed to be serving (Ondoga Ori Amaza 1998, 41–44). Political education focused on being disciplined with weapons and serving the civilian population, in contrast to prior regimes' abusive secu-rity forces. Fighters needed to "subordinate their individual and/or group inter-ests to the demands of the political objectives and intentions of the struggle" (Ondoga Ori Amaza 1998, 43), ideally being "willing to die or sacrifice for the common good" (Weinstein 2007, 141–42) and the NRM's advancement. For both fighters and civilians, NRM indoctrination was supposed to create "nationalistic, patriotic, anti-imperialist, democratic, informed, progressive and pro-people" attitudes (Kabwegyere 2000, 105).

From 1982 onward, the ranks of the NRM swelled with Luwero residents victimized by government forces and UPC youth gangs (Meert 2020; Schubert 2006, 99–100). To try to ensure that recruits internalized NRM ideals, commissars held daily political education sessions for fighters, while seminars and speeches to civilians sought "to enlighten them about the reasons for the war and the methods of the struggle" (Kabwegyere 2000, 105). Absorption of these ideas was uneven, but political education did further legitimize the NRM among some civilians (Kasfir 2005, 285), undercut critics who viewed the group as purely militaristic (Ondoga Ori Amaza 1998, 43), and built internal discipline (Schubert 2006; Weinstein 2007, 141–45).

This emphasis on political education and civilian welfare remained constant throughout the rebellion. When the NRM was retreating in 1983 and 1984, the organization tried to help civilians escape Luwero to refugee camps, under the guidance of RCs (Kasfir 2005, 288–89)—although this assistance may have also been to keep civilians' knowledge from government forces. In 1985, when the NRM decided to expand to the Rwenzori mountains in western Uganda, the organization "invested significant energy in political education and elected village committees" (Kasfir 2005, 289–90). This western front provided a successful testing ground outside Buganda for the RC system and the NRM's political ideas (Burkey 1991, 3–4; Ddungu 1993, 377–78).

Throughout the rebellion, RCs supported NRM fighters but also served as governments. RCs varied across regions, but they undertook administrative tasks autonomously or in cooperation with the NRM, including issuing travel passes, resolving disputes, managing local security through roadblocks and militia patrols, and providing for refugees (Ddungu 1993). RCs built on the foundations of *mayumba kumi*, ten-house cells that Amin's government put in place and Obote continued, which were employed for dispute resolution but also used for surveillance, repression, and regulations enforcement (Burkey 1991; Oloka-Onyango 1989; Tidemand 1994). Yet RCs had powers of "legislation, implementation and adjudication which had until then been the preserve of appointed officials and party nominees" (Burkey 1991, 3–4) or colonially appointed village chiefs (Mamdani 1988, 1173–74), providing a first taste of local democracy. RCs thus came to symbolize the NRM ideal of popular empowerment during the rebellion, and wartime ideals and institutions continued shaping NRM policies and governance in power from 1986 on.

Transition to Power

The NRM's success in gaining civilian support and territorial control eroded Obote's power, but the military ultimately toppled him. Northern Ugandan soldiers dominated the military, and tensions among northern ethnic groups grew during the war. Obote promoted the members of his own Langi ethnic group at the expense of the more numerous Acholis, who received more dangerous combat assignments (e.g., Mutibwa 1992, 161–63). In July 1985, Acholi generals Tito Okello and Bazilio Olara-Okello overthrew Obote, naming Okello president. The NRM remained skeptical that Okello and his military clique would institute political reforms (Kutesa 2006, 207); Okello and other Acholi military leaders thought that the NRM wanted to disempower northerners (Tripp 2010, 47), and so fighting continued.

The NRM kept consolidating territory and building administrative structures, including establishing an interim government in western Uganda in October 1985 (Kutesa 2006, 218; Mutibwa 1992, 172). NRM planning focused on security and economic recovery, including an economic Minimum Recovery Programme (NRM 1990, ii). NRM forces advanced toward Kampala in November, and government soldiers increasingly deserted or defected (Katumba-Wamala 2000, 168).

The NRM finally captured Kampala on January 26, 1986, taking over a country devastated by decades of misrule and violence. Political violence killed an estimated 800,000 Ugandans between 1971 and 1985 (Tripp 2004, 4). Uganda was economically shattered, with high inflation, per capita income standing at 60 percent lower than it was in 1971, and the informal economy predominating (Flanary and Watt 1999; Kiyaga-Nsubuga 2004, 89; Larkin 1987). Security remained tenuous in most areas. According to Pecos Kutesa (2006, 259), capturing power "marked the beginning rather than the end of the revolution . . . an opportunity and the challenge to translate the convictions and promises of the NRM's five-year armed struggle into reality."

Yet this was not a social revolution. The Ten-Point Programme provided basic guidelines for governing, but it was "no more than a guide to the philosophy of the NRM leadership—it says nothing about how the movement's aims are carried out in practice" (Mutibwa 1992, 179). In practice, the NRM prioritized security and economic revitalization above all else. Museveni (1990, 8) stated in 1989:

> When we captured power, we decided to start the huge job of rehabilitation by attending to eight priority areas: 1. Defence; 2. Agriculture; 3. Roads, railways and water transport; 4. Commercial trucks; 5. Repair of light goods industries in order to save foreign exchange; 6. Repair of utilities, especially electricity and water for industrial use; 7. Restoration of construction capacity; 8. Restoration of storage capacity.

Social transformation and welfare were to be, at most, externalities resulting from other priorities.

The NRM had mainly operated in the Luwero Triangle and western mountains so "no previous Ugandan political organisation was less well-known" on taking power (Kasfir 2000, 63). Leaders decided to incorporate other sociopolitical groups into the new government and to institutionalize the RC system nationwide to legitimize NRM control and displace lingering old regime structures. This brought new actors into a coalition with the NRM, especially from the Buganda-centered DP, while the NRC became the national legislature. Museveni, acting as president, presided over the cabinet. The NRC was elected, but candidates could not run based on partisan affiliation, maintaining the NRM's nonsectarianism principle and blunting the remaining power of political parties. Embracing outside politicians in cabinet positions gave the NRM's claims of inclusiveness greater legitimacy through broadened representation outside the NRM's Banyankole core (Muhumuza 2009, 25–26; Tripp 2010, 48–49), and during the NRM's first decade in power, former official Augustine Ruzindana (U-1) said, "There was a lot of collectivity, consultation, and attention to values." Museveni and core NRM leaders retained the final say, however, and a Banyankole-Baganda alliance dominated the government, alienating northerners and some members of the NRM's supposedly broadened base (Fisher 2020, 103–4; Lindemann 2011).

The NRM was not necessarily seeking to enact political and economic equality, but rather denying differences existed. Inclusion for all Ugandans within the NRM's "movement" was designed "to distinguish the NRM from all previous parties and governments by characterizing them as inherently sectarian and thus incapable of ruling Ugandans democratically," inspiring the political party ban and the denial of class differences (Kasfir 1998, 58). Negating differences, however, kept the NRM from addressing inequalities and truly working to represent and benefit all Ugandans, relying more on security forces than infrastructural power to hold Uganda together.

Developing Coercive Power

At his inauguration, Museveni (1992, 21) promised the NRM would bring "fundamental change," but security was the immediate priority amid worries about new rebel rivals. As Sjögren (2013, 102–3) argues, the new government needed "to secure a minimum of political and economic stabilisation in terms of security and resource extraction within a very volatile political context." Museveni believed, as he later said, that security forces were "pillars" without which "you will not have a viable State" (Museveni 1990, 53).

NRM forces needed reorganization to build a new security apparatus after many army deserters and bandwagon supporters joined during the final march toward Kampala. The new military retained the National Resistance Army name until 1995, when it became the Uganda People's Defence Force. NRM forces numbered around ten thousand at victory in 1986 (Republic of Uganda 1990a, 126). Then they rapidly expanded through both recruitment and the integration of former rebels until there were almost eighty thousand NRA soldiers in 1989 (Weinstein 2007, 68), before gradually declining to fifty thousand by 1996 (International Institute for Strategic Studies 1996, 268).

In early 1986, the NRM began overseeing urban police operations (*Weekly Focus* 1986), but Museveni (1992, 32) admitted that, "in many areas, neither the police force nor the administration is functioning," with only three thousand police officers nationwide. By 1996, the national police had seventeen thousand officers, standardized training, and more equipment (Kabwegyere 2000, 48), although this force remained too small for a robust presence across rural Uganda and faced constant equipment shortfalls, prompting complaints among legislators and ministers (e.g., Republic of Uganda 1990a, 2, 17, 78–81).

Instead of building up the police, the NRM decentralized policing authority by tasking local RCs with administering law and order in their communities (Lewis 2012; Tapscott 2023; Tidemand 1994). This continued the RCs' rebellion-era function as both local administrations and the government's eyes and ears where police and military presence was thin (Museveni 1992, 22–23)—especially in the restive north (Branch 2011, 69)—and RCs held greater local policing authority than the Amin- and Obote-era mayumba kumi had (Tidemand 1994, 55). RCs contributed to a clear decline over time in the ability of rebel groups to organize as intelligence networks grew denser (Lewis 2012, 2020). In rural areas where rebellions or cattle raiding occurred, the NRM also created militias called Local Defence Units (LDUs) that were connected to state security forces and RCs (Rukooko 2005). LDUs were under-resourced and undertrained, however, and legislators and citizens expressed concern about their lack of uniforms, unclear chain of command, and limited coordination with the military and police (Nsambu 1993; Republic of Uganda 1991a, 251, 315).

From the military down to RCs and militias, political education remained a priority. Building on structures established when the NRM was rebelling (Bell 2016, 504–5; Kabwegyere 2000, 106–7), the military quickly established the Central School for Political Education where officers undertook four months of classes "such as 'Introduction to Political Education,' 'Revolutionary Methods of Work,' and 'The Importance of Ideological Development for Leaders'" (Bell 2016, 505). The military also maintained the rebellion-era institutions of political officers in units and consultative meetings across ranks, helping build cohesion, integrate new troops, and enforce civilian protection norms (Bell 2016). Over time, however, emphasis on political education began eroding, contributing to service members' declining identification with the NRM project and weakening discipline (Museveni 1994b; Ondoga Ori Amaza 1998, 51).

Political and military education programs extended to NRM partisans and citizens more generally. Throughout Uganda, courses called *mchakamchaka* were organized to engage citizens politically and provide basic military training—although northern areas tended to be neglected because of both instability and government distrust of local populations (Verma 2013). Between 1986 and 1991, approximately sixty thousand people graduated from mchakamchaka courses, and while mchakamchaka was initially targeted toward civil servants, the scope expanded from 1991 onward (Kayunga 2001, 91–94; Lewis 2012, 237–38). Uptake of political concepts was not always high, but weapons handling was reportedly popular (Joseph 1993). Rubongoya (2007, 64) says that these courses helped gain trust by showing that the government was willing to help citizens learn "to defend themselves against state tyranny." Museveni (1992, 97) presented mchakamchaka this way, saying it continued the NRM's efforts as rebels to "democratize" force, for "tyrannical rulers would never do such a thing because their existence depends on the mystification and monopolisation of the gun."

Yet resistance to state tyranny was not the goal, but rather greater NRM legitimacy and building stronger rural defense and counterinsurgency capacity so citizens would "fight anti-people elements in their society and remain a reserve force in case of external attacks" (Tumwine 1989). Mchakamchaka courses provided structured settings to press civilians in unstable areas not to support rebel movements and also built surveillance capacity by monitoring individuals and recruiting some as informants or new military and intelligence service members (Lewis 2012). In insecure contexts, absorbing political content was less important than citizens being perceived as loyal to the NRM, while mchakamchaka offered citizens a promise of greater safety by being closer to the potentially violent state. When mchakamchaka was finally instituted in Acholiland in the north after 2006, one trainee said, "When you are at the right end of the gun barrel, you feel a kind of security. At the other end you are poorly off" (Verma 2013, 116).

Despite efforts to build ground-level intelligence and security networks, the NRM did not establish consolidated coercive capacity throughout Uganda's territory in its first decade in power, and it is unclear that this was truly a priority. Museveni criticized prior governments' failure to establish nationwide authority (e.g., Museveni 1992, 182), yet NRM security forces would suddenly withdraw from areas suffering from cattle raiding, communal violence, and rebel attacks, leaving undersupplied militias to defend their towns alone (e.g., Branch 2011, 72–73). The military abandoned large areas of northern and eastern Uganda to rebels and cattle raiders (Ochan 1989), leading many residents and analysts to conclude that the NRM was not concerned with residents' well-being in these regions (Branch 2005, 2011; Verma 2013). Military strength was not the issue, force distribution was: at the same time the NRM's security forces were failing to defend domestic territory, they intervened in the Democratic Republic of the Congo and engaged in peacekeeping elsewhere.

Political Reform and Infrastructural Power

Beyond security, what else did the NRM seek to accomplish with the state? The principal aims espoused by NRM leaders and the Ten-Point Programme were democracy and economic development. While a by-product of the rebellion (e.g., Tapscott and Urwin 2024), the NRM fully embraced elected RCs as the institutional manifestation of their commitment to democracy—although this was democracy at the local level rather than the national level (Kasfir 1998; Kayunga 2001). The economic recovery plan, meanwhile, aimed more for subsidized liberalism than socialism, calling for import-substitution industrialization and an economy involving "the majority of economic activities being carried out by private entrepreneurs . . . with the state, however, taking part in selected . . . sectors" (NRM 1986).

The RC system marked a transformation throughout the national territory, with Hansen and Twaddle (1991, 4) describing the creation of elected local-level governments as a "revolutionary change in politics" in Uganda. RCs became the building block for governance, creating a five-tiered system, from RC1 at the village level to RC5 at the regional level, and the national legislature, the NRC, at the top. Ddungu (1993, 368–69) highlights four views of the RCs' in operation:

> The bureaucratic view sees RCs as mere appendages of civil service created to implement government policy more effectively. . . . The democratic view . . . sees RCs as more of popular organs created to counter and hold in check abuses of the civil servants and all other state functionaries: that is, as organs of the people. . . . The third view sees RCs as organs of one political group, NRM, with its socialist proclivity. This is the view held by organized political parties. . . . The fourth view which could be taken as the semi-official version takes RCs as organs of the people, organs of the Movement, and organs of the state.

The reality was an amalgam of all these views: RCs varied over time and space in how the NRM government used them and how responsive they were to constituents, with the NRM taking credit for RCs' good actions and disowning unpopular ones (Burkey 1991; Ddungu 1993; Tapscott and Urwin 2024; Tidemand 1994).

RCs gave communities a sense of political engagement, but politics and policymaking grew increasingly distant from the grassroots level of the original RCs. Local RCs' (RC1s) authority diminished from almost all everyday governance during the rebellion to "uniting people, propagating NRM policy, reconciliation of disputes, promotion of self-help projects, maintenance of law and order in their areas and moral rehabilitation" (Ddungu 1993, 377–78). The NRM had little interest in dealing with everyday local governance, and so it deployed few cadres or bureaucrats in much of the country to interact with RC1s, which tended to "reproduce organic village authority" rather than acting as "an extension of the state apparatus or the political regime" (Tidemand 1994, 95, 97). Limited state provision of resources and reliance on voluntary labor for organizing and carrying out projects meant many RC1s withered after initial postvictory excitement wore off (Golooba-Mutebi 2004).

RCs at higher levels became bureaucratic machinery for implementing top-down directives, a situation legally institutionalized in 1987 in the Resistance Councils Statute, which subordinated the RCs to the national minister of local government and centrally appointed district administrators. Jaberi Bidandi Ssali said that when he became minister of local government in 1989, he was "charged with transforming RCs and connecting them at different levels," but power rested with the national government (U-5). The pattern of creating lower-level structures for citizen participation and then subordinating them to national-level leaders' plans was repeated in the late 1980s and early 1990s constitutional reform process, when NRM elites largely ignored an impressively wide consultative exercise (Furley and Katalikawe 1997).

RCs and the NRM party remained the primary political institutions through which the new government organized the population. The NRM did not devote significant effort to building corporatist, state-controlled unions or other mass organizations, like the FSLN did in Nicaragua. For example, women were integral in the NRM's rebellion and grew in political influence and participation from 1986 onward, yet the NRM government did not develop a nationwide women's organization (Ottemoeller 1999; Tripp 1994, 2001). Politicians sought women's votes (Ottemoeller 1999) and tried to "coopt women and youth into state structures" (U-4, Miria Matembe), but the NRM did not seek greater social influence through the women's movement, and an autonomous civil society sector emerged instead (Tripp 2001). With the women's movement, youth organizations, and trade unions, the NRM sought to establish regulating bodies to try to keep civil society in line versus exercising direct control in and through these sectors like Obote and Amin had done (Mujaju 1997). Thus, this was a change but not one requiring significant new institution building or mobilization, pulling the state back rather than redeveloping infrastructural power in a new way. Meanwhile, the NRM officially pushed ethnic and religious identities and actors out of politics but never directly challenged their cultural and social influence. In practice, ethnicity continued shaping NRM political appointments, resource distribution, and citizens' understandings of politics (e.g., Alava and Ssentongo 2016, 680–81; Green 2006; Lindemann 2011).

Reconstruction and development rather than transformation were the NRM's main economic priorities, and NRM leaders were willing to reverse course rapidly when initial policies performed poorly. The Ten-Point Programme called for a mixed economy, and in 1984, Museveni said that he envisioned this as "largely based on private production by peasants but also by middle classes in certain sectors like commerce and industry plus state participation in selected areas on the basis of profitability" (New Vision 1990). Rebuilding an economy damaged by war and corruption and reining in the informal economy posed serious challenges, however (Larkin 1987, 163). A year after victory, Museveni (1992, 45) stated that the government was committed "to effecting fundamental economic changes so that our economy best serves the interests of the majority . . . by restoring the social and economic infrastructures and by creating conditions for expanded economic production." Yet he remained vague about how this would be accomplished, and the NRM had "yet to adopt a national budget or draft any major guidelines for the future economy of Uganda" (Larkin 1987, 163).

The NRM initially implemented a set of "interim economic measures" that called for some state intervention, controlling prices for essential goods, and giving some state companies monopolies on a number of products while privatizing other parastatals (Kiyaga-Nsubuga 1997; Loxley 1989). This program was not accompanied by structural changes: leaders denied "that there were any basic economic cleavages dividing Ugandans" (Kasfir 1998, 58), and even more left-leaning NRM leaders "wanted to reform rather than dismantle the existing apparatus" (Brett 1994, 64; see also Nabudere 1990). The interim economic measures bankrupted the country by not including revenue generation measures and lacked deep commitment among top NRM leaders (e.g., Loxley 1989), who abandoned them in 1987, within a year, in favor of liberalization and structural adjustment.

Sjögren (2013, 119, 148) argues that economic liberalization was a "bitter pill for the NRM to swallow," but that it was necessary "to guarantee a revenue basis for stabilisation and recovery." The NRM quickly embraced international financial institutions (IFIs), however, both reevaluating their own plans and recognizing that liberalization was necessary to secure external support

(Kiyaga-Nsubuga 1995, 256–57, 1997). As early as 1984, Museveni himself had stated that he could "work with anybody including the IMF" (*New Vision* 1990), so the shift toward liberalization was not as radical as some observers thought (Mamdani 1988, 1163). Top leaders already favored it, and capitalism became fully entrenched as the NRM's dominant economic paradigm (Brett 1994). By 1993, Uganda's economic model was "one of only very few in sub-Saharan Africa today to which the donors, and particularly the World Bank, can point with some pride" (Independent Working Group 1993, 10)—even with corruption and mismanagement during privatization (Tangri and Mwenda 2001). Despite credible accusations of ethnoregional favoritism toward western Uganda and Buganda (Branch 2011; Lindemann 2011; Omara-Otunnu 1987), clientelism in resource distribution diminished compared to previous governments (Kjaer 2004, 407). Underlying economic systems remained largely the same, however, and the rising macroeconomic tide left many Ugandans behind. A decade into NRM rule, a legislator protested that "when I was going through the Budget . . . you will find that those that have got more are actually facilitated more and those that are poor in the rural, remote areas, even the little they have is somehow being taken away" (Republic of Uganda 1996a, 104).

Beyond security, democracy, and macro-level economic development, the other items included in the Ten-Point Programme were never strongly emphasized during the rebellion and remained limited priorities for the NRM once it took power. There was general success in curtailing corruption during the first decade in power, although dedication to anticorruption efforts eroded after 1993 (Flanary and Watt 1999; Tangri and Mwenda 2001, 2008). The project of "settling the Karimojong," the seminomadic northern ethnic group, and further developing the north was given little effort outside counterinsurgency campaigns until the mid-2000s (Czuba 2019; Kandel 2018; Ogwang 2023; Verma 2013). Macro-level economic development was expected to lift up impoverished Ugandans rather than the NRM directly implementing pro-poor measures such as land reform (Ssewakiryanga 2008, 74–77), and the NRM passed only limited land reforms in 1998, after elections became competitive (Green 2006; Okuku 2006). Public service improvement likewise remained on the NRM agenda more in rhetoric than in practice.

Social Services

The NRM never considered service provision a strong priority, following earlier governments' mixed legacies. Amin's regime increased investment and expanded the number of health and education facilities from 1971 to 1975, but service delivery and quality rapidly deteriorated from 1975 to 1986 under

Obote and Okello (Nagubuzi 1995), so there were opportunities and needs for expanding and improving public services. In the first postvictory decade, the NRM invested export income in government service provision, but health care remained focused on curative care in hospitals (Sjögren 2013, 81–82), while parents and nongovernmental actors primarily funded and organized education (Wiebe and Dodge 1987).

Improving social services was the Ten-Point Programme's sixth point, with aims to increase the number of medical practitioners and access to drugs, "wipe out" illiteracy, and work toward universal primary and secondary education (NRM 1986). Efforts to achieve these goals were sporadic and limited. In 1990, legislators pressed NRM leadership to increase spending on services. Representative Kisamba Mugerwa argued that there was a need to balance budget priorities because "defence is allocated 10 billion [Ugandan shillings]. The only Ministry following it nearer is Education which is five billion, otherwise, and Health two billion . . . we have to sustain defence but we have now to uplift Health and Education which are equally very fundamental" (Republic of Uganda 1990b, 19–20). This admonition went largely unheeded. Free public services were held up as an ideal, yet the NRM repeatedly deemed them too expensive or infeasible, instead promoting cost sharing in line with leaders' liberal ideals and structural adjustment guidelines (Nagubuzi 1995, 203–4).

Health Care

The NRM government made few meaningful efforts to expand health-care infrastructure or access. When the NRM took power, "structures for health care were dilapidated" (Sjögren 2013, 102). Decades of instability and conflict had seen Uganda's infant mortality rate and disease incidence rise, while repression and war caused death, disabilities, and poor epidemic management (Macrae, Zwi, and Gilson 1996). In 1986, UNICEF's representative in Uganda suggested two possible paths for rehabilitating the health sector: "to rebuild the health service to its 1970s levels of functioning, or to more radically redefine it to meet equity and sustainability objectives . . . a major restructuring of health provision in favour of the rural poor" (Macrae, Zwi, and Gilson 1996, 1098). The NRM government rhetorically endorsed the latter path of emphasizing primary health care, with Deputy Minister of Health James Batwala in December 1986 saying that "we are going to continue to invest into . . . curative treatment, but our emphasis is going to go into preventive and promotive measures" (Republic of Uganda 1986, 92). In practice, however, the NRM showed little interest in reorganizing health-care provision or undertaking new duties that might require expanding state infrastructural power.

In 1987, the new Health Policy Review Commission issued broad recommendations for reconstructing the health system to improve preventive and primary health-care capacity. There were funding difficulties and a shortage of health-care personnel but also a "lack of political interest in the health sector," with little effort to implement the commission's recommendations until 1991 (Okuonzi and Macrae 1995, 126)—by which point Uganda had twice as many people per physician as the developing country average (Ministry of Health 1993, 8). The government funded and managed hospitals, but most primary health-care provision was left to nongovernmental organizations (NGOs) (Okuonzi and Macrae 1995; Sjögren 2013, 134).

The Ugandan National Programme on Immunisation (UNEPI), for instance, was funded by UNICEF and run by Save the Children, with ground-level cooperation from local health workers (Macrae, Zwi, and Gilson 1996). UNEPI increased national immunization coverage and reduced maternal and infant mortality, achievements Museveni trumpeted in speeches (Museveni 1992, 72; Muwanga 1993, 40). There were suspicions, however, that the government overreported immunizations and underreported mortality (Macrae, Zwi, and Gilson 1996), and the NRM did not build domestic immunization capacity. Immunization rates declined in the early 1990s as donor-supplied facilities broke down and external funding fell (Amooti 1994; Bitangaro 1995; Lamwaka 1996). Improvements in preventive care were further undermined by continuing structural problems. The NRM government's failure to expand public water provision, for example, contributed to disease outbreaks and impeded sterilization at health facilities (Republic of Uganda 1988, 54–58).

Because the NRM did not seek to establish state-run primary health-care provision nationwide, RCs were not integrated into health-care planning and implementation beyond the construction of some local health posts and promoting hygiene and immunization drives (Republic of Uganda 1991b, 203; *Weekly Topic* 1989). This overlooked an opportunity to build additional state connections with the population and to facilitate policy implementation throughout Uganda. In 1986, Health Minister Ruhakana Rugunda (1987) announced plans for locally elected "health unit committees" to increase popular participation in health policy, prevention, and primary health-care provision, but the idea was never implemented nationally. Museveni argued in 1989 that "through the RC system the NRM Government had found a practical solution" to implement primary health-care plans throughout the country (Kagoro 1989), but state actions never matched his rhetoric.

The government was biased overall toward health-care delivery in urban settings (Macrae, Zwi, and Gilson 1996; Sjögren 2013), leaving other areas behind. Prime Minister Samson Kisekka, a doctor, stated in December 1987,

"We have gone on spending big sums of money in developing what we call curative services when in fact the alternative would have been done at less than half the price" (Kisekka 1992, 163). Kisekka (1992, 61–62) admitted in 1990 that in immunization and rural health care, "the rural grassroot is fully involved with the assistance of mainly NGOs" rather than the government. Even with the NRM's urban bias, in the 1990s, residents of Kampala, Uganda's wealthiest area, were still "not much healthier than the poor lot in the rural areas, looking at infant deaths and malnutrition figures" (Amooti 1995). Despite his title, training, and early involvement in the NRM, Kisekka was not in the inner circle of leadership; instead, Museveni and other NRM leaders' disinterest drove health-care policy and its poor funding.

In 1986 and 1987, the NRM funded the Ministry of Health at 6.4 percent of its 1970 level—a ratio that only improved to 16.1 percent by 1988 and 1989—while just 4 percent of government expenditures were on health, a quarter of the international average for low-income countries (Macrae, Zwi, and Gilson 1996). Even while enjoying donor assistance, the NRM sought to introduce user fees for historically free public curative services (Ablo and Reinikka 1998; Ministry of Health 1990; Okuonzi and Macrae 1995). By 1992, health spending was still only one-fourth of the World Health Organization's recommended level for developing countries, with the Ministry of Health (1993, 4) blaming "underfunding of government services and the low level of coverage." Over half of Ugandans still lived more than five kilometers from a basic health facility offering essential drugs and immunizations, including three-quarters of northern Ugandans (Ministry of Health 1993, 7).

These systemic issues led to a policy shift in the 1993 National Health Plan (NHP), which followed World Bank guidelines by adopting a fee-for-service model (Okuonzi and Macrae 1995, 128). The NHP report concluded that "the state's role in the health sector should be redefined from provider to policy maker and supervisor of various private providers," with limited state provision of preventive care (Sjögren 2013, 155–56). This solution was produced not only by donors' fiscal concerns but also by the NRM government's own liberal bias favoring markets over state intervention (Nagubuzi 1995, 203–4; Sjögren 2013, 155–56). The NRM's idea to demonstrate continuing commitments to primary health care was promoting voluntary self-help projects where communities would manage and maintain health-care provision and facilities (Bitangaro 1993; Ministry of Health 1993; Museveni 1994a, 40), but there was poor direction and little central government follow-through. Local governments struggled to fund projects and depended on donors and central government grants, which impeded capacity building (Ablo and Reinikka 1998).

Health-care spending overall doubled between 1991 and 1996 (Ablo and Reinikka 1998), but NGOs still provided nearly two-thirds of Uganda's health-care funding (Harrison 2001, 668–69). In 1995, about 85 percent of the Ugandan government's health budget went to hospitals and only 15 percent toward primary health care, diverging from the NRM's supposed priorities and reflecting a failure to build a more extensive, well-resourced primary health-care system (Mugisa 1995). In 1996, legislators and officials still bemoaned funding shortfalls and their impacts on health workers and quality of care throughout the health-care system (Namutebi 1996; Republic of Uganda 1996b, 585–86).

Under the NRM, Uganda was seen internationally as a health success for its HIV/AIDS prevention and treatment efforts at a time when other countries were ignoring or downplaying the crisis. The NRM was reportedly convinced that it was "wise to open the gates to national and international efforts to control AIDS" (Kisekka 1992, 69) and began hosting international HIV/AIDS workshops once it was in power (*Focus* 1987). Yet government rhetoric and programs were also inconsistent, reflecting NRM discomfort with responsibility for primary health care and prevention. For instance, Museveni promoted abstinence and traditional herbal medicine rather than condom use and pharmaceuticals (Museveni 1992, 274–77; Muwanga 1993, 40–41). NRM officials' outspokenness about HIV/AIDS and the establishment of institutions like the Uganda AIDS Commission were better than many governments' policies, however, and did help change behavior, likely saving thousands of lives (Parkhurst 2001; Parkhurst and Lush 2004; Putzel 2004).

In general, NRM rhetoric about health-care systems that could benefit all Ugandans was not followed up with committed efforts. As Susan Dicklitch (1998, 70) aptly noted in the mid-1990s, "With an estimated recurrent expenditure on health less than US$2 per capita per annum, the spending priorities of the regime seem to be mixed up." Instead of a functioning, publicly provided health-care system, the NRM moved to de facto total privatization: "Almost all elements of the system which were once public have been incorporated into the private business activity of the health workers. . . . The result is that very few free services are delivered in the public health facilities, and almost none at all are delivered to the poor" (Asiimwe et al. 1997, 54–55). This pattern of lofty NRM rhetoric and only modest actions for public benefit was mirrored in the education sector, too.

Education

NRM strategy documents recognized education's potential to build national unity and promote civic values but also placed strong emphasis on education's economic potential (Republic of Uganda 1986, 76, 1992), with broader education access a back-burner priority. Earlier Ugandan governments had privileged higher education over primary education (Wiebe and Dodge 1987, 7), and the debate over when or how to achieve universal primary education dominated the education agenda throughout the NRM's first decade in power. It remained a lesser concern for Museveni and top officials, however, who moved toward action only with the advent of increased political competition in 1996.

In budget debates in 1986, Minister of State for Education John Ntimba declared the government's chief aims as the "universalization of education beginning with the primary school level," and eradicating illiteracy (Republic of Uganda 1986, 76). Museveni (1992, 57) in 1989 said that it was "an NRM long-term aim to ensure free universal and compulsory primary and, when possible, secondary education." The next year, he again proclaimed, "We must aim at providing universal education up to the twelfth year of school" (Museveni 1992, 195).

Yet even as rising school fees caused parents to withdraw their children (*The Citizen* 1990; *Financial Times* 1990), the NRM constantly pushed off into the future any implementation of universal and free education, and "more often than not, schools [were] left to the parents to run" (*The Guide* 1989). In 1992, even after the economy had improved, Museveni argued that "although education must be universal and compulsory this must be attained through the possibility of cost sharing and not free" (Muwanga 1993, 33).

The number of government-aided schools grew, but the NRM government struggled to keep up with population growth and demand, and teachers were often untrained or undertrained, especially in primary schools. In 1986, 60 percent of primary school teachers were not formally trained (Republic of Uganda 1986, 78), while nearly 47 percent of primary school teachers and 46 percent of secondary school teachers were still not formally trained in 1989 (Khan 1991, 9–10; Republic of Uganda 1989a, 103). A 1987 internal ministry of education report decried "the appalling situation," amid fraud, overpayment, negligence, abuse of authority, and payment for fake students and employees (*New Vision* 1987). The situation was worse in northern Uganda, where war frequently disrupted schooling and damaged facilities (e.g., Moro 1996; Republic of Uganda 1988, 27).

Government education spending fluctuated, with the percentage of total spending devoted to education rising from 10.7 percent in 1986 and 1987 to 12.5 percent the next academic year, before falling back to 10.9 percent in 1989 and 1990 (Khan 1991, 15). During this period, the NRM government gave some assistance to most educational institutions, but NGOs provided approximately 30 percent of educational services without state assistance (Bitamazire 1991, 22), and parents' associations often paid or supplemented teachers' salaries. Spending also still skewed heavily toward higher levels: in 1988 and 1989, the average expenditure per pupil was 11 times higher for secondary schools than for primary schools, and 183 times higher for Kampala's Makerere University (Khan 1991, 20).

Primary and secondary school enrollment from 1987 to 1996 appeared relatively stable according to official government data (Ablo and Reinikka 1998; Tumusiime 1992), but funding was rising, prompting questions about where resources were going. A World Bank survey of 250 government-aided primary schools in nineteen districts found that official statistics were highly implausible, with enrollments actually rising 60 percent during the period and the student-teacher ratio increasing from 26:1 to 37:1 from 1991 to 1995 (Ablo and Reinikka 1998). Parents' contributions to salaries, supplies, and building rehabilitation and maintenance doubled between 1991 and 1995, suggesting continued inadequate government investment and diversion of government funding (Ablo and Reinikka 1998).

The NRM continually pleaded that Uganda's macroeconomic weakness made fully funding education too difficult. In 1989, Minister of Education Amanya Mushega rejected calls for universal education, arguing against the idea "that Uganda is a very rich country and hence can more or less afford to run and sustain a welfare system" (Republic of Uganda 1989b, 36). These same economic factors, however, made it difficult for Uganda's poor majority to afford fees in the government's cost-sharing model—precluding the increased literacy and educated workforce the NRM deemed necessary for economic development (Kiiza 1993). Schools and students in poorer rural areas faced especially great difficulties (Kawamara 1993; Lucima 1993; Mirembe and Kaheru 1994). Yet even in urban areas, the government consistently blamed lack of funds for educational shortcomings and called on parents to contribute more (Wanzusi and Azabo 1989). The NRM government kept making excuses in the early 1990s and refusing to abandon cost sharing (Akiiki 1994; Obbo and Kabusingye 1994), while the Constituent Assembly rejected including a right to free primary education in the 1994 constitution (Stasavage 2005, 58). At the same time that the NRM was seeking to avoid responsibility for primary and secondary education, it was cutting back government spending and involvement in higher education, which had previously been more robustly supported (Mamdani 2007).

When the political system began opening to opposition party competition ahead of the 1996 elections, however, universal education returned to the agenda as an NRM and Museveni campaign promise. Museveni (1994a, 34–35) announced plans in 1994 "to make primary education universal by 1997," with parents being responsible for uniforms and supplies and the state paying for teacher training and salaries, facilities, and textbooks. Through 1995, however,

Museveni's economic liberalism still made him reluctant to fund education. He instead prioritized infrastructure "on the logic that road building would facilitate participation in the market economy, allowing Ugandans to earn income which could be used in part to pay school fees" while denigrating education as a "non-productive" economic sector (Stasavage 2005, 58–59).

Museveni explicitly promised to provide government-funded primary education for up to four children per family, but education remained a low priority (Stasavage 2005, 59). Public responses to the pledge, however, convinced NRM officials to follow through and increase educational investment throughout the late 1990s (Stasavage 2005, 68–69). Museveni was quick to claim credit in his 1996 state of the nation address. He said that the government was ready to roll out universal primary education and reduce or eliminate cost sharing because, "over the last ten years, we have been able to carry out a number of experiments in providing cheap or free education to the children of the poor rural families"—although he named only military schools, eight schools around Lake Mburo, and one in Kisozi as examples (Republic of Uganda 1996a, 47–48).

The NRM government also did not tackle illiteracy as promised. Deputy Minister of Information and Broadcasting Maumbe-Mukwana complained to UNESCO representatives in 1988 that "lack of communication equipment hinders [the Ministry] from effectively combating illiteracy in the country," while the visiting experts noted a lack of coordination across government ministries and NGOs (Rwakaara 1988). The government started some literacy education efforts but never in a coordinated, nationwide manner (Mugote 1989; Okech et al. 2001, 6). A donor-assisted program called Integrated Nonformal Basic Education began in 1992 to teach adults in parts of eight districts (Okech et al. 2001, 6), but efforts to scale up were slow to materialize. In a 1995 speech on International Literacy Day, Prime Minister Kintu Musoke reiterated the Ten-Point Programme's commitment "to eradicating illiteracy in order to enhance development" but lamented that 45 percent of men and 55 percent of women over the age of ten remained illiterate (Onyango-Kakoba 1995). In 1996, the government developed plans to expand adult literacy programs to twenty-six of Uganda's forty-five districts by the end of 1998. However, "the programs operate[d] only in small parts of a district," reaching just 140,000 participants and leaving NGOs to carry out literacy education to accommodate the high level of demand nationwide (Okech et al. 2001, 7–9).

Despite the NRM never treating education as a right, universal primary education was eventually implemented *after* the NRM's first decade in power. The NRM's foot-dragging was self-defeating even for their own idea that education would provide human capital leading to economic development because education spending was positively correlated with Uganda's economic output (Musila and Balassi 2004). Greater efforts earlier in the NRM's time in power could have yielded larger and faster educational improvements and economic growth, but this did not align with leaders' ideology and priorities. Even when the NRM did finally increase public education provision, this was not part of a move toward more programmatic governance; it was instead a clientelist effort to offer services in exchange for votes rather than treating universal primary education as something good and necessary for the NRM-controlled state to deliver.

Considering Alternative Explanations

Following decades of dictatorship, conflict, and state collapse, Oloka-Onyango (1993, 513) argues that the NRM were presented with a unique opportunity: "to attempt to make amends and reconstruct the . . . framework of governance that we live under" in Uganda. Around this critical juncture, how did the influence of the NRM's ideology and rebellion-era institutions compare to other factors that could have shaped postvictory statebuilding and service provision?

As Weinstein (2007) discusses, the NRM did not have access to natural resources or significant foreign funding during its rebellion, which may have kept the organization from gravitating toward opportunism like the NPFL. Yet this does not necessarily explain why the NRM did not become more programmatic like the FSLN. Museveni's ideological leanings when organizing FRO-NASA were inspired by Mozambique's programmatic-inclusive Frelimo rebels, and some NRM members wanted to push the organization in a leftist direction. Instead, Museveni and the leaders around him asserted their agency and influence to develop the NRM around a more liberal vision of limited state and capitalist economic development. This was a clearly articulated ideological program, unlike that of the NPFL, and Museveni and other NRM leaders did not try to use charisma to substitute for political appeals (Gerdes 2013). Their Movement ideology, however, did not compel the NRM to try to build FSLN-style infrastructural power programmatically for two reasons. First, ideals of individual freedoms and limited state intervention in economic and social life are biased against expanding state infrastructural power. Second, liberalism had already shaped prior Ugandan politics and state structures as the predominant ideological leaning in the postindependence period (Engholm and Mazrui 1967; Mazrui 2000). The NRM thus did not need or desire societal transformation to implement liberal political and economic policies, while its aims also did not lead it to try to serve all Ugandans inclusively. Conservative economic ideologies can be adopted by more programmatic groups and compel them to build infrastructural power but only where the future or "return to the past" they desire requires transforming or overturning existing societal structures, like in Spain, where victorious nationalist rebels sought to uproot and reverse prior left-leaning transformations (e.g., Payne 1987).

Territorial control shaped where the NRM engaged in rebel governance but did not necessarily have longer-term implications for statebuilding and service provision. The NRM consolidated liberated territory in the Luwero Triangle after its first year of fighting, and while resistance committees developed initially to gather food and supplies for the NRM fighters, they became a new form of local administrative structure. Many in the NRM's military wing wanted to avoid involvement in civilian affairs, thus granting wide autonomy to the resistance committees in nonmilitary matters (Kasfir 2005, 287–88; Tidemand 1994, 80–81) and forgoing opportunities to engage in service provision or more extensive ideological indoctrination.

Territorial control did tend to overlap with ethnic divisions because the NRM was founded by Banyankole and Banyarwanda from western Uganda and then built up its rebellion in the Luwero Triangle, the Baganda heartland in central Uganda (Lindemann 2011; Omara-Otunnu 1987, 176–78). On the surface, the NRM's coercive approach to northern Uganda, the base of the NRM's Obote-era rivals, would appear to align with Liu's (2024) theory. Did the NRM's wartime bases affect targeting of statebuilding and service provision efforts? The Luwero Triangle's experience suggests not because, despite being where the NRM rebellion forged the strongest civilian ties, Luwero's people felt abandoned after victory. The NRM declared that children in the Luwero Triangle would receive free primary education (Wiebe and Dodge 1987, 7), but this promise and most other parts of the announced reconstruction program for the region were never accomplished (Kiwanuka 1994; *Monitor* 1996). It was not only the north, therefore, where the NRM neglected noncoercive statebuilding or development efforts. And while the NRM developed RCs in non-northern areas where they had little influence as rebels, they did not develop the bureaucratic infrastructure or funding streams that might have co-opted residents' support, as Liu (2024) envisions.

Did Uganda's ethnic heterogeneity dissuade the NRM from more extensive statebuilding and service provision efforts? Early in its rebellion, the NRM in fact proclaimed a desire to *transcend* ethnicity in governance, claiming ethnic differences were only impediments when exploited by politicians (NRM 1990, 123–24). The NRM tolerated ethnic differences, most prominently by culturally (but not politically) recognizing historical kingdoms, including Buganda, and their kings. This reversed Obote's confrontational stance toward the kingdoms and did not seek to break kingdoms' social influence, yet the NRM retained political control and could act against the kings' will when desired (Lindemann

2011; Mazrui 2000; Okuku 2002; Rubongoya 2007). Even in northern Uganda, where citizens have long accused the NRM government of ethnic bias, the NRM has shown it can engage in statebuilding and service provision when it so chooses, even amid continuing insecurity (Branch 2011). Ethnic concerns thus should not have prevented NRM efforts to build infrastructural power or expand service provision if these had been priorities.

Meanwhile, prior state institutions did not constrain NRM planning because the preexisting state apparatus had largely ceased to function by the middle of their rebellion, and the military disintegrated and fled north at victory. Some colonial administrative legacies and appointed chiefs remained, but, as the NRM saw it, most colonial structures "were abandoned" by the Obote and Amin governments, who then "failed to think of institutions with which to replace them" (Museveni 1992, 94–95). There was thus a large scope for reshaping the state and society. The NRM changed politics structurally with the resistance council system, yet it did not seek to enact major economic transformations or to build and utilize mass mobilization capacity beyond addressing security issues. RCs had the potential to extend state infrastructural power down to the village level, but—while they were democratizing—the NRM used RCs to decentralize responsibility for local government and leave local-level social welfare to self-help rather than taking a more active state role (Golooba-Mutebi 2004; Ottemoeller 1996; Tidemand 1994).

International political pressures and influence on Uganda in the late 1980s and early 1990s were also weaker than those other states experienced. The NRM carefully avoided entanglement in Cold War politics or capitalism-versus-socialism debates. Once in power, they also largely ignored the democratization agenda advanced by the Western powers and NGOs. Susan Dicklitch (1998, 95) highlighted that "Uganda is one of the few countries in Africa that can brush off political liberalization, and still have the strong backing of the IFIs and foreign donors. Why? Because Uganda is also one of a handful of African countries that has fully embraced economic liberalization." The NRM could therefore forge its own policy path domestically, even resisting unwanted donor demands, rather than external policies being forcibly imposed (Dijkstra and Van Donge 2001).

Did security threats affect the type or forms of statebuilding and service provision attempted by the NRM? The various rebellions faced by the NRM after taking power (see Day 2011; Lewis 2020) certainly created resource constraints, with defense consuming money and energy that could have been used for social programs (Mutibwa 1992, 196). Yet even if more of the military budget had been available for other purposes, the NRM lacked the political desire to build infrastructural power or take state responsibility for service provision. Security threats also did not lead the NRM to seek more extensive state control through-out Uganda's national territory. The NRM remained content with areas of lim-ited control within Uganda, leaving portions of the north and east to the mercies of the Lord's Resistance Army and cattle raiders (Branch 2005, 2011), all while sending the military on interventions and peacekeeping missions abroad. The NRM was comfortable ultimately with a state that could wield political and coercive influence throughout Uganda when desired, but one that was not a consistent presence in seeking to noncoercively shape Ugandan society.

NRM Rebel Victory and Its Legacies

Almost a decade after the NRM seized power, Mahmood Mamdani (1995, i–ii) argued that the organization retained its emphasis on practical issues rather than transformation, "a pragmatism that judges everything by results, nothing by principles." The NRM took power with a set of ideas and aims involving remaking the political system, but the group never dedicated itself to more thorough state-led social and economic change. Core leaders, and especially Museveni, never embraced more left-wing NRM supporters' idea that the group should achieve a social revolution by restructuring society to improve all citi-zens' lives and opportunities. Instead, the NRM developed coercive power and political control but left most everyday governance and service provision to other actors.

The Movement system that the NRM put in place was an audacious political experiment, creating "an economy without state involvement; a state without political parties; and . . . monarchies without power . . . to maximise market returns [and] minimize ethnic rivalries" (Mazrui 2000, 133). Like many experi-ments born of rebellion, it had mixed and at times unintended results (Kasfir 2024; Tapscott and Urwin 2024). The RC system created meaningful opportu-nities for representation and eventually, from 1992 onward, greater subnational control of resources (e.g., Lambright 2011; Nsibambi 1998). Yet socioeconomic transformation was elusive: there were "improvements of a quantitative, rather than qualitative nature" because social and economic structures did not become "more responsive to the basic needs of the people" (Ondoga Ori Amaza 1998, 226).

The NRM did retain strong influences from the rebel period, which leaders frequently invoked. In a 1989 speech to the NRC, Museveni (1990, 55) called for renewing the rebellion's collective spirit: "You should, therefore, take an active interest in the experiences and history of the NRM, especially the Army. Together we can consolidate and develop this experience and thus be able to close some of the loopholes which are still causing drawbacks." The NRM's wartime experience and ideology were based around displacing political elites and structures and replacing them with the Movement and the RC system. This allowed Museveni and NRM elites to consolidate long-term control while giving the illusion of more decentralized power (Khisa 2013; Muhumuza 2009; Tapscott 2021).

Once the NRM was in Kampala, its more economically liberal tendencies kept it from working to build infrastructural power beyond the organization's central and western bases or providing services inclusively. A coercive approach to engagement with northern Uganda was accompanied by a fragmented approach to establishing state influence elsewhere, with the NRM state an ambiguous, unpredictable presence (Tapscott 2021). The NRM has retained power, but this approach has had long-term consequences for socioeconomic equality and outcomes. Amid common perceptions of Uganda as a development success based on macroeconomic indicators, the country has in fact formed an archipelago of islands of infrastructure and service provision (Hickey, Bukenya, and Matsiko 2023), between which "there is the rest of the country which, for the most part, is far from 'development'" (Jones 2009, 8–9).

Rather than the "independent economic development" the NRM envisioned in the Ten-Point Programme, foreign capital and aid remained vital to Uganda's functioning (Jones 2009; Obwona 2001). In their first two decades in power, NRM political and military leaders did not generally enrich themselves personally, or they disseminated wealth through party structures and patronage networks (Tripp 2010, 129–31), but they still perpetuated inequalities. A more interventionist Ugandan state would not necessarily have provided better outcomes for all. By failing to build infrastructural power, however, and leaving the state an inconsistent, distant, or more coercive actor in many Ugandans' lives, the NRM perpetuated the fragmentation and sectarianism it once fought against.

The Museveni-led NRM has continued controlling Uganda through the time of writing in early 2025. In 2016, when I was conducting research in Uganda, the NRM marked thirty years since victory, and Museveni won an unfair election to gain another five years in office (Abrahamsen and Bareebe 2016). The pressure of open political competition beginning in the mid-1990s did push the NRM to take statebuilding and service provision more seriously. As noted above, the NRM finally adopted universal primary education in 1996 after years of delays (Stasavage 2005), and Museveni introduced universal secondary education ahead of the 2006 elections (Tripp 2010, 188). It required electoral concerns, not any new ideological drive, for the NRM and Museveni to increase their service provision efforts. Some less coercive state engagement with northern Uganda also emerged over time with increasing government development and political education efforts in the 2000s, but security has remained the primary focus (Branch 2011; Czuba 2019; Nsibambi 2014; Tapscott 2017; Verma 2013). Feelings of neglect have persisted in other regions where the NRM has paid little attention (Jones 2009; Leopold 2005). More competitive elections might have spurred the NRM toward greater mass mobilization and building greater infrastructural power, like Slater (2008) found in some Southeast Asian democracies, yet the NRM has instead stifled competition over time, primarily to Museveni's benefit.

Like the contemporary FSLN, the NRM has grown more personalized under Museveni, especially after the early 2000s. To preserve his primacy, Museveni pushed out other NRM politicians who were seen as threats or felt it was their turn to lead. Opposition actors have continued trying to challenge Museveni and the NRM's power, but the regime has withstood them through a combination of electoral manipulation, repression, co-optation, and patronage, while abandoning rebellion-era appeals (Abrahamsen and Bareebe 2021; Khisa 2019, 2023; Reuss and Titeca 2017; Tapscott 2021). Museveni's current presidential term ends in 2026, but he has not suggested that he will give up power, and his son, General Muhoozi Kainerugaba, continues positioning himself to succeed Museveni and establish a family dynasty that could rule Uganda for decades more.

Part III
EXTENSIONS AND IMPLICATIONS

ANTICOLONIAL REBELLION'S DIVERGENT PATHS

Political Orders in Angola's Civil Wars

The Frente Sandinista de Liberación Nacional (FSLN), National Patriotic Front of Liberia (NPFL), and National Resistance Movement (NRM) fought in diverse regions at different times. In this chapter, I compare three separate rebel organizations that developed during the Angolan war of independence against Portuguese colonial rule to demonstrate that leaders may adopt and follow very different ideologies even when facing similar structural conditions. The Movimento Popular de Libertação de Angola (MPLA), Frente Nacional de Libertação de Angola (FNLA), and União Nacional para a Independência Total de Angola (UNITA) all began rebellions around the same time in the early 1960s. They faced a common enemy within the same territory until Portugal ceased fighting in 1974. Yet their leaders took their organizations down very different paths. While independence was a common aim, their other goals and ideals diverged, leading them to adopt different policy positions, patterns of recruitment and socialization, and relations with civilians—and to fight each other.

These cases help allay any concerns that the formation or survival of a specific type of organization does not depend on the time in which an organization is fighting, the type of government it is combatting, the country in which it is active, or the polity it wishes to control. The MPLA, FNLA, and UNITA were all center-seeking groups that aimed to topple the Portuguese colonial regime and to govern an independent Angolan state, and all three had difficulty carving out significant control of populated areas before independence in 1975 (Conte 1972; Marcum 1969). I do not examine the secessionist Frente para a Libertação do Enclave de Cabinda (FLEC), which sought and continues to fight

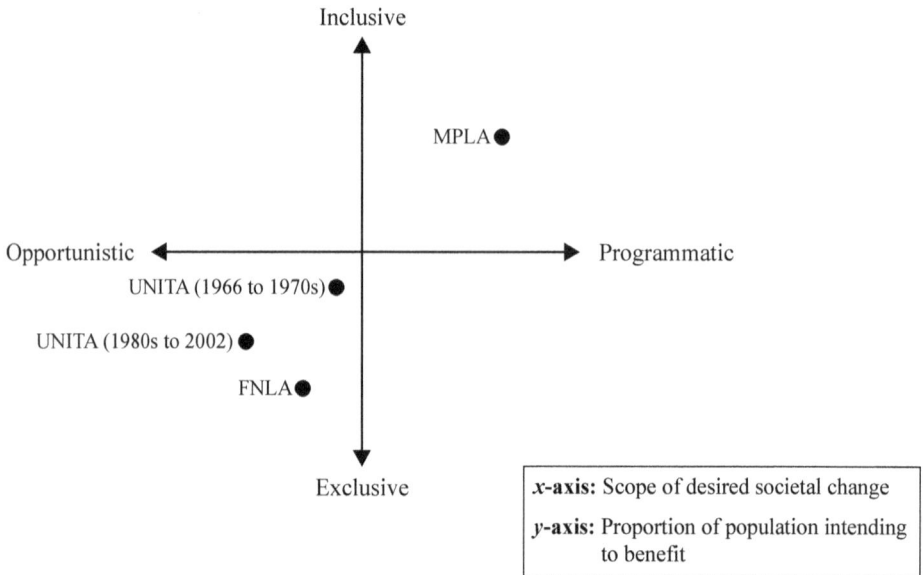

FIGURE 5.1.   Rebel organizational types in Angola

for independence for the oil-rich Cabinda region that is separated from the rest of Angola by the Democratic Republic of the Congo.

The MPLA was more programmatic-inclusive. The ethnonationalist FNLA was more exclusive and somewhat opportunistic. UNITA began fighting in the 1960s and 1970s with a mix of opportunistic and programmatic aims, and had some sense of working toward broader benefits, within limits. After independence, when the MPLA was in government and UNITA continued fighting for control of the Angolan state, UNITA shifted toward a more opportunistic direction. Figure 5.1 displays the three Angolan rebel groups' positions on the programmatic-opportunistic and inclusive-exclusive axes, with UNITA split across two time periods to reflect the organization's ideological evolution. The MPLA's behavior shifted in a more opportunistic direction from the late 1980s onward after President José Eduardo dos Santos, in office beginning in 1979, became increasingly entrenched in power, although this happened after the MPLA's first postvictory decade and thus beyond my theory's scope.

Origins of the MPLA

The MPLA formed out of an alliance of leftist and nationalist organizations that joined forces in 1956. The organization developed a diverse collective leadership group composed of black, *mestiço* (mixed-race), and white Angolans (Marcum 1969). In the 1950s and early 1960s, the MPLA largely engaged in nonviolent pro-independence activism, although it did claim responsibility for directing a November 1961 attack on a prison in the capital, Luanda, to free jailed nationalists. The MPLA's original manifesto called for "'a single front of all the anti-imperialist forces of Angola,' setting aside for this purpose all considerations of political opinion, social status, religious beliefs, or philosophical views" (Marcum 1969, 30–31). However, these unification efforts were largely unsuccessful.

The group reorganized in 1962 as growing violence by the FNLA and Portuguese reprisals heightened the crisis in Angola. The MPLA adopted a programmatic stance seeking not only independence but also embracing the group's roots in the Angolan Communist Party by calling for socioeconomic transformation. Although Chabal (2001, 226) describes the MPLA as "from its inception strongly (orthodox) Marxist," initial leader Agostinho Neto took a more pragmatic stance, believing that Marxist-Leninist goals and principles needed to be adjusted to the Angolan context (Andrew and Mitrokhin 2006, 444–45). In manifestos and propaganda, the MPLA proclaimed a program aiming to achieve clear breaks from the exploitative colonial regime: "No more exploitation but minimum guaranteed wages and equal pay for equal work; an end to discrimination on the grounds of race, ethnic origin, sex or age; and free public health and education" (Wolfers and Bergerol 1983, 109). This leftist program brought Soviet and Cuban support during the independence war, although the MPLA also maintained economic and diplomatic ties to Western countries (Gleijeses 2002; Somerville 1984; Stevens 1976). Robert Hultslander, the US Central Intelligence Agency (CIA) station chief in Luanda in 1975, said that he and the US consul both believed that, while many MPLA leaders "outwardly embraced Marxism, they were much closer to European radical socialism than to Soviet Marxist-Leninism" and that "the MPLA was the least tribal of the three movements . . . more effective, better educated, better trained and better motivated" (Onslow and van Wyk 2013, 84–85).

The MPLA's support base was concentrated among the mestiço and Mbundu populations, but the organization consistently espoused ideals of interethnic and interracial unity, even arguing against the targeting of white Portuguese settlers and following these policies on the ground (Thaler 2012). There were tensions within the organization, however. Neto's efforts to establish a broad, inclusive base by forming a coalition with small ethnic and moderate parties alienated some members who advocated more ethnically specific appeals, prompting the departure of leading Bakongo and Ovimbundu members in 1968 (Marcum 1964, 4, 1975, 5). The remaining MPLA leadership continued to espouse a nonethnic line. The MPLA suffered from continuing factional conflicts between different leaders up through independence, but Neto and his allies retained control over decision making (Malaquias 2007; Marcum 1969).

In 1963, the MPLA began guerrilla operations against the Portuguese in Cabinda, expanding from 1964 to 1966 into mainland Angola and slowly carving out a degree of territorial control that allowed the group to start implementing some of its goals for sociopolitical transformation (Brinkman 2003b, 308; Fortunato 1977; Marcum 1969). The Portuguese strategy of resettling civilians and isolating them in *aldeamentos* (collective villages) made it difficult for the MPLA to consolidate significant populated liberated zones. Yet they sought to free civilians from the aldeamentos and also resettled some civilians in MPLA-controlled collective villages in this "war for people" (Brinkman 2005; Davidson 1975, 28). The MPLA established village committees in the protected villages near guerrilla bases and provided literacy lessons and medical care (Davidson 1975, 26–29; Wolfers and Bergerol 1983, 109). In 1968, the MPLA began holding "regional party conferences" inside Angola (Collelo 1991, 31). Clandestine committees were established in urban areas, providing an organized base and nascent administrative structures in cities and towns closer to the time of independence (Wolfers and Bergerol 1983), and the MPLA also used radio broadcasts to spread its ideas beyond its areas of operations (Pearce 2012, 450). There were strict prohibitions on violence against civilians, which the MPLA took seriously and punished, and the organization engaged in political education both to indoctrinate fighters and to build adherence from the population (Davidson 1975; Thaler 2012; Wolfers and Bergerol 1983).

Development of the FNLA

During this early period of the conflict, the MPLA was competing—sometimes violently—with the FNLA. Founded in 1956 by Holden Roberto as the União dos Povos do Norte de Angola and then renamed the União das Populações de Angola (UPA) two years later, the organization initially held separatist goals of reestablishing the historical Bakongo kingdom, with Roberto as its leader. In 1960, Roberto rejected MPLA overtures to form a united anticolonial front, in line with his earlier rejection of aid offers from Senegalese and Portuguese Marxist-Leninists (Marcum 1969, 43, 67–68). Despite rejecting a united rebel effort, Roberto had shifted the UPA by this time toward national aspirations and proclaimed support for ethnic unity, arguing in a radio broadcast that "Angola was not 'a composite of tribes' but 'one nation'" (Marcum 1969, 86–87).

After the UPA organized a wave of violence against Portuguese settlers in 1961, the group merged with another nationalist organization to form the FNLA, reinforcing a shift to national-level aims. There was little effort to establish a clear political program beyond the end of Portuguese rule. Roberto was "a pragmatist rather than an ideologist" (Marcum 1964, 5) and "reserved all considerations of ideology, and in an operational sense, political education, for sometime *after* Angolan independence" (Marcum 1975, 7, emphasis in the original). This opportunistic stance saw the FNLA seek and take weapons from whatever countries would provide them, as well as recruit former Portuguese soldiers.

The FNLA failed to leave its exclusive Bakongo ethnonationalism behind, however, and did not significantly appeal to or aim to include other Angolans, remaining throughout its first decade "strongly tribalist" (Stevens 1976, 138). Roberto had made political contacts among some Mbundu in the late 1950s (Marcum 1969, 66) but did not seek to incorporate them into the organization. The FNLA put on a multiethnic face when it was politically expedient, recruiting officers "carefully selected to represent a balance of ethnic groups" at the start (Marcum 1964, 4) and naming Rosario Neto (no relation to Agostinho), an Mbundu, as an official in its office in exile in the newly independent Congo (Brinkman 2003a, 199–200; Marcum 1969, 84). Roberto truly trusted only other Bakongo as close advisers, however, and non-Bakongo members were pushed aside in moments of heightened conflict and contestation (Marcum 1975).

Following the initial outbreak of violence in 1961 and 1962, the FNLA began attacking the MPLA in northern Angola (Brinkman 2003a, 198; Marcum 1969, 210–21), allegedly in exchange for US support (Wolfers and Bergerol 1983, 3). In villages where the FNLA operated within northern Angola, visitors observed some efforts at governance and civic education (Houser 1962). The FNLA also sought to gain external legitimacy by establishing the Governo Revolucionârio de Angola no Exilio (GRAE) in Kinshasa, providing basic services to Angolan refugees there (Marcum 1964). The GRAE achieved an initial coup by securing recognition from the Organization for African Unity (OAU) as the representatives of the Angolan independence movement. The OAU walked this back, however, and recognized the MPLA as an equally legitimate liberation movement (Ekaney 1976, 226; Whitaker 1970, 19). With each FNLA success also came setbacks, and in 1964, Ovimbundu recruits "mutinied amid charges that Roberto was unwilling to extend the war beyond his own northern Bakongo bailiwick" (Marcum 1967, 10). Ovimbundu student activist Jonas Savimbi, then serving as the GRAE's foreign minister, arranged for Chinese support to counter the MPLA's Soviet backing, but Savimbi then took the Chinese contacts and resources with him when he split from the FNLA to start his own organization, UNITA (Stevens 1976, 139). Such command-and-control problems continued plaguing the FNLA throughout its organizational life: in 1975, US Secretary of

Defense James Schlesinger expressed worries about backing the FNLA because of its "weak capacity to enforce discipline" (Onslow and van Wyk 2013, 80), with a lack of foreign support ultimately helping doom the FNLA.

UNITA's Beginnings

Jonas Savimbi left the FNLA in 1965 after delivering the scathing indictment that Holden Roberto "was an American puppet and a tribalist, and that in the absence of a programme the FNLA was mercenary in spirit" (Stevens 1976, 138). Savimbi also accused Roberto of "monopolizing the revolutionary movement and decision-making as if they were his business alone" and sought increased armed activity within Angola versus the FNLA's stronger focus on the GRAE as a government-in-exile (Ekaney 1976, 225–26). Savimbi also viewed the MPLA with suspicion (Heywood 1989, 52). In 1966, Savimbi founded UNITA, which he led from the outset in a "unified and unchallenged" manner (Collelo 1991, 32).

UNITA's social base was in the center and south of Angola among the Ovimbundu ethnic group, who made up about one-third of the Angolan population and had a long history of nationalist mobilization against Portuguese rule (Marcum 1969; Heywood 1989; Pearce 2015b; Péclard 2015). UNITA's pretensions to being a nationalist independence movement necessitated some non-Ovimbundu support, and the group sought to attract other young Angolans unhappy with their status in the MPLA or FNLA (Heywood 1989, 53). UNITA's constitution inclusively called for "a government proportionally representative of all ethnic groups, clans, and classes" (Collelo 1991, 32), although UNITA's practices did not always match this.

UNITA's clear core constituency was among the Ovimbundu, and UNITA displayed an enduring interest in Ovimbundu nationalism (Heywood 1989), but the group developed as a more personalized project for Savimbi, with policies opportunistically shifting according to his "ideological flexibility" (Maier 1997, 5). Savimbi sought to tap into Ovimbundu spiritual traditions and the model of the "hunter-king" (Heywood 1998, 164–65), although he presented himself far differently to external audiences, like the NPFL's Charles Taylor later did in Liberia. The broader Ovimbundu nationalist movement had local leaders "who had established independent churches, clinics, and especially schools, where the lore of the guerrillas was integrated into the curriculum," and as UNITA received increasing Ovimbundu recruits in the late 1960s and the beginning of the 1970s, they began replicating these structures in villages in liberated zones (Heywood 1989, 53–54). UNITA's plan was to set up a system of elected village councils reporting up to an elected central committee (Collelo 1991), although in practice Savimbi retained top-down control. Savimbi claimed "that Unita was not an organisation for only one ethnic group" and did incorporate Lundas and Chokwes (Heywood 1989, 54–55; see also Pearce 2012). In practice, however, there were limited meaningful overtures to other ethnic groups or nonrhetorical attempts to establish UNITA as a more inclusive organization during the independence struggle.

Savimbi's main qualities were "driving ambition to be president of Angola, an ability to tell foreigners what they want to hear, and bitterness about mulattos and whites in Angola" (Bender 1981, 59). This fed not only enmity toward the multiracial MPLA but also ideological swings, from Savimbi denouncing US imperialism and spokespeople presenting UNITA as Marxist-Leninist to claims of being Maoist, to seeking and relying upon white and US support (Bender 1981, 59–60; Marcum 1975; Wolfers and Bergerol 1983). UNITA's proclaimed affinity for Maoism earned it limited Chinese support, and in the late 1960s, the group received some Cuban training and arms, but it was quick to shift around in the political winds, and Cuba pulled its support in response to UNITA's continued attacks on the MPLA and refusal to form a common front (Domínguez 1989, 131–32). In 1974, Savimbi, "never one to be bound by the yoke of political consistency, dropped all Maoist rhetoric, and campaigned for support among Angola's 325,000 whites," who he had previously derided (Marcum 1975, 8). This willingness to change UNITA's ostensible ideology rapidly in response to openings for support is emblematic of the organization's opportunism; in the postindependence period, UNITA leaders adopted anticommunism and later Christian democracy as the group's ideological cladding.

Maoism, even if not fully embraced ideologically, did shape UNITA's strategy and tactics, especially in its early emphasis on the importance of relations with and control of civilian populations (see especially Weigert 2011). As a former UNITA lieutenant told Austin Doctor (personal communication, 2018), UNITA officers and fighters were given a set of twelve commandments related to their conduct:

1. Speak delicately.
2. Pay honestly for everything you buy.
3. Give back everything you borrow.
4. Pay for everything that you damage.
5. Do not disrespect other people.
6. Do not damage the people's crops.
7. Do not assault other people's women.
8. Do not steal and do not divert the general assets of anyone.

9. Do not use drugs.
10. Do not abuse alcohol.
11. Love and respect above all your party.
12. Be responsible and conscious of your mission.

Many UNITA fighters followed these guidelines, but others ignored them, especially when it came to interacting with non-Ovimbundu communities or in contested areas, and Savimbi's interests overruled those of all others within UNITA.

Competition, Independence, and Civil War

Where UNITA's operations overlapped with those of the FNLA and MPLA in the late 1960s, internecine fighting emerged. As its status began to slip, the FNLA concentrated more and more on attacking its rival nationalist organizations. This included opening a new eastern front in 1969 (Whitaker 1970, 20–21), breaking from an earlier tacit truce between the FNLA and UNITA (Marcum 1975, 10, n63). This was symptomatic of larger patterns in the conflict, in which the MPLA concentrated most on attacking Portuguese forces, while its competitors were more concerned with their fratricidal struggle. Portuguese intelligence documents attributed "nearly two-thirds of all guerrilla attacks to the MPLA and over a third to the FNLA, but just 4% to UNITA" (Ciment 1997, 41). In 1961, a US diplomat who met Savimbi reported that he "showed much more animosity toward other rebel groups in Angola than he did against the Portuguese" (Bender 1981, 59), a stance that clearly continued. The MPLA and FNLA meanwhile thought Savimbi was a saboteur supported by the CIA and aiming to split up their movements, distrust that only deepened when documents emerged tying Savimbi and UNITA to Portuguese intelligence (Minter 1988; Conte 1972).

The Portuguese ceased to be any group's focus, however, following the April 1974 military coup in Portugal that deposed the Salazar-Caetano dictatorship, installing in its place a group of younger military officers unhappy with the long colonial wars. The new government made clear its plans to grant independence to Portugal's colonies and began withdrawing troops and administrators.

As the Portuguese withdrew and independence loomed in 1975, Angola's three armed factions engaged in negotiations organized by the OAU. In the January 1975 Alvor Accord, they agreed to put forward slates of candidates for a transitional government, to hold elections in October for an independence date of November 11, 1975, and to establish joint national armed forces. There was little trust among the three sides, however, and the period between the Portuguese coup and planned elections was marked by an arms race and a scramble to consolidate territory. In 1974, UNITA was by far the weakest of the three movements, maintaining fewer than one thousand troops, yet it had seized the opportunity presented by the regime change in Portugal to declare a ceasefire and ramp up recruitment quickly (Péclard 2015, 315–17). Each organization also solicited increased foreign support, with the FNLA receiving aid from China, the United States, and Zaire; the MPLA receiving Soviet and Cuban aid; and UNITA getting help from Zambia, France, West Germany, and South Africa, and likely the United States, too (Gleijeses 2002; Marcum 1975; Noer 1993; Somerville 1984). While some negotiations continued and MPLA and UNITA officials claimed they supported elections, the mistrust and history of violence between the three groups created a security dilemma: no group was willing to disarm or felt confident that the winner of an election would treat them fairly and honor the Alvor Accord (Rio Tinto 2017).

After many smaller clashes throughout 1975, tensions broke on November 10, the day before scheduled independence. The FNLA, backed by white Portuguese settlers and Zairean and South African forces, attacked the MPLA and advanced toward Luanda. The MPLA, aided by newly arrived Cuban forces, stopped the attack at the Battle of Quifandongo and held onto Luanda, where they declared independence the next day. The three competing groups all claimed to be the legitimate governors of Angola: the "MPLA backed by Cuban troops controlled Luanda, the capital, and little else; UNITA controlled Huambo, the second largest city and several southern provinces with South African help, while FNLA, supported by Zairian troops, held the northern provinces" (Malaquias 2007, 39). Cuba and the Soviet-aligned Eastern Bloc countries recognized the MPLA as the legitimate government, and, despite US pressure, the majority of African countries quickly followed; no African government officially recognized the FNLA or UNITA's claims to power (Noer 1993, 777). After a brief, failed attempt at an alliance with UNITA (Wolfers and Bergerol 1983, 48–51), the FNLA gradually collapsed between 1975 and 1979, losing its bases in Zaire and other international support and seeing its domestic support dissipate.

The MPLA in Power

The MPLA now acted as the central government, although its authority and ability to project power beyond urban areas and the coast remained limited. Where it developed influence, however, the programmatic-inclusive MPLA began state-building efforts in line with its ideology and the policies it proposed during the independence war. Creating a single, fused party-state, the MPLA engaged in political education of those citizens in areas under its control and built mass organizations for laborers, women, and youth. The MPLA also transformed the economic model, seeking a transition from the capitalism of the colonial regime to state-led socialist industrialization (Ferreira 2002; Young 1988).

Facing insurgencies from FLEC and UNITA and South African intervention, this project of infrastructural power building was also intimately connected with establishing and expanding the security apparatus. Conscription provided opportunities for further political education, and the MPLA presented the military as defenders of the nation and partners in national development (Pearce 2012; Ferreira 2002). The MPLA sought to involve the population in defense and to extend its reach further throughout society and the national territory by establishing popular militias, comprising (officially) hundreds of thousands of members with military and civil defense training (Wolfers and Bergerol 1983, 121–22). This strong security apparatus was also used to police internal dissent because the MPLA's victory had not smoothed over some of its divisions. In May 1977, MPLA official Nito Alves and a group of supporters launched what they considered an act of rebellion "advancing the cause of the poor, black Angolan majority against a well-to-do creole and mixed-race ruling elite," but for the mainline MPLA, this was a counterrevolutionary coup attempt (Pearce 2015a, 112; see also Wolfers and Bergerol 1983, chap. 6). Alves and his supporters were crushed and hundreds, if not thousands, of alleged Alves supporters were killed in an episode that remains taboo to discuss today with the MPLA still in power in 2025 (Heywood 2011; Pearce 2015a; Saul 2014).

Beyond the security sector, the MPLA also used mass organizations to deliver inclusive services. The MPLA expanded access to free health care and education and undertook mass literacy and vaccination campaigns by engaging members of MPLA civic organizations (Pearce 2012, 455–56; Wolfers and Bergerol 1983, 111–16). Education was seen as so integral to the MPLA political project that "schoolteachers could sometimes obtain exemption from military service on the grounds that teaching was a 'frontline activity'" (Pearce 2012, 456) in the battle to reshape Angolan society and citizens' attitudes.

UNITA's Postindependence Rebel Governance

After a series of losses against MPLA and Cuban forces, UNITA regrouped in Angola's central highlands in late 1975, held together by Savimbi's charisma and appeal to his Ovimbundu base as well as South African intervention.

Savimbi aimed to frustrate MPLA statebuilding efforts in central Angola and to maintain Ovimbundu peasant support, trying to build local administrative structures similar to the Protestant Ovimbundu villages that UNITA emulated during the independence war (Heywood 1989, 58–60; Péclard 2015). UNITA's political appeal was strongest among those who "had never experienced the control of any [other] political movement" and who felt excluded from the MPLA's nationalist vision (Pearce 2012, 454). UNITA's ideology, at least in terms of foreign ties, remained flexible and opportunistic after independence, with Savimbi and other UNITA leaders, on a 1976 trip in Namibia, "mourning [recently deceased Mao Tse-Tung] while consorting with apartheid generals" (Pearce 2017, 21). UNITA sought legitimacy domestically, however, by making "state-like claims, claims based on responsibilities of social organisation and welfare provision, and on prerogatives of violence in defence of a nation" (Pearce 2017, 25). These appeals and national vision were still largely restricted, however, to the Ovimbundu and a few smaller allied ethnic groups. Pearce (2017, 25) clearly distills the disconnect between UNITA's foreign policy and what was prioritized domestically by the group's constituents in the central highlands; the relationship with the regional hegemon, apartheid South Africa, was, "in the eyes of the UNITA elite, affirmation of the movement's state-like potential. But for most of UNITA's adherents, the movement's aspirations to statehood were most convincingly embodied in Jamba, the bush capital . . . that existed from the early 1980s until the end of the 20th century."

By the late 1980s, UNITA's territories in the central highlands, now also housing some non-Ovimbundu, reportedly included local schools and health centers funded by timber and diamond revenues. This service provision was organized by UNITA representatives, sometimes local leaders who had been forcibly recruited (Pearce 2017), in exchange for villagers providing food, recruits, and intelligence, with more stable, state-like structures around the group's capital at Jamba (Heywood 1989; Pearce 2012, 2017). In some regions further from Jamba, however, UNITA demanded that civilians provide fighters with food but offered little in the way of protection or services in exchange (Brinkman 2003a, 213–14).

The depth of UNITA's commitment to multiethnic politics or a deeper ideology, remained unclear, however, even in the late 1980s, and the organization continued making common cause with the apartheid government of South Africa and right-wing political actors in the United States (e.g., Windrich 1992). Among the Ovimbundu, Savimbi continued appealing "to black resentment of whites and mulattos in positions of power" in the MPLA government (Bender 1981, 61). Political education in UNITA's core territories emphasized a civil vision of receiving services in exchange for giving labor or food to UNITA, presenting the order the group established at Jamba in opposition to the "predatory" MPLA and "invading" Cubans, but with little vision for societal transformation that might expand its appeal (Pearce 2012, 2017). When an agreement was struck in 1988 for Cuban and South African forces to withdraw from Angola, the conditions made clear that "Unita's brand of nationalism can only survive on unfaltering support from the United States" (Heywood 1989, 65). UNITA had still not convinced non-Ovimbundu Angolans that it had a clear vision for governing Angola beyond the Protestant conservatism that the group pitched to the United States.

Protracted Conflict and Political Stagnation

As the war dragged into the late 1980s, the MPLA's ideological commitment eroded, and UNITA became more openly predatory and personalistic. The MPLA "abandoned its commitment to people-centred ideals in favour of a more elitist and, ultimately, kleptocratic system of governance" (Malaquias 2007, 20; see also Hodges 2001; Ziemke 2008, 74). War weariness and foreign pressure led both sides to the negotiating table, resulting in the 1991 Bicesse Accords and elections in 1992.

When Savimbi did not win a majority in the first round of the presidential election, he refused to participate in a runoff and returned to the battlefield. From this time on, UNITA focused primarily on exploiting the population and extracting natural resource wealth, abandoning the possibility of peacefully entering politics (Malaquias 2007, 2010; Stedman 1997). UNITA retained some support from civilians who had historically lived in areas under the group's control (Pearce 2012), but many more abandoned the group in the face of its violence and increasing hardship. The MPLA engaged in both forced resettlement and outreach to local leaders to break popular ties to UNITA. When Savimbi was killed in an ambush in 2002, UNITA's remaining leaders agreed to a ceasefire and demobilization, suggesting that Savimbi's personal ambitions had remained paramount as long as he held decision-making power within the organization.

The MPLA continues ruling Angola, with UNITA, now proclaiming itself as ideologically Christian Democratic, the main opposition party. Politics have remained tightly controlled by the MPLA and highly corrupt, even after President José Eduardo dos Santos, in power since Agostinho Neto's death in 1979, was replaced in 2017 (e.g., Roque 2021; Soares de Oliveira 2015).

Considering Alternative Explanations

The cases of the FNLA, UNITA, and MPLA reveal how rebel organizations formed in the same context can adopt divergent sets of ideals and practices. All three groups enjoyed foreign support during the independence war and fought in a setting rich in natural resources (although these resources were difficult to exploit commercially during the independence war). Yet they took very different approaches to their visions for a postvictory society and relationships with the population, and divergences continued after independence as the groups kept fighting each other following the MPLA gaining control of the state.

FNLA

The FNLA had goals first for Bakongo independence and then for Bakongo political predominance in an independent Angola. Yet the organization developed little of a political program beyond this, and it remained exclusive and only instrumentally included some members of other ethnic groups. The FNLA's "national claims hardly went beyond the rhetorical sphere" (Malaquias 2007, 59), and the group did not aim to develop close ties to the population or engage in significant governance, even though secessionist aims have stimulated rebel governance in other cases (see Stewart 2018). The FNLA "neither implemented fundamental social changes nor re-organised the rural population within its operating zones" (Henriksen 1976, 379), not even seeking to benefit Bakongo civilians significantly with greater services. While the FNLA did not control significant natural resources, international aid from Zaire, China, and the United States helped it build up its forces in the early to mid-1970s. The FNLA had been active since the early 1960s, and its ideology was already well established, however, versus being reshaped at this juncture by the availability of financial resources or a desire to appeal to foreign backers—especially since the United States' and China's own ideologies were at odds.

Ethnic concerns and a desire for Bakongo political empowerment through secession or controlling independent Angola clearly shaped the FNLA's ideology and behavior, but as the MPLA demonstrates, an organization with a strong constituency among one ethnic group did not mean that same organization would have ethnically exclusive aims. Instead, we should look to the priorities of the FNLA's paramount leader, Holden Roberto. Roberto consistently sought to maintain personal dominance in the FNLA and the broader nationalist movement, remaining more opportunistic and exclusive, to the detriment of the organization's national competitiveness (Malaquias 2007, 60–62). Roberto had neither the charisma nor the popular policies to help the FNLA mobilize more supporters, which contributed to the organization's demise shortly after independence, even as UNITA, which split off from the FNLA, adapted and endured.

UNITA

UNITA changed publicly claimed ideologies like changing hats, with little sincerity demonstrated in the group's external discourse and presentation. As Young (1988, 166) put it, "no one now takes Jonas Savimbi's 'Maoist' past seriously." Savimbi did utilize his charisma to try to build a cult of personality, but this was not the group's only source of popularity among supporters. UNITA maintained a core interest in the advancement of the Ovimbundu people; tapped into symbols and discourses resonating with Ovimbundu peasants (Heywood 1989, 1998); and made UNITA affinity a durable political identity in rural central and southern Angola, where the group was active (Pearce 2012, 2015b). The group sought to replicate the forms of social organization previously established by Protestant communities among the Ovimbundu in Angola's central highlands and delivered benefits and rudimentary social services more exclusively to members and supporters before and after independence (e.g., Collelo 1991, 104). UNITA generally adopted preexisting structures rather than being more programmatic and creating a transformative new model in Angola, and the organization before independence remained primarily focused on military goals (Pearce 2012, 457–58; Péclard 2015), while increasingly focusing on economic accumulation from the 1980s on.

UNITA presented its political-administrative model as one that it could apply to the rest of Angola, which would have required some statebuilding to implement. Leaders' vision remained exclusionary, however, rather than multiethnic. This was not only based on prejudice against non-black Angolans but also on Savimbi's conviction that "the Ovimbundu represented the majority, UNITA represented the Ovimbundu, Savimbi led UNITA, therefore he was destined to rule Angola. . . . All that mattered was to get there" (Malaquias 2007, 68). UNITA's strong central territorial and ethnic base, and other regions being more associated with rival organizations does leave open the possibility that UNITA might have governed in line with Liu's (2024) theory if it had taken over the state—mobilizing the population in supportive areas, trying to install loyal bureaucrats and co-opt people with goods and services in neutral areas, and repressing rivals' constituencies. It is uncertain how much interest

Savimbi and other leaders would have had in any noncoercive governance out-side their central highland stronghold, however, because they had not previ-ously engaged in significant outreach beyond their core constituency, despite controlling territory.

UNITA's lack of serious and thorough planning for what to do with state power made it difficult to appeal nationally for support when its members were rebels and when the group first entered electoral politics in 1992, but it allowed flexibility in seeking foreign support. UNITA changed its external marketing to try to gain support from China and then the United States and South Africa, but the group neither adopted nor abandoned more deeply held ideological stances or goals in response to foreign incentives or pressures. The core aims of aggrandizement for Savimbi and benefits for Ovimbundu supporters remained the same.

Weinstein (2007, 283–87) rightly notes that UNITA grew more opportunis-tic and violent over time, decreasing its reliance on civilians and focusing more on natural resource extraction. While Weinstein argues that UNITA was ini-tially an "activist" rebellion, or more programmatic, I consider UNITA initially in the middle ground, although slightly more opportunistic and exclusive because of the limited societal transformation it sought, the ethnically narrow group of its intended beneficiaries, and the focus on Savimbi's personal empow-erment over other political goals. Savimbi might have restrained or hidden his opportunistic aspirations initially to be more competitive with the FNLA and MPLA for supporters (Tokdemir et al. 2021). Or UNITA's trend toward increased opportunism over time may have resulted, as Weinstein (2007, 283–87) sug-gests, from shifting resource endowments. I would argue, however, that the trigger for UNITA's opportunism was the frustration of Savimbi's aspirations for postindependence rule. Savimbi's sudden willingness to drop Chinese sup-port and ostensible Maoism for appeals to white Portuguese Angolans and US and South African allies came as he worried about shoring up his political posi-tion and his ability to gain control of the central state. Savimbi's single-minded-ness about gaining power, UNITA's postindependence extraction of natural resources for wealth, and the group's high level of violence against civilians were similar to Charles Taylor and the NPFL. Unlike their Liberian counterparts, however, Savimbi and UNITA never managed to capture the state.

MPLA

The MPLA had the clearest ideology of the three organizations, developing a pan-ethnic Marxist "political culture" and an open economic commitment to state socialism (Young 1988, 167). This was reflected in the MPLA's commitment to racial and ethnic inclusion, its political education efforts, and its programmatic attempts to develop new governance structures and deliver services inclusively in regions where it consolidated some degree of control, challenging both the colonial regime and traditional social structures (Henriksen 1976, 382–83). Like the FSLN in Nicaragua, the MPLA had collective leadership despite early leader Agostinho Neto's charisma.

The MPLA maintained an ethnically inclusive, Marxist-Leninist sociopolitical program throughout the independence war and put it into action during its first decade in control of the state. The group sought to build infrastructural power to reorganize society and work for the benefit of all Angolans, not just Mbundu, mestiços, or MPLA supporters. There were still conflicts among MPLA leaders, however, about whether enough benefits and political influence were making their way into the hands of poorer urban residents, which was one of the sources of contention behind Nito Alves's 1977 coup attempt (Birmingham 1978; Wolfers and Bergerol 1983). Still, the MPLA's inclusive stance contrasted with the ethnonationalist FNLA, its earliest major competitor. While rebel organizations sometimes adapt their ideologies in response to competition (Tokdemir et al. 2021), inclusiveness was not an attempt to seek competitive advantages but instead a product of MPLA leaders' ideological convictions focusing their attention more on class and nation.

Statebuilding is costly, and the MPLA as the internationally recognized postindependence government no longer had to prove to the international community that they were capable of governing (Stewart 2018, 2021). Yet leaders pushed forward with their rebellion-era agenda after victory and developed new institutions rather than simply adopting the administrative structures the Portuguese had used or preexisting sociocultural structures. The security threats posed by the FNLA and UNITA as rebel rivals, and then by South African intervention and US support for UNITA, may have helped solidify MPLA unity (other than the Alves conflict), but MPLA efforts to build infrastructural power were responses to ideological tenets, not threats.

Implementation of the MPLA's program, however, was impeded by the war. And the MPLA gradually abandoned transformation and full inclusion after its first decade in power as dos Santos and associated leaders moved the organization in a more opportunistic-exclusive direction of continued authoritarian control, but with increasingly private benefits. This shift toward personalism and opportunistic behavior coincided with increasing exploitation of Angola's petroleum and mineral resources (Hodges 2001), but it occurred in the MPLA's second decade in power, outside the scope of both Weinstein's (2007) theory and my own.

Angolan Rebel Ideologies and Their Legacies

Despite fighting in the same context, the MPLA, FNLA, and UNITA developed distinct ideologies, aims, and practices. Their different organizational types emerged from leaders' decisions about how to orient their respective organizations and their visions of who should benefit from the state in a postindependence Angola (see also Chabal 1993), which then were institutionalized within the organizations and in relations with civilians. The more programmatic-inclusive MPLA's Marxist-Leninist ideology and pan-ethnic appeals were relatively durable through independence and its first decade in power, although leaders' ideological commitment eroded afterward. The more opportunistic-exclusive FNLA maintained relatively narrow Bakongo ethnonationalist aims from its founding, despite claims to have national interests at heart. The initially middle-ground UNITA remained ideologically flexible, especially in its international relations, and fought primarily to advance the interests of Jonas Savimbi and his Ovimbundu ethnic group; however, it demonstrated some desire to build institutions and deliver services. UNITA grew more opportunistic and exclusive over time, especially as its aspirations to hold central power were frustrated.

Looking within these three groups illustrates the importance of agency and ideas in rebel organizational development. Decisions made early in an organization's life can have long-lasting, path-dependent consequences that may endure long after civil wars end, with Angolan politics still dominated by the MPLA and UNITA five decades after independence.

6

WHEN RELIGIOUS REBELS WIN
Examining Islamist Victors

In the preceding chapters, this book has shown how rebel ideology shapes wartime institutions and statebuilding and service provision once rebel groups are in power across organizations in Angola, Liberia, Nicaragua, and Uganda. The groups examined generally organized around secular ideologies, or ideologies in which religion was present, but was not the main focus, like liberation theology in the Frente Sandinista de Liberación Nacional's (FSLN) Sandinismo or Protestant social institutions shaping the União Nacional para a Independência Total de Angola's (UNITA) initial vision for civilians. Religion is central to many rebel ideologies, however, and groups espousing such ideologies aim to restructure society according to their interpretations of religious law. Are religious rebels like other programmatic groups when it comes to statebuilding? And how do victorious religious rebel organizations vary in inclusiveness or exclusiveness?

I examine these questions through a comparative analysis of Islamist rebel victors. Since the turn of the twenty-first century, most religious rebel groups involved in civil wars and the majority of rebel organizations around the world have been Islamist (Walter 2017b). The world's most recent victorious rebel groups, the Taliban in Afghanistan in 2021 and Hayat Tahrir al-Sham (HTS) in Syria in 2024, are both Islamist. Understanding how Islamist rebel organizations appeal to and treat civilians and what they might do with power is therefore a key concern of policymakers, practitioners, and citizens around the world. Islamist rebel groups, and Islamist political parties or social organizations in general, can vary widely, however, in their ideologies and practices

(Ahmad 2024; Cammett and Luong 2014; Hegghammer 2014; Schuck 2013; Shepard 1987; Yadav 2010).

To account for variation in Islamist groups' ideologies, I examine three quite different victors. The anticolonial Front de Libération Nationale (FLN) in Algeria developed an ideology combining nationalism, Islamic ideals, and socialism, and took power at independence in 1962. Iran's Islamist revolutionaries seized power in 1979 to establish a Shi'a theocracy, but one also aiming to modernize and economically develop the country. The Taliban in Afghanistan captured the capital, Kabul, in 1996 and ruled Afghanistan until 2001 as ethnically inspired Sunni traditionalists; they returned to power in 2021 with a slightly broader vision of Islamist nationalism, including greater state-led efforts for economic transformation and infrastructural development than before. These three case studies can help us understand how different Islamist ideologies have shaped rebel victors' approaches to the state and their consequences.

The FLN in Algeria

France considered Algeria an integral part of its national territory rather than an overseas colony. Arab and Berber (Amazigh) Algerians had different views as they endured subordination to French settlers and colonial administrators in their own land. Reforms enacted in 1947 were supposed to enfranchise and incorporate native Algerians into the French political system, but French settlers used gerrymandering, vote rigging, and other illegal practices to prevent Algerian nationalist parties from gaining electoral representation. This radicalized nationalists and contributed to the rebel FLN's formation in 1954.

The FLN emerged from earlier organizations, and several leaders had previous combat experience in the French Army (Jureldini 1963, 73–74; Stone 1997, 36). FLN followers initially came from the rural lower classes before expanding to include a broader swath of Algerian Muslim society. The leadership structure also evolved because the FLN absorbed other organizations in its first two years (Krause 2017, 112–16), but it remained consistent from 1958 to 1962 at the height of armed struggle (Jureldini 1963, 74–75, 82–92).

The FLN announced its main goals in a proclamation in November 1954. The FLN primarily sought independence for a "sovereign, democratic and social Algerian state, within the framework of Islamic principles" but respecting "fundamental liberties without distinction of race or religion" (FLN 1954b). Popular mobilization was key in this programmatic vision, with an aim to create a new independent society by "assembling and organization of all the healthy energies of the Algerian people to liquidate the colonial system" (FLN 1954b).

While the FLN was inclusive in its aims to represent and serve Algeria's Muslim majority, French settlers living in Algeria would have to choose between French nationality or a new Algerian nationality. Because few settlers would likely opt for the latter, FLN leaders saw this as another way "to create a cleavage between the Algerians and the French" (Jureldini 1963, 76). Based on his experiences collaborating with the FLN, Frantz Fanon (1963, 45) wrote that a settler would no longer have "any interest in remaining or in co-existing" once colonial dominance has been ended or reversed. As he predicted, even many settlers who supported Algerian independence still left for France within a few years (Barclay, Chopin, and Evans 2018, 125).

Islam was central to FLN thinking and planning, focusing on the "libera-tion of the spirit" and valorizing the "*Moudjahid*, or fighter for the faith" (Revere 1973, 482), while the group's military "Ten Commandments" ordered fighters to "follow the principles of Islam" when combating enemy forces (FLN 1954a). Alongside these religious elements, the FLN also had a goal of socialist modernization (Revere 1973, 482), which meant that, while Islamic principles guided FLN policies, actions, and planning, "the primacy of socialism and nationalism subordinated Islam to secular goals" (Amirouche 1998, 88) rather than the organization seeking to build a theocracy. The FLN was still an Islamist organization, however, and FLN members who put together the 1956 Soummam Platform calling for a fully secular and democratic state were purged or marginalized and their allies, like Fanon, were later "dismissed as irrelevant and out of touch for not understanding the power of Islam" (Gibson 2015, 13).

During the war, the FLN's goals were further refined as the initially urban leadership interacted increasingly with rural communities and organized and collaborated with "Village Councils" to govern rural areas (Revere 1973, 487), like the National Resistance Movement's (NRM) resistance councils in Uganda. The FLN also set targets for Algerian popular economic and social well-being in the 1957 *Manual of the Algerian Militant*, calling for economic growth, full employment, universal education and health care, and housing provision (Revere 1973, 484–85). These programmatic aspirations guided governance once the FLN took power in 1962 after an independence referendum. The bru-tal independence war killed over half a million people (many due to nationalist infighting), and colonial state structures collapsed (Stone 1997, 40–41; Stora 2004, 121–24). This presented both opportunities and major tasks for the FLN as Algeria's new government.

Factional power struggles in the FLN broke out in 1962, killing approximately fifteen thousand people (Stone 1997, 43–45), but once these struggles were resolved, surviving leaders began building a new Algerian state based on rebellion-era goals. Having transformed the political system by taking power and replacing the colonial state, the FLN viewed its next task as not only economic development but also the "transformation of mentalities" (Byrne 2009, 427). The FLN instituted a socialist system, and many of its policies were justified on a revolutionary basis; for instance, "agrarian reform and land redistribution were justified as a reward for heroic revolutionary contributions on the part of the peasant" and were modeled on the Yugoslav experience and the concept of worker "self-management" of farms (Revere 1973, 486–87), which was also extended to factories (Byrne 2009, 433; Stora 2004, 133–36; Tessler, Konold, and Reif 2004, 190). The FLN worked internally and publicly to reconcile the leftist and Islamic components of its ideology, but through its first decade in power, rebellion-era ideals continued guiding policy (Byrne 2009; Hazard 1981, 245; Revere 1973; Stora 2004, 133–36).

Beyond the socialist state-led approach to developing agriculture and industry, the FLN's ideology was put into action through a "relatively egalitarian and effective program of mass education, health care, and social services" (Tessler, Konold, and Reif 2004, 189–90), including increased Arabization and Islamization of education and government administration (Stone 1997, 49). These policies were initially developed under the leadership of Ahmed Ben Bella, but Ben Bella was toppled and replaced in 1965 in a bloodless coup by Houari Boumediene, who ruled until his death in 1978. The emphasis on Arabic language and Arab culture was a particular point of contention because many early FLN leaders were from the Kabyle Berber community and had hoped that Tamazight, the Berber language, and their own culture would have greater state recognition and support. This more pluralist approach had been prominent among the FLN leaders involved with the Soummam Platform, but Ben Bella's group pushed it aside (Quandt 1973; Roberts 1982; Stone 1997, chap. 9). Some Kabyle leaders later split off, and unrest in Kabylia became a problem in the later decades of FLN rule, especially from 1980 on. Kabyle communities benefited from FLN state policies and service delivery efforts, and many Kabyles stuck with the FLN and worked in the government, but the state's failure to respect Kabyle culture remained a source of conflict (Maddy-Weitzman 2011; Roberts 1982, 1993), like the FSLN's experience in Nicaragua's Atlantic Coast region.

The FLN under Boumediene followed a vanguard party model as the political accompaniment to socialism, implementing policies including "the nationalization of industry, import-substitution, state funding of the industrial sector," and providing "mass education and health care" (Ruedy 1992, 207–30 in Tessler, Konold, and Reif 2004, 190; see also Ottaway and Ottaway 1970; Stone 1997, 50–54). Boumediene sought to extend state reach and inclusiveness, targeting development programs to the "poorest regions of the country" without regard for cost or identity and providing "free education, free medical care, full employment, and electricity and gas to the most remote mountain areas" (Amirouche 1998, 88).

After Boumediene's death in 1978, there was a peaceful transition to the military-allied Chadli Benjedid, who gradually centralized power, reduced mass organizations' autonomy, and privatized some state-owned enterprises; this moved away from the early FLN's more transformative, inclusive ideals (Amirouche 1998; Zoubir 1993). The FLN's efforts to incorporate the masses and build infrastructural power under Ben Bella and Boumediene, however, had a clear and durable effect on Algerians (Tessler, Konold, and Reif 2004), carrying the FLN rebellion's legacies forward.

Alternative Explanations and the FLN

During its fight for Algerian independence, the FLN developed an ideology integrating nationalism, socioeconomic development and equality, and religion—like the FSLN's ideology in Nicaragua, although with religion emphasized more. Algeria was a largely agrarian country at the time of the FLN's fight, although oil exploration was beginning, holding possibilities for postindependence natural resource wealth. Oil was only found in 1956, however, after the FLN's founding and the development of the core of its ideology. As the French state began exploiting Algerian oil, FLN leaders also started thinking about how oil might shape the postindependence political economy. The FLN did not have access to oil wealth during its rebellion, and although leaders built strategic contacts with the Italian oil company ENI (Ente nazionale idrocarburi) and signaled that they wanted to continue developing oil infrastructure and production once in power (Musso 2017), they did not offer future contracts in exchange for wartime material support, what Ross (2004) calls "booty futures." The agreements ending the war left France and allied companies with significant influence over Algeria's oil industry, even as the FLN sought more control for their new national oil company (Musso 2017, 79–82). The Algerian state now had access to large amounts of oil wealth, but FLN leaders did not direct this toward their own benefit. They instead sought to use it throughout their first decade in power for heavy state spending on industrialization, economic diversification, and the development of public goods and services, in line with their more programmatic-inclusive ideology (Addi 1995).

During the independence struggle, the FLN was competing against other Algerian nationalist movements for primacy. This competition shaped its behavior at times, for instance, leading the FLN to launch armed attacks first to seize momentum and influence in the nationalist movement (Krause 2017, 108–9). Competition was not necessarily the source of leaders' efforts to develop the FLN's ideology, however, even as a rival group tried to outbid the FLN with stricter, more fundamentalist Islamist rebel governance and policy proposals (Krause 2017, 111)—although the FLN did incorporate some ideas and leaders, like Ferhat Abbas, from other factions it outcompeted or absorbed (Krause 2017, 112–16).

Like the National Patriotic Front of Liberia (NPFL) or the Frente Nacional de Libertação de Angola (FNLA) and UNITA in Angola, the FLN devoted significant resources to fighting with other Algerian nationalist groups and their supporters, in addition to its battle with the French. In contrast to those groups and some of its more exclusive rivals in Algeria and elsewhere, the FLN "work[ed] to integrate Algerians of all ethnicities, religions, and ideologies—as long as they were nationalist," including by absorbing former rivals (Krause 2017, 115). This also helped the FLN from the mid-1950s on to build a broader base among the Algerian population, and in power they continued seeking to build infrastructural power and deliver benefits throughout the country rather than restricting them to the FLN's initial urban base or narrower constituencies. There was an increasing tendency after the Soummam Platform's defeat, however, toward privileging Arab and Muslim identities and cultural values, making the FLN less pluralist in its vision of the nation. This especially upset some of the Kabyle Berber leaders who had participated heavily in the rebellion. Yet despite Berbers' language and cultures not being officially recognized and taught in the postvictory education system, Berber leaders continued being included in government bodies under both Ben Bella and Boumediene, and the FLN state invested resources in Berber areas like they did elsewhere (e.g., Roberts 1982; Stone 1997, chap. 9).

Having defeated or absorbed most rivals during the war of independence, the FLN faced limited domestic threats in its first decade in power (Levitsky and Way 2022, 193); most threats came from within the FLN from leaders disenchanted with the group's direction, like Hocine Aït-Ahmed's 1963 rebellion in Kabylia, or those seeking greater control over the regime, like Boumediene (Revere 1970). The primary external threat came from Morocco, which invaded in 1963 in response to border disputes. War with Morocco helped to mobilize and unify much of the population behind the new FLN-led regime on nationalist grounds, and the Algerian-Moroccan rivalry continued later with disagreements and competition around the conflict in Western Sahara and with other geostrategic issues (Zoubir 2020). The threat posed by Morocco stimulated the development of coercive power near the border (Zoubir 2020) but was perhaps not severe enough that it could unify the FLN's leadership, as Levitsky and Way (2022, 197–98) note, and the level of external threat did not drive the FLN's decisions around domestic governance and development of infrastructural power.

The destruction of the colonial state gave the FLN space to rebuild Algeria in line with its vision. The FLN built infrastructural power and used it to reshape society, including through education, health care, and other service provision in line with the Islamist and socialist components of their ideology (e.g., Johnson 2016; Stone 1997, 49), while also working to reduce economic dependency and develop a more centrally controlled and industrialized economy. These approaches were vastly different from the colonial regime, which prioritized French settlers and French culture and maintained Algeria's economic dependency for French benefit. Ben Bella was charismatic, and the FLN was attuned to the international environment, but they leveraged this toward their preferred programmatic ends versus using charisma to substitute for public-oriented action or changing tack in response to international pressures. FLN leaders took up the mantle of anticolonial struggle and cultivated support from "Third World" independent postcolonial countries and liberation movements but hewed to their own principles and suffered their own contradictions (Byrne 2016; Connelly 2003; Krause 2017, 120–21; Malley 2023). They also pledged adherence to international law to contrast themselves with the repressive French regime (e.g., Greenberg 1970; Johnson 2016), but this did not stop the FLN from committing violence against both Algerian and French civilians. After independence, the FLN and the Algerian state it built became a model for other movements seeking nationalist and socialist liberation around the world, and the FLN continued to try to play other international actors off each other to protect and advance Algerian interests under Ben Bella and even more under Boumediene (Malley 2023, chap. 5).

The FLN's leadership was not fully consolidated until independence, and even then divisions remained. The overall ideological direction endured from the earlier days of rebellion, however, with programmatic aims for a new independent state based on Islamic and socialist principles and an inclusive vision of serving the majority of Algerians (albeit limiting Berbers' cultural inclusion). The most significant dispute within the FLN was over the primacy of political leaders, many of whom had been in exile during the rebellion, versus military leaders who had been on the front lines—a common occurrence among rebel victors (see Ashley 2024; Roessler 2016). Boumediene's successful coup did not lead to a shift toward opportunism or exclusion, however, but instead continued the FLN's path of seeking to transform Algeria and serve the population.

Iran's Islamic Revolutionaries

Iran's revolution, like Nicaragua's, came after a long, mostly fruitless guerrilla struggle turned into mass urban uprisings in 1978 and 1979, pitting a wide political and social coalition against the US-supported regime of Shah Reza Pahlavi (Farhi 1990; Foran and Goodwin 1993; Parsa 2000). The opposition's most prominent figure, Ayatollah Khomeini, and his supporters had been clashing openly with the shah's regime politically and in the streets since 1963, even after Khomeini's exile in 1964. Armed struggle against the shah began in 1971, when multiple guerrilla groups emerged.

Most guerrilla organizations were aligned with Khomeini in seeking to overthrow the shah and transform Iran, but they differed from him ideologically. Several guerrilla organizations quickly came to oppose the theocratic rule that Khomeini-led clerics began establishing in 1979, including both secular leftist organizations (especially the Fedayi) and religious but economically progressive organizations (especially the Islamic Mojahedin). These groups were decimated or forced into exile in the early 1980s (Abrahamian 1985, 1989; Zabih 1988).

While Iran experienced a social revolution (see Skocpol 1982), this was different from most cases of rebel victory: there was not a clear preexisting rebel organization at the center of the postvictory government. Pro-Khomeini militias remained relatively autonomous until close to the shah's fall, and other organizations were more active in the armed struggle, but members of Khomeini's faction were central players in a successful regime change conflict. Analyzing how the Khomeinist ideology (Abrahamian 1993) developed and influenced postvictory statebuilding, however, helps illustrate a key variant of Islamist revolutionary thought—one Iran's clerical regime has tried to export to this day by sponsoring rebels and friendly governments (e.g., Khatib 2021; Ostovar 2016; Takeyh 2009).

Khomeini developed a vision for an Islamic political system in Iran based in Shi'a laws and doctrines and led by clerics (Khomeini 2002). Because religious scholars were the rightful interpreters of Islamic law and the prophet Mohammed's teachings, they should ensure that these dictates were implemented throughout society. Beyond a religious council overseeing government ministries to enact Islamic laws and programs, Khomeini in 1970 offered few details about what this would mean for statebuilding. However, his calls for "the removal of the Shah and the establishment of Islamic government [were] clear and consistent demands that the whole country could understand . . . which . . . increasingly made him the focal point for opposition to the Shah" (Axworthy 2013, 140). Khomeini emphasized not only religion but also addressing "real economic, social, and political grievances" against the shah's exclusionary state (Abrahamian 1993, 3) and its uneven benefits (Arjomand 1988, 106–14; Harris 2017). This programmatic ideology thus envisioned religious law aligning with a more thorough, inclusive transformation of society.

Even in exile, Khomeini remained the most popular opposition figure during the uprisings of 1978 and 1979. When the shah fled Iran in mid-January 1979, Khomeini called on the shah-appointed government under Shapur Bakhtiar to resign and formed the Islamic Revolutionary Council to establish a provisional government and organize a constituent assembly to write a new constitution (Nikazmerad 1980, 345). When Khomeini returned to Iran in February, these calls intensified, and Khomeini's supporters "took virtual control of the administrative, police, and judicial functions" in several major cities (Nikazmerad 1980, 348). Local voluntary groups, or *komitehs*, had formed nationwide in 1978 (often around mosques) to fulfill administrative tasks in place of the shah's state. Komitehs began seizing control and forming or working with militias, often while coordinating with Khomeini's representatives, giving the Islamic Revolutionary Council reach around the country (Axworthy 2013, 145–46; Salehi 1996). Then, in mid-February 1979, the military defected against the government, Bakhtiar resigned, and a Khomeini-approved provisional government under Mehdi Bazargan took power.

Khomeini and the Islamic Revolutionary Council officially shared control with the provisional government, but they had a broad popular legitimacy that Bazargan lacked. Khomeini and allied clerics worked to ensure their coercive power by setting up alternative Islamic security forces to counterbalance the surviving military. Out of the revolutionary masses and komitehs with Islamist sympathies, the clerics formed the Islamic Revolutionary Guard Corps, or *Pasdaran*. Along with Islamist militias, the Pasdaran enforced Khomeini's and the Islamic Revolutionary Council's will and attacked rivals, displacing Bazargan's ostensible authority at the same time as the military was being purged (Hickman 1982; Katzman 1993; Ostovar 2016). In the judicial sector, Islamic revolutionary courts and komitehs administered justice according to their interpretations of sharia law. Throughout Iran's territory and institutions, Bazargan and his allies were left "demoralized and rendered almost superfluous by the creation of new Khomeini-aligned bodies" (Axworthy 2013, 147–48).

Rather than a constituent assembly, a seventy-five-member Assembly of Experts was elected in November 1979. Its members were informed by Khomeini that this "Constitution and other laws in this Republic must be based one hundred per cent on Islam" (Ramazani 1980, 181–82). The experts began work right when Bazargan and his cabinet resigned, leaving the Islamic Revolutionary Council in control until elections in 1980. The new constitution, ratified in

December 1979, committed not only to an Islamic system of government, with unelected clerical bodies alongside an elected president and legislature, but also to socioeconomic transformation in implementing Islamic law in society and developing a new welfare state (see Ramazani 1980 for a translation). Both would require infrastructural power, leading the new regime to rely "on popular mobilization to embed state organizations deeper into Iranian society" (Harris 2017, 16). This statebuilding occurred amid a devastating war with Iraq beginning in 1980, which provided further grounds for mass mobilization—and more opportunities for the clerics and their security forces to usurp control from newly elected President Abolhassan Bani-Sadr and the military.

Nationalizations ensured that the "state and the foundations allied to it soon controlled about two-thirds of Iran's enterprises and labor force" (Keddie 2006, 256). Prominent among the quasi-governmental foundations was the Imam Khomeini Relief Committee, which used relief and development projects to serve and politically incorporate previously excluded groups and to lower poverty (see Harris 2017, chap. 3). Khomeini and the clerics opted for a pragmatic path of state-led development while maintaining markets, and were willing to make economic policy changes based on what they saw as popular and necessary amid war and domestic crisis (Abrahamian 1993; Harris 2017; Maloney 2015)—though they retained a focus on ensuring that the economy served all citizens, unlike the NRM in Uganda's shift to structural adjustment-style liberalization. Iran's revolutionary government sought to support the lower and middle classes through expanded public employment and subsidies, while also using oil revenues to try to develop other industries and diversify the economy. Agrarian reform and land redistribution never went as far as many rural Iranians had hoped, but there was still significant land redistribution and some agricultural collectivization (Harris 2017; Maloney 2015; Shakoori 2001). The right to housing, guaranteed in the constitution, was implemented through a "Reconstruction Jihad" that "mobilized youth by sending them to rural areas to aid the poor [by building] cheap or free housing" (Keddie 2006, 246), similarly to how the FSLN had mobilized citizens to carry out its national literacy campaign.

Most of Iran's ethnic and religious minorities were included in leaders' conception of their subjects and constituents, although there were particularly harsh policies toward the Baha'i and many minority groups opposed the revolutionary regime (Elling 2013; Saleh 2013). Women's rights were not constitutionally guaranteed, and there were new religious restrictions on women's dress and behavior, but women were included in the Islamic revolutionaries' visions for social development and universal education. Literacy among young women increased rapidly after the revolution, from 42 percent in 1975 and 1976 to 65 percent in 1985 and 1986 (Harris 2017, 10–11). The revolutionary government also built a transformative new primary health-care system in previously underserved areas even amid war, one that began prioritizing women's health and eventually family planning and modern contraception (see, e.g., Harris 2017). Iran's revolutionary regime evolved over time with Khomeini's 1989 death and the end of war with Iraq, but many of Khomeini's ideas and the early vision of the Islamic Revolutionary Council and 1979 constitution have continued guiding the Iranian state.

Alternative Explanations and Iranian Revolutionaries

Like the FLN, Iran's victorious Islamist revolutionaries did not have access to the country's oil resources before taking power, and they similarly saw oil wealth as a tool to forge geopolitical independence and to advance their plans for sociopolitical and economic transformation. Khomeini employed his charisma to consolidate authoritarian control, and it enabled him and his backers to outcompete rivals who had been engaged in organized armed struggle against the shah for longer. Rather than focusing on self-aggrandizement, however, Khomeini used his popularity to legitimize a deeply programmatic and relatively more inclusive ideology, focusing on implementing Islamist policies and redistributive economic practices. And while Khomeini and his allies were sometimes willing to be pragmatic, their ideological convictions were sincere rather than having been adopted to seize a political opportunity later in the shah's reign.

While not traditional rebels, the Islamist revolutionaries allied with Khomeini did have territorial influence and particular constituencies while opposing the shah. The Khomeinist cause had its strongest support among radical clerics and religious students, religious members of the merchant class, and segments of the urban and rural poor. This was a relatively broad base, and there was territorial reach around Iran through mosques and komitehs, which was reflected in postvictory efforts to mobilize the population nationwide and provide relatively inclusive benefits. There were exceptions, however, because certain religious and ethnic minorities either were not included or did not feel represented in the Islamist revolutionary regime's vision of its constituents, and the regime often turned toward repression, not co-optation, to deal with dissent (Elling 2013; Saleh 2013).

Certain state institutions survived the shah's downfall, but Khomeini and his Islamist allies were determined to build a new state in line with their ideological vision and refused to be constrained by past structures and precedents. They used the komitehs to develop local-level infrastructural power, established new Islamic courts and governing bodies, rewrote the constitution, and transformed the economic structure. The clearest clash between the revolutionary victors and the old state's remnants came in the security sector because much of the old regime military survived. Moderates in the provisional government behind Bazargan wanted to preserve the military, but the Islamic Revolutionary Council was determined to dismantle the military to replace it with the Pasdaran and loyal militias (e.g., Ostovar 2016; Schahgaldian and Bakhordarian 1987).

This desire to transform the security sector also made the new revolutionary regime vulnerable domestically and internationally. Security threats and the need to respond to them did eventually strengthen the new Islamic regime as Levitsky and Way (2022, chap. 6) suggest, helping it consolidate coercive power and build infrastructural power through mass mobilization; however, these threats could have been the young regime's undoing. Instead of the military, which had counterinsurgency expertise, Khomeini and the Islamic Revolutionary Council deployed the Pasdaran to tackle domestic rebels in Kurdistan and elsewhere; this helped build Pasdaran effectiveness, but it was likely slower than allowing the military to continue these fights (e.g., Alemzadeh 2023). More damaging was the purging of the military at the same time that Khomeini and his allies were antagonizing neighboring Iraq and the United States, which had been the military's primary supplier and adviser (Herzog 1989; Hickman 1982; Schahgaldian and Bakhordarian 1987). When Iraq invaded in 1980, Iranian forces were disorganized and unable to respond effectively because of the purges, and throughout the ensuing war, Khomeinist clerics' focus on domestic power struggles and the Pasdaran-military rivalry undermined Iran's fighting effectiveness (Thaler forthcoming). The consensus among scholars and analysts is that only hesitation by Iraqi leader Saddam Hussein kept invading Iraqi forces from overthrowing the new revolutionary regime in 1980 and preventing later regime consolidation and statebuilding (Cordesman and Wagner 1990; Ostovar 2016; Talmadge 2015). Iran's Islamist revolutionaries used threats to mobilize domestic militia volunteers and supporters and to engage in statebuilding; yet this was downstream of their ideology, which required transforming the Iranian state and society (leading to domestic backlash) and spreading their ideology abroad to Iraq and elsewhere in the region (leading to external threats).

Revolutionary Iran's aggressive foreign policy also led to international trade restrictions, which required the development of new domestic industries and new foreign trading relationships. This reinforced Khomeini's and his allies' plans for state-led economic development, however, rather than inspiring them in the first place. Cold War politics meant Iran's leftist rebel groups might have more readily secured international support if they won, but Iran's victorious

Islamist revolutionaries actively reshaped the international environment, providing a hub for Shi'a Islamist organizing and supporting militant Islamist movements abroad (e.g., Ostovar 2016). Even if international counterpressure constrained some of their regional ambitions in the first postvictory decade, Iran's revolutionary regime has continued competing against the United States and regional rivals for influence, including in Afghanistan.

The Taliban in Afghanistan: 1994 to 2001

Afghanistan was one of the major Cold War battlegrounds. The United States worked through Pakistan to fund and arm the Mujahedin rebels who fought through the 1980s against the Soviet-backed People's Democratic Party of Afghanistan (PDPA) communist regime until it collapsed in 1992. A powerless government in Kabul replaced the PDPA, while regional warlords carved out power around the country.

In 1994, the Taliban coalesced into a new rebel force in Afghanistan, building on previous networks of Islamist Mujahedin fighters. Early accounts suggested that the Taliban formed from younger men educated in madrassas in Pakistan that advocated for a strict interpretation of the Koran, teaching their *taliban* (students) about "the ideal Islamic society created by the prophet Mohammed 1,400 years ago, [which] they wanted to emulate" (Rashid 2001, 23). Many older leaders were educated in Afghanistan, however, and sought a return to Islamic norms as practiced in rural Pashtun areas of southern Afghanistan. Older leaders believed that the PDPA's statebuilding project since 1979 had interrupted these Pashtun traditions (see Gopal and van Linschoten 2017, 17; Murtazashvili 2016, 53–55) and that they needed to be restored and revitalized through strict enforcement of Islamic law to combat the "malaise of vice that had infected all of Afghan society" (Gopal and van Linschoten 2017, 25). The Taliban's Islamism was therefore less modernizing than the FLN and Iranian revolutionaries' developmentalist ideologies, but it was certainly programmatic in calling for transforming society from its post-1979 status and implementing a Pashtun traditionalist vision of society beyond their southern stronghold.

Early Taliban leaders were unhappy with Afghanistan's descent into warlordism and banditry, calling for "peace, security, and Islam" (Gopal and van Linschoten 2017, 23). Taliban leaders built on their legitimacy as religious scholars, with a history beginning in the 1980s of religious students and teachers running courts and resolving disputes in many areas (Giustozzi and Baczko 2014, 201; Gopal and van Linschoten 2017, 19–20). The Taliban portrayed themselves as opposites of rapacious warlords or corrupt politicians, appealing to citizens based on their religious conviction and morality, which can give Islamists a reputational advantage (see Cammett and Luong 2014). Leaders' decision to label themselves as the Taliban signaled "that they were a movement for cleansing society rather than a party trying to grab power" (Rashid 2001, 22–23).

After initially organizing in September 1994, the Taliban gathered followers and earned support from the Pakistani state and Afghan businessmen, who were tired of warlords impeding cross-border trade and wanted a favorable government in Kabul (Ahmad 2017; Ibrahimi 2017, 951). The Taliban swept through Kandahar disarming militias, burning opium poppy fields, and establishing strict order based on Islamic law and tribal customary law (Matinuddin 1999; Rashid 2001; Sullivan 2007). The Taliban's ideology also provided a transnational mobilizing resource, attracting refugees in Pakistan and volunteers further abroad (Goodson 2001, 83). The initial Taliban campaign that captured Kandahar began a push toward Kabul, imposing the group's version of Islamic law in areas under their control.

By mid-1995, a Taliban leadership council in Kandahar, headed by Mullah Omar, wielded influence over half of Afghanistan, including beyond Pashtun areas (Matinuddin 1999, 41–42; Sinno 2008, 228). The Taliban captured Kabul in September 1996 and became Afghanistan's de facto rulers. Although only Pakistan, Saudi Arabia, and the United Arab Emirates officially recognized the Taliban as Afghanistan's government, their control was widely accepted in practice internationally. Mullah Omar centralized power over time and reduced regional commanders' and councils' autonomy, with a Supreme Council in Kandahar overseeing the government and supervising the more administration-focused Council of Ministers in Kabul (Ibrahimi 2017; Rashid 2001; Sinno 2008, 247). Despite the Council of Ministers officially being in charge of administrative functions, the Supreme Council exercised overall control (Ibrahimi 2017, 952–53).

Taliban leaders put their professed principles into practice, using security forces, intelligence networks, and government ministries to enforce their vision of Islamic law harshly; this was especially the case in urban and northern areas, where the PDPA government had more influence or where ethnoregional norms differed from Pashtun culture (see Gopal and van Linschoten 2017, 28–30; Ibrahimi 2017, 955–59). Once in power, the Taliban scrapped the remaining vestiges of the prior state (Rashid 2001, 101–2). Leaders instead sought to use preexisting social structures and new institutions to enact their vision of transforming Afghanistan back into an idealized vision of the past while also tapping into earlier Afghan patterns and symbols of (often coercive) statebuilding and legitimacy (Gopal and van Linschoten 2017, 9, 30).

Taliban commanders continued living austerely, despite the availability of funds from trade and taxation. They did not have a vision initially for rebuilding or reorganizing the economy, however, leading to unemployment and food insecurity (Maley 2009, 195; Matinuddin 1999, 38). Parts of the country remained under the control of the rebel Northern Alliance forces, and the Taliban devoted much of their energy and resources to developing their coercive power further and defeating this enemy. Even if Taliban security forces were "fragmented and lacked a clear hierarchical structure" (Levitsky and Way 2022, 268) in comparison to a traditional state military, they were able to develop effectiveness over time. The Taliban gradually gained control over the majority of Afghanistan, claiming to hold 90 to 95 percent of the country by 2000 (Ghufran 2001; Ibrahimi 2017, 960; Sullivan 2007, 103). With their increasing territorial control, the Taliban regulated and taxed economic activity, including transnational smuggling and opium production until 2000 (Felbab-Brown 2021; Gopal and van Linschoten 2017, 30–32; Maley 2009, 197). These revenues were not designed to benefit Taliban leaders themselves, although there were certainly instances of corruption (Ghufran 2001; Rubin 2000, 1799).

The order established by the Taliban was based significantly on fear, and Taliban troops and police were quick to use their coercive capacity (Gopal and van Linschoten 2017; Ibrahimi 2017; Maley 2009, 195–96). The brutal punishment of criminals through amputations and executions was considered the application of Koranic law, administered through a "three-tiered judicial system" (Sinno 2008, 247). Alongside coercion, however, the Taliban also sought to develop infrastructural power, using social institutions to try to establish an Islamic state.

War and disorder "had destroyed much of Afghanistan's social capital as communities and institutions were dispersed or destroyed" (Rubin 2000, 1794). The Taliban enjoyed social networks and prestige in many regions, however, stemming from their madrassa education and ethnic ties, thus enabling them both to build new institutions and to leverage remaining social institutions. The Taliban carefully used their knowledge of Pashtun society and kinship ties to win over local leaders and militia commanders, and then established local councils and drew on clerical networks to administer areas (Dorronsoro 2005, 270–75; Sinno 2008, 236–45). Where they had fewer ties, the Taliban generally governed civilians directly while collaborating with trusted preexisting village or regional leaders rather than setting up new civilian political institutions (Murtazashvili 2016, 61–63; Rashid 2001). Institution building was slow, and despite Taliban claims in 1997 to have functioning ministries for issues like education, refugees, and planning, the initial priority was security and order (Ibrahimi 2017). Other aspects of society were expected to fall into place if Islamic law was followed, hence the Taliban state's three aims in 1997: "restoration of peace; collection of weapons; implementation of the *shariah*" (Matinuddin 1999, 41–43). This paucity of additional planning and the group's "administrative incompetence" initially impeded the establishment of noncoercive authority (Sullivan 2007, 102). Taliban leaders then adjusted and increasingly worked through provincial governors and local administrators more closely connected to the population throughout the country (Ghufran 2001, 473–74; Rubin 1999, 81), extending infrastructural power more effectively.

To many eyes, the Taliban's social vision appears oppressive or anachronistic, yet the organization's leaders were acting in what they believed ideologically to be the public interest, and foreign pressures for greater inclusiveness did not lead them to deviate. Pashtuns dominated the Taliban, but ethnic appeals were not the primary mobilizing strategy (Dorronsoro 2005, 258). The organization tried to paint itself as a multiethnic movement, emphasizing unifying Islamic symbols and ideals and incorporating non-Pashtun leaders, although many non-Pashtuns remained unconvinced, and the Hazara, a Shi'a ethnic minority, faced significant violence (Gopal and van Linschoten 2017; Ibrahimi 2017, 954–55). Afghanistan's small non-Muslim population was not considered part of the Taliban's ideal society, but there was a degree of tolerance toward them, even if life remained uncomfortable (PBS 2001). The Taliban still considered women part of their constituency, but they severely and violently curtailed women's freedom (e.g., Physicians for Human Rights 1998), believing that they were "protecting" women from impurity and dishonor.

Until the 2001 US invasion, the Taliban remade social life throughout Afghanistan, including providing services with the limited resources they had available and cooperating with international and nongovernmental organizations (NGOs) to allow service delivery—as long as it aligned with Taliban ideals (Ibrahimi 2017, 963–64). One of the most drastic changes was restricting women's access to education, which the Taliban presented as a temporary measure until they could develop a curriculum aligned with their values (Ghufran 2001, 475–76; Rubin 1999, 90), the same approach as Iran's revolutionaries. Men's education was modeled on the madrassas where Taliban leaders and cadres themselves had studied. Women's access to health care faced some restrictions in line with the Taliban's interpretation of Islamic law, while health-care provision was otherwise regulated and somewhat limited beyond urban areas and NGO clinics (Cook 2003; Faiz 1997; Reyburn et al. 1997).

In a short time, the Taliban overcame barriers to collective action and organization that had hobbled other groups' aspirations for controlling Afghanistan (Sinno 2008; Sullivan 2007) and successfully "transformed themselves from a movement into a ruling government" (Ghufran 2001, 470). This was thanks to the cohesion and purpose provided by the Taliban's strict Islamist ideology. Exercising significant coercive power but also building influence through state institutions, clerical networks, tribal structures, and new administrative councils, the Taliban transformed life in the majority of Afghanistan in line with their vision of an "Islamic Emirate." Their policies were unpopular among many Afghans (e.g., Terpstra 2020, 1156–57). The Taliban brought order, however, and nearly succeeded in gaining control of the entire national territory: on September 9, 2001, they assassinated Ahmad Shah Massoud, commander of the rebel organization that was the "last bastion of resistance" (Sinno 2008, 249).

The Taliban's treatment of women and those who did not share their interpretation of Islam was normatively reprehensible, yet the organization was implementing a vision for transforming society that they genuinely believed benefited Afghanistan's Sunni Muslim majority, *including* women, focusing on the spiritual benefits of protecting "virtue." The Taliban were therefore clearly programmatic and exhibited a mix of inclusivity and exclusivity, aiming (in their minds) to benefit most Afghans but restricting opportunities and services that did not fit their narrow views, especially for women and religious minorities. It ultimately took heavy US intervention—after the September 11 attacks and Taliban refusal to hand over al-Qaeda leader Osama bin Laden—to dislodge the Taliban from power, beginning a new chapter for the organization.

The Taliban in Afghanistan: From 2001 Onward

The Taliban were sent on the run from late 2001, yet their persistence as both an armed organization and a political force attests to the legitimacy and social embeddedness the Taliban built during their time in power—as well as the missteps of the US occupation and the Afghan national government it supported. Surviving Taliban leaders and foot soldiers tried to blend back into society or fled abroad before returning to an insurgency in 2003.

The post-2001 US occupation and new Afghan national government were not "revolutionising Afghan society" or attacking Islam more generally in the country like the PDPA had (Gopal and van Linschoten 2017, 32–33), but they still sought to implement an ambitious liberal peace-building program of democratization, economic liberalization, and human rights (Suhrke 2007). These post-Taliban statebuilding efforts struggled, however, to change society outside Kabul and a few other regions. This was a product of empowering anti-Taliban warlords who were then folded into the new national government but also of failures to engage productively with customary institutions and to convince people to follow international actors' and the national government's vision for Afghanistan's future (Malejacq 2020; Mukhopadhyay 2014; Murtazashvili 2016; Suhrke 2007, 2013; Weigand 2022). Abusive militias, corruption, and the international occupation bred resentment, especially in rural areas. Many Afghans also viewed corruption and the occupation as affronts to Islam (Farrell and Giustozzi 2013; Gopal and van Linschoten 2017; Ladbury 2009). Most wanted peace and stability, however, more than necessarily the Taliban's return (Kaltenthaler, Kruglanski, and Knuppe 2024; van Bijlert 2021a; Weigand 2022).

The Taliban's post-2001 ideology and trajectory differed from its fight in the 1990s. Leaders spent time in Pakistan and in the Persian Gulf countries, absorbing international ideas about Islamism and adopting a more nationalistic and inclusive ideal that (at least in principle) incorporated Afghanistan's minority groups (Farrell and Giustozzi 2013, 853–54; Gopal and van Linschoten 2017, 33–34, 40; Terpstra 2020, 1161). When returning to fighting within Afghanistan and gradually carving out territory, the Taliban placed less emphasis on strict Islamic appearance or learning in a more "modernist" Islamism (Gopal and van Linschoten 2017, 39–40), especially among younger Taliban leaders and recruits (Samim 2022a). Yet the group could also rely on preexisting networks, structures, and legitimacy for rebel governance and avoid depending on arms alone. The Taliban operated a "shadow judiciary" of judges and Promotion of Virtue and Prevention of Vice commissions that became the preferred and most trusted option for dispute resolution in most places where the group had a presence; less influential "shadow governors" exerted influence in contested areas (Farrell and Giustozzi 2013, 862–63; Giustozzi and Baczko 2014; Samim 2022a; Terpstra 2020, 1157–59).

In some areas, state presence was very limited, which allowed the Taliban's shadow government to expand. With the gradual drawdown of international armed forces starting in 2014, the Taliban carved out more influence and consolidated its position as a government-in-waiting in over half of Afghanistan; there were "Taliban officials for military operations, recruitment, and intelligence as well as health directors, tax collectors, judges, education monitors, and officials responsible for negotiating aid access with nongovernmental organizations," and they controlled administration and service provision (Jackson and Weigand 2019, 144–45). This consolidation of a new Taliban order accelerated further after the 2020 announcement that US forces would withdraw by September 2021. US and international partner forces curtailed their operations, while Afghan national forces' morale sank as fighting continued. The Taliban captured dozens of districts by mid-2021 before taking over Kabul in late August.

Throughout the insurgency, the Taliban were less cohesive than in the 1990s. Control was more fragmented and policies varied by region and commander (e.g., Giustozzi and Baczko 2014; Samim 2022a). There were divides during the insurgency and after victory between conservatives and more modernist leaders and members (Abbas 2023; Samim 2022a, 2022b), despite top commanders' efforts to forge cohesion while setting up a new government (van Bijlert 2021b). This manifested, for instance, around the issue of girls' education. During the insurgency and in power, there were debates between younger and modernist Taliban who supported education even for older girls and young women, while conservative leaders wanted a return to more severe restrictions; the latter gained the upper hand over time (Abbas 2023; Kazemi and Clark 2022; Jackson 2022; Samim 2022b), as had occurred around 2000 and 2001 (Cornell 2006, 279–81).

Unlike in the 1990s, when the Taliban had to build from scratch in a collapsed state, they captured more established state structures in 2021. The Taliban could decide which institutions to keep, remake, or discard, while reviving their previous cabinet structure (UNAMA Human Rights Service 2022, 7–8). Hamoon and Tawakkoli (2024, 126) describe the stark contrast between the first and second Taliban victories: "Unlike their first entry in Kabul in 1996, this time, the Taliban inherited a government well equipped, functional, and modernized. The first Taliban government's Finance Ministry in their last year in power, 2001, did not have a single computer. In 2021, however, they found the ministry digitally equipped with robust financial management systems run by qualified civil servants," with the Taliban asking male employees to continue working and dismissing only senior officials.

The Taliban began reorienting remaining state institutions toward their own ideological program, but otherwise Taliban infrastructural power was largely already in place because local leaders had collaborated with rebel governance during the fight to recapture the country, and people across Afghanistan already knew what Taliban governance meant. This reduced some of the effort that a completely new rebel victor might have needed to generate compliance and gain cooperation. This time, however, the Taliban has focused to a greater extent on economic transformation than it did in the 1990s and early 2000s, alongside a continuing focus on security and enforcement of religious law (Hamoon and Tawakkoli 2024). The Taliban did still face protests in some cities, along with pockets of armed resistance and threats from Islamic State-Khorasan Province (IS-K) militants (e.g., UNAMA Human Rights Service 2022). To ensure their coercive power, the Taliban solidified their security apparatus, using military equipment abandoned by the old regime and international forces and building up the police and the General Directorate of Intelligence (Abbas 2023; Jackson and Weigand 2023).

As this book goes to press, it remains too early to know how Taliban governance will unfold over the rest of the decade. Even amid a crushing economic crisis and international pressure, however, the Taliban have stuck to their ideals. The Taliban adopted a more moderate approach in fighting their way back to power than they had in the 1990s, being more flexible with recruits and accepting the importance of modern media and communications (Abbas 2023; Gopal and van Linschoten 2017); in power, the Taliban has continued to be somewhat looser about media technologies and sports than in the past for communications and soft power, while also taking on new service provision tasks like polio vaccination (Noack 2023, 2024a, 2024b). Yet their Islamist ideological core meant they have still sought programmatically to enact societal changes—such as banning opium production in a reprise of their 2000 policy—while also growing more comfortable with the practicalities of statecraft, for instance, increasing tax collection to replace foreign donor dependence and investing in major infrastructure projects (Abbas 2023; Bjelica and Clark 2022; Clark 2022; Hamoon and Tawakkoli 2024; Jackson and Weigand 2023, 146; Shih 2023b). Economic struggles and international isolation, however, have meant that the Taliban has struggled to bring planned development and infrastructure projects to fruition (Isar 2025; Noack and Van Houten 2025).

The Taliban's slightly greater inclusivity in rhetoric and in recruitment while rebelling could have been a façade because more conservative leaders have asserted greater control once the Taliban was in power, with a Pashtun-dominated government and harsh restrictions on women in public life (Abbas 2023; Akbari and True 2022; Jackson 2022; van Bijlert 2021b). Women initially had more legal rights than they did in the 1990s, and Taliban treatment of ethnoreligious minorities like the Hazara has also seen some (if still limited) improvements (Abbas 2023, 112–19, 243–44), but conservatives may continue pushing Taliban governance in a stricter direction now that their leadership is secure, similarly to their first stint in power (Cornell 2006, 279–81). Regardless of the trajectory the Taliban continues to take in power, however, the group's resilience and return to government show the organizing power of more programmatic ideologies and how they can persist over time.

Alternative Explanations and the Taliban

As rebels in the 1990s, the Taliban did not have access to significant natural resources, but they benefited from foreign funding, mainly from Pakistan, and taxed trade across the Pakistani border. Warlord rivals already had access to war chests from international support in the 1980s, exploitation of the opium trade, and local taxation, but the Taliban's strict Islamist ideology and behavior enabled them to gain popularity and legitimacy and outcompete rivals, who were seen as perpetuating instability and corruption (Ahmad 2017; Felbab-Brown 2006). Having initially pledged to eradicate opium cultivation, the Taliban shifted to allowing and taxing opium cultivation but not production of heroin; they also reversed this stance after a few years and regulated and taxed heroin producers, although this reversal was "not driven by any acute financial need" and was instead based on a recognition of opium's key role in the rural economy (Felbab-Brown 2006, 136–38). The Taliban attempted to adopt an eradication policy again in 2000, but then backed off because of its unpopularity (Mansfield 2016, chap. 6).

When returning to rebellion after 2001, "the Taliban reconstituted itself in Pakistan between 2002 and 2004 without access to large profits from drugs, rebuilding its material base largely from donations from Pakistan and the Middle East," and again participating in and taxing the smuggling of licit goods across the Afghanistan-Pakistan border (Felbab-Brown 2013b, 192). As they developed greater control within Afghanistan over the course of the 2000s, the Taliban began drawing revenue from the opium trade again. This was far from their only funding source, however, and they mostly relied on taxing licit and illicit industries versus directly controlling them (Felbab-Brown 2013a, 163). After victory, the Taliban in 2022 again sought to eradicate opium cultivation and heroin production. Like before, they have struggled to implement this policy, even while attempting to offer alternative economic opportunities for rural farmers and seeking to rely on infrastructural power and not coercion alone (Noack and Van Houten 2024; Shih 2023a).

Among Taliban leaders in the first period, Mullah Omar emerged as a relatively charismatic figure, but this did not substitute for collective goals or policy planning and implementation, and he remained focused on the Taliban's strict Islamist ideology. Devout Islamists enjoy a reputational advantage of being seen as strict but following a rule of law and imposing a more predictable order (Cammett and Luong 2014; Walter 2017a). In the context of unpredictable violence and corruption amid state collapse and warlord rule in the 1990s and then in regions where corrupt warlords had been returned to power after the US invasion, the Taliban used their reputation to gain legitimacy and eventually seize power. The political environment presented opportunities for a radical Islamist rebel organization, but Taliban leaders' convictions appear to have been sincere (see, e.g., Cornell 2006) rather than adopted instrumentally.

The Taliban had a clear territorial base and ethnic constituency, especially in the group's first period, among Pashtuns in southern Afghanistan and in refugee camps in Pakistan. While Taliban leaders professed a desire to create order and a religiously righteous society to benefit all Muslim Afghans, their policies were based on Pashtun culture without acknowledging other ethnic groups' interests, and the Taliban accepted only those Muslims who followed their strict vision of Sunni Islam. The Taliban used significant force in northern and non-Pashtun areas where the prior government and warlord rivals had more influence (Gopal and van Linschoten 2017, 28–30; Ibrahimi 2017, 955–59). In rural Pashtun areas, meanwhile, less effort was needed to get the population to comply with Taliban policies. This generally aligns with Liu's (2024) argument about wartime constituencies and postvictory governance, but the order the Taliban implemented was backed by coercive force and threats everywhere in Afghanistan, not only in regions previously controlled by rivals.

In their second rebellion and since retaking power, the Taliban became somewhat more inclusive, working more to address ethnic minority groups' interests and incorporating them into leadership. The Taliban's incorporation of more non-Pashtun leaders has parallels to Liu's (2024) idea of rebel victors co-opting populations where they and rivals previously had more limited influence because, after 2001, Afghan governments had their own favored and excluded constituencies. Ideology still shaped policies and practices, however, with the Taliban especially persecuting and committing violence against the Hazara ethnic minority, who did participate significantly in the post-2001 state but are also primarily Shi'a, in contrast to the Taliban's Sunni beliefs (Hakimi 2023).

When the Taliban first took power in 1996, little was left of the prior Afghan state, and the group set about organizing the state as leaders saw fit to implement their ideological vision. In 2021, however, there was a different situation. After 2001, international actors and the Afghan governments they supported modernized the military, developed new infrastructure projects, and extended service provision in urban areas and certain regions, although gaps remained (e.g., Suhrke 2007, 2013). When US and allied forces withdrew in 2021, the Taliban could seize many of the fruits of these efforts, yet they still primarily relied on the model of an "Islamic Emirate" from their first stint in power and on the institutions they built while rebelling.

After seizing Kabul in 1996, the Taliban faced continuing threats from domestic warlord rivals. They then confronted an increased US threat after 1998, when al-Qaeda, which was based in Afghanistan and closely allied with the Taliban, bombed the US embassies in Kenya and Tanzania, prompting a US missile attack on Afghanistan. These threats did help unify Taliban leadership (Dorronsoro 2005, 274), but as Levitsky and Way (2022, 269) describe them, these were already "*highly ideological* top leaders" (emphasis added). Threats may have stimulated further cohesion and development of coercive power, but they did not provoke a shift in ideology or in the type of state Taliban leaders wanted to build.

After the Taliban regained power in 2021, there was a brief domestic threat from anti-Taliban rebels in the north (O'Grady et al. 2021) as well as a continuing threat from the IS-K militant group, who had also clashed with the Taliban before 2021 (Ibrahimi and Akbarzadeh 2020). These threats perhaps helped maintain some cohesion among Taliban's now-looser coalition and gave impetus to strengthening coercive power (e.g., Abbas 2023, 192), but they did not greatly affect policy planning and statebuilding efforts. Some argue that the IS-K extremist threat has pushed Taliban leaders toward more radical stances to maintain Islamist legitimacy, despite telling foreign audiences they would be more moderate when they first retook power (e.g., Verma and Ali 2023). Pledges of moderation might have simply been cheap talk to assuage international worries about the Taliban returning to power. Yet if they were sincere, I would argue this was simply part of the long-standing internal push and pull between more religiously conservative, Kandahar-based Taliban leaders and somewhat more moderate, administratively focused leaders around Kabul, a situation that existed during the Taliban's first stint in power (see Cornell 2006) and continued in 2021 and beyond, even after major changes in personnel. There has been little threat of renewed US intervention since 2021, and despite Pakistani allegations of Taliban support for Pakistani Islamist rebels and occasional cross-border strikes on Afghanistan (RFE/RL 2024), a Pakistani threat does not appear to be mounting. Neither domestic nor foreign threats, however, appear key to understanding the Taliban's contemporary approach to statebuilding, which builds on their ideologically informed prior patterns of governance, now utilizing the remaining state institutions they have inherited.

The Taliban have enjoyed support from some international allies, but more often they have faced international condemnation and pressure because of their extremely restrictive policies and coercive enforcement of them, especially regarding women's rights and education. International incentives and opportunities have sometimes attracted Taliban leaders, but they have always approached them on their own terms, and they have been willing to reverse course if desired results are not achieved. For instance, the Taliban were ideologically opposed to drug production and use, but they sought to take advantage of international antinarcotics pressures to receive aid and diplomatic recognition in exchange for their opium eradication efforts in the late 1990s to 2001; advances or drawbacks in eradication campaigns, however, depended more on Taliban leaders' whims and domestic economic calculations than international actors' decisions and incentives (Cornell 2006, 281–85; Felbab-Brown 2006; Mansfield 2016, chap. 6). This has continued to be the case since 2021 (Shih 2023a; Noack and Van Houten 2024). As discussed above, significant international pressures and incentives to loosen restrictions on women's rights have borne limited sustained results because the Taliban quickly returned to many of the same policies as the 1990s (Mukhopadhyay 2022); in response to international condemnation of new restrictions on women in 2024, a leading Taliban spokesman declared that "foreign moralizing 'will not sway the Islamic Emirate from its commitment to upholding and enforcing Islamic law'" (Tharoor 2024). On other policies, the Taliban have frustrated and ignored even their allies when they have been pushed to make changes. The Saudi and Pakistani states both supported the Taliban's rise in the 1990s, yet neither could sway Taliban leaders around key issues, like the extradition or expulsion of Osama bin Laden or Taliban recognition of Pakistan's preferred border demarcation (Cornell 2006, 273–75). Since returning to power in 2021, Taliban leaders have retained desires for international recognition and financing, yet they have continued implementing their own "ideologically driven and ideologically consistent policymaking" (Malejacq and Terpstra 2023), refusing to sacrifice control regardless of international incentives.

Lessons of Islamist Rebels' Ideological Diversity

While Islamist organizations fight in different contexts and vary significantly in their ideologies, ideology remains critical to understanding how they mobilize and govern. The FLN, Iranian revolutionaries, and the Taliban were all programmatic, seeking to transform the societies they fought to govern. All three built new states and worked to establish influence throughout their countries and societies; in Iran and Afghanistan, they often worked through religious institutions. In Algeria, Iran, and in the Taliban's second act, there were efforts to change not only politics and society but also the economy by undertaking major development projects. There was also a focus on aligning service provision with the organizations' particular ideological principles, with the FLN and Iran's revolutionary regime, for example, providing more services to women than the Taliban did. The FLN was the most inclusive overall, with fewer exclusionary restrictions on women and minorities than the Iranian revolutionaries or the Taliban, although it still maintained a pro-Arab cultural bias.

The FLN lost power in the 1990s, but it has returned to prominence and has remained Algeria's largest and most cohesive political party, even if it no longer enjoys majority control. The Iranian revolutionary regime remains in power and is a powerful political actor around the world. The Taliban, meanwhile, endured defeat and evolved to reclaim the Afghan state. These three cases make clear Islamist ideologies' potential for organizing not only rebellions but also durable postconflict parties and states.

Contemporary Islamist rebellions or transnational jihadist groups may be viewed as exceptional in the larger study of civil wars (Walter 2017b), but there is more to be gained than lost by considering Islamist rebels in broader comparative perspective (Kalyvas 2015a). Like other rebels, Islamist groups can differ vastly in their sociopolitical goals and how inclusionary or exclusionary they are in the constituencies they aim to serve. Some organizations may consider only adherents of the same sect as members of their ideal polity (e.g., the Islamic State's Sunni supremacism), while others may embrace Muslims more broadly. Other organizations may seek to govern based on Islamic principles but embrace non-Muslims as part of their constituency. Hezbollah in Lebanon, an armed organization that also engages in electoral politics, delivers services primarily to fellow Shi'a but also provides services to outgroup members, including non-Muslims (Cammett 2011; Cammett and Issar 2010). Sufi organizations were "the most prevalent forces of armed anti-colonial struggle in the Islamic world" (Motadel 2014, 16), and Sufi political organizations today have tended to be more inclusive in their governance (Stepan 2012). Islamist groups may also be based around a particular ethnic identity, with top FLN leaders ultimately prioritizing Arab Algerians, and the Taliban's ideology and recruitment centered on Afghanistan's Pashtun community, provoking conflict with minority groups like the Kabyle and Hazara, respectively.

This diversity of ideologies and approaches to governing highlights the importance of focusing on the specificities of Islamist rebel organizations and victors rather than lumping them together and expecting them to behave similarly. Even jihadist organizations vary significantly and can evolve over time (Ahmad 2024; Drevon 2024), with many groups' and their members' motivations and aims more local than global. Responses to Islamist rebel groups and attempts to engage with the governments Islamist rebel victors form must be based on a clear understanding of each group's ideology in order to have a chance of succeeding.

CONCLUSION
Understanding and Responding to Rebel Victory

This book has traced the paths along which rebel groups' ideologies led them to recruit and socialize members in different manners; to treat civilians in their areas of operations differently while fighting as rebels; to formulate varied policies and plans for governing if they were to succeed in taking power; and to pursue divergent visions for the postvictory state once they captured power in diverse contexts across Africa, Asia, and Latin America. The organizations examined all aimed to build the security apparatus to secure coercive power, but only some sought to build infrastructural power and extend the state beyond the national core to reach toward the periphery and throughout society. The organizations also varied on whether they sought to use state resources to benefit a narrow, exclusive constituency or a broader, more inclusive public.

This conclusion to the book discusses additional insights from the cases that suggest some potential issues that future research should explore, with special attention to rebel leadership structures and rebel victors' longer-term legacies. I conclude with the book's implications for policymakers across governments, international organizations, and nongovernmental organizations (NGOs), and how they should understand and engage with rebel organizations and rebel victors.

Future Research on Ideology and Rebel Victory

One of this book's goals has been to make the case for the importance of ideology in shaping rebel group policies and behavior before and after victory, an importance that did not go away with the end of the Cold War (see especially Ugarriza 2009). Ideology is not a singular or constant cause of actions by rebel organizations or governments, but ideas can have powerful effects on decision making and deserve continued focus in research on civil wars (Gutiérrez Sanín and Wood 2014; Maynard 2019). Taking ideology seriously can also help us understand when it may be overshadowed by other, more salient factors. When examining ideology, however, we must not conflate discourse alone with ideological adherence. Ideology in general is not mere cheap talk, but some groups' rhetoric and deeds may diverge significantly, so a full consideration of ideology should include both discourse *and* practice.

Drawing such distinctions demands deep engagement with cases on their own terms and triangulating between multiple sources of evidence to come as close as possible to a more complete picture of an organization's ideology and how it is translated into action. For both research and policy, comparison is important, but analysts must also resist the temptation to assume that groups with similar overarching ideologies have the same aims and will behave in the same manner. "Islamist" and "leftist" are convenient short-hand terms, but underneath their umbrellas, rebel groups and victorious rebel governments vary widely. This is especially important in the post-2001 world of the so-called War on Terror, where groups being classed as jihadist has led to the assumption that they and their members are all similarly radical and beyond the realm of negotiation or productive engagement by governments or civil society organizations. Jihadist groups, however, are far from uniform (Ahmad 2024; Hegghammer 2014).

For instance, two Islamist rebel organizations in the Democratic Republic of the Congo (DRC) and Mozambique both pledged allegiance to the Islamic State and have developed ties to each other (Warner et al. 2021; UN Group of Experts on the Democratic Republic of the Congo 2023), yet the groups have different bases and have often behaved differently. The branch in the DRC was formed by the Allied Democratic Forces (ADF), which has roots in Uganda, while Mozambique's branch, known locally as al-Shabaab (although it is separate from the Somali group), developed domestically. Their Congolese counterparts have reportedly criticized the Mozambican leadership for engaging in too much violence against civilians and not enough governance (Repórteres CJI 2022); the groups' approaches to civilians more generally differ because the ADF operates mainly in Christian areas, and al-Shabaab operates generally in Muslim-majority parts of Mozambique (Bofin 2024). The two groups also illustrate potential differences across and within organizations when it comes to recruitment. The ADF, thanks to its Ugandan origins and having few Muslims to appeal to in its DRC areas of operations, has drawn heavily from non-Congolese recruits (e.g., Warner et al. 2021, chap. 9). Some foreign fighters joined Mozambique's al-Shabaab because of commitments to global jihad or prospects of new wives, which also attracted a smaller portion of Mozambican recruits. Most Mozambicans, however, joined because of coercion or locally focused grievances that have little to do with the implementation and enforcement of sharia law. Voluntary recruits were attracted to the group by the prospect of economic opportunities and a chance to resist the Frente de Libertação de Moçambique (Frelimo) government after its decades of neglect of Mozambique's Muslim north (Ewi et al. 2022; Feijó 2021; Habibe, Forquilha, and Pereira 2019; Matsinhe and Valoi 2019). These distinctions are crucial to characterize these and other jihadist groups' aims, practices, and constituencies accurately, and to identify nonmilitary possibilities for engaging with or challenging the organizations.

Analysis of rebel ideology and its effects must also consider the nuances of each organization's ideology and how it is understood not only by leaders but also by rank-and-file members and supporters. There are often disconnects between official narratives and the aspects of an organization's ideology that actually appeal to recruits. Knowledge about ground-level members' and supporters' beliefs and preferences is often tightly controlled by leaders, and individuals may be reluctant to say much beyond the organization's official line (Thaler, Juelich, and Ashley 2024), but researchers should continue finding ways to garner this critical information.

There is (rightly) a great deal of research on civil war termination in general and on negotiated settlements; however, as this book has illustrated, it is important to further understand rebel victories' varying effects on postconflict political, social, and economic life (Toft 2009; Huang 2016b; Day and Woldemariam 2024; Liu 2022), which will be shaped by their ideology. Such consideration of the causes or impacts of rebel victories should be integrated into a process-oriented view of civil wars, looking across the prewar, wartime, and postwar periods (Wood 2008; Shesterinina 2022). One way to do this is to treat civil wars as critical junctures, moments of contingency in a state and society's history and development that can have long-lasting effects (Thaler 2024a). Civil wars open up possibilities for transformative change, but they can also reinforce existing dynamics. As Fidel Castro proclaimed, "A revolution is a fight to the death between the future and the past" (Castro 1961). Further research on how civil wars shape subsequent politics can explore what prewar conditions remain the same or are reinforced, and what aspects of civil wars shift postwar trajectories following rebel victories or other outcomes. I now turn to two issues emerging from my case analyses that deserve further scholarly attention: leadership structure and rebel victors' longer-term trajectories.

Leadership Structure

One issue I have not examined in depth is leadership structure and its potential effects while a group is rebelling and once it is in power. Jonas Savimbi's hegemony within the União Nacional para a Independência Total de Angola (UNITA) and his role as a veto player in Angola's peace process, and Charles Taylor's centrality in the National Patriotic Front of Liberia (NPFL) versus the Frente Sandinista de Liberación Nacional's (FSLN) collective leadership model suggest that perhaps I have underplayed the importance of leadership structure. Leadership structure is likely somewhat dependent on whether the leaders who emerge are more programmatic and inclusive or opportunistic and exclusive, with opportunists more inclined toward personalism. More programmatic ideological programs and personalism can coexist within rebel organizations (Duyvesteyn 2004), however; programmatic-inclusive leaders may stay relatively true to their publicly interested principles even when enjoying more individualized power if they are truly committed to their ideological aims. Opportunistic rebel organizations appear unlikely to sustain collective leadership, but if we look to rebel groups' analogs among military coup makers, there is still variation based on leaders' goal orientation rather than leadership structure alone. Military regimes in Gambia, Liberia, and Sierra Leone, which initially had collective leadership, were characterized by opportunism, lack of institution building, and exclusive distribution of resources, as well as increasing concentration of power in the hands of one individual (Kandeh 1996). In Peru, meanwhile, Juan Velasco Alvarado was the primary leader of a more programmatic-inclusive military government that instituted social and economic reforms to benefit the masses and expanded the state's scope and reach (Einaudi 1973; Lowenthal 1975).

What effects might leadership structure have on rebel organizations? Having a single leader as the primary decision maker within an organization may increase the potential variance of the group's ideals, goals, and policies regardless of organizational type. The more programmatic Sendero Luminoso in Peru, which mixed inclusive and exclusive tendencies, had some collective leadership at times, but it developed a cult of personality around primary leader Abimael Guzmán. Sendero Luminoso experienced fractures, sharp changes of tactics and goals, and eventually almost complete collapse after Guzmán was captured in 1992; this came despite having challenged the government throughout the country, operating in twenty-one of twenty-four departments in 1991 (e.g., Taylor 2017). In Angola, UNITA suffered a similar military collapse when long-time leader Savimbi was killed, and it agreed almost immediately to end the decades-long rebellion and turn toward electoral politics. In Liberia, Charles Taylor and the NPFL's political party, the National Patriotic Party

(NPP), endured, but drastically lost public support when Taylor stepped down and fled into exile. In 1997, Taylor won 75.3 percent of the presidential vote, and the NPP captured twenty-one of twenty-six Senate seats and forty-nine of sixty-four House of Representatives seats (Harris 1999). In 2005, after Taylor's fall, the NPP won a mere 4.1 percent of first-round presidential ballots, three of thirty Senate seats, and four of sixty-four House seats (National Elections Commission n.d.). Some groups with personalized leadership may therefore be able to survive, but their future often depends on how leaders and potential successors approach the transition (Mendelsohn 2024).

The FSLN and its legacy, meanwhile, raise interesting questions about how collective leadership might act to constrain individuals with divergent goals. During the rebellion, the FSLN always maintained collective leadership, despite many leaders' personal and strategic disagreements. This carried over into the group's time in power from 1979 to 1990, with the FSLN National Directorate basing decisions about goals, strategy, and policies on ideologically motivated priorities. Daniel Ortega's personal motivations and degree of ideological commitment during the rebellion and revolutionary government periods are impossible to know. In retrospect, however, some FSLN cadres I interviewed argue that Ortega's more personalist motivations became clear after victory (names omitted due to risks of repression as this book goes to press).

Ortega became the only FSLN National Directorate member on the Junta of the Government of National Reconstruction (JGRN) after victory, and he chaired the junta. He was then elected president in the 1984 elections and sought to use the presidency's symbolic weight to consolidate power and become first-among-equals among the FSLN leaders in the National Directorate. After the FSLN left power in 1990, Ortega steadily centralized control of the FSLN as it shifted from ruling to opposition party, pushing out rivals and moving away from the organization's programmatic policies and roots (Close 2016; Thaler 2017; Martí i Puig and Serra 2020). Had Ortega been able to break free from the FSLN's collective power structure to impose his own will earlier in the rebellion or postvictory periods, the FSLN's statebuilding and service provision efforts might have looked less programmatic.

Overall, leadership structure does appear to have an effect on organizations' trajectories and the potential elasticity of their policies and behavior, yet it is unlikely to be determinate. More programmatic organizations can have more collective or more personalized leadership structures. A collective leadership structure, however, can increase the likelihood of continuity in a programmatic group's ideals, goals, and practices in the event of leadership turnover, even when there are early charismatic leaders. Frelimo in Mozambique, for example, had a well-developed collective leadership structure that helped the group maintain its ideological commitments and cohesion despite the assassination of founding president Eduardo Mondlane in 1969 and the alleged assassination of his successor, Samora Machel, in 1986, a decade after victory (Marcum 2018). In contrast, an ideal of personal empowerment and benefit makes it hard to sustain coalitions and pursue collective goals, so opportunistic-exclusive organizations are more likely to experience centrifugal tendencies toward the centralization of power around a single leader; without a hegemonic leader to impose order in such an organization, it would be extremely difficult to coordinate and divide the spoils of plunder without descending into chaotic infighting. Further untangling these relationships between ideology, leadership structure, and organizational behavior is a promising avenue for future work.

Rebel Victors' Longer-Term Trajectories

The FSLN, National Resistance Movement (NRM), and cases like the Movimento Popular de Libertação de Angola (MPLA) show that rebel victors' programmatic and inclusive ideals may erode or be abandoned over time. Leaders and organizations may decide they prefer retaining power over any other priorities. Ideological erosion or change does not necessarily undermine rebel victors' hold on power because we can see more programmatic and middle-ground organizations retaining control for decades (Lachapelle et al. 2020; Levitsky and Way 2022), even as they shift ideologically. The Chinese Communist Party (CCP) gradually abandoned its socialist economic ideals for state-led capitalism, but its grip on power has not loosened (Saich 2021; Pearson, Rithmire, and Tsai 2023). Rebel victors in Laos and Vietnam are following similar trajectories (Bolesta 2017), and Cuba's revolutionary regime has accepted smaller-scale capitalism amid continuing economic struggles but continues cracking down on any political opposition (Mesa-Lago 2023). The initially middle-ground Zimbabwe African National Union (ZANU) grew more personalistic and exclusive under long-standing leader Robert Mugabe. Mugabe retained power from ZANU's victory in 1980 until 2017, when the military forced him out and helped former Vice President Emmerson Mnangagwa take power, preserving ZANU elites' repressive hold on the state and its resources (Beardsworth, Cheeseman, and Tinhu 2019). In 2023, Mnangagwa declared at campaign rallies that ZANU "will keep on ruling and ruling and ruling for eternity" (Steinhauser and Mpofu 2023)—before claiming victory in elections marked by voter intimidation and fraud.

Rebel victories' long-term impacts deserve greater comparative study, but ideological change in victorious rebel organizations is an especially promising area for research. When and why do elites and rank-and-file members retain rebellion-era ideological principles, and when do they shift in other directions?

In some cases, rebel group members are dismayed by leaders who stray from their professed ideals (e.g., Oppenheim et al. 2015), but others stay in line, whether they are swayed by propaganda or by once-inclusive benefits now being directed only to followers (e.g., Chamorro 2020). Understanding changes in ideology or ideological adherence at the organizational and individual levels will clarify the mechanisms and processes behind ideological shifts and when exactly rebellion-era ideals and institutions lose salience among rebel victors.

Policy Implications

A better understanding of how ideology affects rebel behavior and governance, before and after victory, can improve policymakers' and practitioners' engagement with rebels and victorious rebel organizations. Caution is needed, though. Civil wars are constantly evolving, and it takes sustained observation, diverse sources, and contextual knowledge to make reasoned inferences about rebel organizations. The same care should also be given to understanding the interests and attitudes of civilians, civil society organizations, and other domestic actors, which can be key for conflict resolution, peace building, and statebuilding efforts' success (e.g., Autesserre 2017; Radin 2020).

Counterinsurgency

Counterinsurgent governments take seriously the potential for rebel organizations to develop governance institutions and legitimacy that challenge and may usurp those of the state (Staniland 2012). The Assad regime's bombing campaign during Syria's civil war (with significant Russian aid), for example, aimed to disrupt and destroy rebels' provision of food and health care as threats to central state authority (Ciro Martínez and Eng 2018).

The Assad regime had little interest in any concessions to rebels, but if governments are open to negotiations and a potential political settlement, my theory does have one key lesson: the menu of options for policy changes or concessions to resolve the conflict may be limited by groups' ideologies. Where rebel organizations have more opportunistic and exclusive aims, it may be easier to buy them off with promises of political positions and material resources. If rebel organizations have more programmatic goals, however, it may be difficult to reach an agreement without promising larger structural changes and, if organizations are inclusive, resource-intensive expansion of service provision. These rebellion-era aims will likely continue shaping how rebels use whatever power and resources they gain in power-sharing agreements.

Government efforts to undertake reforms or shift resource distribution to address rebels' grievances can potentially undercut programmatic-inclusive rebels' popular appeals and bases of support so that rebellions peter out or rebel leaders are forced to seek a settlement. Given the diversity of interests among rank-and-file rebel group members and followers (e.g., Arjona and Kalyvas 2012; Humphreys and Weinstein 2008)—and sometimes leaders, too—good-faith efforts to address grievances can also fragment rebel groups, leading members whose grievances have been addressed to seek peace and isolating those who want to continue fighting. This is the case even for jihadist groups. In the case of Mozambique's al-Shabaab, despite the group's brutal violence, the local nature of many members' concerns led Mozambican analysts to affirm that there—and elsewhere—it is "possible to negotiate with terrorists" (Dgedge 2024), with only certain leaders and foreign recruits unlikely to be responsive. If there are hardcore members who want to keep fighting when others have forged agreements and laid down their arms, then splitting off and isolating these radicals makes it easier to tackle them militarily.

International Support for Rebels

The book's lessons about rebel ideology and how rebels govern if they win are likely to be more relevant for international actors. Rebel victories are an unlikely outcome in civil wars, but they remain possible, as the Taliban's 2021 takeover of Afghanistan and Syrian rebels' 2024 victory showed. During the Cold War, there were more "robust insurgencies" by rebels possessing high levels of organization, resources, and international support, which enabled them to challenge and often defeat governments (Kalyvas and Balcells 2010). The return of multipolar great power competition and regional competition could facilitate increasingly robust insurgencies again; alongside international interventions, this could lead to more rebel victories in the future. Russia's support for insurgents in Eastern Ukraine turned into an international war, but a weakened Russia could seek to support rebels elsewhere to continue competition with Western Europe and the United States through other means. There are worries that US-China competition may turn into competitive support for rival sides in civil wars around Asia (Tierney 2021; Mumford 2013). Iran, Saudi Arabia, Turkey, and other countries have been involved in direct and indirect interventions in the civil wars in Libya, Syria, and Yemen (Bergen et al. 2022). International interventions in civil wars have often counterbalanced each other and led to quagmires (Anderson 2025), but in other circumstances, they might facilitate rebel victory: Turkish backing helped Hayat Tahrir al-Sham (HTS) and other rebels in Syria topple the Russian-supported Assad regime (Kardaş 2025).

Governments and international organizations considering supporting rebels must weigh the potential statebuilding strategy and governing orientation that a rebel organization might implement if it took power. Early in the Syrian civil war, there were significant debates among Western actors about whether and how to support "good rebels" to counter the Assad regime and the Islamic State (Lynch 2013; Mukhopadhyay and Howe 2023; Yassin-Kassab 2013). Rebels' ideological discourse and how it is implemented through institutions and rebel governance offer a strong indication of how they might act when controlling the state. It can be difficult to sort through fact, fiction, and propaganda, but by triangulating between rebel statements, on-the-ground reporting, information from communities in rebel areas of operations, and intelligence sources, international actors can gain a good sense of rebels' priorities and how they are attempting to put them into practice. As efforts to support "good rebel governance" in Syria revealed, however, rebel groups remain dependent on their particular appeals and constituencies, and those leaders who are most keen to work with international partners may find it difficult to maintain local, let alone national, legitimacy (Mukhopadhyay and Howe 2023).

Relief and Development Work

Careful data collection about rebel groups and rebel victors' ideologies and practices can also inform relief and development organizations' decisions because they often must work with rebel organizations in order to serve conflict-affected populations (Mampilly 2011; Matfess 2022). These international actors will face different opportunities and risks, however, depending on rebels' aims and priorities before and after victory.

In the Afghan context, for instance, the Taliban's gender policies constrain possibilities for action by certain international organizations. For the United Nations, UN Women has been able to maintain a presence in Afghanistan, but it has limited scope for action directly aimed at tackling gender inequality and restrictions on women's rights. Other UN agencies, however, like UNICEF and the UN Development Programme, have been able to use their programs supporting education, health care, nutrition, and pregnant and nursing mothers to carry out work that benefits Afghan women and girls, even if delivering the full rights and opportunities they deserve remains impossible (UN Women 2024).

Rebel Victors' Policies and Regime Consolidation

Even if we possess the requisite knowledge to infer what type of statebuilding and service provision a rebel organization might pursue if it gained power, this does not provide a key to which groups will govern "best." Programmatic organizations are more likely to build infrastructural power, which holds greater potential for stability, but infrastructural power is value neutral: it depends on how it is used and one's viewpoint. An organization like the Taliban can use its infrastructural power to pursue policies that those who value human rights find abhorrent. The FSLN's attempts at statebuilding and service provision on Nicaragua's Atlantic Coast and in rural areas were seen by many in those regions as structural and cultural violence against their establish ways of life (Hale 1994; Horton 1998; Bendaña 1991; CIPRES 1991).

International actors may decide that the quality of governance matters less than stability after a civil war. Rebel victory can reduce the likelihood of renewed conflict in the short-term (Toft 2009; Licklider 1995) and may lead to some initial increases in democratic institutions, inclusion, and economic development (Huang 2016b; Toft 2009; Weinstein 2005). Even for programmatic-inclusive organizations, however, short- or medium-term stability likely comes at the cost of the centralization of power and authoritarian tendencies over time (Lyons 2016a; Levitsky and Way 2022). As former NRM government official Augustine Ruzindana put it in an interview, "All regimes that capture power through armed struggle have the same structure . . . there is on the horizon the possibility of losing or giving up power. That eventually affects their behavior because they have to retain power" (U-1). In Uganda and in other countries ruled by rebel victors, this results, in the long term, in greater repression and new conflicts, increasing human and economic costs.

One issue policymakers have debated, especially after international interventions or negotiated settlements, is how soon after civil wars end to hold elections in order to build stability and democracy (Brancati and Snyder 2011; 2013). What happens if a rebel organization's political arm wins the first post-conflict elections? This can lead to democratic consolidation. Communist Party of Nepal-Maoist (CPN-M) rebels reluctantly accepted democratic constraints once in power, despite their strong position after the civil war. The Frente Revolucionária de Timor-Leste Independente (Fretilin) in Timor-Leste accepted open democratic competition more willingly because it took power after an international intervention and had already mostly shifted from armed struggle to nonviolent activism over the previous fifteen years (Strating 2016; Kammen 2019), so Fretilin had less coercive capacity to try to enforce their will or threaten voters and rivals into submission than many other rebel victors. Both the CPN-M and Fretilin accepted losses in later elections.

Elsewhere, however, rebels have taken electoral victory as merely a stamp of approval to govern autocratically. Only major rebellions and intense international pressure broke the NPFL and Charles Taylor's hold on power, while

ZANU remains in power today over four decades after winning Zimbabwe's first elections. If rebel leaders are not ideologically committed to electoral democracy, then it may be difficult to keep them on a democratic path after they win post-conflict elections, so domestic and international actors must think about what guardrails they can put in place.

International actors can try to push or incentivize victorious rebels toward their preferred policies and to arrest slides toward autocracy, but one finding across cases in this book is that international actors' ability to influence rebel organizations can be quite limited. Whether international pressures or incentives mediate organizational type's effects may depend in part on how connected an organization is to international actors and the sway those actors have, what Levitsky and Way (2010), discussing democratization, call international linkage and leverage. Before and after victory, however, rebel organizations often ignore or subvert international actors' advice and demands. This is the case even for organizations that were heavily supported or created by foreign powers. Rwanda and Uganda formed the Alliance des Forces Démocratiques pour la Libération du Congo (AFDL) and installed Laurent-Désiré Kabila as leader, but he turned on his sponsors once he was in power in the DRC. In Uganda, even after the NRM in 1987 officially accepted the Bretton Woods institutions' structural adjustment plans to stabilize the economy, there remained internal NRM debates about how economic reforms should be carried out (Sjögren 2013, 148)—and the NRM government refused to implement international financial institutions' plans fully. In Liberia, Charles Taylor and the NPFL ignored diplomatic pressure about human rights and meddling abroad, with Taylor unwilling to temper his ambitions or forgo opportunities to funnel resource wealth into his bank accounts.

Putting the Focus Back on People

We must not lose sight of the fact that civil wars are inherently violent processes. In some cases, rebellion is worth the risks, and victory by rebel forces offers better prospects for human rights and welfare than continuing under an existing repressive regime. Other times, rebels are worse than those they replace. When rebels are facing repressive, tyrannical regimes, it can be ethically just to support the rebels, although international actors must be careful in how they do so, and international interests may not always match those of rebels (Finlay 2022; Renzo 2018). Rebels in Myanmar's current civil war are fighting against a brutal military that crushed the country's fledgling democracy, so support for that fight is justified, but there are multiple rebel organizations with varying ideologies, behaviors, and alliances that complicate the picture (e.g., Brenner 2024; Vrieze 2023). Attempts to support "good rebels" and their governance efforts in Myanmar or in other conflicts should take lessons from Syria and elsewhere, and accept the limits of international interventions and the primacy of local interests (Mukhopadhyay and Howe 2023). Across conflicts, while rebel leaders, foreign politicians, and other power brokers may seek to advance their own agendas, it is critical to maintain a focus on humanitarian concerns and not only political ones, to seek better outcomes for citizens in both the short and long term so they do not need to resort to rebellion again in the future.

Appendix A

CASES OF REBEL VICTORY, 1945–2023

ORGANIZATION	GOVERNMENT OPPONENT	CIVIL WAR YEARS
Haganah/Irgun	United Kingdom (Palestine/Israel)	1933–1948
Indonesian People's Army	Netherlands (Indonesia)	1946–1949
People's Liberation Army	China	1946–1949
Viet Minh	France (Vietnam)	1946–1954
Neo Destour	France (Tunisia)	1952–1956
Pathet Lao	Laos	1953–1975
Movimiento 26 de Julio (M-26-J)	Cuba	1953–1959
Front de Libération Nationale (FLN)	France (Algeria)	1954–1962
Movimento Popular de Libertação de Angola (MPLA)	Portugal (Angola)	1961–1974
Frente Sandinista de Liberación Nacional (FSLN)	Nicaragua	1961–1979
Partido Africano da Independência da Guiné e Cabo Verde (PAIGC)	Portugal (Guinea-Bissau and Cape Verde)	1963–1974
National Liberation Front (NLF)	South Yemen	1963–1967
Frente de Libertação de Moçambique (Frelimo)	Portugal (Mozambique)	1964–1974
Eritrean People's Liberation Front (EPLF)	Ethiopia (Eritrea)	1964–1991
Zimbabwean African National Union (ZANU)	Rhodesia (Zimbabwe)	1965–1980
South-West African People's Organization (SWAPO)	South Africa (Namibia)	1966–1988
Khmer Rouge	Cambodia	1967–1975

(*Continued*)

(*Continued*)

ORGANIZATION	GOVERNMENT OPPONENT	CIVIL WAR YEARS
Mukti Bahini	Pakistan (Bangladesh)	1971–1971
Ethiopian People's Revolutionary Democratic Front (EPRDF)	Ethiopia	1974–1991
Frente Revolucionária de Timor-Leste Independente (Fretilin)	Indonesia (Timor-Leste)	1974–1998
Forces Armées Populaires/Gouvernement d'Union Nationale de Transition (FAP/GUNT)	Chad	1976–1979
African National Congress (ANC)	South Africa	1976–1994
Islamic revolutionaries (Khomeinists)	Iran	1978–1979
Forces Armées Nationales (FAN)	Chad	1979–1982
Mujahideen	Afghanistan	1979–1992
National Resistance Army (NRA)	Uganda	1981–1986
Sudanese People's Liberation Army (SPLA)	Sudan (South Sudan)	1983–2011
Mouvement Patriotique de Salut (MPS)	Chad	1989–1990
National Patriotic Front of Liberia (NPFL)	Liberia	1989–1996
Rwandan Patriotic Front (RPF)	Rwanda	1990–1994
Croatian separatists	Yugoslavia (Croatia)	1991–1991
Sassou-Nguesso/Cobras	Republic of Congo	1993–1997
Taliban	Afghanistan	1994–1996
Alliance des Forces Démocratique pour la Libération du Congo (AFDL)	Zaire (Democratic Republic of the Congo)	1996–1997
Northern Alliance	Afghanistan	1996–2001
Communist Party of Nepal-Maoist (CPN-M)	Nepal	1996–2006
Kosovo Liberation Army	Yugoslavia (Kosovo)	1998–1999
Forces Nouvelles	Côte d'Ivoire	2002–2011
National Transitional Council	Libya	2011–2011
Taliban	Afghanistan	2001–2021

Note: Must have retained control of the state for at least one year.
Sources: Compiled from Toft (2010), Fearon and Laitin (2003), Lyall and Wilson (2009), and Themnér and Wallensteen (2012), with modifications and updates.

INTERVIEWEES

Nicaragua

2015

N-1	Dora María Téllez, Comandante Guerrillera; FSLN Political Commissioner for Managua (1979–1985); Vice President of Council of State (1980–1984); Minister of Health (1985–1990)
N-2	Juventud Sandinista leader during revolution; education scholar
N-3	Elvira Cuadra Lira, security scholar
N-4	Joaquín Cuadra, Comandante Guerrillero; general and Chief of Staff of the EPS (1979–1990); Vice Minister of Defense (1980–1990)
N-5	Edmundo Jarquín, economic adviser and ambassador to Spain and to Mexico in the 1980s
N-6	Hugo Torres, Comandante Guerrillero; Vice Minister of Interior (1979–1982) and Secretary of Consejo del Estado (1980–1982); general and director of the political directorate of the EPS (1982–1990)
N-7	Lea Guido, FSLN militant and women's leader; Minister of Social Welfare (1979–1980); Minister of Health (1980–1985); other government posts (1985–1990)
N-8	Roberto Cajina, military historian; staff at Ministry of Defense (1984–1990)
N-9	Journalist active in the 1980s, including working on the Atlantic Coast
N-10	Hugo Torres (2)
N-11	FSLN guerrilla and later EPS staff officer
N-12	Antonio Lacayo, political opponent of FSLN; Minister of the Presidency (1990–1995)
N-13	Luis Carrión, leader of Proletarian Tendency and Comandante de la Revolución; member of Dirección Nacional; Vice Minister of Defense (1979–1980); Vice Minister of Interior (1980–1988); Minister of Economy, Industry, and Commerce (1988–1990)

(Continued)

N-14	NGO official during the 1980s
N-15	Jaime Wheelock Román, leader of Proletarian Tendency and Comandante de la Revolución; member of Dirección Nacional and Minister of Agriculture and Agrarian Reform (1979–1990)
N-16	Víctor Hugo Tinoco, Comandante Guerrillero; Ambassador to the UN (1979–1980); Vice Minister of Foreign Affairs (1981–1990)
N-17	Arturo Cruz Sequeira, Contra political leader and later academic
N-18	Oscar René Vargas, early FSLN militant and leading FSLN ideologue
N-19	Father Fernando Cardenal, member of Grupo de los Doce; leader of National Literacy Crusade (1979–1980); Minister of Education (1984–1990)

2017

N-20	Carlos Tünnerman, member of Grupo de los Doce; Minister of Education (1979–1984); ambassador to the United States (1984–1988)
N-21	Alejandro Bendaña, ambassador to the UN (1981–1982); Secretary General of the Foreign Ministry (1984–1990)

Liberia

2015 Only

L-1	NPFL member, then SSU and ATU during Taylor presidency
	NPFL member, then progovernment militia during Taylor presidency
	NPFL member, then progovernment militia during Taylor presidency
	NPFL member
L-2	NPFL member
	NPFL member, then joined INPFL, then rejoined NPFL
L-3	NPFL member, then NSA during Taylor presidency
	NPFL member, then ATU during Taylor presidency
	NPFL member
	NPFL member
L-4	NPFL member, then SSU during Taylor presidency
	NPFL member, then SSU during Taylor presidency
	NPFL member, then ATU during Taylor presidency
L-5	NPFL member
L-6	NPFL member, then SSU during Taylor presidency
	NPFL member, then progovernment militia during Taylor presidency
L-7	NPFL member, then ATU during Taylor presidency
	NPFL member
	NPFL member
	NPFL member

L-8	NPFL member, then AFL during Taylor presidency
	NPFL member, then ATU during Taylor presidency
L-9	Former AFL member, then joined NPFL, then AFL during Taylor presidency
L-10	Former United Nations High Commissioner for Refugees official
L-11	NPFL member, then SSU during Taylor presidency
	NPFL member, then AFL during Taylor presidency
L-12	Community leader in Monrovia
L-13	NPFL member, then SSU and ATU during Taylor presidency
	NPFL member, then ATU during Taylor presidency
	NPFL member, then ATU during Taylor presidency
	NPFL member
L-14	Community leader in Monrovia
L-15	Former AFL colonel, left before war, rejoined AFL during Taylor presidency
L-16	NPFL member, then ATU and SSU during Taylor presidency
	NPFL member, then ATU during Taylor presidency
L-17	NPFL member, then member of Executive Mansion staff during Taylor presidency
L-18	Former AFL member, then joined NPFL, then joined police during Taylor presidency
	Former AFL member, then joined police during Taylor presidency
	NPFL member
	NPFL member, then LURD during Taylor presidency
	NPFL member, then LURD during Taylor presidency
	INPFL member, then joined NPFL, then LURD during Taylor presidency
L-19	NPFL member, then ATU during Taylor presidency
	NPFL member, then ATU during Taylor presidency
L-20	NPFL member, then AFL during Taylor presidency
	NPFL member, captured and joined LPC, then AFL during Taylor presidency
	INPFL member, then joined police during Taylor presidency
	NPFL member, then progovernment militia during Taylor presidency
	NPFL member
	NPFL member
	ULIMO member, then joined LPC, then LURD during Taylor presidency
L-21	NPFL member
	NPFL member
	NPFL member
	NPFL member, then ULIMO
	Progovernment (Taylor) militia member, then joined LURD
L-22	Former AFL member, then joined NPFL, then AFL during Taylor presidency
	NPFL member, then joined AFL during Taylor presidency
	NPFL member
L-23	NPFL, then joined AFL during Taylor presidency

(Continued)

L-24	INPFL member, then joined NPFL, then AFL during Taylor presidency
L-25	NPFL member
	NPFL member
	NPFL member
	NPFL member
	War widow of NPFL officer
L-26	NPFL member
	NPFL member
	NPFL member
	Former journalist from NPFL-controlled areas
L-27	NPFL member, then joined ATU during Taylor presidency
	NPFL member, then joined progovernment militia during Taylor presidency
	NPFL member, then joined AFL during Taylor presidency
	NPFL member
L-28	NPFL member, then joined SSU during Taylor presidency
L-29	NPFL, then joined ATU during Taylor presidency
L-30	NPFL member, then joined military police during Taylor presidency
	NPFL member, then joined SSU during Taylor presidency
L-31	Former AFL member
	Former AFL member
L-32	NPFL member, then joined progovernment militia during Taylor presidency
	NPFL member, then joined ATU during Taylor presidency
L-33	Former AFL member
	Former AFL member, then joined NPFL, then AFL during Taylor presidency
L-34	Former AFL member
L-35	Joseph Saye Guannu, political historian and professor, University of Liberia and Cuttington University
L-36	Nathaniel Barnes, Minister of Finance (1999–2002) in Taylor government
L-37	Reverend J. Emmanuel Bowier, historian, former government minister
L-38	Philip N. Wesseh, journalist
L-39	Representative George Mulbah, NPP vice chair, worked with Taylor in Gbarnga and became superintendent for Bong County in Taylor government
L-40	Reverend J. Emmanuel Bowier (2)
L-41	Hassan Bility, journalist and human rights advocate
L-42	Kenneth Y. Best, journalist
L-43	Representative Jefferson S. Kanmoh, rural political activist in the 1980s and 1990s
L-44	Senator Prince Y. Johnson, former NPFL general and INPFL commander in chief
L-45	S. Byron Tarr, social scientist, former political activist and government minister
L-46	Senator Peter Coleman, Minister of Health and Social Welfare in Taylor government
L-47	S. Byron Tarr (2)
	Nakomo Duche, legal scholar and former United Nations official

L-48	Monie Captan, Minister of Foreign Affairs (1997–2003) in Taylor government, former professor and newspaper publisher
L-49	Jonathan Taylor, Minister of State for Presidential Affairs (2000–2003) in Taylor government, professor and dean at University of Liberia
L-50	E. Reginald Goodridge, Deputy Minister of State for Presidential Affairs and Press Secretary, later Minister of Information, Culture, and Tourism in Taylor government
L-51	S. Byron Tarr (3)
L-52	John T. Richardson, former NPFL commander and political official, Minister of Public Works and National Security Advisor in Taylor government
L-53	Senator Conmany Wesseh, former student leader and peace negotiator, IGNU member
L-54	Reverend J. Emmanuel Bowier (3)

Uganda

2016 Only

U-1	Augustine Ruzindana, Inspector General of Government (1986–1996)
U-2	Lieutenant Colonel Fred Mwesigye, founding NRM guerrilla; military officer after victory; member of parliament
U-3	Elijah Mushemeza, Constituent Assembly and parliament member (1994–1996); NRA/M political official; academic
U-4	Miria Matembe, NRC and Constituent Assembly member; Minister of Ethics and Integrity (1998–2003); human rights lawyer
U-5	Jaberi Bidandi Ssali, Minister of Local Government (1989–2004)

References

ARCHIVAL LOCATIONS FOR CASE STUDIES

Nicaragua

Digital National Security Archive, United States (online). *Collections*: "Nicaragua: The Making of U.S. Policy, 1978–1990."

Hoover Institution, Stanford University. *Collections*: Anaya; Bermúdez; Fagen; Fuerza Democrática Nicaragüense; Hassan; Miranda; Nicaragua, Ministerio de Defensa; Nicaragua, Ministerio del Interior; Pastora; Resistencia Nicaragüense (Organización) Ejercito; and Robelo.

Instituto de Historia de Nicaragua y Centroamérica (IHNCA), Universidad Centroamericana, Managua.

Liberia

Defense Intelligence Agency FOIA Electronic Reading Room, United States (online).

Residual Special Court for Sierra Leone Document and Video Archive, The Hague (online). *Collections*: Charles Taylor (SCSL-03-01).

Uganda

Centre for Basic Research (CBR), Kampala. *Collections*: Newspaper clippings 1989–1996 in the folders NRM; NRA; National Resistance Council/Parliament; Resistance Councils/Local Councils; education; health; and human rights.

Makerere Institute for Social Research, Kampala.

Makere University Library (MUL), Kampala. *Collections*: Newspapers 1986–1989.

Parliamentary Library, Kampala. *Collections*: Legislative transcripts 1986–1996.

PRIMARY AND SECONDARY SOURCES

Abbas, Hassan. 2023. *The Return of the Taliban: Afghanistan After the Americans Left.* Yale University Press.

Abbink, Jon. 2009. "The Ethiopian Second Republic and the Fragile 'Social Contract.'" *Africa Spectrum* 44 (2): 3–28.

Abbott, Jared A., Hillel David Soifer, and Matthias vom Hau. 2017. "Transforming the Nation? The Bolivarian Education Reform in Venezuela." *Journal of Latin American Studies* 49 (4): 885–916.

Ablo, Emmanuel, and Ritva Reinikka. 1998. "Do Budgets Really Matter? Evidence from Public Spending on Education and Health in Uganda." *World Bank Policy Research*. Policy Research Working Paper. World Bank. https://doi.org/10.1596/1813-9450-1926.

Abrahamian, Ervand. 1985. "The Guerrilla Movement in Iran, 1963–77." In *Iran: A Revolution in Turmoil*, edited by Haleh Afshar, 149–74. MacMillan.

Abrahamian, Ervand. 1989. *The Iranian Mojahedin*. Yale University Press.

Abrahamian, Ervand. 1993. *Khomeinism: Essays on the Islamic Republic*. University of California Press.

Abrahamsen, Rita, and Gerald Bareebe. 2016. "Uganda's 2016 Elections: Not Even Faking It Anymore." *African Affairs* 115 (461): 751–65.

Abrahamsen, Rita, and Gerald Bareebe. 2021. "Uganda's Fraudulent Election." *Journal of Democracy* 32 (2): 90–104.

Acosta, Benjamin, Reyko Huang, and Daniel Silverman. 2022. "Friends in the Profession: Rebel Leaders, International Social Networks, and External Support for Rebellion." *International Studies Quarterly* 66 (1): sqab085.

Addi, Lahouari. 1995. "Algeria's New Oil Strategy." In *Oil in the New World Order*, edited by Kate Gillespie and Clement M. Henry, 89–102. University Press of Florida.

Adebajo, Adekeye. 2002a. *Building Peace in West Africa: Liberia, Sierra Leone, and Guinea-Bissau*. International Peace Academy/Lynne Rienner.

Adebajo, Adekeye. 2002b. *Liberia's Civil War: Nigeria, ECOMOG, and Regional Security in West Africa*. Lynne Rienner.

Adikhari, Aditya. 2014. *The Bullet and the Ballot Box: The Story of Nepal's Maoist Revolution*. Verso.

Africa Confidential. 1993. "The Battle for Gbarnga." *Africa Confidential* 34 (11): 1–2.

Ahmad, Aisha. 2017. *Jihad & Co.: Black Markets and Islamist Power*. Oxford University Press.

Ahmad, Aisha. 2024. "Jihadist Governance in Civil Wars." In *Oxford Research Encyclopedia of International Studies*. Oxford University Press. https://doi.org/10.1093/acrefore/9780190846626.013.763.

Akbari, Farkhondeh, and Jacqui True. 2022. "One Year on from the Taliban Takeover of Afghanistan: Re-Instituting Gender Apartheid." *Australian Journal of International Affairs* 76 (6): 624–33.

Akiiki, Kenturah Kamugasa. 1994. "Free Universal Education Needs Joint Effort." *New Vision*, September 17. CBR-Primary Education-1.

Alao, Abiodun. 1998. *The Burden of Collective Goodwill: The International Involvement in the Liberian Civil War*. Ashgate.

Alava, Henni, and Jimmy Spire Ssentongo. 2016. "Religious (de)Politicisation in Uganda's 2016 Elections." *Journal of Eastern African Studies* 10 (4): 677–92.

Alemzadeh, Maryam. 2023. "The Attraction of Direct Action: The Making of the Islamic Revolutionary Guards Corps in the Iranian Kurdish Conflict." *British Journal of Middle Eastern Studies* 50 (3): 589–608.

Alexander, Jocelyn. 1994. "State, Peasantry and Resettlement in Zimbabwe." *Review of African Political Economy* 21 (61): 325–45.

Americas Watch. 1985a. *Human Rights in Nicaragua: Reagan, Rhetoric and Reality*. Americas Watch.

Americas Watch. 1985b. *Violations of the Laws of War by Both Sides in Nicaragua, 1981–1985*. Americas Watch.

Americas Watch. 1989. *The Killings in Northern Nicaragua*. Americas Watch.

Aminzade, Ronald, Jack A. Goldstone, and Elizabeth J. Perry. 2001. "Leadership Dynamics and Dynamics of Contention." In *Silence and Voice in the Study of Contentious Politics*, edited by Ronald Aminzade, Jack A. Goldstone, Doug McAdam, Elizabeth J. Perry, William H. Sewell, Sidney Tarrow, and Charles Tilly, 126–54. Cambridge University Press.

Amirouche, Hamou. 1998. "Algeria's Islamist Revolution: The People Versus Democracy?" *Middle East Policy* 5 (4): 82–103.

Amnesty International. 1989. *Nicaragua: The Human Rights Record, 1986–1989*. Amnesty International.

Amooti, Ndayakira. 1994. "Child Immunization Drops." *New Vision*, December 2. CBR-Health-2.

Amooti, Ndayakira. 1995. "Urban Health Appalling." *New Vision*, January 20. CBR-Health-2.

Anderson, Noel. 2025. *Wars Without End: Competitive Intervention, Escalation Control, and Protracted Conflict*. Oxford University Press.

Andrew, Christopher, and Vasili Mitrokhin. 2006. *The World Was Going Our Way: The KGB and the Battle for the Third World*. Basic Books.

Aning, Emmanuel Kwesi. 1998. "Gender and Civil War: The Cases of Liberia and Sierra Leone." *Civil Wars* 1 (4): 1–26.

Aráuz Ruiz, José. 1989. "La Disciplina Militar." *Revista Segovia* 2 (35): 15–17.

Arjomand, Said Amir. 1988. *The Turban for the Crown: The Islamic Revolution in Iran*. Oxford University Press.

Arjona, Ana. 2014. "Wartime Institutions: A Research Agenda." *Journal of Conflict Resolution* 58 (8): 1360–89.

Arjona, Ana. 2016. *Rebelocracy: Social Order in the Colombian Civil War*. Cambridge University Press.

Arjona, Ana, and Stathis N. Kalyvas. 2012. "Recruitment into Armed Groups in Colombia: A Survey of Demobilized Fighters." In *Understanding Collective Political Violence*, edited by Yvan Guichaoua, 143–71. Palgrave Macmillan.

Arjona, Ana, Nelson Kasfir, and Zachariah Cherian Mampilly, eds. 2015. *Rebel Governance in Civil War*. Cambridge University Press.

Arnove, Robert F. 1986. *Education and Revolution in Nicaragua*. Praeger.

Arríen, Juan B., and Róger Matus Lazo. 1989. *Nicaragua: Diez Años de Educación En La Revolución*. Ministerio de Educación. IHNCA,PAA,917.

Ashley, Sean Paul. 2023. "Rebel Victory, State Power, and the Durability of Rebel Regimes." PhD diss., Harvard University.

Ashley, Sean Paul. 2024. "Comrades in Arms? Rebel Leadership Roles and Coups in Rebel Regimes." *International Studies Quarterly* 68 (2): sqae059.

Asiimwe, D., F. Mwesigye, B. McPake, and P. Streefland. 1997. *Informal Health Markets and Formal Health Financing Policy in Uganda: Final Report*. Makerere Institute of Social Research and African Studies Association.

Autesserre, Séverine. 2017. "International Peacebuilding and Local Success: Assumptions and Effectiveness." *International Studies Review* 19 (1): 114–32.

Axworthy, Michael. 2013. *Revolutionary Iran: A History of the Islamic Republic*. Oxford University Press.

Azam, Jean-Paul. 2006. "On Thugs and Heroes: Why Warlords Victimize Their Own Civilians." *Economics of Governance* 7 (1): 53–73.

Azango, Bertha Baker. 1997. "Problems and Conflicts in Liberian Education: A Road to National Peace." *Liberian Studies Journal* 22 (1): 67–77.

Azevedo, Mario J. 1998. *Roots of Violence: A History of War in Chad*. Gordon and Breach.

Bakke, Kristin M., Kathleen Gallagher Cunningham, and Lee J. M. Seymour. 2012. "A Plague of Initials: Fragmentation, Cohesion, and Infighting in Civil Wars." *Perspectives on Politics* 10 (2): 265–83.

Balcells, Laia. 2017. *Rivalry and Revenge: The Politics of Violence During Civil War*. Cambridge University Press.

Balcells, Laia, and Stathis N. Kalyvas. 2014. "Does Warfare Matter? Severity, Duration, and Outcomes of Civil Wars." *Journal of Conflict Resolution* 58 (8): 1390–1418.

Baltodano, Mónica. 1999. "Cayendo Estelí, Somoza Salió Disparado." Memorias de La Lucha Sandinista. https://memoriasdelaluchasandinista.org/view_stories.php?id=79.

Barbosa Miranda, Francisco. 2009. *Historia Militar de Nicaragua: Antes Del Siglo XV al XXI*. Francisco Barbosa Miranda.

Barclay, Anthony. 2002. "The Political Economy of Brain Drain at Institutions of Higher Learning in Conflict Countries: Case of the University of Liberia." *African Issues* 30 (1): 42–46.

Barclay, Fiona, Charlotte Ann Chopin, and Martin Evans. 2018. "Introduction: Settler Colonialism and French Algeria." *Settler Colonial Studies* 8 (2): 115–30.

Barma, Naazneen H. 2017. *The Peacebuilding Puzzle: Political Order in Post-Conflict States.* Cambridge University Press.

Barricada. 1979a. "Ahora: Consolidar La Revolución." *Barricada,* July 25. IHNCA.

Barricada. 1979b. "Arrancó La Reforma Agraria En León." *Barricada,* July 29. IHNCA.

Barricada. 1979c. "Carretera Río Blanco-Siuna: Llave Para Acercarnos al Caribe." *Barricada,* November 14. IHNCA.

Barricada. 1979d. "Casas Sandinistas En Los Barrios." *Barricada,* July 31. IHNCA.

Barricada. 1979e. "Declaración de Alfonso Robelo: Patriotismo Es Hoy Sustituir El Concepto 'Utilidad' Por El de Beneficio Social." *Barricada,* August 14. IHNCA.

Barricada. 1979f. "Educación Impulsará Campaña de Alfabetización." *Barricada,* August 3. IHNCA.

Barricada. 1979g. "Estudiantes Se Integran En Un Solo Organismo de Lucha." *Barricada,* August 15. IHNCA.

Barricada. 1979h. "Habla El Ejército Sandinista." *Barricada,* July 25. IHNCA.

Barricada. 1979i. "La Salud Llega a Toda La Población." *Barricada,* August 12. IHNCA.

Barricada. 1979j. "Ni Pena de Muerte Ni Maltrato a Prisioneros." *Barricada,* July 29. IHNCA.

Barricada. 1979k. "Nombramiento de Funcionarios." *Barricada,* July 26. IHNCA.

Barricada. 1979l. "Por Todo El País La Organización Avanza." *Barricada,* August 9. IHNCA.

Barricada. 1979m. "Pueblo Leonés Elige Junta Local de Reconstrucción." *Barricada,* August 10. IHNCA.

Barricada. 1979n. "Será Gigantesca Labor de Salud." *Barricada,* August 5. IHNCA.

Barricada. 1979o. "Trabajando Intensamente Con Milicias Populares." *Barricada,* July 31. IHNCA.

Barricada. 1979p. "Vasto Programa de Educación Rural." *Barricada,* August 9. IHNCA.

Barricada. 1979q. "Verdadera Reincorporación de La Costa Atlántica Hará FSLN." *Barricada,* August 2. IHNCA.

Barry, Michele, Mark R. Cullen, James E. P. Thomas, and Rene H. Loewenson. 1990. "Health Care Changes After Independence and Transition to Majority Rule." *Journal of the American Medical Association* 263 (5): 638–40.

Bass, Bernard M. 1985. *Leadership and Performance Beyond Expectations.* Free Press.

Bates, Robert H. 2010. *Prosperity and Violence: The Political Economy of Development.* Norton.

Baxter, Craig. 1998. *Bangladesh: From a Nation to a State.* Westview.

Beardsworth, Nicole, Nic Cheeseman, and Simukai Tinhu. 2019. "Zimbabwe: The Coup That Never Was, and the Election That Could Have Been." *African Affairs* 118 (472): 580–96.

Bell, Andrew M. 2016. "Military Culture and Restraint Toward Civilians in War: Examining the Ugandan Civil Wars." *Security Studies* 25 (3): 488–518.

Bell, Curtis. 2011. "Buying Support and Buying Time: The Effect of Regime Consolidation on Public Goods Provision." *International Studies Quarterly* 55 (3): 625–46.

Bell, John Patrick. 1971. *Crisis in Costa Rica: The 1948 Revolution.* University of Texas Press.

Bendaña, Alejandro. 1991. *Una Tragedia Campesina: Testimonios de La Resistencia.* Editora de Arte.

Bender, Gerald J. 1981. "Angola: Left, Right, and Wrong." *Foreign Policy*, no. 43, 53–69.

Bennett, Andrew, and Jeffrey T. Checkel, eds. 2015. *Process Tracing: From Metaphor to Analytic Tool*. Cambridge University Press.

Berdal, Mats, and David Keen. 1997. "Violence and Economic Agendas in Civil Wars: Some Policy Implications." *Millennium: Journal of International Studies* 26 (3): 795–818.

Berg, Louis-Alexandre. 2022. *Governing Security After War: The Politics of Institutional Change in the Security Sector*. Oxford University Press.

Bergen, Peter, Candace Rondeaux, Daniel Rothenberg, and David Sterman, eds. 2022. *Proxy Warfare and the Future of Conflict: Battlegrounds and Strategies Reshaping the Greater Middle East*. Oxford University Press.

Berhe, Aregawi. 2009. *A Political History of the Tigray People's Liberation Front (1975–1991): Revolt, Ideology and Mobilisation in Ethiopia*. Tsehai.

Besley, Timothy, and Torsten Persson. 2008. "Wars and State Capacity." *Journal of the European Economic Association* 6 (2–3): 522–30.

Besley, Timothy, and Torsten Persson. 2014. "Why Do Developing Countries Tax So Little?" *Journal of Economic Perspectives* 28 (4): 99–120.

Birmingham, David. 1978. "The Twenty-Seventh of May: An Historical Note on the Abortive 1977 'Coup' in Angola." *African Affairs* 77 (309): 554–64.

Bitamazire, G. N. 1991. "Management and Administration of Education in Uganda." In *Education for Development*, edited by Syed A. H. Abidi, 21–30. Foundation for African Development.

Bitangaro, Barbara. 1993. "New Plan Released." *New Vision*, October 29. CBR-Health-2.

Bitangaro, Barbara. 1995. "Immunization Rate Drops." *New Vision*, May 12. CBR-Health-2.

Bjelica, Jelena, and Kate Clark. 2022. "The New Taleban's Opium Ban: The Same Political Strategy 20 Years On?" Afghanistan Analysts Network. https://www.afghanistan-analysts.org/en/reports/economy-development-environment/the-new-talebans-opium-ban-the-same-political-strategy-20-years-on/.

Blair, Robert A., and Benjamin S. Morse. 2021. "Policing and the Legacies of Wartime State Predation: Evidence from a Survey and Field Experiment in Liberia." *Journal of Conflict Resolution* 65 (10): 1709–37.

Blattman, Christopher, and Edward Miguel. 2010. "Civil War." *Journal of Economic Literature* 48 (1): 3–57.

Bøås, Morten. 2001. "Liberia and Sierra Leone—Dead Ringers? The Logic of Neopatrimonial Rule." *Third World Quarterly* 22 (5): 697–723.

Bob, Clifford. 2005. *The Marketing of Rebellion: Insurgents, Media, and International Activism*. Cambridge University Press.

Bofin, Peter. 2024. "IS Propaganda Presents ISM Leaders with a Problem." *Cabo Ligado Monthly*, May. https://www.caboligado.com/monthly-reports/cabo-ligado-monthly-may-2024.

Bolesta, Andrzej. 2017. "The Post-Socialist Developmental State in Asia." In *Post-Communist Development: Europe's Experiences, Asia's Challenges*, edited by Andrzej Bolesta, 11–36. Collegium Civitas.

Booth, John A. 1982. *The Nicaraguan Revolution: The End and the Beginning*. Westview.

Borge, Tomás. 1980. "El Poder Tienen Las Clases Tradicionales Explotadas." *Cuadernos de Marcha* 1 (5): 85–89.

Bourgois, Philippe, and Jorge Grünberg. 1980. *La Mosquitia y La Revolución: Informe de Una Investigación Rural En La Costa Atlántica Norte (1980)*. Instituto Nicaragüense de Reforma Agraria. IHNCA/FN,972.850,B773.

Brancati, Dawn, and Jack Snyder. 2011. "Rushing to the Polls: The Causes of Premature Postconflict Elections." *Journal of Conflict Resolution* 55 (3): 469–92.

Brancati, Dawn, and Jack Snyder. 2013. "Time to Kill: The Impact of Election Timing on Postconflict Stability." *Journal of Conflict Resolution* 57 (5): 822–53.

Branch, Adam. 2005. "Neither Peace nor Justice: Political Violence and the Peasantry in Northern Uganda, 1986–1998." *African Studies Quarterly* 8 (2): 1–31.

Branch, Adam. 2011. *Displacing Human Rights: War and Intervention in Northern Uganda*. Oxford University Press.

Brautigam, Deborah A. 2000. *Aid Dependence and Governance*. Almkvist & Wiksell.

Brenner, David. 2024. "Myanmar in 2023: Revolution in an Escalating War." *Asian Survey* 64 (2): 330–40.

Brett, Edward A. 2005. "From Corporatism to Liberalization in Zimbabwe: Economic Policy Regimes and Political Crisis, 1980–97." *International Political Science Review* 26 (1): 91–106.

Brett, Edwin A. 1993. *Providing for the Rural Poor: Institutional Decay and Transformation in Uganda*. Fountain.

Brett, Edwin A. 1994. "Rebuilding Organisation Capacity in Uganda Under the National Resistance Movement." *Journal of Modern African Studies* 32 (1): 53–80.

Brinkman, Inge. 2003a. "War and Identity in Angola: Two Case Studies." *Lusotopie*, no. 10, 195–221.

Brinkman, Inge. 2003b. "War, Witches and Traitors: Cases from the MPLA's Eastern Front in Angola (1966–1975)." *Journal of African History* 44 (2): 303–25.

Brinkman, Inge. 2005. *A War for People: Civilians, Mobility, and Legitimacy in South East Angola During the MPLA's War for Independence*. Koppe.

Brown, Timothy C. 2001. *The Real Contra War: Highlander Peasant Resistance in Nicaragua*. University of Oklahoma Press.

Buckley-Zistel, Susanne. 2006. "Dividing and Uniting: The Use of Citizenship Discourses in Conflict and Reconciliation in Rwanda." *Global Society* 20 (1): 101–13.

Bunce, Valerie. 1981. *Do New Leaders Make a Difference? Executive Succession and Public Policy Under Capitalism and Socialism*. Princeton University Press.

Burkey, Ingvild. 1991. "People's Power in Theory and Practice: The Resistance Council System in Uganda." BA thesis, Department of Political Science, Yale University.

Byrne, Jeffrey James. 2009. "Our Own Special Brand of Socialism: Algeria and the Contest of Modernities in the 1960s." *Diplomatic History* 33 (3): 427–47.

Byrne, Jeffrey James. 2016. *Mecca of Revolution: Algeria, Decolonization, and the Third World Order*. Oxford University Press.

Byrnes, Rita M., ed. 1992. *Uganda: A Country Study*. Library of Congress.

Cabezas, Omar. 1980. "Palabras de Inauguración." In *La Universidad y La Revolución*, edited by Víctor Tirado, Omar Cabezas, and Carlos Núñez, 5–10. Comisión Política Universitaria, UNAN.

Cabezas, Omar. 1985. *Fire from the Mountain*. Plume.

Cabrales Domínguez, Sergio. 2020. "La Oleada de Protestas del 2018 en Nicaragua: Procesos, Mecanismos y Resultados." In *Anhelos de Un Nuevo Horizonte: Aportes Para Una Nicaragua Democrática*, edited by Alberto Cortés Ramos, Umanzor López Baltodano, and Ludwing Moncada Bellorin, 79–95. FLACSO.

Cajina, Roberto J. 1996. *Transición Política y Reconversión Militar En Nicaragua, 1990–1995*. CRIES.

Cammett, Melani. 2011. "Partisan Activism and Access to Welfare in Lebanon." *Studies in Comparative International Development* 46 (1): 70–97.

Cammett, Melani, and Sukriti Issar. 2010. "Bricks and Mortar Clientelism: Sectarianism and the Logics of Welfare Allocation in Lebanon." *World Politics* 62 (3): 381–421.

Cammett, Melani, and Pauline Jones Luong. 2014. "Is There an Islamist Political Advantage?" *Annual Review of Political Science* 17: 186–206.

Cammett, Melani, and Lauren Morris MacLean, eds. 2014. *The Politics of Non-State Social Welfare.* Cornell University Press.

Capoccia, Giovanni, and R. Daniel Kelemen. 2007. "The Study of Critical Junctures: Theory, Narrative, and Counterfactuals in Historical Institutionalism." *World Politics* 59 (3): 341–69.

Captan, Monie R. 2000. "Statement by His Excellency Monie R. Captan, Minister of Foreign Affairs, Republic of Liberia." United Nations General Assembly. http://www.un.org/ga/webcast/statements/liberiaE.htm.

Cardenal, Ernesto. 2003. *La Revolución Perdida.* Anamá.

Cardenal, Fernando. 2008. *Sacerdote en la Revolución,* vol. 2. Anamá.

Cardenal, Fernando, and Valerie Miller. 1981. "Nicaragua 1980: The Battle of the ABCs." *Harvard Educational Review* 51 (1): 1–26.

Castro, Fidel. 1961. "Discurso Pronunciado por el Comandante Fidel Castro Ruz, Primer Ministro del Gobierno Revolucionario, en el Desfile Efectuado en la Plaza Civica, El 2 de Enero de 1961." Departamento de Versiones Taquigráficas Del Gobierno Revolucionario. http://www.cuba.cu/gobierno/discursos/1961/esp/f020161e.html.

Cederman, Lars-Erik, Kristian Skrede Gleditsch, and Halvard Buhaug. 2012. *Inequality, Grievances and Civil War.* Cambridge University Press.

Cederman, Lars-Erik, and Manuel Vogt. 2017. "Dynamics and Logics of Civil War." *Journal of Conflict Resolution* 61 (9): 1992–2016.

Centeno, Miguel Angel. 2002. *Blood and Debt: War and the Nation-State in Latin America.* Pennsylvania State University Press.

Chabal, Patrick. 1993. "Emergencies and Nationalist Wars in Portuguese Africa." *Journal of Imperial and Commonwealth History* 21 (3): 235–49.

Chabal, Patrick. 2001. "Angola and Mozambique: The Weight of History." *Portuguese Studies* 17 (1): 216–32.

Chakrabarti, Kaustav. 2021. "Underground Governance: Rules-Based Order by Armed Groups in Northeast India." PhD diss., Brown University.

Challoner, Kathryn R., and Nicolas Forget. 2011. "Effect of Civil War on Medical Education in Liberia." *International Journal of Emergency Medicine* 4 (1): 6.

Chamorro, Luciana. 2020. "'Love Is Stronger Than Hate': Authoritarian Populism and Political Passions in Post-Revolutionary Nicaragua." PhD diss., Columbia University.

Chamorro, Pedro Joaquín. 1979. "Letter from Pedro Joaquín Chamorro to the Compañeros Responsables del Frente Sandinista de Liberación Nacional." May 27. IHNCA/FSLN,D11G2,0045.

Cheng, Christine. 2018. *Extralegal Groups in Post-Conflict Liberia: How Trade Makes the State.* Oxford University Press.

Chiozza, Giacomo, and Aijin Choi. 2003. "Guess Who Did What: Political Leaders and the Management of Territorial Disputes, 1950–1990." *Journal of Conflict Resolution* 47 (3): 251–78.

Ciment, James. 1997. *Angola and Mozambique: Post-Colonial Wars in Southern Africa.* Facts on File.

CIPRES. 1991. *La Guerra en Nicaragua.* Centro para la Investigación, la Promoción y el Desarrollo Rural y Social.

Ciro Martínez, José, and Brent Eng. 2018. "Stifling Stateness: The Assad Regime's Campaign Against Rebel Governance." *Security Dialogue* 49 (4): 235–53.

Clapham, Christopher. 1998. "Introduction: Analysing African Insurgencies." In *African Guerrillas,* edited by Christopher Clapham, 1–18. Indiana University Press.

Clark, John F. 2008. *The Failure of Democracy in the Republic of Congo.* Lynne Rienner.

Clark, Kate. 2022. "Taxing the Afghan Nation: What the Taleban's Pursuit of Domestic Revenues Means for Citizens, the Economy and the State." Afghanistan Analysts Network. https://www.afghanistan-analysts.org/en/reports/economy-development-environment/new-aan-special-report-taxing-the-afghan-nation-what-the-talebans-pursuit-of-domestic-revenues-means-for-citizens-the-economy-and-the-state-2/.

Clarke, Killian. 2023. "Revolutionary Violence and Counterrevolution." *American Political Science Review* 117 (4): 1344–60.

Close, David. 1990. "Responding to Low-Intensity Conflict: Counterinsurgency in Sandinista Nicaragua." *New Political Science* 9 (1–2): 5–19.

Close, David. 1999. *Nicaragua: The Chamorro Years.* Lynne Rienner.

Close, David. 2016. *Nicaragua: Navigating the Politics of Democracy.* Lynne Rienner.

Coalition for International Justice. 2005. *Following Taylor's Money: A Path of War and Destruction.* Coalition for International Justice.

Cochran, Augustus B., and Catherine V. Scott. 1992. "Class, State, and Popular Organizations in Mozambique and Nicaragua." *Latin American Perspectives* 19 (2): 105–24.

Coggins, Bridget L. 2015. "Rebel Diplomacy: Theorizing Non-State Actors' Strategic Use of Talk." In *Rebel Governance in Civil War,* edited by Ana Arjona, Nelson Kasfir, and Zachariah Mampilly, 98–118. Cambridge University Press.

Coggins, Bridget L. 2016. *Power Politics and State Formation in the Twentieth Century: The Dynamics of Recognition.* Cambridge University Press.

Colburn, Forrest D. 1990. *Managing the Commanding Heights: Nicaragua's State Enterprises.* University of California Press.

Collelo, Thomas, ed. 1991. *Angola: A Country Study.* Federal Research Division, Library of Congress.

Collier, Paul. 1999. "On the Economic Consequences of Civil War." *Oxford Economic Papers* 51 (1): 168–83.

Collier, Paul. 2007. *The Bottom Billion: Why the Poorest Countries Are Failing and What Can Be Done About It.* Oxford University Press.

Collier, Paul, and Anke Hoeffler. 2004. "Greed and Grievance in Civil War." *Oxford Economic Papers* 56 (4): 563–95.

Connell, Dan. 2002. *Rethinking Revolution: New Strategies for Democracy and Social Justice.* Red Sea.

Connelly, Matthew. 2003. *A Diplomatic Revolution: Algeria's Fight for Independence and the Origins of the Post-Cold War Era.* Oxford University Press.

Conte, Gilbert. 1972. "Angolan Nationalists in Need of a Miracle." *Survival* 14 (2): 70–74.

Cook, Judith. 2003. "Post-Conflict Reconstruction of the Health System of Afghanistan: Assisting in the Rehabilitation of a Provincial Hospital-Context and Experience." *Medicine, Conflict and Survival* 19 (2): 128–41.

Cordesman, Anthony H., and Abraham R. Wagner. 1990. *The Lessons of Modern War, Volume II: The Iran-Iraq War.* Westview.

Cornell, Svante E. 2006. "Taliban Afghanistan: A True Islamic State?" In *The Limits of Culture: Islam and Foreign Policy,* edited by Brenda Shaffer, 263–90. MIT Press.

Cremer, Jacques. 1986. "Cooperation in Ongoing Organizations." *Quarterly Journal of Economics* 101 (1): 33–50.

Cruz, Arturo J. 2002. *Nicaragua's Conservative Republic 1853–1893.* Palgrave Macmillan.

Cruz, Eduardo. 2021. "Daniel Ortega, el Candidato Que No Hace Campaña Electoral." *La Prensa,* March 7.

Cuadra Lira, Elvira. 2020. "La Perversión de la Fuerza: El Ejército y la Policía en la Crisis Nicaragüense." In *Anhelos de un Nuevo Horizonte: Aportes para una Nicaragua*

Democrática, edited by Alberto Cortés Ramos, Umanzor López Baltodano, and Ludwing Moncada Bellorin, 377–96. FLACSO.

Czuba, Karol. 2019. "Karamojan Politics: Extension of State Power and Formation of a Subordinate Political Elite in Northeastern Uganda." *Third World Quarterly* 40 (3): 558–77.

Daly, Sarah Zukerman. 2022. *Violent Victors: Why Bloodstained Parties Win Postwar Elections*. Princeton University Press.

Darden, Keith, and Anna Grzymala-Busse. 2006. "The Great Divide: Literacy, Nationalism, and the Communist Collapse." *World Politics* 59 (1): 83–115.

David, Soniia. 1993. "Health Expenditure and Household Budgets in Rural Liberia." *Health Transition Review* 3 (1): 57–76.

Davidson, Basil. 1975. *In the Eye of the Storm: Angola's People*. Penguin.

Day, Christopher. 2011. "The Fates of Rebels: Insurgencies in Uganda." *Comparative Politics* 43 (4): 439–58.

Day, Christopher, and Michael Woldemariam. 2024. "From Rebelling to Ruling: Insurgent Victory and State Capture in Africa." *Studies in Conflict and Terrorism* 47 (5): 476–501.

Ddungu, Expedit. 1993. "Popular Forms and the Question of Democracy: The Case of Resistance Councils in Uganda." In *Uganda: Studies in Living Conditions, Popular Movements, and Constitutionalism*, edited by Mahmood Mamdani and J. Oloka-Onyango, 365–404. JEP.

Defense Intelligence Agency. 1990. "More Notes on Rebels at Harbel." Defense Intelligence Agency, June 14. http://www.dia.mil/FOIA/FOIA-Electronic-Reading-Room/FOIA-Reading-Room-Africa/FileId/140848/.

Defense Intelligence Agency. 1994. "Krahn/NPFL/ECOMOG Activity." Defense Intelligence Agency, September 1. http://www.dia.mil/FOIA/FOIA-Electronic-Reading-Room/FOIA-Reading-Room-Africa/FileId/140847/.

Dennis, Philip A. 1993. "The Miskito-Sandinista Conflict in Nicaragua in the 1980s." *Latin American Research Review* 28 (3): 214–34.

Derderian, Katharine, Helene Lorinquer, and Stéphan Goetghebuer. 2007. "Post-War Liberia: Healthcare in the Balance." *Forced Migration Review* 1 (28): 19–20.

Desrosiers, Marie-Eve, and Susan Thomson. 2011. "Rhetorical Legacies of Leadership: Projections of 'Benevolent Leadership' in Pre- and Post-Genocide Rwanda." *Journal of Modern African Studies* 49 (3): 429–53.

"Developments in Liberia." 1999. *Liberia Review* 1 (1): 31–38.

de Villers, Gauthier, and Jean Omasombo Tshonda. 2002. "An Intransitive Transition." *Review of African Political Economy* 29 (93–94): 399–410.

Dgedge, Rui. 2024. "'É Possível Negociar Com Os Terroristas.'" *O País*, January 18. https://opais.co.mz/e-possivel-negociar-com-os-terroristas/.

Dicklitch, Susan. 1998. *The Elusive Promise of NGOs in Africa: Lessons from Uganda*. MacMillan.

Dijkstra, A. Geske, and Jan Kees Van Donge. 2001. "What Does the 'Show Case' Show? Evidence of and Lessons from Adjustment in Uganda." *World Development* 29 (5): 841–63.

Dinerman, Alice. 2006. *Revolution, Counter-Revolution and Revisionism in Postcolonial Africa: The Case of Mozambique, 1975–1994*. Routledge.

Dirección Política E.P.S. 1984. *Preparación Política: Clases, Soldados y Marineros*. Dirección Política del Ejército Popular Sandinista. IHN/FN,355.31,D597c.

Doctor, Austin C. 2021. "Rebel Leadership and the Specialisation of Rebel Operations." *Civil Wars* 23 (3): 311–42.

Domínguez, Jorge I. 1989. *To Make a World Safe for Revolution: Cuba's Foreign Policy*. Harvard University Press.

Donahue, John M. 1986. *The Nicaraguan Revolution in Health*. Bergin & Garvey.

Dorman, Sara Rich. 2006. "Post-Liberation Politics in Africa: Examining the Political Legacy of Struggle." *Third World Quarterly* 27 (6): 1085–1101.

Dorronsoro, Gilles. 2005. *Revolution Unending: Afghanistan, 1979 to the Present*. Columbia University Press.

Downton, James V. 1973. *Rebel Leadership: Commitment and Charisma in the Revolutionary Process*. Free Press.

Drevon, Jerome. 2024. *From Jihad to Politics: How Syrian Jihadis Embraced Politics*. Oxford University Press.

Dukuly, Abdullah. 2004. "Education-Liberia: Civil War Leaves School System in Tatters." *Inter Press News Service*, June 16. http://www.ipsnews.net/2004/06/education-liberia-civil-war-leaves-school-system-in-tatters/.

Dunn, D. Elwood. 1999. "The Civil War in Liberia." In *The Civil War in Liberia*, edited by Taisier M. Ali and Robert O. Matthews, 88–121. McGill-Queen's University Press.

Dunn, D. Elwood. 2009. *Liberia and the United States During the Cold War: Limits of Reciprocity*. Palgrave Macmillan.

Dunn, D. Elwood. 2012. *Liberia and Independent Africa, 1940s to 2012: A Brief Political Profile*. Africana Homestead Legacy.

Dunn, Kevin C. 2002. "A Survival Guide to Kinshasa: Lessons of the Father, Passed Down to the Son." In *The African Stakes of the Congo War*, edited by John F. Clark, 53–74. Palgrave Macmillan.

Duyvesteyn, Isabelle. 2004. *Clausewitz and African War: Politics and Strategy in Liberia and Somalia*. Frank Cass.

Dwyer, Jonny. 2015. *American Warlord*. Knopf.

Easterly, William. 2006. *The White Man's Burden: Why the West's Efforts to Aid the Rest Have Done So Much Ill and So Little Good*. Penguin.

Einaudi, Luigi R. 1973. "Revolution from Within? Military Rule in Peru Since 1968." *Studies in Comparative International Development* 8 (1): 71–87.

Ekaney, Nkwelle. 1976. "Post-Mortem of a Conflict." *Présence Africaine* 1976/2 (98): 211–33.

Elling, Rasmus Christian. 2013. *Minorities in Iran: Nationalism and Ethnicity After Khomeini*. Palgrave Macmillan.

Ellis, Stephen. 1995. "Liberia 1989–1994: A Study of Ethnic and Spiritual Violence." *African Affairs* 94 (375): 165–97.

Ellis, Stephen. 2007. *The Mask of Anarchy: The Destruction of Liberia and the Religious Dimension of an African Civil War*. New York University Press.

Engholm, G. F., and Ali A. Mazrui. 1967. "Violent Constitutionalism in Uganda." *Government and Opposition* 2 (4): 585–99.

Enriquez, Laura J. 1991. *Harvesting Change: Labor and Agrarian Reform in Nicaragua, 1979–1990*. University of North Carolina Press.

Envío Team. 1984. "Partidos y Movimientos Políticos en Nicaragua (I Parte)." *Envío*, no. 38. https://www.revistaenvio.org/articulo/428.

Esteban, Joan. 1976. "The Economic Policy of Francoism: An Interpretation." In *Spain in Crisis: The Evolution and Decline of the Franco Regime*, edited by Paul Preston, 82–100. Harvester.

Everingham, Mark. 1996. *Revolution and the Multiclass Coalition in Nicaragua*. University of Pittsburgh Press.

Ewi, Martin, Liesl Louw-Vaudran, Willem Els, Richard Chelin, Yussuf Adam, and Elisa Samuel Boerekamp. 2022, August. "Violent Extremism in Mozambique: Drivers and Links to Transnational Organised Crime." Institute for Security Studies.

Faiz, A. 1997. "Health Care Under the Taliban." *Lancet* 349 (9060): 1247–48.

Falleti, Tulia G., and Julia F. Lynch. 2009. "Context and Causal Mechanisms in Political Analysis." *Comparative Political Studies* 42 (9): 1143–66.

Fanon, Frantz. 1963. *The Wretched of the Earth*. Grove.

Farhi, Farideh. 1990. *States and Urban-Based Revolutions: Iran and Nicaragua*. University of Illinois Press.

Farrell, Theo, and Antonio Giustozzi. 2013. "The Taliban at War: Inside the Helmand Insurgency, 2004–2012." *International Affairs* 89 (4): 845–71.

Fearon, James D., and David D. Laitin. 2003. "Ethnicity, Insurgency, and Civil War." *American Political Science Review* 97 (1): 75–90.

Feijó, João. 2021. "Characterization and Social Organization of the Machababos from the Discourses of Kidnapped Women." Observador Rural. Observatório do Meio Rural. https://omrmz.org/observador/or-109-caracterizacao-e-organizacao-social-dos-machababos/.

Felbab-Brown, Vanda. 2006. "Kicking the Opium Habit? Afghanistan's Drug Economy and Politics Since the 1980s: Analysis." *Conflict, Security & Development* 6 (2): 127–49.

Felbab-Brown, Vanda. 2013a. *Aspiration and Ambivalence: Strategies and Realities of Counterinsurgency and State Building in Afghanistan*. Brookings Institution Press.

Felbab-Brown, Vanda. 2013b. "Counterinsurgency, Counternarcotics, and Illicit Economies in Afghanistan: Lessons for State-Building." In *Convergence: Illicit Networks and National Security in the Age of Globalization*, edited by Michael Miklaucic and Jacqueline Brewer, 189–209. National Defense University Press.

Felbab-Brown, Vanda. 2021. "Pipe Dreams: The Taliban and Drugs from the 1990s into Its New Regime." *Small Wars Journal*, September 15. https://smallwarsjournal.com/jrnl/art/pipe-dreams-taliban-and-drugs-1990s-its-new-regime.

Ferreira, Manuel Ennes. 2002. "Angola: Civil War and the Manufacturing Industry." In *Arming the South: The Economics of Military Expenditure, Arms Production and Arms Trade in Developing Countries*, edited by Jurgen Brauer and J. Paul Dunne, 251–74. Palgrave Macmillan.

Financial Times. 1990. "Parents in Fees Agony." *Financial Times*, January 12. CBR-Primary Education-1.

Finlay, Christopher J. 2022. "Assisting Rebels Abroad: The Ethics of Violence at the Limits of the Defensive Paradigm." *Journal of Applied Philosophy* 39 (1): 38–55.

Fisher, Jonathan. 2020. *East Africa After Liberation: Conflict, Security and the State Since the 1980s*. Cambridge University Press.

Flanary, Rachel, and David Watt. 1999. "The State of Corruption: A Case Study of Uganda." *Third World Quarterly* 20 (3): 515–36.

FLN. 1954a. "Les Dix Commandements de l'A.L.N." Front de Libération Nationale. http://theirwords.org/media/transfer/doc/dz_fln_aln_01-b15da539a9a5da1468140eca-0d60e3a7.pdf.

FLN. 1954b. "Proclamation au Peuple Algérien." Front de Libération Nationale. https://perspective.usherbrooke.ca/bilan/servlet/BMDictionnaire?iddictionnaire=1841.

Florea, Adrian. 2014. "De Facto States in International Politics (1945–2011): A New Data Set." *International Interactions* 40 (5): 788–811.

Focus. 1987. "Uganda Hosts International Seminar on AIDS." *Focus*, December 15. CBR.

Fonseca, Carlos. 1964. "Desde La Carcel, Yo Acuso La Dictadura." Centro de Documentación de los Movimientos Armados. http://www.cedema.org/ver.php?id=97.

Foran, John. 2005. *Taking Power: On the Origins of Third World Revolutions*. Cambridge University Press.

Foran, John, and Jeff Goodwin. 1993. "Revolutionary Outcomes in Iran and Nicaragua: Coalition Fragmentation, War, and the Limits of Social Transformation." *Theory and Society* 22 (2): 209–47.

Forrest, Joshua B. 1987. "Guinea-Bissau Since Independence: A Decade of Domestic Power Struggles." *Journal of Modern African Studies* 25 (1): 95–116.

Fortin, Jessica. 2009. "A Tool to Evaluate State Capacity in Post-Communist Countries, 1989–2006." *European Journal of Political Research* 49 (5): 654–86.

Fortunato, José, ed. 1977. *Angola: Documentos Do MPLA, 1o Volume.* Ulmeiro.

Fragoso, Heleno Claudio, and Alejandro Artucio. 1980. *Human Rights in Nicaragua: Yesterday and Today.* International Commission of Jurists.

Freeden, Michael. 2003. *Ideology: A Very Short Introduction.* Oxford University Press.

FSLN. 1960. "La Lucha por la Transformación de Nicaragua." Centro de Documentación de los Movimientos Armados. http://www.cedema.org/ver.php?id=1794.

FSLN. 1969. "Programa Histórico del FSLN." Centro de Documentación de los Movimientos Armados. http://www.cedema.org/ver.php?id=3399.

FSLN. 1978a. "La Consigna Es: Muerte al Somocismo." Centro de Documentación de los Movimientos Armados. http://www.cedema.org/ver.php?id=3787.

FSLN. 1978b. "Operación: 'Muerte al Somocismo' 'Carlos Fonseca Amador.'" Centro de Documentación de los Movimientos Armados. http://www.cedema.org/ver.php?id=4604.

FSLN. 1978c. "Por Qué Lucha El FSLN Junta al Pueblo?" Centro de Documentación de los Movimientos Armados. http://www.cedema.org/ver.php?id=3325.

FSLN. 1978d. *Programa Mínimo del F.S.L.N.* Frente Sandinista de Liberación Nacional. IHNCA,AV,324.21.

FSLN. 1979. "Comunicado Unitario de las Tres Tendencias del FSLN." Centro de Documentación de los Movimientos Armados. http://www.cedema.org/ver.php?id=3641.

FSLN. 1984. "Bases Para el Plan de Lucha del FSLN." Frente Sandinista de Liberación Nacional. IHNCA/FN,324.23,F879D,c1.

Fukuyama, Francis. 2004. "The Imperative of State-Building." *Journal of Democracy* 15 (2): 17–31.

Fukuyama, Francis. 2013. "What Is Governance?" *Governance* 26 (3): 347–68.

Furley, O., and J. Katalikawe. 1997. "Constitutional Reform in Uganda: The New Approach." *African Affairs* 96 (383): 243–60.

Galtung, Johan. 1969. "Violence, Peace, and Peace Research." *Journal of Peace Research* 6 (3): 167–91.

Garfield, Richard, and Glen Williams. 1992. *Health Care in Nicaragua: Primary Care Under Changing Regimes.* Oxford University Press.

Gebregziabher, Tefera Negash, and Wil Hout. 2018. "The Rise of Oligarchy in Ethiopia: The Case of Wealth Creation Since 1991." *Review of African Political Economy* 45 (157): 501–10.

Geddes, Barbara. 1990. "How the Cases You Choose Affect the Answers You Get: Selection Bias in Comparative Politics." *Political Analysis* 2 (1): 131–50.

George, Alexander, and Andrew Bennett. 2005. *Case Studies and Theory Development.* MIT Press.

Gerdes, Felix. 2013. *Civil War and State Formation: The Political Economy of War and Peace in Liberia.* Campus Verlag.

Gershoni, Yekutiel. 1997. "Military and Diplomatic Strategies in the Liberian Civil War." *Liberian Studies Journal* 22 (2): 199–239.

Gertzel, Cherry. 1980. "Uganda After Amin: The Continuing Search for Leadership and Control." *African Affairs* 79 (317): 461–89.

Ghobarah, Hazem Adam, Paul Huth, and Bruce Russett. 2004. "The Post-War Public Health Effects of Civil Conflict." *Social Science & Medicine* 59 (4): 869–84.

Ghufran, Nasreen. 2001. "The Taliban and the Civil War Entanglement in Afghanistan." *Asian Survey* 41 (3): 462–87.

Gibson, Nigel. 2015. "The Rationality of Revolt and Fanon's Relevance, 50 Years Later." *Karib* 2 (1): 9–25.

Gilbert, Dennis. 1988. *Sandinistas: The Party and the Revolution*. Basil Blackwell.

Giustozzi, Antonio, and Adam Baczko. 2014. "The Politics of the Taliban's Shadow Judiciary, 2003–2013." *Central Asian Affairs* 1 (2): 199–224.

Gleditsch, Nils Petter, Peter Wallensteen, Mikael Eriksson, Margareta Sollenberg, and Havard Strand. 2002. "Armed Conflict 1946–2001: A New Dataset." *Journal of Peace Research* 39 (5): 615–37.

Gleijeses, Piero. 2002. *Conflicting Missions: Havana, Washington and Africa 1959–1976*. University of North Carolina Press.

Global Witness. 2001. *Taylor-Made: The Pivotal Role of Liberia's Forests and Flag of Convenience in Regional Conflict*. Global Witness.

Gobat, Michel. 2005. *Confronting the American Dream: Nicaragua Under U.S. Imperial Rule*. Duke University Press.

Golooba-Mutebi, Frederick. 2004. "Reassessing Popular Participation in Uganda." *Public Administration and Development* 24 (4): 289–304.

Goodson, Larry P. 2001. *Afghanistan's Endless War: State Failure, Regional Politics, and the Rise of the Taliban*. University of Washington Press.

Goodwin, Jeff. 2001. *No Other Way Out: States and Revolutionary Movements, 1945–1991*. Cambridge University Press.

Gopal, Anand, and Alex Strick van Linschoten. 2017. "Ideology in the Afghan Taliban." Afghanistan Analysts Network. https://www.afghanistan-analysts.org/publication /aan-papers/ideology-in-the-afghan-taliban-a-new-aan-report/.

Gorman, Stephen M., and Thomas W. Walker. 1985. "The Armed Forces." In *Nicaragua: The First Five Years*, edited by Thomas W. Walker, 91–118. Praeger.

Graham, Helen. 2005. *The Spanish Civil War: A Very Short Introduction*. Oxford University Press.

Green, Elliott D. 2006. "Ethnicity and the Politics of Land Tenure Reform in Central Uganda." *Commonwealth & Comparative Politics* 44 (3): 370–88.

Greenberg, Eldon van Cleef. 1970. "Law and the Conduct of the Algerian Revolution." *Harvard International Law Journal* 11 (1): 37–72.

Guevara, Che. 1961. *Guerrilla Warfare*. Monthly Review Press.

Guevara, Ernesto "Che." 2001. *The African Dream: The Diaries of the Revolutionary War in the Congo*. Grove.

Gurr, Ted Robert. 1970. *Why Men Rebel*. Princeton University Press.

Gutiérrez Sanín, Francisco, and Elisabeth Jean Wood. 2014. "Ideology in Civil War: Instrumental Adoption and Beyond." *Journal of Peace Research* 51 (2): 213–26.

Habibe, Saide, Salvador Forquilha, and João Pereira. 2019. "Radicalização Islâmica No Norte De Moçambique: O Caso Da Mocímboa Da Praia." *Cadernos IESE*. Instituto de Estudos Sociais e Económicos.

Hagmann, Tobias, and Jon Abbink. 2011. "Twenty Years of Revolutionary Democratic Ethiopia, 1991 to 2011." *Journal of Eastern African Studies* 5 (4): 579–95.

Hakimi, Medhi. 2023. "Relentless Atrocities: The Persecution of Hazaras." *Michigan Journal of International Law* 44 (1): 157–217.

Hale, Charles R. 1994. *Resistance and Contradiction: Miskitu Indians and the Nicaraguan State, 1894–1987*. Stanford University Press.

Hall, Peter A. 2006. "Systematic Process Analysis: When and How to Use It." *European Management Review* 3 (1): 24–31.

Hamoon, Waheedullah, and Ahmad Omid Tawakkoli. 2024. "National Budgeting and Revenue Collection Under the Taliban." *Journal of Social and Political Sciences* 7 (1): 122–34.

Hansen, Holger Bernt, and Michael Twaddle. 1991. "Introduction." In *Changing Uganda: The Dilemmas of Structural Adjustment & Revolutionary Change*, edited by Holger Bernt Hansen and Michael Twaddle, 1–19. James Currey.

Hanson, Jonathan K., and Rachel Sigman. 2021. "Leviathan's Latent Dimensions: Measuring State Capacity for Comparative Political Research." *Journal of Politics* 83 (4): 1495–1510.

Hanson, Stephen E. 2010. *Post-Imperial Democracies: Ideology and Party Formation in Third Republic France, Weimar Germany, and Post-Soviet Russia*. Cambridge University Press.

Harris, David. 1999. "From 'Warlord' to 'Democratic' President: How Charles Taylor Won the 1997 Liberian Elections." *Journal of Modern African Studies* 37 (3): 431–55.

Harris, David. 2012. *Civil War and Democracy in West Africa: Conflict Resolution, Elections and Justice in Sierra Leone and Liberia*. Tauris.

Harris, Kevan. 2017. *A Social Revolution: Politics and the Welfare State in Iran*. University of California Press.

Harrison, Graham. 2001. "Post-Conditionality Politics and Administrative Reform: Reflections on the Cases of Uganda and Tanzania." *Development and Change* 32 (4): 657–79.

Hater, John J., and Bernard M. Bass. 1988. "Superiors' Evaluations and Subordinates' Perceptions of Transformational and Transactional Leadership." *Journal of Applied Psychology* 73 (4): 695–702.

Hazard, John N. 1981. "Socialism and Law in Algeria." *Review of Socialist Law* 7 (3): 243–60.

Hegghammer, Thomas. 2014. "Jihadi-Salafis or Revolutionaries? On Religion and Politics in the Study of Militant Islamism." In *Global Salafism: Islam's New Religious Movement*, edited by Roel Meijer, 245–66. Oxford University Press.

Heninger, Lori, Carolyn Makinson, Faye Richardson, Miranda Duncan, and Julia Aker Duany. 2006. *Help Us Help Ourselves: Education in the Conflict to Post-Conflict Transition in Liberia*. Women's Commission for Refugee Women and Children.

Henriksen, Thomas H. 1976. "People's War in Angola, Mozambique, and Guinea-Bissau." *Journal of Modern African Studies* 14 (3): 377–99.

Herbst, Jeffrey. 2000. *States and Power in Africa*. Princeton University Press.

Hernández, Plutarco. 1982. *El FSLN por Dentro: Relatos de un Combatiente*. Talleres Gráficos Trejos Hermanos.

Herrera, Leticia. 2013. *Guerrillera, Mujer y Comandante de la Revolución Sandinista: Memorias de Leticia Herrera*. Edited by Alberto González Casado, Maria Antònia Sabater Montserrat, and Maria Pau Trayner Vilanova. Icaria.

Herzog, Chaim. 1989. "A Military-Strategic Overview." In *The Iran-Iraq War: Impact and Implications*, edited by Efraim Karsh, 255–68. Palgrave Macmillan.

Heywood, Linda M. 1989. "Unita and Ethnic Nationalism in Angola." *Journal of Modern African Studies* 27 (1): 47–66.

Heywood, Linda M. 1998. "Towards an Understanding of Modern Political Ideology in Africa: The Case of the Ovimbundu of Angola." *Journal of Modern African Studies* 36 (1): 139–67.

Heywood, Linda M. 2011. "Angola and the Violent Years 1975–2008: Civilian Casualties." *Portuguese Studies Review* 19 (1–2): 311–32.

Hickey, Sam, Badru Bukenya, and Haggai Matsiko. 2023. "The Politics of PoEs in Uganda: Trapped Between Neoliberal State-Building and the Politics of Survival?" In *Pockets of Effectiveness and the Politics of State-Building and Development in Africa*, edited by Sam Hickey, 173–205. Oxford University Press.

Hickman, William F. 1982. *Ravaged and Reborn: The Iranian Army*. Brookings Institution.

Hobsbawm, Eric. 1959. *Primitive Rebels: Studies in Archaic Forms of Social Movement in the 19th and 20th Centuries*. Manchester University Press.

Hodges, Tony. 2001. *Angola: From Afro-Stalinism to Petro-Diamond Capitalism*. Indiana University Press.

Holden, Robert H. 2004. *Armies Without Nations: Public Violence and State Formation in Central America, 1821–1960*. Oxford University Press.

Hoover Green, Amelia. 2016. "The Commander's Dilemma: Creating and Controlling Armed Group Violence." *Journal of Peace Research* 53 (5): 619–32.

Horowitz, Donald L. 1985. *Ethnic Groups in Conflict*. University of California Press.

Horton, Lynn R. 1998. *Peasants in Arms: War and Peace in the Mountains of Nicaragua, 1979–1994*. Ohio University Center for International Studies.

Horton, Lynn R. 2004. "Constructing Conservative Identity: Peasant Mobilization Against Revolution in Nicaragua." *Mobilization: An International Quarterly* 9 (2): 167–80.

Houser, George M. 1962. "Journey to Rebel Angola." *Africa Today* 9 (2): 4–7.

Howe, Herbert. 1996. "Lessons of Liberia: ECOMOG and Regional Peacekeeping." *International Security* 21 (3): 145–76.

Huang, Reyko. 2016a. "Rebel Diplomacy in Civil War." *International Security* 40 (4): 89–126.

Huang, Reyko. 2016b. *The Wartime Origins of Democratization: Civil War, Rebel Governance, and Political Regimes*. Cambridge University Press.

Huband, Mark. 1998. *The Liberian Civil War*. Frank Cass.

Humphreys, Macartan, and Jeremy M. Weinstein. 2008. "Who Fights? The Determinants of Participation in Civil War." *American Journal of Political Science* 52 (2): 436–55.

Huntington, Samuel P. 1968. *Political Order in Changing Societies*. Yale University Press.

Ibáñez, Ana María, Ana Arjona, Julián Arteaga, Juan C. Cárdenas, and Patricia Justino. 2023. "The Long-Term Economic Legacies of Rebel Rule in Civil War: Micro Evidence from Colombia." *Journal of Conflict Resolution* 68 (9): 1825–55.

Ibrahim, Amira. 2009. *Libya: A Critical Review of Tripoli's Sub-Saharan African Policies*. Institute for Security Studies.

Ibrahimi, Niamatullah, and Shahram Akbarzadeh. 2020. "Intra-Jihadist Conflict and Cooperation: Islamic State–Khorasan Province and the Taliban in Afghanistan." *Studies in Conflict & Terrorism* 43 (12): 1086–1107.

Ibrahimi, S. Yaqub. 2017. "The Taliban's Islamic Emirate of Afghanistan (1996–2001): 'War-Making and State-Making' as an Insurgency Strategy." *Small Wars and Insurgencies* 28 (6): 947–72.

Independent Working Group. 1993. *Report on the Ugandan Economy*. Government Printer.

INEC. 1990. *ESDENIC '85: Encuesta Socio-Demográfica Nicaragüense, Informe General*. Instituto Nacional de Estadísticas y Censos. IHNCA/FN,304.6,I59r.

Ingelaere, Bert, Réginas Ndayiragije, and Marijke Verpoorten. 2022. "Political Representation in the Wake of Ethnic Violence and Post-Conflict Institutional Reform: Comparing Views from Rwandan and Burundian Citizens." WIDER Working Paper 2022 /142. UNU-WIDER. https://doi.org/10.35188/UNU-WIDER/2022/275-1.

Innes, Michael A. 2005a. "Denial-of-Resource Operations and NPFL Radio Dominance in the Liberian Civil War." *Civil Wars* 7 (3): 288–309.

Innes, Michael A. 2005b. "Reading Guerrilla Radio in Wartime Liberia." *Small Wars & Insurgencies* 16 (2): 241–51.

Inter-American Commission on Human Rights. 1978. *Report on the Situation of Human Rights in Nicaragua.* Inter-American Commission on Human Rights, Organization of American States.

Interim National Council. 2011. "A Vision of a Democratic Libya." *The Guardian,* March 29.

International Institute for Strategic Studies. 1996. *The Military Balance 1996–1997.* International Institute for Strategic Studies. https://doi.org/10.1080/04597229608460099.

Iqbal, Zaryab. 2010. *War and the Health of Nations.* Stanford University Press.

Isar, Sarajuddin. 2025. "Taliban Economy and Regional Integration: Challenges, Pitfalls and Prospects." Andiana Foundation. https://www.andianafoundation.org/_files/ugd/612119_eeaede03300f42298424ffb15fc0113e.pdf.

Ishiyama, John. 2016. "Introduction to the Special Issue 'From Bullets to Ballots: The Transformation of Rebel Groups into Political Parties.'" *Democratization* 23 (6): 969–71.

Jackson, Ashley. 2022. "The Ban on Older Girls' Education: Taleban Conservatives Ascendant and a Leadership in Disarray." Afghanistan Analysts Network. https://www.afghanistan-analysts.org/en/reports/rights-freedom/the-ban-on-older-girls-education-taleban-conservatives-ascendant-and-a-leadership-in-disarray/.

Jackson, Ashley, and Florian Weigand. 2019. "The Taliban's War for Legitimacy in Afghanistan." *Current History* 118 (807): 143–48.

Jackson, Ashley, and Florian Weigand. 2023. "How the Taliban Are Losing the Peace in Afghanistan." *Current History* 122 (843): 143–48.

Jackson, Robert H., and Carl G. Rosberg. 1982. "Why Africa's Weak States Persist: The Empirical and the Juridical in Statehood." *World Politics* 35 (1): 1–24.

Jacobs, Alan M. 2015. "Process Tracing the Effects of Ideas." In *Process Tracing: From Metaphor to Analytic Tool,* edited by Andrew Bennett and Jeffrey T. Checkel, 41–73. Cambridge University Press.

James, Larry. 1986. "Quiwonkpa's Fatal Gamble." *Africa Report* 31 (1): 47–49.

Jarquín, Edmundo, ed. 2016. *El Régimen de Ortega: ¿Una Nueva Dictadura Familiar en el Continente?* PAVSA.

Jarquín, Mateo. 2020. "A la Sombra de la Revolución Sandinista: Nicaragua, 1979–2019." In *Anhelos de un Nuevo Horizonte: Aportes para una Nicaragua Democrática,* edited by Alberto Cortés Ramos, Umanzor López Baltodano, and Ludwing Moncada Bellorin, 55–77. FLACSO.

Jarquín, Mateo. 2024. *The Sandinista Revolution: A Global Latin American History.* University of North Carolina Press.

Jo, Hyeran. 2015. *Compliant Rebels: Rebel Groups and International Law in World Politics.* Cambridge University Press.

Johnson, Chalmers A. 1962. "Civilian Loyalties and Guerrilla Conflict." *World Politics* 14 (4): 646–61.

Johnson, Jennifer. 2016. *The Battle for Algeria: Sovereignty, Health Care, and Humanitarianism.* University of Pennsylvania Press.

Johnson, Prince Yeduo. 1991. *The Gun That Liberates Should Not Rule: The Philosophy of the I.N.P.F.L.* Pax Cornwell.

Johnston, Patrick. 2004. "Timber Booms, State Busts: The Political Economy of Liberian Timber." *Review of African Political Economy* 31 (101): 441–56.

Johnston, Patrick. 2008. "The Geography of Insurgent Organization and Its Consequences for Civil Wars: Evidence from Liberia and Sierra Leone." *Security Studies* 17 (1): 107–37.

Jones, Ben. 2009. *Beyond the State in Rural Uganda*. Edinburgh University Press.

Joseph, Were. 1993. "Inside Mchakamchaka: 'Amin Tried, UPC Good, NRM Best.'"
Monitor, September 21. CBR-NRM-1.

Judah, Tim. 2000. *Kosovo: War and Revenge*. Yale University Press.

Junta de Gobierno de Reconstrucción Nacional. 1979. *Programa de Gobierno de Reconstrucción Nacional*. Ministerio de Educación. IHNCA/FN,324.23,N583a.

Jureldini, Paul A. 1963. *Case Studies in Insurgency and Revolutionary Warfare: Algeria
1954–1962*. Special Operations Research Office, American University.

Kabwegyere, Tarsis Bazana. 2000. *People's Choice, People's Power: Challenges and Prospects of Democracy in Uganda*. Fountain.

Kagoro, Barbara. 1989. "Boost Health Spending—YM." *New Vision*, April 25.
CBR-Health-1.

Kaldor, Mary. 1999. *New and Old Wars: Organized Violence in a Global Era*. Stanford
University Press.

Kaldor, Mary. 2013. "In Defence of New Wars." *Stability* 2 (1): art. 4. https://doi
.org/10.5334/sta.at.

Kaltenthaler, Karl, Arie W. Kruglanski, and Austin J. Knuppe. 2024. "The Paradox of
the Heavy-Handed Insurgent: Public Support for the Taliban Among Afghan
Pashtuns." *Studies in Conflict and Terrorism* 47 (12): 1699–1723.

Kalyvas, Stathis N. 2006. *The Logic of Violence in Civil War*. Cambridge University
Press.

Kalyvas, Stathis N. 2009. "Civil Wars." In *The Oxford Handbook of Comparative Politics*, edited by Carles Boix and Susan C. Stokes, 416–34. Oxford University Press.

Kalyvas, Stathis N. 2015a. "Is ISIS a Revolutionary Group and if Yes, What Are the
Implications?" *Perspectives on Terrorism* 9 (4): 42–47.

Kalyvas, Stathis N. 2015b. "Rebel Governance During the Greek Civil War, 1942–1949."
In *Rebel Governance in Civil War*, edited by Ana Arjona, Nelson Kasfir, and
Zachariah Mampilly, 119–37. Cambridge University Press.

Kalyvas, Stathis N., and Laia Balcells. 2010. "International System and Technologies of
Rebellion: How the End of the Cold War Shaped Internal Conflict." *American
Political Science Review* 104 (3): 415–29.

Kammen, Douglas. 2019. *Independent Timor-Leste: Between Coercion and Consent*.
Cambridge University Press.

Kandeh, Jimmy D. 1996. "What Does the 'Militariat' Do When It Rules? Military
Regimes: The Gambia, Sierra Leone and Liberia." *Review of African Political
Economy* 23 (69): 387–404.

Kandel, Matt. 2018. "State Formation and the Politics of Land in North-Eastern
Uganda." *African Affairs* 117 (467): 261–85.

Kanyongo, Gibbs Y. 2005. "Zimbabwe's Public Education System Reforms: Successes
and Challenges." *International Education Journal* 6 (1): 65–74.

Kardaş, Şaban. 2025. "Turkey's Long Game in Syria: Moving Beyond Ascendance."
Middle East Policy 32 (1): 22–37.

Karugire, Samwiri. 1996. *Roots of Instability in Uganda*. Fountain.

Kasfir, Nelson. 1976. *The Shrinking Political Arena: Participation and Ethnicity in African Politics, with a Case Study of Uganda*. University of California Press.

Kasfir, Nelson. 1998. "'No-Party Democracy' in Uganda." *Journal of Democracy* 9 (2):
49–63.

Kasfir, Nelson. 2000. "'Movement' Democracy, Legitimacy and Power in Uganda." In *No-Party Democracy in Uganda: Myths and Realities*, edited by Justus Mugaju and J. Oloka-Onyango, 60–78. Fountain.

Kasfir, Nelson. 2005. "Guerrillas and Civilian Participation: The National Resistance Army in Uganda, 1981–86." *Journal of Modern African Studies* 43 (2): 271–96.

Kasfir, Nelson. 2015. "Rebel Governance—Constructing a Field of Inquiry: Definitions, Scope, Patterns, Order, Causes." In *Rebel Governance in Civil War*, edited by Ana Arjona, Nelson Kasfir, and Zachariah Mampilly, 21–46. Cambridge University Press.

Kasfir, Nelson. 2024. "Legacies of Victors' Rebel Governance." *Civil Wars*, forthcoming. https://doi.org/10.1080/13698249.2024.2318686.

Kasozi, A. B. K. 1994. *The Social Origins of Violence in Uganda, 1964–1985*. McGill-Queen's University Press.

Kasza, Gregory J. 1995. *The Conscription Society: Administered Mass Organizations*. Yale University Press.

Katumba-Wamala, Edward. 2000. "The National Resistance Army (NRA) as a Guerrilla Force." *Small Wars & Insurgencies* 11 (3): 160–71.

Katzman, Kenneth. 1993. "The Pasdaran: Institutionalization of Revolutionary Armed Force." *Iranian Studies* 26 (3–4): 389–402.

Kawamara, Sheila. 1993. "Rural Pupils Fail PLE." *New Vision*, February 3. CBR-Primary Education-1.

Kayunga, Sallie Simba. 2001. "The No-Party System of Democracy and the Management of Ethnic Conflicts in Uganda." PhD diss., Roskilde University.

Kazemi, S. Reza, and Kate Clark. 2022. "Who Gets to Go to School? (2) The Taleban and Education Through Time." Afghanistan Analysts Network. https://www.afghanistan-analysts.org/en/reports/rights-freedom/going-back-to-school-2-looking-at-the-taleban-and-education-through-time/.

Keddie, Nikki R. 2006. *Modern Iran: Roots and Results of Revolution*. Yale University Press.

Khan, Qutub. 1991. "Primary Education in Uganda—Some Observations." In *Education for Development*, edited by Syed A. H. Abidi, 9–20. Foundation for African Development.

Khatib, Dania Koleilat. 2021. "Iran and 'Exporting' the Revolution: The Syrian Case." In *The Syrian Crisis: Effects on the Regional and International Relations*, edited by Dania Koleilat Khatib, 69–86. Springer.

Khisa, Moses. 2013. "The Making of the 'Informal State' in Uganda." *Africa Development* 38 (1–2): 191–226.

Khisa, Moses. 2019. "Shrinking Democratic Space? Crisis of Consensus and Contentious Politics in Uganda." *Commonwealth and Comparative Politics* 57 (3): 343–62.

Khisa, Moses. 2023. "Uganda's Ruling Coalition and the 2021 Elections: Change, Continuity and Contestation." *Journal of Eastern African Studies* 17 (1–2): 325–43.

Khomeini, Ruhollah. 2002. *Islamic Government: Governance of the Jurist*. Institute for Compilation and Publication of Imam Khomeini's Works.

Kieh, George Klay. 1992. "Combatants, Patrons, Peacemakers, and the Liberian Civil Conflict." *Studies in Conflict & Terrorism* 15 (2): 125–43.

Kieh, George Klay. 2007. "The Human Development Crisis in Liberia: Taproot and Dimensions." *Journal of Sustainable Development in Africa* 9 (1): 78–94.

Kieh, George Klay. 2024. "The Movement for Justice in Africa and Democratisation in Liberia." In *Revolutionary Movements in Africa: An Untold Story*, edited by Paolo Bianchini, Ndongo Samba Sylla, and Leo Zeilig, 121–40. Pluto.

Kiiza, Julius. 1993. "The Cost and Implications of Cost-Sharing in the Education Sector of Developing Countries: Lessons from Uganda." Presented at the Workshop on

Institution Building and Institutional Reform, Makerere University, Kampala, December 12.

Kinzer, Stephen. 2007. *Blood of Brothers: Life and War in Nicaragua*. David Rockefeller Center for Latin American Studies, Harvard University.

Kisekka, Samson. 1992. *Challenges to Leadership in the Developing World: Speeches of Dr. Samson Kisekka, Vice-President of the Republic of Uganda*. Kisekka Foundation.

Kiwanuka, Frederick. 1994. "Luwero: 'We Won the War to No Avail.'" *Sunday Vision*, January 16. CBR.

Kiyaga-Nsubuga, John. 1995. "Political Instability and the Struggle for Control in Uganda, 1970–1990." PhD diss., University of Toronto.

Kiyaga-Nsubuga, John. 1997. "From 'Communists' to Neo-Liberals: The Transformation of the National Resistance Movement (NRM) Regime's Economic Policy, 1986–1989." Working Paper, Department of Political Science and Public Administration, Makerere University.

Kiyaga-Nsubuga, John. 2004. "Uganda: The Politics of 'Consolidation' Under Museveni's Regime, 1996–2003." In *Durable Peace: Challenges for Peacebuilding in Africa*, edited by Taisier M. Ali and Robert O. Matthews, 86–112. University of Toronto Press.

Kjaer, Anne Mette. 2004. "'Old Brooms Can Sweep Too!' An Overview of Rulers and Public Sector Reforms in Uganda, Tanzania and Kenya." *Journal of Modern African Studies* 42 (3): 389–413.

Knott, Eleanor. 2019. "Beyond the Field: Ethics After Fieldwork in Politically Dynamic Contexts." *Perspectives on Politics* 17 (1): 140–53.

Kornbluh, Peter. 1988. "Nicaragua: U.S. Proinsurgency Warfare Against the Sandinistas." In *Low-Intensity Warfare*, edited by Michael T. Klare and Peter Kornbluh, 136–57. Pantheon.

Kornbluh, Peter. 1991. "The U.S. Role in the Counterrevolution." In *Revolution & Counterrevolution in Nicaragua*, edited by Thomas W. Walker, 323–49. Westview.

Krause, Peter. 2017. *Rebel Power: Why National Movements Compete, Fight, and Win*. Cornell University Press.

Kruijt, Dirk. 2008. *Guerrillas: War and Peace in Central America*. Zed.

Kruijt, Dirk. 2017. *Cuba and Revolutionary Latin America: An Oral History*. Zed.

Kubota, Yuichi. 2017. "Imagined Statehood: Wartime Rebel Governance and Post-War Subnational Identity in Sri Lanka." *World Development* 90 (2): 199–212.

Kun, Katherine. 2008. "Counting the Costs of War: Human Rights Abuses in Montserrado County During the Liberian Conflict." *Women's World*, no. 43, 15–18.

Kutesa, Pecos. 2006. *Uganda's Revolution: How I Saw It*. Fountain.

Lachapelle, Jean, Steven Levitsky, Lucan A. Way, and Adam E. Casey. 2020. "Social Revolution and Authoritarian Durability." *World Politics* 72 (4): 557–600.

Lacher, Wolfram. 2020. *Libya's Fragmentation: Structure and Process in Violent Conflict*. Tauris.

Ladbury, Sarah. 2009. "Testing Hypotheses on Radicalisation in Afghanistan." Cooperation for Peace and Unity. http://dx.doi.org/10.2458/azu_acku_pamphlet_ds371 _3_l333_2009.

Lai, Brian, and Clayton Thyne. 2007. "The Effect of Civil War on Education, 1980–97." *Journal of Peace Research* 44 (3): 277–92.

Lake, David A. 2016. *The Statebuilder's Dilemma: On the Limits of Foreign Intervention*. Cornell University Press.

Lake, David A., and Matthew A. Baum. 2001. "The Invisible Hand of Democracy: Political Control and the Provision of Public Services." *Comparative Political Studies* 34 (6): 587–621.

Lambright, Gina M. S. 2011. *Decentralization in Uganda: Explaining Successes and Failures in Local Governance*. FirstForum.

Lamwaka, Caroline. 1996. "TB Immunisation Drops." *New Vision*, July 19. CBR-Health-2.

Landau-Wells, Marika. 2018. "High Stakes and Low Bars: International Recognition of Governments During Civil Wars." *International Security* 43 (1): 100–137.

Larkin, Greg. 1987. "NRM and Uganda's Realities." *Ufahamu: A Journal of African Studies* 15 (3): 156–66.

Lawoti, Mahendra, and Anup Kumar Pahari, eds. 2010. *The Maoist Insurgency in Nepal: Revolution in the Twenty-First Century*. Routledge.

Lawson, George. 2019. *Anatomies of Revolution*. Cambridge University Press.

Lee, Melissa M. 2022. "International Statebuilding and the Domestic Politics of State Development." *Annual Review of Political Science* 25: 261–81.

Lee, Melissa M., and Nan Zhang. 2016. "Legibility and the Informational Foundations of State Capacity." *Journal of Politics* 79 (1): 118–32.

LeoGrande, William M. 1996. "Making the Economy Scream: US Economic Sanctions Against Sandinista Nicaragua." *Third World Quarterly* 17 (2): 329–48.

Leopold, Mark. 2005. *Inside West Nile*. James Currey.

Levi, Margaret. 1988. *Of Rule and Revenue*. University of California Press.

Levitsky, Steven, and Lucan Way. 2010. *Competitive Authoritarianism: Hybrid Regimes After the Cold War*. Cambridge University Press.

Levitsky, Steven, and Lucan Way. 2022. *Revolution and Dictatorship: The Violent Origins of Durable Authoritarianism*. Princeton University Press.

Levitt, Jeremy I. 2005. *The Evolution of Deadly Conflict in Liberia*. Carolina Academic Press.

Lewis, Janet I. 2012. "How Rebellion Begins: Insurgent Group Formation and Viability in Uganda." PhD diss., Harvard University.

Lewis, Janet I. 2020. *How Insurgency Begins: Rebel Group Formation in Uganda and Beyond*. Cambridge University Press.

Liberty, C. E. Zamba. 1998. "Butuo: A Lilliputian Testament to a Struggle–The NPFL Journey to State-Power: How Charles Taylor Upset the Bowl of Rice and Took Home the Whole Hog . . ." *Liberian Studies Journal* 23 (1): 135–207.

Licklider, Roy. 1995. "The Consequences of Negotiated Settlements in Civil Wars, 1945–1993." *American Political Science Review* 89 (3): 681–90.

Lidow, Nicholai. 2016. *Violent Order: Understanding Rebel Governance Through Liberia's Civil War*. Cambridge University Press.

Liebenow, J. Gus. 1969. *Liberia: The Evolution of Privilege*. Cornell University Press.

Liebenow, J. Gus. 1987. *Liberia: The Quest for Democracy*. Indiana University Press.

Lieberman, Evan S. 2002. "Taxation Data as Indicators of State-Society Relations: Possibilities and Pitfalls in Cross-National Research." *Studies in Comparative International Development* 36 (4): 89–115.

Lijphart, Arend. 1977. *Democracy in Plural Societies: A Comparative Exploration*. Yale University Press.

Lindemann, Stefan. 2011. "Just Another Change of Guard? Broad-Based Politics and Civil War in Museveni's Uganda." *African Affairs* 110 (440): 387–416.

Linz, Juan J. 1975. "Totalitarian and Authoritarian Regimes." In *Handbook of Political Science*, vol. 3, edited by Fred I. Greenstein and Nelson W. Polsby, 175–411. Addison-Wesley.

Liu, Shelley X. 2022. "Control, Coercion, and Cooptation: How Rebels Govern After Winning Civil War." *World Politics* 74 (1): 37–76.

Liu, Shelley X. 2024. *Governing After War: Rebel Victories and Post-War Statebuilding*. Oxford University Press.

López Baltodano, Umanzor. 2020. "Del Sultanismo a la Democracia: El Régimen Político de Nicaragua." In *Anhelos de un Nuevo Horizonte: Aportes para una Nicaragua Democrática*, edited by Alberto Cortés Ramos, Umanzor López Baltodano, and Ludwing Moncada Bellorin, 135–74. FLACSO.

Lowenkopf, Martin. 1976. *Politics in Liberia: The Conservative Road to Development.* Hoover Institution Press.

Lowenkopf, Martin. 1995. "Liberia: Putting the State Back Together." In *Collapsed States: The Disintegration and Restoration of Legitimate Order*, edited by I. William Zartman, 91–108. Lynne Rienner.

Lowenthal, Abraham, ed. 1975. *The Peruvian Experiment: Continuity and Change Under Military Rule.* Princeton University Press.

Lowenthal, Richard. 1970. "Development vs. Utopia in Communist Policy." In *Change in Communist Systems*, edited by Chalmers Johnson, 33–116. Stanford University Press.

Loxley, John. 1989. "The IMF, the World Bank and Reconstruction in Uganda." In *Structural Adjustment in Africa*, edited by Bonnie K. Campbell and John Loxley, 67–91. MacMillan.

Loyle, Cyanne E., Kathleen Gallagher Cunningham, Reyko Huang, and Danielle F. Jung. 2023. "New Directions in Rebel Governance Research." *Perspectives on Politics* 21 (1): 264–76.

Luciak, Ilja A. 1990. "Democracy in the Nicaraguan Countryside: A Comparative Analysis of Sandinista Grassroots Movements." *Latin American Perspectives* 17 (3): 55–75.

Lucima, Otim. 1993. "Why Rural Primary Schools Perform Badly." *Weekly Topic*, April 16. CBR-Primary Education-1.

Luttwak, Edward N. 1999. "Give War a Chance." *Foreign Affairs* 78 (4): 36–44.

Lyall, Jason. 2015. "Process Tracing, Causal Inference, and Civil War." In *Process Tracing: From Metaphor to Analytic Tool*, edited by Andrew Bennett and Jeffrey T. Checkel, 186–207. Cambridge University Press.

Lyall, Jason, and Isaiah Wilson. 2009. "Rage Against the Machines: Explaining Outcomes in Counterinsurgency Wars." *International Organization* 63 (1): 67–106.

Lynch, Marc. 2013. "Shopping Option C for Syria." *Foreign Policy*, February 14. http://foreignpolicy.com/2013/02/14/shopping-option-c-for-syria/.

Lyons, Terrence. 1998a. "Peace and Elections in Liberia." In *Postconflict Elections, Democratization, and International Assistance*, edited by Krishna Kumar, 177–94. Lynne Rienner.

Lyons, Terrence. 1998b. *Voting for Peace: Postconflict Elections in Liberia.* Brookings Institution Press.

Lyons, Terrence. 2016a. "From Victorious Rebels to Strong Authoritarian Parties: Prospects for Post-War Democratization." *Democratization* 23 (6): 1026–41.

Lyons, Terrence. 2016b. "The Importance of Winning: Victorious Insurgent Groups and Authoritarian Politics." *Comparative Politics* 48 (2): 167–84.

Lyons, Terrence. 2019. *The Puzzle of Ethiopian Politics.* Lynne Rienner.

Lyons, Terrence. 2021. "The Origins of the EPRDF and the Prospects for the Prosperity Party." *Journal of Asian and African Studies* 56 (5): 1051–63.

Macrae, Joanna, Anthony B. Zwi, and Lucy Gilson. 1996. "A Triple Burden for Health Sector Reform: 'Post'-Conflict Rehabilitation in Uganda." *Social Science & Medicine* 42 (7): 1095–1108.

Maddy-Weitzman, Bruce. 2011. *The Berber Identity Movement and the Challenge to North African States.* University of Texas Press.

Maier, Karl. 1997. "Angola: Peace at Last?" *Refugee Survey Quarterly* 16 (2): 1–23.

Malaquias, Assis. 2007. *Rebels and Robbers: Violence in Post-Colonial Angola.* Nordiska Afrikainstitutet.

Malaquias, Assis. 2010. "UNITA's Insurgency Lifecycle in Angola." In *Violent Non-State Actors in World Politics*, edited by Klejda Mulaj, 293–317. Hurst.

Malejacq, Romain. 2020. *Warlord Survival: The Delusion of State Building in Afghanistan*. Cornell University Press.

Malejacq, Romain, and Dipali Mukhopadhyay. 2016. "The 'Tribal Politics' of Field Research: A Reflection on Power and Partiality in 21st-Century Warzones." *Perspectives on Politics* 14 (4): 1011–28.

Malejacq, Romain, and Niels Terpstra. 2023. "Why International Leverage Has Failed with the Taliban." *Lawfare*, July 30. https://www.lawfaremedia.org/article/why-international-leverage-has-failed-with-the-taliban.

Maley, William. 2009. *The Afghanistan Wars*. Palgrave Macmillan.

Malley, Robert. 2023. *The Call from Algeria: Third Worldism, Revolution, and the Turn to Islam*. University of California Press.

Maloney, Suzanne. 2015. *Iran's Political Economy Since the Revolution*. Cambridge University Press.

Mamdani, Mahmood. 1976. *Politics and Class Formation in Uganda*. Monthly Review Press.

Mamdani, Mahmood. 1988. "Uganda in Transition: Two Years of the NRA/NRM." *Third World Quarterly* 10 (3): 1155–81.

Mamdani, Mahmood. 1995. *And Fire Does Not Always Beget Ash: Critical Reflections in the NRM*. Monitor.

Mamdani, Mahmood. 2007. *Scholars in the Marketplace: The Dilemmas of Neo-Liberal Reform at Makerere University, 1989–2005*. CODESRIA.

Mampilly, Zachariah. 2011. *Rebel Rulers: Insurgent Governance and Civilian Life During Civil War*. Cornell University Press.

Mampilly, Zachariah, and Megan A. Stewart. 2021. "A Typology of Rebel Political Institutional Arrangements." *Journal of Conflict Resolution* 65 (1): 15–45.

Mangen, S. P. 2001. *Spanish Society After Franco: Regime Transition and the Welfare State*. Palgrave Macmillan.

Manion, Megan, Robert Ralston, Thandi Matthews, and Ian Allen. 2017. "Budget Analysis as a Tool to Monitor Economic and Social Rights: Where the Rubber of International Commitment Meets the Road of Government Policy." *Journal of Human Rights Practice* 9 (1): 146–58.

Mann, Laura, and Marie Berry. 2016. "Understanding the Political Motivations That Shape Rwanda's Emergent Developmental State." *New Political Economy* 21 (1): 119–44.

Mann, Michael. 1986. *The Sources of Social Power: A History of Power from the Beginning to A.D. 1760*, vol. 1. Cambridge University Press.

Mann, Michael. 1988. *The Autonomous Power of the State: Its Origins, Mechanisms and Results*. Basil Blackwell.

Mann, Michael. 1993. *The Sources of Social Power: Volume 2, The Rise of Classes and Nation-States, 1760–1914*. Cambridge University Press.

Manning, Carrie, Ian O. Smith, and Ozlem Tuncel. 2024. "Rebels with a Cause: Introducing the Post-Rebel Electoral Parties Dataset." *Journal of Peace Research* 61 (2): 294–303.

Mansfield, David. 2016. *A State Built on Sand: How Opium Undermined Afghanistan*. Oxford University Press.

Mao, Tse-Tung. 1962. *On Guerrilla Warfare*. Praeger.

Marcum, John A. 1964. "The Angola Rebellion: Status Report." *Africa Report* 9 (2): 3–7.

Marcum, John A. 1967. "Three Revolutions." *Africa Report* 12 (8): 8–22.

Marcum, John A. 1969. *The Angolan Revolution, Vol. 1: Anatomy of an Explosion*. MIT Press.

Marcum, John A. 1975. "The Anguish of Angola: On Becoming Independent in the Last Quarter of the Twentieth Century." *Issue: A Journal of Opinion* 5 (4): 3–11.

Marcum, John A. 2018. *Conceiving Mozambique*. Palgrave Macmillan.

Markoff, John, and Silvio R. Duncan Baretta. 1985. "Professional Ideology and Military Activism in Brazil: Critique of a Thesis of Alfred Stepan." *Comparative Politics* 17 (2): 175–91.

Martí i Puig, Salvador. 2010. "The Adaptation of the FSLN: Daniel Ortega's Leadership and Democracy in Nicaragua." *Latin American Politics and Society* 52 (4): 79–106.

Martí i Puig, Salvador, and Macià Serra. 2020. "Nicaragua: De-Democratization and Regime Crisis." *Latin American Politics and Society* 62 (2): 117–36.

Martin, Philip A. 2021. "Commander–Community Ties After Civil War." *Journal of Peace Research* 58 (4): 778–93.

Martin, Philip A., Giulia Piccolino, and Jeremy S. Speight. 2022. "The Political Legacies of Rebel Rule: Evidence from a Natural Experiment in Côte d'Ivoire." *Comparative Political Studies* 55 (9): 1439–70.

Matfess, Hilary. 2022. "Alms, Arms, and the Aftermath: The Legacies of Rebel Provision of Humanitarian Aid in Ethiopia." *African Affairs* 121 (483): 197–220.

Matfess, Hilary, and Terrence Lyons. 2023. "Proxy Wars in the Horn of Africa." In *Routledge Handbook of Proxy Wars*, edited by Assaf Moghadam, Vladimir Rauta, and Michel Wyss, 311–25. Routledge.

Matinuddin, Kamal. 1999. *The Taliban Phenomenon Afghanistan 1994–1997*. Oxford University Press.

Matsinhe, David M., and Estacio Valoi. 2019. "The Genesis of Insurgency in Northern Mozambique." Southern Africa Report 27. Institute for Security Studies.

Maynard, Jonathan Leader. 2019. "Ideology and Armed Conflict." *Journal of Peace Research* 56 (5): 635–49.

Maynard, Jonathan Leader, and Kai Thaler. 2018. "Correspondence: Ideological Extremism in Armed Conflict." *International Security* 43 (1): 186–90.

Mazrui, Ali A. 2000. "Between Domestic Policy and Regional Power: The Role of Ideology in Uganda." In *No-Party Democracy in Uganda: Myths and Realities*, edited by Justus Mugaju and J. Oloka-Onyango, 127–40. Fountain.

McClintock, Cynthia. 1998. *Revolutionary Movements in Latin America: El Salvador's FMLN and Peru's Shining Path*. US Institute of Peace Press.

McDonough, David S. 2008. "From Guerrillas to Government: Post-Conflict Stability in Liberia, Uganda and Rwanda." *Third World Quarterly* 29 (2): 357–74.

McDoom, Omar Shahabuddin. 2022. "Securocratic State-Building: The Rationales, Rebuttals, and Risks Behind the Extraordinary Rise of Rwanda After the Genocide." *African Affairs* 121 (485): 535–67.

McGovern, Mike. 2010. *Making War in Côte d'Ivoire*. University of Chicago Press.

Meert, Abigail. 2020. "Suffering, Consent, and Coercion in Uganda: The Luwero War." *International Journal of African Historical Studies* 53 (3): 389–412.

Melber, Henning. 2002. "From Liberation Movements to Governments: On Political Culture in Southern Africa." *African Sociological Review* 6 (1): 161–72.

Mendelsohn, Barak. 2024. "Casting Shadow: Founders and the Unique Challenges of a Terrorist Group's First Leadership Change." *Studies in Conflict & Terrorism* 47 (10): 1147–71.

Meringer, Eric Rodrigo. 2019. "The Company Times: Neocolonialism and Ethnic Relations on Nicaragua's Caribbean Coast in the Twentieth Century." In *Indigenous*

Struggles for Autonomy: The Caribbean Coast of Nicaragua, edited by Luciano Baracco, 33–51. Lexington Books.

Mesa-Lago, Carmelo. 2023. "Cuba's Economy in Times of Crisis: 2020–2022 and Prospects for 2023." *Cuban Research Institute Occasional Papers*. Florida International University. https://cri.fiu.edu/_assets/docs/cuba-economic-crisis.pdf.

MIDINRA. 1984. *Notas Sobre Campesinado, Revolución y Contrarrevolución: Zelaya Central*. Dirección General de Reforma Agraria, Centro de Investigación y Estudio de la Reforma Agraria. IHNCA/FN,305.563,3,N583.

Migdal, Joel. 1988. *Strong Societies and Weak States: State-Society Relations and State Capabilities in the Third World*. Princeton University Press.

Migdal, Joel. 2001. *State in Society: Studying How States and Societies Transform and Constitute One Another*. Cambridge University Press.

Millett, Richard L. 1977. *Guardians of the Dynasty*. Orbis.

MINED. 1980a. *La Educación en el Primer Año de la Revolución Popular Sandinista*. Ministerio de Educación. IHNCA/FN,379.24,N583c.

MINED. 1980b. *Manual del Brigadista*. Cruzada Nacional de Alfabetización, Ministerio de Educación. IHNCA/FN,374.012,N583a.

MINED. 1982. *La Educación En Tres Años de Revolución*. Ministerio de Educación. IHNCA/FN,379.972 85,N583a.

Ministerio del Desarollo Agropecuario. 1980. *La Encuesta a los Trabajadores del Campo: Levantada por los Brigadistas de la Cruzada Nacional de Alfabetización*. Centro de Investigación y Estudio de la Reforma Agraria. IHCA/FN,305.563,N583.

Ministerio del Interior. 1989. *El MINT En Cifras, 1979–1989*. Ministerio del Interior. IHCA/FN,363.1,N583.

Ministry of Health. 1990. *Health Cost-Sharing Policy: Statement by Honourable Z. K. R. Kaheru, Minister of Health*. Ministry of Health.

Ministry of Health. 1993. *The Three Year Health Plan Frame, 1993/94–1995/96*. Ministry of Health.

MINSA. 1980. *Salud: Políticas, Logros y Limitaciones*. Ministerio de Salud. IHNCA/FN,353.6,N583e.

MINSA. 1981. *Informe 1980*. Ministerio de Salud. IHNCA/FN,7656.

MINSA. 1989a. *Leyes Relativas a Salud, 1979–1989*. Ministerio de Salud. IHNCA/AV,362.1c.

MINSA. 1989b. *Principales Logros de la Revolución en Salud (Gráficos)*. Ministerio de Salud. IHNCA/FN,362.1,N583y.

Minter, William, ed. 1988. *Operation Timber: Pages from the Savimbi Dossier*. Africa World Press.

Mirembe, Sarah, and Hamis Kaheru. 1994. "Education in Crisis, 100,000 Fail Exams." *Monitor*, January 28. CBR-Primary Education-1.

Mittelman, James H. 1975. *Ideology and Politics in Uganda: From Obote to Amin*. Cornell University Press.

Monitor. 1996. "10 Years of NRM: The Good and Bad." *Monitor*, January 26. CBR-NRM-5.

Montgomery, Tommie Sue. 1982. *Revolution in El Salvador: Origins and Evolution*. Westview.

Moore, David B. 1991. "The Ideological Formation of the Zimbabwean Ruling Class." *Journal of Southern African Studies* 17 (3): 472–95.

Moro, Justine. 1996. "Kony Rebels Kill 70 Teachers." *New Vision*, July 18. CBR-Primary Education-2.

Mosinger, Eric. 2019. "Balance of Loyalties: Explaining Rebel Factional Struggles in the Nicaraguan Revolution." *Security Studies* 28 (5): 935–75.

Mosinger, Eric, Kai M. Thaler, Diana Paz García, and Charlotte Fowler. 2022. "Civil Resistance in the Shadow of the Revolution: Historical Framing in Nicaraguan's Sudden Uprising." *Comparative Politics* 54 (2): 253–77.

Motadel, David. 2014. "Introduction." In *Islam and the European Empires*, edited by David Motadel, 1–32. Oxford University Press.

MPEA and UNDP Liberia. 2006. *National Human Development Report 2006 Liberia: Mobilizing Capacity for Reconstruction and Development*. Ministry of Planning and Economic Affairs and United Nations Development Programme.

Mudde, Cas, and Cristóbal Rovira Kaltwasser. 2013. "Exclusionary vs. Inclusionary Populism: Comparing Contemporary Europe and Latin America." *Government and Opposition* 48 (2): 147–74.

Mueller, John. 2004. *The Remnants of War*. Cornell University Press.

Mugisa, Anne. 1995. "'Health Budget Stresses Cure.'" *New Vision*, December 5. CBR-Health-2.

Mugote, Teddy. 1989. "Illiteracy Campaign to Be Launched Soon." *New Vision*, May 29. MUL-New Vision-April/June.

Muhumuza, William. 2009. "From Fundamental Change to No Change: The NRM and Democratization in Uganda." *IFRA-Les Cahiers*, no. 41, 21–42.

Mujaju, Akiiki B. 1997. "Civil Society at Bay in Uganda." In *The State and Democracy in Africa*, edited by Georges Nzongola-Ntalaja and Margaret C. Lee, 42–52. Africa World Press.

Mukhopadhyay, Dipali. 2014. *Warlords, Strongman Governors, and the State in Afghanistan*. Cambridge University Press.

Mukhopadhyay, Dipali. 2022. "The Taliban Have Not Moderated." *Foreign Affairs*, March. https://www.foreignaffairs.com/afghanistan/taliban-have-not-moderated.

Mukhopadhyay, Dipali, and Kimberly Howe. 2023. *Good Rebel Governance: Revolutionary Politics and Western Intervention in Syria*. Cambridge University Press.

Müller-Crepon, Carl, Philipp Hunziker, and Lars Erik Cederman. 2021. "Roads to Rule, Roads to Rebel: Relational State Capacity and Conflict in Africa." *Journal of Conflict Resolution* 65 (2–3): 563–90.

Mumford, Andrew. 2013. "Proxy Warfare and the Future of Conflict." *RUSI Journal* 158 (2): 40–46.

Munive, Jairo. 2011. "A Political Economic History of the Liberian State, Forced Labour and Armed Mobilization." *Journal of Agrarian Change* 11 (3): 357–76.

Munslow, Barry, ed. 1985. *Samora Machel: An African Revolutionary, Selected Speeches and Writings*. Zed.

Murtazashvili, Jennifer Brick. 2016. *Informal Order and the State in Afghanistan*. Cambridge University Press.

Museveni, Yoweri K. 1971. "Fanon's Theory of Violence: Its Verification in Liberated Mozambique." In *Essays on the Liberation of Southern Africa*, edited by N. M. Shamuyarira, 1–24. Tanzanian Publishing House.

Museveni, Yoweri K. 1986. *Selected Articles on the Uganda Resistance War*. NRM Publications.

Museveni, Yoweri K. 1990. *Consolidating the Revolution*. Government Printer.

Museveni, Yoweri K. 1992. *What Is Africa's Problem?* NRM Publications.

Museveni, Yoweri K. 1994a. *Tackling the Tasks Ahead: Election Manifesto*. NRM Publications.

Museveni, Yoweri K. 1994b. "The Value of Political Education." *Daily Topic*, May 16. CBR-NRA-2.

Museveni, Yoweri K. 1997. *Sowing the Mustard Seed: The Struggle for Freedom and Democracy in Uganda*. MacMillan.

Musila, Jacob Wanjala, and Walid Balassi. 2004. "The Impact of Educational Expenditure on Economic Growth in Uganda: Evidence from Time Series Data." *Journal of Developing Areas* 38 (1): 123–33.

Musso, Marta. 2017. "'Oil Will Set Us Free': The Hydrocarbon Industry and the Algerian Decolonization Process." In *Britain, France and the Decolonization of Africa*, edited by Andrew W. M. Smith and Chris Jeppesen, 62–84. UCL Press.

Mutibwa, Phares. 1992. *Uganda Since Independence: A Story of Unfulfilled Hopes*. Fountain.

Muwanga, M. Mike, ed. 1993. *Selected Reminiscences of President Yoweri Museveni: Uganda's Exports*. Recent Magazine.

Nabudere, Dani Wadada. 1990. "The IMF-World Bank's Stabilisation and Structural Adjustment Policies and the Uganda Economy, 1981–1989." ASC Research Reports 39/1990. African Studies Centre Leiden.

Nagel, Joane, and Conrad W. Snyder. 1989. "International Funding of Educational Development: External Agendas and Internal Adaptations: The Case of Liberia." *Comparative Education Review* 33 (1): 3–20.

Nagubuzi, Emmanuel. 1995. "Popular Initiatives in Service Provision in Uganda." In *Service Provision Under Stress in East Africa*, edited by Joseph Semboja and Ole Therkildsen, 192–208. Centre for Development Research.

Namutebi, Joyce. 1996. "Uganda's Health Expenditure Low." *New Vision*, November 18. CBR-Health-5.

National Elections Commission. n.d. "Results Portal." Republic of Liberia National Elections Commission. https://results.necliberia.org/index.php.

New Vision. 1987. "Cadres Expose School Fraud." *New Vision*, August 18. CBR.

New Vision. 1990. "A 1984 Interview with Museveni." *New Vision*, January 26. CBR-NRM-1.

Ngoga, Pascal. 1998. "Uganda: The National Resistance Army." In *African Guerrillas*, edited by Christopher Clapham, 91–106. Indiana University Press.

Nikazmerad, Nicholas M. 1980. "A Chronological Survey of the Iranian Revolution." *Iranian Studies* 13 (1–4): 327–68.

Noack, Rick. 2023. "After Long Banning Polio Campaigns, Taliban Declares War on the Disease." *Washington Post*, December 5. https://www.washingtonpost.com/world/2023/12/05/taliban-afghanistan-polio-vaccination/.

Noack, Rick. 2024a. "Taliban Sets Sights on Making Afghanistan a Global Power in Cricket." *Washington Post*, March 7. https://www.washingtonpost.com/world/2024/02/27/afghanistan-kabul-taliban-cricket-sports/.

Noack, Rick. 2024b. "The Taliban Once Smashed TVs. Now It Fosters YouTubers to Promote Its Image." *Washington Post*, March 9. https://www.washingtonpost.com/world/2024/03/09/afghanistan-taliban-media-youtube-influencers/.

Noack, Rick, and Carolyn Van Houten. 2024. "As Climate Change Imperils Taliban's Shift from Opium, Impact Could Be Felt Worldwide." *Washington Post*, June 21. https://www.washingtonpost.com/world/2024/06/21/afghanistan-taliban-opium-climate-change/.

Noack, Rick, and Carolyn Van Houten. 2025. "A Taliban Highway Could Lead to the Future. But It's Stuck in the Past." *Washington Post*, February 1. https://www.washingtonpost.com/world/2025/02/01/wakhan-corridor-highway-afghanistan-china/.

Noer, Thomas J. 1993. "International Credibility and Political Survival: The Ford Administration's Intervention in Angola." *Presidential Studies Quarterly* 23 (4): 771–85.

Nolan, David. 1984. *FSLN: The Ideology of the Sandinistas and the Nicaraguan Revolution*. Institute of Inter-American Studies, University of Miami.

Nolutshungu, Sam C. 1996. *Limits of Anarchy: Intervention and State Formation in Chad*. University Press of Virginia.

NRM. 1986. *Ten-Point Programme of NRM*. NRM Publications.

NRM. 1990. *Mission to Freedom: Uganda Resistance News 1981–1985*. NRM Secretariat.

Nsambu, Hillary. 1993. "Policy on LDUs to Be Issued Soon." *New Vision*, July 15. CBR-RCs/NRC-4.

Nsibambi, Apolo, ed. 1998. *Decentralisation and Civil Society in Uganda: The Quest for Good Governance*. Fountain.

Nsibambi, Apolo. 2014. *National Integration in Uganda 1962–2013*. Fountain.

Obbo, Sam, and Joan Kabusingye. 1994. "NRC Debates Education." *New Vision*, May 11. CBR-RCs/NRC-5.

Obwona, Marios B. 2001. "Determinants of FDI and Their Impact on Economic Growth in Uganda." *African Development Review* 13 (1): 46–81.

Ochan, Charles. 1989. "LDUs Start Training in Soroti." *New Vision*, April 10. MUL-New Vision-April/June.

Ocón, Jaime. 1981. *Una Nueva Concepción Del Sistema Estadístico Nacional*. Instituto Nacional de Estadística y Censos. IHNCA/FN,4008.

O'Donnell, Guillermo. 1993. "On the State, Democratization and Some Conceptual Problems: A Latin American View with Glances at Some Postcommunist Countries." *World Development* 21 (8): 1355–69.

O'Grady, Siobhán, Rachel Pannett, Haq Nawaz Khan, and Ezzatullah Mehrdad. 2021. "Panjshir Valley, Last Resistance Holdout in Afghanistan, Falls to the Taliban." *Washington Post*, September 7. https://www.washingtonpost.com/world/2021/09/06/afghanistan-kabul-taliban-updates/.

Ogwang, Tom. 2023. "Development Interventions and Post Conflict Reconstruction in Northern Uganda." PhD diss., Makerere University.

Okech, Anthony, Roy A. Carr-Hill, Anne R. Katahoire, et al. 2001. *Adult Literacy Programs in Uganda*. Edited by Roy A. Carr-Hill. World Bank.

Okuku, Juma. 2002. "Ethnicity, State Power and the Democratisation Process in Uganda." Discussion Paper 17. Nordiska Afrikainstitutet.

Okuku, Juma. 2006. "The Land Act (1998) and Land Tenure Reform in Uganda." *Africa Development* 31 (1): 1–26.

Okuonzi, Sam Agatre, and Joanna Macrae. 1995. "Whose Policy Is It Anyway? International and National Influences on Health Policy Development in Uganda." *Health Policy and Planning* 10 (2): 122–32.

Oloka-Onyango, Joe. 1989. "Law, Grassroots Democracy, and the National Resistance Movement in Uganda." *International Journal of the Sociology of Law* 17 (4): 465–80.

Oloka-Onyango, Joe. 1993. "Judicial Power and Constitutionalism in Uganda: A Historical Perspective." In *Uganda: Studies in Living Conditions, Popular Movements, and Constitutionalism*, edited by Mahmood Mamdani and Joe Oloka-Onyango, 463–517. JEP.

Olson, Mancur. 1993. "Dictatorship, Democracy, and Development." *American Political Science Review* 87 (3): 567–76.

Omara-Otunnu, Amii. 1987. *Politics and the Military in Uganda, 1890–1985*. MacMillan.

Ondoga Ori Amaza, Godfrey. 1998. *Museveni's Long March from Guerrilla to Statesman*. Fountain.

Onslow, Sue, and Anna-Mart van Wyk, eds. 2013. *Southern Africa in the Cold War, Post-1974*. Woodrow Wilson International Center for Scholars.

Onyango-Kakoba. 1995. "NRM Will Fight Illiteracy—Premier." *New Vision*, September 12. CBR-Primary Education-2.

Oppenheim, Ben, Abby Steele, Juan F. Vargas, and Michael Weintraub. 2015. "True Believers, Deserters, and Traitors: Who Leaves Insurgent Groups and Why." *Journal of Conflict Resolution* 59 (5): 794–823.

Oppenheim, Ben, and Michael Weintraub. 2017. "Doctrine and Violence: The Impact of Combatant Training on Civilian Killings." *Terrorism and Political Violence* 29 (6): 1126–48.

Ortega Saavedra, Daniel. 1985. *Daniel y Los Médicos de Nicaragua: Problemática, Medidas y Compromisos*. Dirección de Información y Prensa de la Presidencia de la República. IHNCA/FN,362.1,O77.

Ortega Saavedra, Humberto. 2004. *Epopeya de La Insurección*. Lea Grupo Editorial.

Ortiz de Zárate, Verónica Valdivia. 2003. "Terrorism and Political Violence During the Pinochet Years: Chile, 1973–1989." *Radical History Review* 2003 (85): 182–90.

Ostovar, Afshon. 2016. *Vanguard of the Imam: Religion, Politics, and Iran's Revolutionary Guards*. Oxford University Press.

Ottaway, David, and Marina Ottaway. 1970. *Algeria: The Politics of a Socialist Revolution*. University of California Press.

Ottemoeller, Dan. 1996. "Institutionalization and Democratization: The Case of the Ugandan Resistance Councils." PhD diss., University of Florida.

Ottemoeller, Dan. 1999. "The Politics of Gender in Uganda: Symbolism in the Service of Pragmatism." *African Studies Review* 42 (2): 87–104.

Paglayan, Agustina S. 2022. "Education or Indoctrination? The Violent Origins of Public School Systems in an Era of State-Building." *American Political Science Review* 116 (4): 1242–57.

Paris, Roland. 2004. *At War's End: Building Peace After Civil Conflict*. Cambridge University Press.

Parkhurst, Justin O. 2001. "The Crisis of AIDS and the Politics of Response: The Case of Uganda." *International Relations* 15 (6): 69–87.

Parkhurst, Justin O., and Louisiana Lush. 2004. "The Political Environment of HIV: Lessons from a Comparison of Uganda and South Africa." *Social Science and Medicine* 59 (9): 1913–24.

Parkinson, Sarah E. 2023. *Beyond the Lines: Social Networks and Palestinian Militant Organizations in Wartime Lebanon*. Cornell University Press.

Parkinson, Sarah Elizabeth, and Sherry Zaks. 2018. "Militant and Rebel Organization(s)." *Comparative Politics* 50 (2): 271–93.

Parsa, Misagh. 2000. *States, Ideologies, and Social Revolutions: A Comparative Analysis of Iran, Nicaragua, and the Philippines*. Cambridge University Press.

Pastor, Robert A. 2002. *Not Condemned to Repetition: The United States and Nicaragua*. Westview.

Payne, Stanley G. 1987. *The Franco Regime, 1936–1975*. University of Wisconsin Press.

PBS. 2001. "Taliban Defends Plan for Labeling Non-Muslims." *PBS Newshour*, May 24. https://www.pbs.org/newshour/politics/asia-jan-june01-afghanistan_05-24.

Pearce, Justin. 2012. "Control, Politics and Identity in the Angolan Civil War." *African Affairs* 111 (444): 442–65.

Pearce, Justin. 2015a. "Contesting the Past in Angolan Politics." *Journal of Southern African Studies* 41 (1): 103–19.

Pearce, Justin. 2015b. *Political Identity and Conflict in Central Angola, 1975–2002*. Cambridge University Press.

Pearce, Justin. 2017. "Global Ideologies, Local Politics: The Cold War as Seen from Central Angola." *Journal of Southern African Studies* 43 (1): 13–27.

Pearce, Justin. 2020. "History, Legitimacy, and Renamo's Return to Arms in Central Mozambique." *Africa* 90 (4): 774–95.

Pearson, Margaret M., Meg Rithmire, and Kellee S. Tsai. 2023. *The State and Capitalism in China.* Cambridge University Press.

Péclard, Didier. 2015. *Les Incertitudes de la Nation en Angola: Aux Racines Sociales de l'Unita.* Éditions Karthala.

Pérez, Andrés. 1992. "The FSLN After the Debacle: The Struggle for the Definition of Sandinismo." *Journal of Interamerican Studies and World Affairs* 34 (1): 111–39.

Pettersson, Therése, and Peter Wallensteen. 2015. "Armed Conflicts, 1946–2014." *Journal of Peace Research* 52 (4): 536–50.

Phimister, Ian. 1987. "Zimbabwe: The Combined and Contradictory Inheritance of the Struggle Against Colonialism." *Transformation* no. 5: 51–59.

Physicians for Human Rights. 1998. *The Taliban's War on Women: A Health and Human Rights Crisis in Afghanistan.* Physicians for Human Rights.

Plaut, Martin, and Sarah Vaughan. 2023. *Understanding Ethiopia's Tigray War.* Oxford University Press.

Podder, Sukanya. 2014. "Mainstreaming the Non-State in Bottom-up State-Building: Linkages Between Rebel Governance and Post-Conflict Legitimacy." *Conflict, Security & Development* 14 (2): 213–43.

Pool, David. 2001. *From Guerrillas to Government: The Eritrean People's Liberation Front.* Ohio University Press.

Popkin, Samuel L. 1979. *The Rational Peasant: The Political Economy of Rural Society in Vietnam.* University of California Press.

Porter, Bruce D. 1994. *War and the Rise of the State: The Military Foundations of Modern Politics.* Free Press.

Portocarrero, Jorge. 1986. "Las Co.P.T.: Vigorosa Expresión de Combatividad Campesina." *Revista Segovia* 2 (6): 27–30.

Posner, Daniel N. 2005. *Institutions and Ethnic Politics in Africa.* Cambridge University Press.

Preston, Paul. 2006. *The Spanish Civil War: Reaction, Revolution, and Revenge.* Harper Perennial.

Prorok, Alyssa K. 2016. "Leader Incentives and Civil War Outcomes." *American Journal of Political Science* 60 (1): 70–84.

Prosecutor v. Charles Ghankay Taylor. 2012. Special Court for Sierra Leone.

Pugel, James. 2007. *What the Fighters Say: A Survey of Ex-Combatants in Liberia, February–March 2006.* UNDP Liberia.

Pugh, Michael. 2004. "Rubbing Salt into Old Wounds." *Problems of Post-Communism* 51 (3): 53–60.

Purdeková, Andrea. 2008. "Building a Nation in Rwanda? De-Ethnicisation and Its Discontents." *Studies in Ethnicity and Nationalism* 8 (3): 502–23.

Putzel, James. 2004. "The Politics of Action on AIDS: A Case Study of Uganda." *Public Administration and Development* 24: 19–30.

Quandt, William B. 1973. "The Berbers in the Algerian Political Elite." In *Arabs and Berbers: From Tribe to Nation in North Africa*, edited by Ernest Gellner and Charles Micaud, 285–303. Duckworth.

Radin, Andrew. 2020. *Institution Building in Weak States: The Primacy of Local Politics.* Georgetown University Press.

Ramazani, Rouhollah K. 1980. "Constitution of the Islamic Republic of Iran." *Middle East Journal* 34 (2): 181–204.

Ramírez, Sergio. 2012. *Adiós Muchachos: A Memoir of the Sandinista Revolution.* Duke University Press.

Rashid, Ahmed. 2001. *Taliban: Militant Islam, Oil and Fundamentalism in Central Asia*. Yale University Press.

Rasler, Karen A., and William R. Thompson. 1989. *War and State Making: The Shaping of the Global Powers*. Unwin Hyman.

Rauch, James E. 2001. "Leadership Selection, Internal Promotion, and Bureaucratic Corruption in Less Developed Polities." *Canadian Journal of Economics* 34 (1): 240–58.

Reed, Jean-Pierre. 2002. "Culture in Action: Nicaragua's Revolutionary Identities Reconsidered." *New Political Science* 24 (2): 235–63.

Reed, William Cyrus. 1996. "Exile, Reform, and the Rise of the Rwandan Patriotic Front." *Journal of Modern African Studies* 34 (3): 479–501.

Reid, Richard J. 2017. *A History of Modern Uganda*. Cambridge University Press.

Reno, William. 1993. "Foreign Firms and the Financing of Charles Taylor's NPFL." *Liberian Studies Journal* 18 (2): 175–88.

Reno, William. 1995a. *Corruption and State Politics in Sierra Leone*. Cambridge University Press.

Reno, William. 1995b. "Reinvention of an African Patrimonial State: Charles Taylor's Liberia." *Third World Quarterly* 16 (1): 109–20.

Reno, William. 1998. *Warlord Politics and African States*. Lynne Rienner.

Reno, William. 2011. *Warfare in Independent Africa*. Cambridge University Press.

Reno, William. 2013. "The Problem of Extraterritorial Legality." In *Interview Research in Political Science*, edited by Layna Mosley, 159–78. Cornell University Press.

Reno, William. 2015. "Predatory Rebellions and Governance: The National Patriotic Front of Liberia, 1989–1992." In *Rebel Governance in Civil War*, edited by Ana Arjona, Nelson Kasfir, and Zachariah Mampilly, 265–85. Cambridge University Press.

Renzo, Massimo. 2018. "Helping the Rebels." *Journal of Ethics and Social Philosophy* 13 (3): 222–39.

Repórteres CJI. 2022. "Cabo Delgado 2017–2022: Um Quinquénio de Terror." *Centro de Jornalismo Investigativo*, October 5. https://cjimoz.org.mz/news/cabo-delgado-2017 -2022-um-quinquenio-de-terror/.

Republic of Liberia. 1993. *Chronology of Terroristic Acts Committed by the National Patriotic Front of Liberia (NPFL) from August 24, 1990, to June 12, 1993*. Ministry of Information, Culture, and Tourism.

Republic of Liberia. 2008. *Poverty Reduction Strategy*. Republic of Liberia.

Republic of Uganda. 1986. *Parliamentary Debates (Hansard), First Session 1986–87, Issue No. 2, 4 December–17 December 1986*. Republic of Uganda.

Republic of Uganda. 1988. *Parliamentary Debates (Hansard), Second Session 1987–88, Issue No. 6, 5 January–21 January 1988*. Republic of Uganda.

Republic of Uganda. 1989a. *Parliamentary Debates (Hansard), Third Session 1989–90, Second Meeting, Issue No. 10, 3 July–3 August 1989*. Republic of Uganda.

Republic of Uganda. 1989b. *Parliamentary Debates (Hansard), Third Session 1989–90, Second Meeting, Issue No. 12, 6 September–25 October 1989*. Republic of Uganda.

Republic of Uganda. 1990a. *Parliamentary Debates (Hansard), Fourth Session 1990–91, Issue No. 13, 30 April–21 June 1990*. Republic of Uganda.

Republic of Uganda. 1990b. *Parliamentary Debates (Hansard), Fourth Session 1990–91, Issue No. 14, 28 June–23 August 1990*. Republic of Uganda.

Republic of Uganda. 1991a. *Parliamentary Debates (Hansard), Fifth Session 1991–1992 Issue No. 18, 23 April–27 June 1991*. Republic of Uganda.

Republic of Uganda. 1991b. *Parliamentary Debates (Hansard), Fifth Session 1991–1992, Second Meeting, Issue No. 20, 1 August–25 September 1991*. Republic of Uganda.

Republic of Uganda. 1992. *Government White Paper on the Implementation of the Recommendations of the Report of the Education Policy Review Commission*. Ministry of Education and Sport.

Republic of Uganda. 1996a. *Parliamentary Debates (Hansard), 1st Session, First Meeting, Issue No. 1, 2–9 July 1996*. Republic of Uganda.

Republic of Uganda. 1996b. *Parliamentary Debates (Hansard), 1st Session, First Meeting, Issue No. 5, 1–30 October 1996*. Republic of Uganda.

Reuss, Anna, and Kristof Titeca. 2017. "When Revolutionaries Grow Old: The Museveni Babies and the Slow Death of the Liberation." *Third World Quarterly* 38 (10): 2347–66.

Revere, Robert B. 1970. "Consensus in Independent Algeria, 1962–1965." PhD diss., New York University.

Revere, Robert B. 1973. "Revolutionary Ideology in Algeria." *Polity* 5 (4): 477–88.

Revista Segovia. 1986. "Los Batallones Ligero Cazadores." *Revista Segovia* 2 (11): 16–19.

Reyburn, Hugh, Mark Rowland, Ahmad Abd el Rahman, and Egbert Sondrop. 1997. "Health Care Under the Taliban." *Lancet* 349 (9069): 1916.

Reyntjens, Filip. 1996. "Rwanda: Genocide and Beyond." *Journal of Refugee Studies* 9 (3): 240–51.

Reyntjens, Filip. 2006. "Post-1994 Politics in Rwanda: Problematising 'Liberation' and 'Democratisation.'" *Third World Quarterly* 27 (6): 1103–17.

Reyntjens, Filip. 2009. *The Great African War: Congo and Regional Geopolitics, 1996–2006*. Cambridge University Press.

Reyntjens, Filip. 2024. "Rwanda: The Eternal Sunshine of the Spotless Election." *African Arguments* (blog). August 8. https://africanarguments.org/2024/08/rwanda-the -eternal-sunshine-of-the-spotless-election/.

RFE/RL. 2024. "Taliban Says It Strikes Back After Deadly Pakistani Strikes." *Radio Free Europe/Radio Liberty*, March 18. https://www.rferl.org/a/afghanistan-taliban -pakistan-airstrikes-bomb/32865938.html.

RFI. 2008. "Liberian General Implicates Burkina Faso President in Predecessor's Assassination." *RFI English*, October 27. http://www1.rfi.fr/actuen/articles/106 /article_1979.asp.

Rio Tinto, Daniel. 2017. "Tracing the Security Dilemma in Civil Wars: How Fear and Insecurity Can Lead to Intra-State Violence." PhD diss., University of Birmingham.

Rivera Quintero, José Francisco, and Sergio Ramírez. 1989. *La Marca del Zorro: Hazañas del Comandante Francisco Rivera Quintero Contadas a Sergio Ramírez*. Nueva Nicaragua.

Roberts, Hugh. 1982. "The Unforeseen Development of the Kabyle Question in Contemporary Algeria." *Government and Opposition* 17 (3): 312–34.

Roberts, Hugh. 1993. "The FLN: French Conceptions, Algerian Realities." In *North Africa: Nation, State, and Region*, edited by George Joffé, 111–40. Routledge.

Rocha, José Luis. 2021. "Why Did Daniel Ortega Imprison His Former Comrades?" *NACLA*, June 21.

Roessler, Philip. 2016. *Ethnic Politics and State Power in Africa: The Logic of the Coup-Civil War Trap*. Cambridge University Press.

Roque, Paula Cristina. 2021. *Governing in the Shadows: Angola's Securitised State*. Oxford University Press.

Ross, Michael L. 2004. "How Do Natural Resources Influence Civil War? Evidence from Thirteen Cases." *International Organization* 58 (1): 35–67.

Rubin, Barnett R. 1999. "Afghanistan Under the Taliban." *Current History* 98 (1): 79–91.

Rubin, Barnett R. 2000. "The Political Economy of War and Peace in Afghanistan." *World Development* 28 (10): 1789–1803.

Rubongoya, Joshua B. 2007. *Regime Hegemony in Museveni's Uganda*. Palgrave Macmillan.

Ruedy, John. 1992. *Modern Algeria: The Origins and Development of a Nation*. Indiana University Press.

Rueschemeyer, Dietrich, and Peter B. Evans. 1985. "The State and Economic Transformation: Toward an Analysis of the Conditions Underlying Effective Intervention." In *Bringing the State Back In*, edited by Peter B. Evans, Dietrich Rueschemeyer, and Theda Skocpol, 44–77. Cambridge University Press.

Rugunda, Ruhakana. 1987. "Foreword." In *Beyond Crisis: Development Issues in Uganda*, edited by Paul D. Wiebe and Cole P. Dodge, vi–vii. Makerere Institute of Social Research and African Studies Association.

Rukooko, A. Byarahunga. 2005. "Protracted Civil War, Civil Militias and Political Transition in Uganda Since 1986." In *Civil Militia: Africa's Intractable Security Menace*, edited by David J. Francis, 213–30. Routledge.

Rwakaara, Beatrice. 1988. "Lack of Equipment Hampers Uganda's Illiteracy Campaign." *New Vision*, July 26. MUL-New Vision-May/August.

Ryan, Phil. 1994. *Fall and Rise of the Market in Sandinista Nicaragua*. McGill-Queen's University Press.

Saich, Tony. 2021. *From Rebel to Ruler: One Hundred Years of the Chinese Communist Party*. Harvard University Press.

Saleh, Alam. 2013. *Ethnic Identity and the State in Iran*. Palgrave Macmillan.

Salehi, M. M. 1996. "Radical Islamic Insurgency in the Iranian Revolution of 1978–1979." In *Disruptive Religion: The Force of Faith in Social Movement Activism*, edited by Christian Smith, 47–63. Routledge.

Samim, Sabawoon. 2022a. "Policing Public Morality: Debates on Promoting Virtue and Preventing Vice in the Taleban's Second Emirate." Afghanistan Analysts Network. https://www.afghanistan-analysts.org/en/reports/rights-freedom/policing-public-morality-debates-on-promoting-virtue-and-preventing-vice-in-the-talebans-second-emirate/.

Samim, Sabawoon. 2022b. "Who Gets to Go to School? (3): Are Taleban Attitudes Starting to Change from Within?" Afghanistan Analysts Network. https://www.afghanistan-analysts.org/en/reports/rights-freedom/who-gets-to-go-to-school-3-are-taleban-attitudes-starting-to-change-from-within/.

Saul, John S. 2014. "'When Freedom Died' in Angola: Alves and After." *Review of African Political Economy* 41 (142): 609–22.

Sawyer, Amos. 1992. *The Emergence of Autocracy in Liberia: Tragedy and Challenge*. ICS Press.

Sawyer, Amos. 2004. "Violent Conflicts and Governance Challenges in West Africa: The Case of the Mano River Basin Area." *Journal of Modern African Studies* 42 (3): 437–63.

Sawyer, Amos. 2005. *Beyond Plunder: Toward Democratic Governance in Liberia*. Lynne Rienner.

Saylor, Ryan. 2014. *State Building in Boom Times: Commodities and Coalitions in Latin America and Africa*. Oxford University Press.

Schahgaldian, Nikola B., and Gina Bakhordarian. 1987. *The Iranian Military Under the Islamic Republic*. RAND.

Schatzberg, Michael G. 1997. "Beyond Mobutu: Kabila and the Congo." *Journal of Democracy* 8 (4): 70–84.

Schroeder, Michael Jay. 1993. "'To Defend Our Nation's Honor': Toward a Social & Cultural History of the Sandino Rebellion in Nicaragua, 1927–1934." PhD diss., University of Michigan.

Schubert, Frank. 2006. "'Guerrillas Don't Die Easily': Everyday Life in Wartime and the Guerrilla Myth in the National Resistance Army in Uganda, 1981–1986." *International Review of Social History* 51 (1): 93–111.

Schuck, Christoph. 2013. "A Conceptual Framework of Sunni Islamism." *Politics, Religion & Ideology* 14 (4): 485–506.

Schuster, Lynda. 1994. "The Final Days of Dr. Doe." *Granta* 48 (48): 40–95.

Schwartz, Rachel A. 2023a. "Rewriting the Rules of Land Reform: Counterinsurgency and the Property Rights Gap in Wartime Nicaragua." *Small Wars and Insurgencies* 34 (6): 1154–79.

Schwartz, Rachel A. 2023b. *Undermining the State from Within: The Institutional Legacies of Civil War in Central America*. Cambridge University Press.

Scott, James C. 1979. "Revolution in the Revolution: Peasants and Commissars." *Theory and Society* 7 (1/2): 97–134.

Scott, James C. 1998. *Seeing Like a State: How Certain Schemes to Improve the Human Condition Have Failed*. Yale University Press.

Scott, James C. 2009. *The Art of Not Being Governed: An Anarchist History of Upland Southeast Asia*. Yale University Press.

Selbin, Eric. 1997. "Revolution in the Real World: Bringing Agency Back In." In *Theorizing Revolutions*, edited by John Foran, 123–36. Routledge.

Selbin, Eric. 1999. *Modern Latin American Revolutions*. Westview.

Serra, Luis Hector. 1985. "The Grassroots Organizations." In *Revolution & Counterrevolution in Nicaragua*, edited by Thomas W. Walker, 49–75. Westview.

Seyon, Patrick L. N. 1998. "A Quick Fix for the Liberian 'Humpty Dumpty': Will It Work? State Transformation and Democratization in Africa: A Lesson from Liberia." *Liberian Studies Journal* 23 (2): 1–60.

Shakoori, Ali. 2001. *The State and Rural Development in Post-Revolutionary Iran*. Palgrave Macmillan.

Sharif, Sally, and Madhav Joshi. 2023. "Territorial Consolidation After Rebel Victory: When Does Civil War Recur?" *Territory, Politics, Governance,* forthcoming. https://doi.org/10.1080/21622671.2023.2243996.

Shaw, Joshua, and Brett Carter. 2021. "The Republic of the Congo: The Colonial Origins of Military Rule." *Oxford Research Encyclopedia of Politics.* https://doi.org/10.1093/acrefore/9780190228637.013.1807.

Shepard, William E. 1987. "Islam and Ideology: Towards a Typology." *International Journal of Middle East Studies* 19 (3): 307–36.

Shesterinina, Anastasia. 2022. "Civil War as a Social Process: Actors and Dynamics from Pre- to Post-War." *European Journal of International Relations* 28 (3): 538–62.

Shih, Gerry. 2023a. "After Taliban Bans Opium, a Guilt-Racked Commander Winks at Harvest." *Washington Post*, June 23. https://www.washingtonpost.com/world/2023/06/23/taliban-opium-ban-dissent-afghanistan/.

Shih, Gerry. 2023b. "Taliban Bringing Water to Afghanistan's Parched Plains via Massive Canal." *Washington Post*, August 20. https://www.washingtonpost.com/world/2023/08/20/afghanistan-taliban-canal-amu-darya/.

Silberfein, Marilyn, and Al Hassan Conteh. 2006. "Boundaries and Conflict in the Mano River Region of West Africa." *Conflict Management and Peace Science* 23 (4): 343–61.

Simwogerere, Kyazze. 1996. "Only NRM Can Ensure Peace." *The Crusader*, January 26. CBR-NRM-5.

Sinno, Abdulkader H. 2008. *Organizations at War in Afghanistan and Beyond*. Cornell University Press.

Sjögren, Anders. 2013. *Between Militarism and Technocratic Governance: State Formation in Contemporary Uganda*. Fountain.

Skocpol, Theda. 1979. *States and Social Revolutions*. Cambridge University Press.

Skocpol, Theda. 1982. "Rentier State and Shi'a Islam in the Iranian Revolution." *Theory and Society* 11 (3): 265–83.

Skocpol, Theda, and Margaret Somers. 1980. "The Uses of Comparative History in Macrosocial Inquiry." *Comparative Studies in Society and History* 22 (2): 174–97.

Slater, Dan. 2008. "Can Leviathan Be Democratic? Competitive Elections, Robust Mass Politics, and State Infrastructural Power." *Studies in Comparative International Development* 43 (3–4): 252–72.

Slater, Dan. 2010. *Ordering Power: Contentious Politics and Authoritarian Leviathans in Southeast Asia*. Cambridge University Press.

Slater, Dan, and Erica Simmons. 2010. "Informative Regress: Critical Antecedents in Comparative Politics." *Comparative Political Studies* 43 (7): 886–917.

Slater, Dan, and Daniel Ziblatt. 2013. "The Enduring Indispensability of the Controlled Comparison." *Comparative Political Studies* 46 (10): 1301–27.

Soares de Oliveira, Ricardo. 2015. *Magnificent and Beggar Land: Angola Since the Civil War*. Hurst.

Soifer, Hillel. 2008. "State Infrastructural Power: Approaches to Conceptualization and Measurement." *Studies in Comparative International Development* 43 (3–4): 231–51.

Soifer, Hillel. 2012. "Measuring State Capacity in Contemporary Latin America." *Revista de Ciencia Política* 32 (3): 585–98.

Soifer, Hillel. 2015. *State Building in Latin America*. Cambridge University Press.

Soifer, Hillel, and Matthias vom Hau. 2008. "Unpacking the Strength of the State: The Utility of State Infrastructural Power." *Studies in Comparative International Development* 43 (3–4): 219–30.

Sollis, Peter. 1989. "The Atlantic Coast of Nicaragua: Development and Autonomy." *Journal of Latin American Studies* 21 (3): 481–520.

Somerville, Keith. 1984. "Angola: Soviet Client State or State of Socialist Orientation?" *Millennium: Journal of International Studies* 13 (3): 292–310.

Soskice, David, Robert H. Bates, and David Epstein. 1992. "Ambition and Constraint: The Stabilizing Role of Institutions." *Journal of Law, Economics, and Organization* 8 (3): 547–60.

Southall, Roger. 2013. *Liberation Movements in Power: Party & State in Southern Africa*. James Currey.

Spatz, Benjamin J., and Kai M. Thaler. 2018. "Has Liberia Turned a Corner?" *Journal of Democracy* 29 (3): 156–70.

Ssewakiryanga, Richard. 2008. "Assessment of the Processes and Politics in the Making of Uganda's PRSP." In *Assessment of Poverty Reduction Strategies in Sub-Saharan Africa: The Case of Uganda*, edited by OSSREA, 74–98. Organisation for Social Science Research in Eastern and Southern Africa.

Ssuuna, Ignatius. 2024. "Provisional Election Results Show Rwanda's Kagame Cruising to Victory, an Outcome That Was Expected." *AP News*, July 15. https://apnews.com/article/rwanda-presidential-election-voting-kagame-c541dcfdc2f90dd3cf3eb508842f365f.

Staniland, Paul. 2012. "States, Insurgents, and Wartime Political Orders." *Perspectives on Politics* 10 (2): 243–64.

Staniland, Paul. 2014. *Networks of Rebellion: Explaining Insurgent Cohesion and Collapse*. Cornell University Press.

Staniland, Paul. 2021. "Leftist Insurgency in Democracies." *Comparative Political Studies* 54 (3–4): 518–52.

Stanton, Jessica. 2016. *Violence and Restraint in Civil War: Civilian Targeting in the Shadow of International Law.* Cambridge University Press.

Stasavage, David. 2005. "The Role of Democracy in Uganda's Move to Universal Primary Education." *Journal of Modern African Studies* 43 (1): 53–73.

Stearns, Jason K. 2022. "Rebels Without a Cause: The New Face of African Warfare." *Foreign Affairs* 101 (3): 143–56.

Stedman, Stephen John. 1997. "Spoiler Problems in Peace Processes." *International Security* 22 (2): 5–53.

Steinberg, Jonny. 2011. *Little Liberia: An African Odyssey in New York.* Jonathan Ball.

Steinhauser, Gabriele, and Bernard Mpofu. 2023. "'Life Was Better Under Mugabe': Disappointment, Fear Cloud Zimbabwe Election." *Wall Street Journal*, August 23. https://www.wsj.com/world/africa/life-was-better-under-mugabe-disappointment-fear-cloud-zimbabwe-election-8ac63d5f.

Stepan, Alfred. 2012. "Rituals of Respect: Sufis and Secularists in Senegal in Comparative Perspective." *Comparative Politics* 44 (4): 379–401.

Stevens, Christopher. 1976. "The Soviet Union and Angola." *African Affairs* 75 (299): 137–51.

Stewart, Megan A. 2018. "Civil War as State Building: Strategic Governance in Civil War." *International Organization* 72 (1): 205–26.

Stewart, Megan A. 2021. *Governing for Revolution: Social Transformation in Civil War.* Cambridge University Press.

Stewart, Megan A. 2023. "Foundations of the Vanguard: The Origins of Leftist Rebel Groups." *European Journal of International Relations* 29 (2): 398–426.

Stone, Martin. 1997. *The Agony of Algeria.* Columbia University Press.

Stora, Benjamin. 2004. *Algeria, 1830–2000: A Short History.* Cornell University Press.

Strating, Rebecca. 2016. *Social Democracy in East Timor.* Routledge.

Straus, Scott. 2015. *Making and Unmaking Nations: War, Leadership, and Genocide in Modern Africa.* Cornell University Press.

Straus, Scott. 2019. "The Limits of a Genocide Lens: Violence Against Rwandans in the 1990s." *Journal of Genocide Research* 21 (4): 504–24.

Straus, Scott, and Lars Waldorf, eds. 2011. *Remaking Rwanda: State Building and Human Rights After Mass Violence.* University of Wisconsin Press.

Suhrke, Astri. 2007. "Reconstruction as Modernisation: The 'Post-Conflict' Project in Afghanistan." *Third World Quarterly* 28 (7): 1291–1308.

Suhrke, Astri. 2013. "Statebuilding in Afghanistan: A Contradictory Engagement." *Central Asian Survey* 32 (3): 271–86.

Sullivan, Daniel P. 2007. "Tinder, Spark, Oxygen, and Fuel: The Mysterious Rise of the Taliban." *Journal of Peace Research* 44 (1): 93–108.

Takeyh, Ray. 2009. *Guardians of the Revolution: Iran and the World in the Age of the Ayatollahs.* Oxford University Press.

Talmadge, Caitlin. 2015. *The Dictator's Army: Battlefield Effectiveness in Authoritarian Regimes.* Cornell University Press.

Tangermann, R. H., H. F. Hull, H. Jafari, B. Nkowane, H. Everts, and R. B. Aylward. 2000. "Eradication of Poliomyelitis in Countries Affected by Conflict." *Bulletin of the World Health Organization* 78 (3): 330–38.

Tangri, Roger, and Andrew M. Mwenda. 2001. "Corruption and Cronyism in Uganda's Privatization in the 1990s." *African Affairs* 100 (398): 117–33.

Tangri, Roger, and Andrew M. Mwenda. 2008. "Elite Corruption and Politics in Uganda." *Commonwealth and Comparative Politics* 46 (2): 177–94.

Tanner, Victor. 1998. "Liberia: Railroading Peace." *Review of African Political Economy* 25 (75): 133–47.

Tapscott, Rebecca. 2017. "The Government Has Long Hands: Institutionalized Arbitrariness and Local Security Initiatives in Northern Uganda." *Development and Change* 48 (2): 263–85.

Tapscott, Rebecca. 2021. *Arbitrary States: Social Control and Modern Authoritarianism in Museveni's Uganda.* Oxford University Press.

Tapscott, Rebecca. 2023. "Vigilantes and the State: Understanding Violence Through a Security Assemblages Approach." *Perspectives on Politics* 21 (1): 209–24.

Tapscott, Rebecca, and Eliza Urwin. 2024. "The Origins and Legacies of Unpredictability in Rebel-Incumbent Rule." *Civil Wars*, forthcoming. https://doi.org/10.1080 /13698249.2024.2302731.

Taylor, Charles. n.d. *Presidential Papers: A Premiere Edition, August 2, 1997–December 31, 1998.* Edited by Reginald B. Goodridge. Department of Public Affairs and Press Secretary to the President.

Taylor, Lewis. 2017. "Sendero Luminoso in the New Millennium: Comrades, Cocaine and Counter-Insurgency on the Peruvian Frontier." *Journal of Agrarian Change* 17 (1): 106–21.

Terpstra, Niels. 2020. "Rebel Governance, Rebel Legitimacy, and External Intervention: Assessing Three Phases of Taliban Rule in Afghanistan." *Small Wars and Insurgencies* 31 (6): 1143–73.

Tessler, Mark, Carrie Konold, and Megan Reif. 2004. "Political Generations in Developing Countries: Evidence and Insights from Algeria." *Public Opinion Quarterly* 68 (2): 184–216.

Thaler, Kai M. 2012. "Ideology and Violence in Civil Wars: Theory and Evidence from Mozambique and Angola." *Civil Wars* 14 (4): 546–67.

Thaler, Kai M. 2017. "Nicaragua: A Return to Caudillismo." *Journal of Democracy* 28 (2): 157–69.

Thaler, Kai M. 2021. "Reflexivity and Temporality in Researching Violent Settings: Problems with the Replicability and Transparency Regime." *Geopolitics* 26 (1): 18–44.

Thaler, Kai M. 2022. "Rebel Mobilization Through Pandering: Insincere Leaders, Framing, and Exploitation of Popular Grievances." *Security Studies* 31 (3): 351–80.

Thaler, Kai M. 2024a. "Civil Wars as Critical Junctures: Conceptual Grounding and Empirical Potential." *Review of International Studies*, forthcoming. https://doi .org/10.1017/S0260210524000871.

Thaler, Kai M. 2024b. "Levels of Analysis and Variation in Civil War Violence and Restraint: Ideology and Contestation in Nicaragua." *Journal of Global Security Studies* 9 (2): ogae018.

Thaler, Kai M. Forthcoming. "Stumbling Out of the Gates: Security Strategy and Military Weakness After Revolutionary Victory." *Security Studies.*

Thaler, Kai M., Antonia H. Juelich, and Sean Paul Ashley. 2024. "From Snapshots to Panoramas: Navigating Power, Space, and Time in the Study of Armed Groups." *Conflict, Security & Development* 24 (6): 725–55.

Thaler, Kai M., and Eric Mosinger. 2022. "Nicaragua: Doubling Down on Dictatorship." *Journal of Democracy* 33 (2): 133–46.

Tharoor, Ishaan. 2024. "Afghan Women Endure Draconian Taliban, 23 Years After 9/11." *Washington Post*, September 11. https://www.washingtonpost.com/world/2024 /09/11/afghanistan-women-taliban-rights/.

The Citizen. 1990. "Parents Strangled over School Fees." *The Citizen*, January 24. CBR-Primary Education-1.

The Guide. 1989. "Give Due Attention to Primary Education to Get Technocrats." *The Guide*, September 27. CBR-Primary Education-1.

Themnér, Anders. 2015. "Former Military Networks and the Micro-Politics of Violence and Statebuilding in Liberia." *Comparative Politics* 47 (3): 334–53.

Themnér, Lotta, and Peter Wallensteen. 2012. "Armed Conflicts, 1946–2011." *Journal of Peace Research* 49 (4): 565–75.

Thies, Cameron G. 2005. "War, Rivalry, and State Building in Latin America." *American Journal of Political Science* 49 (3): 451–65.

Thies, Cameron G. 2006. "Public Violence and State Building in Central America." *Comparative Political Studies* 39 (10): 1263–82.

Thornton, Patricia M. 2007. *Disciplining the State: Virtue, Violence, and State-Making in Modern China*. Harvard East Asia Center.

Tidemand, Per. 1994. "The Resistance Councils in Uganda: A Study of Rural Politics and Popular Democracy in Africa." PhD diss., Roskilde University.

Tierney, Dominic. 2021. "The Future of Sino-U.S. Proxy War." *Texas National Security Review* 4 (2): 49–73.

Tilly, Charles. 1985. "War Making and State Making as Organized Crime." In *Bringing the State Back In*, edited by Peter Evans, Dietrich Rueschemeyer, and Theda Skocpol, 169–87. Cambridge University Press.

Tilly, Charles. 1990. *Coercion, Capital, and the European State, AD 990–1990*. Blackwell.

Toft, Monica Duffy. 2009. *Securing the Peace: The Durable Settlement of Civil Wars*. Princeton University Press.

Toft, Monica Duffy. 2010. "Ending Civil Wars: A Case for Rebel Victory?" *International Security* 34 (4): 7–36.

Tokdemir, Efe, Evgeny Sedashov, Sema Hande Ogutcu-Fu, et al. 2021. "Rebel Rivalry and the Strategic Nature of Rebel Group Ideology and Demands." *Journal of Conflict Resolution* 65 (4): 729–58.

Torres, Hugo. 2005. *Rumbo Norte: Historia de un Sobreviviente*. Hispamer.

Torres, Hugo. 2010. "Chilling Similarities Between Ortega and the Somozas." *Envío*, no. 342. https://www.revistaenvio.org/articulo/4140.

Tripp, Aili Mari. 1994. "Gender, Political Participation and the Transformation of Associational Life in Uganda and Tanzania." *African Studies Review* 37 (1): 107–31.

Tripp, Aili Mari. 2001. "The Politics of Autonomy and Cooptation in Africa: The Case of the Ugandan Women's Movement." *Journal of Modern African Studies* 39 (1): 101–28.

Tripp, Aili Mari. 2004. "The Changing Face of Authoritarianism in Africa: The Case of Uganda." *Africa Today* 50 (3): 2–26.

Tripp, Aili Mari. 2010. *Museveni's Uganda: Paradoxes of Power in a Hybrid Regime*. Lynne Rienner.

Truth and Reconciliation Commission of Liberia. 2008. *Truth and Reconciliation Commission, Volume II: Consolidated Final Report*. Republic of Liberia Truth and Reconciliation Commission.

Tsimpo, Clarence, and Quentin Wodon. 2012a. "Education in Liberia: Basic Diagnostic Using the 2007 CWIQ Survey." In *Poverty and the Policy Response to the Economic Crisis in Liberia*, edited by Quentin Wodon, 35–59. World Bank.

Tsimpo, Clarence, and Quentin Wodon. 2012b. "Health in Liberia: Basic Diagnostic Using the 2007 CWIQ Survey." In *Poverty and the Policy Response to the Economic Crisis in Liberia*, 60–81. World Bank.

Tumusiime, James, ed. 1992. *Uganda 30 Years, 1962–1992*. Fountain.

Tumwine, Alfred. 1989. "330 LDUs Commissioned." *New Vision*, June 5. CBR-RCs/NRC-1.

Ugarriza, Juan E. 2009. "Ideologies and Conflict in the Post–Cold War." *International Journal of Conflict Management* 20 (1): 82–104.

UN Group of Experts on the Democratic Republic of the Congo. 2023. "Letter Dated 13 June 2023 from the Group of Experts on the Democratic Republic of the Congo Addressed to the President of the Security Council." S/2023/431. United Nations. https://digitallibrary.un.org/record/4013781.

UN Women. 2024. "Gender Country Profile: Afghanistan." UN Women Afghanistan. https://www.unwomen.org/en/digital-library/publications/2024/06/gender-country-profile-afghanistan.

UNAMA Human Rights Service. 2022. "Human Rights in Afghanistan: 15 August 2021 to 15 June 2022." United Nations Assistance Mission in Afghanistan Human Rights Service.

UNDP. 2006. *Human Development Report 2006*. United Nations Development Programme.

UNICEF. 1996. *The State of the World's Children 1996*. Oxford University Press.

UNICEF. 1999. *The State of the World's Children 1999*. Oxford University Press.

UNICEF. 2005. *The State of the World's Children 2005*. Oxford University Press.

UNICEF. 2011. "Progress Evaluation of the UNICEF Education in Emergencies and Post-Crisis Transition Programme (EEPCT): Liberia Case Study." UNICEF.

van Bijlert, Martine. 2021a. "Between Hope and Fear: Rural Afghan Women Talk About Peace and War." Afghanistan Analysts Network. https://www.afghanistan-analysts.org/en/wp-content/uploads/sites/2/2021/07/2021-Rural-women-peace-and-war-FINAL-website.pdf.

van Bijlert, Martine. 2021b. "The Focus of the Taleban's New Government: Internal Cohesion, External Dominance." Afghanistan Analysts Network. https://www.afghanistan-analysts.org/en/reports/war-and-peace/the-focus-of-the-talebans-new-government-internal-cohesion-external-dominance/.

Vaughan, Sarah. 2003. "Ethnicity and Power in Ethiopia." PhD diss., University of Edinburgh.

Vaughan, Sarah. 2011. "Revolutionary Democratic State-Building: Party, State and People in the EPRDF's Ethiopia." *Journal of Eastern African Studies* 5 (4): 619–40.

Vaughan, Sarah, and Mesfin Gebremichael. 2011. "Rethinking Business and Politics in Ethiopia: The Role of EFFORT, the Endowment Fund for the Rehabilitation of Tigray." Africa Power and Politics Research Report 2. Overseas Development Institute.

Verhoeven, Harry, and Michael Woldemariam. 2022. "Who Lost Ethiopia? The Unmaking of an African Anchor State and U.S. Foreign Policy." *Contemporary Security Policy* 43 (4): 622–50.

Verma, Cecilie Lanken. 2013. "Guns and Tricks: State Becoming and Political Subjectivity in War-Town Northern Uganda." PhD diss., Copenhagen University.

Verma, Raj, and Shahid Ali. 2023. "How the Islamic State Rivalry Pushes the Taliban to Extremes." *Middle East Policy* 30 (4): 42–55.

Verwimp, Philip. 2003. "Testing the Double-Genocide Thesis for Central and Southern Rwanda." *Journal of Conflict Resolution* 47 (4): 423–42.

Vilas, Carlos M. 1988. *De la Opresión a la Autonomía: Estado, Modernización Capitalista y Revolución Social en la Costa Atlántica de Nicaragua*. CIDCA. IHNCA/FN,972.85,V697a.

Vlavonou, Gino. 2014. "Understanding the 'Failure' of the Séléka Rebellion." *African Security Review* 23 (3): 318–26.

Vrieze, Paul. 2023. "Joining the Spring Revolution or Charting Their Own Path? Ethnic Minority Strategies Following the 2021 Myanmar Coup." *Asian Survey* 63 (1): 90–120.

Vu, Tuong. 2010. *Paths to Development in Asia: South Korea, Vietnam, China, and Indonesia*. Cambridge University Press.

Waldner, David. 1999. *State Building and Late Development.* Cornell University Press.

Walker, Thomas W. 1991. "The Armed Forces." In *Revolution & Counterrevolution in Nicaragua*, edited by Thomas W. Walker, 77–100. Westview.

Walker, Thomas W., and Christine J. Wade. 2011. *Nicaragua: Living in the Shadow of the Eagle.* Westview.

Walt, Stephen M. 1996. *Revolution and War.* Cornell University Press.

Walter, Barbara F. 2004. "Does Conflict Beget Conflict? Explaining Recurring Civil War." *Journal of Peace Research* 41 (3): 371–88.

Walter, Barbara F. 2017a. "The Extremist's Advantage in Civil Wars." *International Security* 42 (2): 7–39.

Walter, Barbara F. 2017b. "The New New Civil Wars." *Annual Review of Political Science* 20 (1): 469–86.

Walter, Knut. 1993. *The Regime of Anastasio Somoza, 1936–1956.* University of North Carolina Press.

Wanzusi, Joseph, and Jolly Azabo. 1989. "Schools Overcrowded." *New Vision*, August 7. CBR-Primary Education-1.

Warner, Jason, Ryan O'Farrell, Héni Nsaibia, and Ryan Cummings. 2021. *The Islamic State in Africa: The Emergence, Evolution, and Future of the Next Jihadist Battlefront.* Hurst.

Warren, T. Camber. 2014. "Not by the Sword Alone: Soft Power, Mass Media, and the Production of State Sovereignty." *International Organization* 68 (1): 111–41.

Waterman, Alex. 2023. "The Shadow of 'the Boys:' Rebel Governance Without Territorial Control in Assam's ULFA Insurgency." *Small Wars & Insurgencies* 34 (1): 279–304.

Waugh, Colin M. 2011. *Charles Taylor and Liberia.* Zed.

Weaver, Eric, and William Barnes. 1991. "Opposition Parties and Coalitions." In *Revolution & Counterrevolution in Nicaragua*, edited by Thomas W. Walker, 117–42. Westview.

Weber, Max. 1946. "Politics as a Vocation." In *From Max Weber: Essays in Sociology*, edited by H. H. Gerth and C. Wright Mills, 77–128. Oxford University Press.

Weber, Max. 1968. *Economy and Society.* Bedminster.

Weekly Focus. 1986. "Police to Resume Full Operations Next Week." *Weekly Focus*, February 7. CBR-NRA-1986.

Weekly Topic. 1989. "RCs Start Health Training." *Weekly Topic*, May 31. CBR-RCs/NRC-1.

Weerdesteijn, Maartje. 2019. "The Rationality and Reign of Paul Kagame." In *Perpetrators of International Crimes: Theories, Methods, and Evidence*, edited by Alette Smeulers, Maartje Weerdesteijn, and Barbora Holá, 224–38. Oxford University Press.

Weigand, Florian. 2022. *Waiting for Dignity: Legitimacy and Authority in Afghanistan.* Columbia University Press.

Weigert, Stephen L. 2011. *Angola: A Modern Military History, 1961–2002.* Palgrave Macmillan.

Weinstein, Jeremy M. 2005. "Autonomous Recovery and International Intervention in Comparative Perspective." Center for Global Development.

Weinstein, Jeremy M. 2007. *Inside Rebellion: The Politics of Insurgent Violence.* Cambridge University Press.

Weissman, Fabrice. 1996. "Libéria, derrière le chaos, crise et interventions internationales." *Relations Internationales et Stratégiques*, no. 24, 82–99.

Weld, Kirsten. 2018. "The Spanish Civil War and the Construction of a Reactionary Historical Consciousness in Augusto Pinochet's Chile." *Hispanic American Historical Review* 98 (1): 77–115.

Wheelock Román, Jaime. 1990. *La Reforma Agraria Sandinista: 10 Años de Revolución en el Campo.* Vanguardia.

Whitaker, Paul M. 1970. "The Revolutions of 'Portuguese' Africa." *Journal of Modern African Studies* 8 (1): 15–35.

Wickham-Crowley, Timothy P. 1987. "The Rise (and Sometimes Fall) of Guerrilla Governments in Latin America." *Sociological Forum* 2 (3): 473–99.

Wickham-Crowley, Timothy P. 1992. *Guerrillas & Revolutionaries in Latin America: A Comparative Study of Insurgents and Regimes Since 1956*. Princeton University Press.

Wiebe, Paul D., and Cole P. Dodge. 1987. "Introduction." In *Beyond Crisis: Development Issues in Uganda*, edited by Paul D. Wiebe and Cole P. Dodge, 1–9. Makerere Institute of Social Research and African Studies Association.

Williams, Philip J. 1994. "Dual Transitions from Authoritarian Rule: Popular and Electoral Democracy in Nicaragua." *Comparative Politics* 26 (2): 169–85.

Willis, Justin, Gabrielle Lynch, and Nic Cheeseman. 2017. "'A Valid Electoral Exercise'? Uganda's 1980 Elections and the Observers' Dilemma." *Comparative Studies in Society and History* 59 (1): 211–38.

Wimmer, Andreas. 2012. *Waves of War: Nationalism, State Formation, and Ethnic Exclusion in the Modern World*. Cambridge University Press.

Windrich, Elaine. 1992. *The Cold War Guerrilla: Jonas Savimbi, the U.S. Media, and the Angolan War*. Greenwood.

Wintrobe, Ronald. 1990. "The Tinpot and the Totalitarian: An Economic Theory of Dictatorship." *American Political Science Review* 84 (3): 849–72.

Woldemariam, Michael, and Yilma Woldgabreal. 2023. "Atrocity Denial and Emotions in the Ethiopian Civil War." *Aggression and Violent Behavior* 73: 101875.

Wolfers, Michael, and Jane Bergerol. 1983. *Angola in the Front Line*. Zed.

Wood, Elisabeth Jean. 2003. *Insurgent Collective Action and Civil War in El Salvador*. Cambridge University Press.

Wood, Elisabeth Jean. 2008. "The Social Processes of Civil War: The Wartime Transformation of Social Networks." *Annual Review of Political Science* 11 (1): 539–61.

Wood, Elisabeth Jean. 2015. "Social Mobilization and Violence in Civil War and Their Social Legacies." In *Oxford Handbook of Social Movements*, edited by Donatella della Porta and Mario Diani, 452–66. Oxford University Press.

Worsnop, Alec. 2017. "Who Can Keep the Peace? Insurgent Organizational Control of Collective Violence." *Security Studies* 26 (3): 482–516.

Wright, Bruce E. 1995. *Theory and Practice in the Nicaraguan Revolution*. Center for International Studies, Ohio University.

Yadav, Stacey Philbrick. 2010. "Understanding 'What Islamists Want': Public Debate and Contestation in Lebanon and Yemen." *Middle East Journal* 64 (2): 199–213.

Yassin-Kassab, Robin. 2013. "Fund Syria's Moderates." *Foreign Policy*, January 23. http://foreignpolicy.com/2013/01/23/fund-syrias-moderates/.

Yates, Peter. 1980. "The Prospects for Socialist Transition in Zimbabwe." *Review of African Political Economy* 7 (18): 68–88.

Young, Enrique Wedgwood, and Adrian Florea. 2025. "Rethinking Rebel Victory in Civil War." *Review of International Studies*, forthcoming. https://doi.org/10.1017/S0260210524000858.

Young, John. 1997. *Peasant Revolution in Ethiopia: The Tigray People's Liberation Front, 1975–1991*. Cambridge University Press.

Young, Tom. 1988. "The Politics of Development in Angola and Mozambique." *African Affairs* 87 (347): 165–84.

Zabih, Sepehr. 1988. "The Non-Communist Left in Iran: The Case of the Mujahidin." In *Ideology and Power in the Middle East*, edited by Peter J. Chelkowski and Robert J. Pranger, 241–58. Duke University Press.

Zaks, Sherry. 2024. "Do We Know It When We See It? (Re)-Conceptualizing Rebel-to-Party Transition." *Journal of Peace Research* 61 (2): 246–62.

Ziemke, Jennifer J. 2008. "From Battles to Massacres." PhD diss., University of Wisconsin–Madison.

Zimmermann, Mathilde. 2001. *Sandinista: Carlos Fonseca and the Nicaraguan Revolution*. Duke University Press.

Zoubir, Yahia H. 1993. "The Painful Transition from Authoritarianism in Algeria." *Arab Studies Quarterly* 15 (3): 83–111.

Zoubir, Yahia H. 2020. "The Algerian-Moroccan Rivalry." In *Shocks and Rivalries in the Middle East and North Africa*, edited by Imad Mansour and William R. Thompson, 179–200. Georgetown University Press.

Zwerling, Philip, and Connie Martin. 1985. *Nicaragua: A New Kind of Revolution*. Lawrence Hill.

Index

Note: Page numbers in italics refer to figures and tables.

Abbas, Ferhat, 161
administrative capacity, 36–37, 46, *47*
Afghanistan. *See* Taliban
Aït-Ahmed, Hocine, 161
Alemán, Arnoldo, 77
Algeria. *See* Front de Libération Nationale (FLN)
Allende, Salvador, 39, 74
Alliance des Forces Démocratiques pour la Libération du Congo (AFDL), 8–9, 28, 191
Allied Democratic Forces (ADF), 182–83
al-Qaeda, 172, 177
al-Shabaab (Mozambique), 182–83, 188
Alves, Nito, 148, 154
Alvor Accord (1975), 146–47
Amin, Idi, 109–10, 115, 118, 122–23, 133
Angola. *See* Frente Nacional de Libertação de Angola (FNLA); Movimento Popular de Libertação de Angola (MPLA); União Nacional para a Independência Total de Angola (UNITA)
anti-colonial nationalism, 8, 43, 139–55, 157–58, 180
Armed Forces of Liberia (AFL), 20, 80, 89, 92
Arnove, Robert F., 70
Assad regime, 5, 187–89
authoritarian regimes, 11, 16, 18, 40, 77–78, 106, 154, 166, 190

Bakhtiar, Shapur, 164
Bakut, Ishaya, 88
Bangladesh, 11, 35
Bani-Sadr, Abolhassan, 165
Barnes, Nathaniel, 100–101
Batta, Ronald, 113
Batwala, James, 124
Bazargan, Mehdi, 164, 167
Ben Bella, Ahmed, 159–62
Bendaña, Alejandro, 58
Benjedid, Chadli, 160
Bicesse Accords (1991), 150
Bility, Hassan, 100
bin Laden, Osama, 172, 179

Borge, Tomás, 53, 55, 62, 71
Boumediene, Houari, 159–62
Burkina Faso, 81–82, 89

Cabezas, Omar, 53
Cabral, Luís, 43
Cape Verde, 43
Captan, Monie, 91
Carrión, Luis, 55, 70, 72–73
Castro, Fidel, 12, 55, 183
Central African Republic, 44
Chabal, Patrick, 141
Chad, 5, 28, 37–38
Chamorro, Pedro Joaquín, 55
Chamorro, Violeta Barrios de, 57, 59
Chile, 39, 74
China, 11, 35, 143, 145, 147, 151, 153, 188
Chinese Communist Party, 27, 186
civil society, 5, 19–21, 37, 45, 187; Islamist rebels and, 182; Nicaragua, 55–56, 75; Uganda, 121–22
civil wars: humanitarian concerns, 191–92; prevalence of, 5; process-oriented view of, 183; scholarship on, 9–10. *See also* rebel group political orientation
civilian constituencies, 12–13, *14*, 26, 29, 35, 38, 48, 177, 189; in Afghanistan, 170–71, 176–77; in Angola, 144, 149, 151–53, 161; in Iran, 165–66; Islamist groups and, 180, 183; in Liberia, 103, 106; in Nicaragua, 72; in Uganda, 41, 112, 121
Cobra militia (Republic of Congo), 4, 38
coercive power, 7, 33, 181; defined, 45; FLN, 162; FSLN, 60–62; infrastructure and, 36; Iran's Islamist revolutionaries, 167; NPFL, 91–93; NRM, 108, 117–20; security forces as measure of, 45, *47*; service provision and, 42; Taliban, 170–72, 174, 177. *See also* security forces
Cold War, 13, 17–18, 104, 113, 133, 167–68, 188
Coleman, Peter, 96–97
Communist Party of Nepal-Maoist (CPN-M), 35–36, 44, 104, 190

Compaoré, Blaise, 82
Conservative Party (Uganda), 110
Contreras, Eduardo, 55
Costa Rica, 44, 54, 56, 62
Côte d'Ivoire, 82, 105
counterinsurgency, 187–88; in Iran, 167; in Nicaragua, 56, 60, 62; in Uganda, 114, 119, 123
Cuadra, Joaquín, 61, 63
Cuba, 27, 35–36, 58, 60, 74, 141, 145, 147, 150, 186

Ddungu, Expedit, 120
democracy, 190–91; in Nicaragua, 75–78; in Uganda, 113–14, 120–23, 135–36
Democratic Party (DP; Uganda), 109–11, 117
Democratic Republic of the Congo (DRC), 8–9, 11, 28, 104, 120, 143, 147, 151, 182–83, 191
Dicklitch, Susan, 127, 133
Doctor, Austin, 145
Doe, Jackson, 84
Doe, Samuel, 80–85, 96, 101–2, 104
Dokie, Samuel, 80
dos Santos, José Eduardo, 140, 150, 154
Downton, James, 24
Duo, Roland, 91
Duopu, Moses, 84

ECOMOG (ECOWAS Monitoring Group), 84–85, 88–89, 92, 103–5
Economic Community of West African States (ECOWAS), 84
economy. *See* resource availability; resource extraction; revenues; taxation
education and literacy campaigns, 35–37, 46–47; in Afghanistan, 171, 174–75, 178–79, 189; in Algeria, 160; in Angola, 142, 148–49; in Iran, 165; in Liberia, 98–100; in Nicaragua, 56, 59, 68–71, 73, 76; in Uganda, 124, 127–31, 135. *See also* political education
Ejército de Liberación Nacional (Costa Rica), 44
El Salvador, 24, 104
Eritrea, 18
Eritrean People's Liberation Front, 36
Ethiopia, 18, 41–42
Ethiopian People's Revolutionary Democratic Front (EPRDF), 41–42
ethnic groups, 13; in Afghanistan, 175; in Angola, 141–42, 145, 149, 151, 154–55; in Iran, 165; Islamist rebel groups and, 180; in Liberia, 86; in Nicaragua, 72–73; programmatic-exclusive rebel organizations, 40–42; in Uganda, 41, 109, 113, 116, 132–33

exclusive benefits, 6–9, 29–30, 35, 47–48, 181; leaders and, 26; opportunistic organizations, 6–9, 37–39; programmatic organizations, 38–42

Fahnbulleh, Boima, 81
Fanon, Frantz, 158
Fonseca, Carlos, 53, 55, 68, 71
foreign investment and support, 13, 34, 39
France, 147; colonialism in Algeria, 157–62
Franco, Francisco, 39
Frente Amplio Opositor (FAO), 56
Frente de Libertação de Moçambique (Frelimo), 8, 24, 27, 36, 110, 112, 131, 183, 185–86
Frente Farabundo Martí para la Liberación Nacional (El Salvador), 24
Frente Nacional de Libertação de Angola (FNLA), 18; development of, 142–44; ethnic groups and, 41, 151, 155; foreign investment and support, 147, 151; leadership, 152; opportunistic-exclusive ideology, 139–40, 151–52, 155; resource availability, 151; security threats, 141, 143, 146–47, 161
Frente Revolucionária de Timor-Leste Independente (Fretilin), 190
Frente Sandinista de Liberación Nacional (FSLN), 3–4, 15–18, 27, 36, 51–78; Afro-descendant and Indigenous communities, 59–60, 62, 64, 70, 72–74; agrarian reform, 59, 63–65, 76; Atlantic Coast and, 56, 60, 62, 64–65, 72–75, 190; authoritarian government, 77–78; civil society, 75; civilian constituencies, 72; coercive power, 60–62; Comités de Defensa Sandinista (CDSs), 62, 74; contras and, 59–62, 65, 74–76; corruption, 76–78; coups and, 52; democracy and, 75–78; Dirección Nacional (DN), 57–59, 64, 185; education and literacy campaigns, 56, 59, 68–71, 73, 76; ethnic groups, 72–73; foreign investment and support, 71, 74; Grupo de los Doce (Group of Twelve), 56–57; Guerra Popular Prolongada (GPP), 55, 58; health care, 56, 59, 65–67, 69, 76; Historical Program, 53–56, 58, 68, 71, 73; human rights and, 53, 61; infrastructural power and service provision, 56–70, 74–78, 102, 121, 190; Interior Ministry (MINT), 58, 60–62; interventionism, 104; Junta of the Government of National Reconstruction (JGRN), 57–59, 66, 69, 185; leadership, 71, 184–85; neoliberalism, 77; opportunistic-exclusive ideology, 77–78, 186; origins and

www.ingramcontent.com/pod-product-compliance
Lightning Source LLC
Chambersburg PA
CBHW030356270326
41926CB00009B/1129

* 9 7 8 1 5 0 1 7 8 4 9 3 4 *